"In this volume, Hays provides his readers with a superb overview of the message and significance of the Old Testament prophets. After introducing prophetic literature in general, Hays guides his readers through each prophetic book. Numerous clear images and helpful sidebars add to the richness of this book. He includes features like suggestions for further reading, discussion questions, and writing assignments that make the book ready-made for classroom use. Hays takes a number of the complicated issues of prophetic literature and provides a clear explanation of this important part of the Old Testament."

—MICHAEL A. GRISANTI, PhD
Professor of Old Testament
The Master's Seminary

"Every once in a while a book comes along that is exceptional in every aspect one may choose to look at it. I have found J. Daniel Hays's *The Message of the Prophets* to be such a book. Not only is it aesthetically pleasing in its graphics and content layout, but it moves easily from introductory matters about the prophets to the message of each of the sixteen writing prophets. I believe it will become a standard textbook for pastors, Bible study leaders, and college and seminary classes on the prophets. I heartily endorse its widest usage for all who love to grasp the message of the Old Testament prophets."

—WALTER C. KAISER JR.
President Emeritus
Gordon-Conwell Theological Seminary

"To the burgeoning interest in the Old Testament prophets and the recent literature reflecting that interest must be added this magnificent overview of the men and their writings that make up a major part of the Old Testament canon. Although presupposing up-to-date scholarship on the prophets in a technically accurate fashion, Hays spares the beginning student the morass of argument pro and con on various issues, preserving instead the crucial facts and facets of the prophets' messages in their historical and cultural contexts. The photographs and other visual assets greatly enhance the beauty and reader-friendliness of the work, making it, with its other virtues, the finest volume of its kind. Highly recommended!"

—EUGENE H. MERRILL, PhD
Distinguished Professor of Old Testament Studies
Dallas Theological Seminary

"*The Message of the Prophets* is an excellent introduction to the prophets of the Old Testament. From the attractive and inviting format, with photographs, maps, and sidebars, to the very fair and even-handed treatment of controversial issues, this book will be of great benefit to any who are seeking to get an understanding of this complex but vital field. The introductory overview is careful and complete, the writing style is clear and engaging, and the contents of the books are effectively summarized without becoming pedantic. In view of all these factors, I predict that this book will become a standard text in the coming years."

—John Oswalt, PhD
Visiting Distinguished Professor of Old Testament
at Asbury Theological Seminary

"J. Daniel Hays gives the students a front-row seat into the world of the prophets. Students will learn to appreciate the struggles of the prophets, their literature, and their theology, plus gain insight into their poetry and eschatological messages. Hays traces their messages and highlights the key theological themes in each major literary unit in both the major and minor prophets. The text is attractively designed with either a large illustrative picture or a sidebar on almost every page. Students will love the beautiful pictures that show what a high place, an olive tree, or a Bedouin tent looks like, plus the maps will raise their consciousness of the land where these events took place. The sidebars explain theological terms, an ancient custom, or an important archaeological discovery that is mentioned in the verses under discussion. The text flows smoothly and is spiced up with modern illustrations and numerous connections to the New Testament."

—Gary Smith
Professor of Christian Studies
Union University

textbook*plus*⁺

Equipping Instructors and Students with
***FREE RESOURCES** for Core Zondervan Textbooks*

Available Resources for The Message of the Prophets

Teaching Resources

- Instructor's manual
- Presentation slides
- Chapter quizzes
- Midterm and final exams
- Sample syllabus
- Image/map library

Study Resources

- Chapter videos
- Quizzes
- Flashcards
- Exam study guides

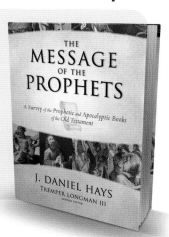

*How To Access Resources

- Go to www.ZondervanAcademic.com
- Click "Sign Up" button and complete registration process
- Find books using search field or browse using discipline categories
- Click "Teaching Resources" or "Study Resources" tab once you get to book page to access resources

www.ZondervanAcademic.com

THE MESSAGE OF THE PROPHETS

A Survey of the Prophetic and Apocalyptic Books of the Old Testament

J. DANIEL HAYS

TREMPER LONGMAN III
GENERAL EDITOR

ZONDERVAN

The Message of the Prophets
Copyright © 2010 by J. Daniel Hays

This title is also available as a Zondervan ebook.
Visit www.zondervan.com/ebooks.

Requests for information should be addressed to:
Zondervan, 3900 *Sparks Dr. SE, Grand Rapids, Michigan 49546*

Library of Congress Cataloging-in-Publication Data

Hays, J. Daniel, 1953–
        Message of the prophets : a survey of the prophetic and apocalyptic books of the Old Testament / J.
    Daniel Hays ; Tremper Longman III, general editor.
            p.   cm.
        Includes bibliographical references and index.
        ISBN 978-0-310-27152-9 (hardcover)
        1. Bible. O.T. Prophets—Textbooks. I. Longman, Tremper. II. Title.
    BS1506.H43—2009
        224'.066—dc22   2009022477

Interior design: Tracey Walker
Maps: International Mapping. Copyright © 2010 by Zondervan. All rights reserved.

Printed in China

16 17 18 /GSC/ 30 29 28 27 26 25 24 23 22 21 20 19 18 17 16 15 14 13 12 11 10 9 8 7

Contents

Contents

PART THREE: THE BOOK OF THE TWELVE

Introduction

Without doubt, the prophetic books of the Old Testament are among the most fascinating, powerful, and important works of literature ever written. What a privilege it is to read them, study them, and engage with them! God speaks through these books both to the ancient audience and to us today. Time spent immersed in the prophets will be time well spent. Welcome!

This book is an introductory survey of the Old Testament prophetic literature. Part One (The Big Picture) will present methodological and background material that will assist the student in understanding the prophets and their message. It also provides an introductory overview of the prophets as a whole. In Part Two we will analyze each of the four "major prophets," and in Part Three we will explore the "Book of the Twelve," commonly called the "minor prophets."

The ministry and the message of the prophets is integrally interconnected to the tumultuous historical events of their day. Thus we will frequently pause to place them into their proper historical setting and to ask the question of what their message meant for those who first heard it. Yet the primary focus of this book is not on historical background but on the *message* of the prophets; thus, we will spend much of our time dealing with literary meaning as expressed in the written form of their proclamation, that is, the books of the prophets as we have them. Likewise, while historical setting will be important to us, we will also explore the meaning implied by canonical location, especially in the "minor prophets" (Book of the Twelve). In addition, while this book seeks to engage with the very best of Old Testament scholarship, especially that of the evangelical tradition, it also seeks to move beyond mere academic study to help the reader ask the bottom-line theological question, "What impact should this have on me?" Thus, throughout the book we will pause from time to time to grapple with theology for today and contemporary application. This will be especially true in the Discussion Questions and Writing Assignments at the end of each chapter.

The Old Testament prophetic books provide a crucial bridge for continuity between God's message in the Old Testament and God's message in the New Testament. The New Testament itself frequently alludes to the prophets, and the New Testament story is difficult to understand accurately without a good grasp of the Old Testament prophets. This book assumes that its readers are Christians and that their ultimate interest is biblical theology, that is, a theology that encompasses the entire Christian canon. Thus, while we will resist the temptation to read the New Testament back into the prophets in an unwarranted allegorical manner, we will, however, frequently point to New Testament connections with the prophets, noting especially how Jesus and the New Testament writers used specific prophetic texts.

Finally, this book attempts to reflect a mainstream, "critical conservative," evangelical approach to the prophets. Within evangelicalism there are several different theological "systems" that influence how people read and understand the predictive passages in the prophets (amillennialism, premillennialism, etc.). This book attempts to stay neutral in this contentious debate, striving to present the range of possible understandings that are held by respectable evangelical Old Testament scholars.

I want to thank my good friends and colleagues Scott Duvall and Marvin Pate for encouraging me in this project and allowing me to borrow freely from works that we have co-authored together (especially *Grasping God's Word; Dictionary of Biblical Prophecy and End Times;* and *Iraq: Babylon of the End Times?*). Likewise, my heartfelt thanks goes to Tremper Longman, the Old Testament editor of this textbook series, for entrusting me with this project and providing helpful advice and guidance. Several people currently and formerly at Zondervan played important roles as well in getting this book produced, and I want to thank all of them—especially Katya Covrett, Jack Kuhatschek, Jim Ruark, Kim Zeilstra, and Jack Kragt, who first suggested the idea to me.

Scripture quotations throughout the book are usually from the New International Version, although I have modified the text by substituting "Yahweh" for "the LORD."

For the transliteration of Hebrew words in English, I have attempted to use the English letters that best approximate the sound of the Hebrew letters rather than follow the standard scholarly transliteration guidelines of the Society of Biblical Literature. Thus I use *sh* instead of *š* and *ts* instead of *ṣ*. Hopefully this will make it easier for English readers who do not know Hebrew to be able to pronounce the words.

PART 1

The Big Picture

CHAPTER 1

Prophets and Prophecy

"And we have the word of the prophets made more certain, and you will do well to pay attention to it, as to a light shining in a dark place...." (2 Peter 1:19)

INTRODUCTION

The apostle Peter underscores the nature of the Old Testament prophetic books when he writes that "no prophecy of Scripture came about by the prophet's own interpretation. For

prophecy never had its origin in the will of man, but men spoke from God as they were carried along by the Holy Spirit" (2 Peter 1:20–21). From the beginning of the Christian faith, the Old Testament prophets have played a critical role in understanding God's great redemptive plan for the world. The New Testament relies on the prophetic books repeatedly for its understanding of God and Jesus the Messiah. Jesus himself interconnects his message and his imagery with that of the Old Testament prophets and links them together inextricably.

Obviously, the prophetic books are an important part of our Scriptures. In fact, the prophetic books take up as much space in the Bible as the entire New Testament does! Clearly this is an important part of the Bible that God wants us to understand and obey.

The prophets are powerful and inspiring. Their criticism of sin and injustice is harsh, scathing, and unyielding. Yet their words to the faithful are gentle and encouraging. Furthermore, in the prophets we are able to engage with God himself, for he is a major character throughout the prophetic material. God speaks and acts. He grieves, hurts, explodes in anger, comforts, loves, rebukes, and restores. God reveals much about himself through the prophets. We see his transcendence—that is, his "otherness." He is sovereign over all the world and in total control of history. Isaiah will ask, Who can comprehend God or his ways? Yet we are also shown God's immanence—his presence with us and his "connectedness" to his people here on earth.

Likewise, the prophets have a lot to say about people. In the prophets we see a story unfold that recounts how the people of Israel (and their neighbors) responded to God and his revelation to them. We see a tragic story of rebellion against God, followed by terrible consequences. Yet at the same time the prophets show us God's great capacity for forgiveness reflected in his constant call for repentance and renewal of the hearts of his wayward people. Although most of the people will reject God's call for repentance, the prophets will also tell us their own personal stories—how they encountered God and then proclaimed his word valiantly and faithfully in dangerous and hostile situations.

Truly the prophetic books of the Old Testament are fascinating, even though they are not always easy to understand. The goal of this book is to help you understand the Old Testament prophets and their significance for you and your life today.

THE PROPHETIC BOOKS OF THE OLD TESTAMENT

In our English Bible, the prophetic corpus begins with the four large books of Isaiah, Jeremiah, Ezekiel, and Daniel, with the small book of Lamentations inserted on the heels of Jeremiah and before Ezekiel. Often these larger books (especially Isaiah, Jeremiah, and Ezekiel) are referred to as the *Major Prophets*. Next come twelve smaller books, often called the *Minor Prophets* (Hosea, Joel, Amos, Obadiah, Jonah, Micah, Nahum, Habakkuk, Zephaniah, Haggai, Zechariah, and Malachi). The terms *major* and *minor* have nothing to do with importance. Rather, they refer to the length of the books. Isaiah, Jeremiah, and Ezekiel are much longer than the twelve minor prophets.

The book of Daniel falls into a special category. Many scholars classify it as "apocalyptic" rather than "prophetic" because both its literary style and its message differ in some respects from that of the rest of the prophets. However, the Christian canon has traditionally included Daniel with the prophets, and thus the book of Daniel is included in this study. Likewise, Lamentations is included with the Writings in the Hebrew Bible, but in the Christian canon this book is associated with Jeremiah and is located immediately after the book of Jeremiah. Thus we will also cover the book of Lamentations in our discussion.

The structure of the Hebrew Bible is slightly different from the Christian Old Testament canon. The Jews refer to the Scriptures as the *Tanak*. This title is an acronym taken from the first letters of the names of the three basic structural units of the Hebrew Bible: the Pentateuch (Torah); the Prophets (Nebi'im); and the Writings (Ketubim). The Prophets section contains two parts: the Former Prophets (Joshua, Judges, 1–2 Samuel, 1–2 Kings), and the Latter Prophets (Isaiah, Jeremiah, Ezekiel, and the Book of the Twelve, i.e., the twelve minor prophets). In the Hebrew Bible, Daniel and Lamentations are included with the Writings (along with Psalms, Job, Ecclesiastes, Ruth, etc.) rather than with the Prophets.

HISTORY OF PROPHECY IN THE OLD TESTAMENT

Beginning in the Pentateuch, the role of the prophet is closely associated with delivering the word of God. In Exodus 7:1 God tells Moses that Moses will be like god to Pharaoh and that Aaron will be his prophet, implying that Aaron's role will be to speak the word of God to Pharaoh. In Deuteronomy, however, it is Moses who is identified as the prophet, primarily because of his important role in delivering the word of God (most of the book of Deuteronomy) to the people. In fact, Deuteronomy 18:14–22 presents guidelines for the

Left to right: Jeremiah, Jonah, Isaiah, Habakkuk, Zephaniah, Joel, Obadiah, Hosea (by John Singer Sargent, 1865 – 1925).

Jerusalem (the city of Zion) plays a prominent role in the prophetic literature.

people concerning prophets and prophecy. In that text God promises to raise up another prophet like Moses, one they should listen to and obey. On the other hand, God strictly commands them to watch out for false prophets and not to listen to them.

In the historical books, especially 1–2 Samuel and 1–2 Kings, several prophets play key roles in the biblical story (Samuel, Nathan, Elijah, Elisha). The role of the prophet takes on a special significance in times when the Israelite monarchy and the Israelite priesthood turn away from God. Beginning in 1–2 Samuel and developing throughout 1–2 Kings, the Israelite monarchy grows both in power and in corruption. Especially in 1–2 Kings, the king often controls the priesthood and thus brings the worship system and its organization into his administration and under his control, often with an idolatrous orientation. Frequently, these Israelite kings worship idols and thus lead the entire nation into idol worship through their control of the priesthood.

God's true prophets, however, will stand outside of this theological and moral corruption and proclaim the true word of God to all of the guilty parties — the king, the priesthood, the false prophets, and the people. The prophets Elijah and Elisha (1 Kings 17–2 Kings 13) predate the literary prophets (Isaiah, Amos, etc.) by about one hundred years, but they set the pattern that many of the literary prophets will follow — confrontation with the king and other ruling powers, a call to repent and return to faithful obedience to Yahweh, and warnings of judgment on those who fail to heed the voice of Yahweh.

> Beginning in the Pentateuch, the role of the prophet is closely associated with delivering the word of God.

TERMINOLOGY

There are three major terms used in the Old Testament to refer to those special people who speak and transmit the word of Yahweh. The most common Hebrew term for such a person is *nabi'* (prophet). Two other terms, "seer" and "man of God," are also used. First Samuel 9:8–10 uses all three terms, indicating that they were nearly synonymous. "Seer" is used in several places throughout 1–2 Samuel as well as in 1–2 Chronicles. As in 1 Samuel

The Names for God in the Prophets

There are two major Hebrew terms for God in the Old Testament. Elohim is a "generic" term, used both for the true God who created the heavens and the earth (Gen. 1:1) and for the false "gods" of the nations. Thus it can be translated as God (i.e., the true God) or as god (i.e., Baal or Molech). Technically, it is a plural form, and thus when used of pagan deities it can be translated as a plural (gods). However, when used of the God of Israel, it always has singular verbs as well as singular pronouns (*he*, not *they*) associated with it, clearly indicating a singular entity. When Elohim is used of the God of Israel, plural Hebrew form functions as a plural of majesty or intensification. Elohim occurs 2,570 times in the Old Testament and is normally translated as "God."

The other major Hebrew term for God in the Old Testament is Yahweh. This term functions more as the personal name of Israel's God. Occurring 6,800 times in the Old Testament, the name Yahweh has strong connotations of personal, covenant relationship. Thus God will frequently say, "I am Yahweh, who brought you up out of Egypt," or something along those lines. The name Yahweh is similar in sound and probably related to the verb "to be." Thus the name is closely associated with God's self-description as "I am who I am" (Exod. 3:14). The name Yahweh is often connected to the term Elohim to stress that Yahweh is Israel's God (Elohim). Thus in the great "Shema" of Deuteronomy 6:4–5, the text reads: "Hear, O Israel: Yahweh our Elohim, Yahweh is one. Love Yahweh your Elohim with all your heart and with all your soul and with all your strength."

In English Bibles the name Yahweh is usually translated as "the LORD" with LORD all in caps. But Hebrew has another word (Adonai) that means "lord." Thus, when you read LORD in your Bible, it is helpful to remember that this is a translation of Yahweh, the specific personal name for God in the Old Testament.

Yahweh is the primary term for God used by the prophets. Because of their emphasis on the covenant relationship between God and Israel, and because God gets very personal in the prophetic literature, the name Yahweh dominates the pages of the prophetic books (with the exception of Daniel). Thus throughout this textbook on the prophets, we will use the name Yahweh most of the time when referring to God, especially when discussing the prophets in their Old Testament context. When referring to the New Testament or to contemporary application, we will use the regular English word *God*.

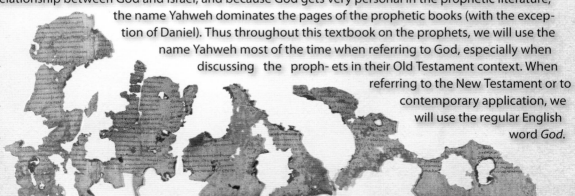

Photo Clara Amit, courtesy Israel Antiquities Authority

9:8–10, sometimes more than one of these terms is used to describe an individual. For example, in 2 Samuel 24:11 Gad is called "the prophet, David's seer." Likewise, when the antagonistic priest Amaziah calls Amos a "seer" in Amos 7:12, Amos replies by declaring that he is neither a "prophet" nor a "son of a prophet" (Amos 7:14). Yet 1 Samuel 9:9 implies that "seer" was perhaps an older designation, while "prophet" was the primary term in usage at the time when 1–2 Samuel was written.

> The term "seer" was apparently an older designation for a prophet, more prevalent in the early history of Israel.

The term "man of God" is closely associated with delivering the word of God. It is used of Moses in postexilic literature a few times (1 Chron. 23:14; Ezra 3:2) as well as of David (Neh. 12:24, 36). It is also used interchangeably with the term "prophet" in the Historical Books. However, "man of God" is not used of any of the literary prophets (Isaiah, Jeremiah, etc.).

Within the prophetic books, the major term used for Yahweh's spokesmen is "prophet." Yet this term is also used of people who speak falsely or who prophesy by the idols. Thus the term "prophet" is used for both true and false prophets.

Prophecy in the Ancient Near East

During the Old Testament era, prophet-like diviners and mediums were probably a common feature in the royal courts throughout the Ancient Near East. On the other hand, firm nonbiblical evidence of prophet-like activity comes primarily from two main contexts: literary texts found at Mari (eighteenth century BC) and Neo-Assyrian texts from the reigns of Esarhaddon (680–669 BC) and Ashurbanipal (668–627 BC). This literature reflects a rather wide range of terms and titles used for those individuals who sought to communicate with the gods and to bring oracles and other messages to (usually) the king. Such titles include "answerer," "cult functionary," "ecstatic," "diviner" (a word similar to the Hebrew *nabi'* or "prophet"), "proclaimer," "revealer" (a word similar to the Hebrew term translated as "seer"), and "sent one." In addition, this literature mentions numerous other individuals who act very much like prophets but who don't carry official titles.

These functionaries (by whatever term they were called) appear to be a fairly powerful class of people with a high standing at court. Generally they backed the king and supported his policies through their oracles and dreams. On a few rare occasions a court prophet might admonish the king, but this is always done mildly and is usually in response to the king's earlier refusal to heed a previous oracle or utterance of the gods.[1]

© The Trustees of the British Museum

Caryn Reeder

Top: An Assyrian prophecy text in cuneiform. *Bottom:* Diviners and prophets in the ANE often used livers to read omens. This is a model of a liver that was used by diviners.

1. H. B. Huffmon, "Prophecy: Ancient Near East," *Anchor Bible Dictionary* 5:477–82.

FALSE PROPHECY

While the act and office of prophecy in Israel in many regards parallels that found in the courts of the Ancient Near East, there were some stark differences as well (especially in regard to the "true prophets" of Yahweh). Deuteronomy 18:9–22 explicitly prohibited many of the specific practices (such as sorcery, necromancy, etc.) of these prophet-like pagan intermediaries.

During the time of the Old Testament prophets, however, the backsliding kings of Israel and Judah often strove to emulate their pagan neighbors, and they established their own "court prophets" rather than listening to and obeying the prophets that Yahweh ordained. This reflected their attempt to bring the prophetic office under royal control. Thus "false prophets" appeared fairly frequently in the royal courts of Israel and Judah. Sometimes these prophets were specifically identified with pagan gods, as in the case of the 450 prophets of Baal and the 400 prophets of Asherah whom Elijah encountered on Mt. Carmel (1 Kings 18:19). These idolatrous prophets were easily recognizable as false prophets. However, in the royal courts of Israel and Judah there were also "prophets" who claimed to prophesy in the name and power of Yahweh, yet who in truth were simply pawns of the king and had not been appointed by Yahweh.

> The prophetic books are somewhat vague in regard to who actually wrote down the words of the book.

The false prophets that Jeremiah encountered, for example, are similar to those functioning in royal courts throughout the region. Since they served the king and not Yahweh, they often collided with true prophets like Jeremiah. Indeed, Yahweh sent his own specially appointed prophets to the Israelite and Judahite kings to confront the false prophets and to remind the king, his court, and the nation that they all serve Yahweh and must be obedient to him and his covenant. Furthermore, Yahweh often pronounced judgment specifically upon these false prophets. In Jeremiah 28, the false prophet Hananiah contradicted Jeremiah and told all the people that Jeremiah was mistaken. At first this "counter-prophecy" created uncertainty in Jeremiah (28:5–11). Yet Yahweh soon clarified the truth for Jeremiah, sending him back to prophesy the death of the false prophet Hananiah, who did indeed die within two months.

AUTHORSHIP AND COMPOSITION OF THE PROPHETIC BOOKS

The prophetic books are somewhat vague in regard to who actually wrote down the words of the book. For example, the book of Isaiah does not open by saying that "these are the words that Isaiah wrote," but it opens by claiming that this is the "vision … that Isaiah … saw" (Isa. 1:1). Similarly, Jeremiah opens with "The words of Jeremiah …" (Jer. 1:1), quickly followed by the claim that these words are also the words of Yahweh (1:2, 4, etc.). Other books open with the identification of the book with the word of Yahweh. Joel, for example, begins with "The word of Yahweh that came to Joel …" (Joel 1:1).

Likewise, the prophetic books are similar to anthologies; that is, they are collections of materials from different genres (oracles, sermons, narratives, etc.) that have been arranged rhetorically for effect (we will discuss this some more in chapter 3). Was this material arranged in this order by the prophet himself or by someone else? When the book claims to be the "words of Jeremiah" or the "word of Yahweh that came to Joel," does that imply (or insist) that Jeremiah and Joel both heard/spoke the word as well as wrote it down and edited it into its final form? This has been the subject of quite a lot of scholarly discussion over the last one hundred and fifty years.

Throughout the latter half of the nineteenth century and into the twentieth century there was a strong movement in Western academic circles to apply "scientific" methods to all areas of study, including religion. Thus many scholars in the top universities (and even some seminaries) of the Western academy began analyzing Scripture apart from the presupposition that the Scriptures were divinely inspired. As part of this approach, they dropped the traditional claims of authorship for the prophetic books (i.e., that Isaiah had written the book of Isaiah) and began analyzing the content against the changing historical background to try to determine when different portions of each book were written and how the composition of each book developed. The driving feature of this methodology was the attempt to place texts into the actual historical context in which they were written and not just to accept the traditional assumed setting. Often, in determining the date of a passage, this line of study attempted to minimize divine activity in the formation of the prophetic books. Thus the scholars employing this methodology were usually skeptical of predictive prophecy, and they generally assumed that if a prophetic book mentioned an event or an individual, then that text must have been written after the event and either concurrent with or after the life of the individual mentioned in the book. For example, the book of Isaiah mentions Cyrus, king of Persia, three times (Isa. 44:28; 45:1, 13). The prophet Isaiah (as identified in Isa. 1:1), however, lived in the eighth century BC, while Cyrus came to power in the sixth century BC. Thus many scholars concluded that it was much more likely that someone during (or after) the time of Cyrus wrote the passages that mention him by name than that Isaiah the prophet, who lived two centuries earlier, wrote them.

There was an accompanying skepticism regarding the historicity of much of the Bible in many circles of Western biblical scholarship at this time, and often there was direct disavowal of the actual historicity of some events described in Scripture, especially miraculous events. Thus, evangelicals and other conservatives during the early twentieth century were frequently occupied with defending the veracity of the Bible against the skepticism of what was becoming the dominant view in the mainstream Western religion academy. During the first half of the twentieth century, this "liberal vs. conservative" battle over the truth of the Bible spilled over into the issue of authorship and composition of the prophetic books. Regarding Isaiah, for example, most nonevangelical scholars came to accept (almost without question) that the prophet Isaiah from the eighth century wrote only Isaiah 1–39 (at most). Isaiah 40–66, they concluded, was written by two other individuals or groups at a much later date. Many conservatives, on the other hand, felt that denying Isaianic authorship of the second half of Isaiah was a denial of the veracity of the Bible (especially since Jesus quoted from this portion and referred to the author as Isaiah), and would undermine the faith of believers. The rift between "liberals" and "conservatives" during this time was quite deep over issues like this concerning the veracity of the Bible, and

> During the first half of the twentieth century, the "liberal vs. conservative" battle over the truth of the Bible spilled over into the issue of authorship and composition of the prophetic books.

there was little dialogue between the two groups. The study of the prophets by evangelicals during the first half of the twentieth century was conducted in this context.

Toward the end of the twentieth century, however, and certainly as Old Testament scholarship entered into the twenty-first century, there was some moderating of both views. The mainstream nonevangelical academy began to recognize many of the unifying factors within each prophetic book that the evangelicals had been pointing to as an indication of unitary authorship. These nonevangelicals didn't necessarily conclude that the prophet for whom the book was named was the unitary author, but they did tend more and more to acknowledge significant input from the original prophet into the final product. Along with this, a scholarly trend began among some in mainstream nonevangelical American and British Old Testament scholarship (which continues still) that focuses on each prophetic book in its final, completed form as the primary point of study rather than slicing it up into smaller units to be analyzed individually based on the historical setting of the assumed time of composition for each small part (as was the main approach earlier in the twentieth century).[1] At the same time, nonevangelical Old Testament scholarship at the end of the twentieth century and into the beginning of the twenty-first experienced a general movement away from the more liberal views of the earlier generations and a movement toward a more "centrist" view that tended to temper some of the skepticism of divine activity in the Scriptures. For example, writing in the Anchor Bible commentary on Isaiah 1–39 regarding authorship of the total book, Blenkinsopp states, "For the majority of critical scholars this view of the matter is not, as conservative polemicists argue, dictated by a disposition to rule out the possibility of predictive prophecy. Critical commentators for whom this is still an issue would probably want to ask why inspiration should be denied to *anonymous* biblical authors."[2]

Many evangelical scholars likewise began reassessing their traditional conservative views on authorship in the prophetic books. While still holding to inspiration and inerrancy of Scripture, they began discussing just exactly what the Bible did say about authorship in the prophetic books. Their goal was to affirm all that the Bible claimed about authorship, but not to read into the text or to simply assume what could or could not have happened regarding the composition of the prophetic books. In some instances, evangelical scholars concluded that the original prophet did truly speak the word of Yahweh, and perhaps even wrote some of these oracles, visions, and sermons down, but that their material was then (later?) edited and finalized by someone else (perhaps a close associate, like Baruch in Jeremiah). These evangelical scholars were thus suggesting that the concept of inspiration could be applied both to the original prophet and to the later editor. Mark Boda, an

---

1. See, for example, Donald Gowan, *Theology of the Prophetic Books* (Louisville: Westminster John Knox, 1998); Brevard Childs, *Isaiah,* The Old Testament Library (Louisville: Westminster John Knox, 2001); Walter Brueggemann, *Like Fire in the Bones: Listening for the Prophetic Word in Jeremiah* (Minneapolis: Fortress, 2006); Christopher R. Seitz, *Isaiah 1–39,* Interpretation (Louisville: Westminster John Knox, 1993); and Terence E. Fretheim, *Jeremiah,* Smyth & Helwys Bible Commentary (Macon, GA: Smyth & Helwys, 2002).

2. Joseph Blenkinsopp, *Isaiah 1–39,* Anchor Bible (New York: Doubleday, 2000), 82.

evangelical Old Testament scholar, states this newly evolving evangelical view succinctly: "It is consistent with an evangelical view of Scripture that close associates of the prophets took the words revealed to the prophets by God and shaped them into a powerful message for later generations to read and profit from."[3]

Today evangelical Old Testament scholars are tending more and more to accept some editorial activity by someone other than the prophet himself. However, many evangelicals stress that the editor was probably a close associate of the prophet and that the final editing took place fairly soon after the prophet's death. Bullock, for instance, writes, "But it is unlikely that more than a generation intervened between the life of the prophet and the final edition of his book."[4] Not all evangelicals agree, especially about the extent and the time of the editing, and the discussion continues.

> Just exactly what does the Bible say about authorship in the prophetic books?

In general, therefore, the rift between evangelical and nonevangelical scholarship regarding the authorship of the prophetic books has grown smaller in the last generation. As the nonevangelical scholars focus more and more on the final form of the prophetic books, and as evangelical scholars open up to some editorial activity, the two groups are more able to engage and dialogue in the study of the prophets, although significant differences do still exist.

CONCLUSION AND CONTEMPORARY RELEVANCE

The Old Testament prophetic books comprise a large portion of our Bibles. As part of the Word of God, they beckon us to study them—to analyze, to reflect, to listen, to obey. As you will see throughout this book, the prophets are integrally connected to the New Testament. The prophets provide the primary link between the Old Testament and the New Testament. Indeed, much of the theology of the New Testament is built upon the prophets, and the New Testament is difficult to understand apart from the message they proclaimed. In addition, most of Jesus' colorful imagery (e.g., springs of living water, fishers of men, bride and bridegroom) is drawn from the imagery of the prophets.

> The prophets provide the primary link between the Old Testament and the New Testament.

As Scripture, the prophets have much to teach us about a wide range of issues. God is a major character in the prophetic books, and thus we can learn much about the nature and character of God from our study. The prophets present insight into many aspects of God's character—his loyal love, his patience, his anger and wrath, his pain, his power, his justice, and his sense of humor. Likewise, the prophets spend a lot of time addressing how God's people ought to live. The themes of social justice and right living are frequent. The prophets decry hypocrisy and superficial worship and call for sincere faith that manifests itself in the way people treat each other day by day. And finally, the prophets proclaim comfort and hope for those who suffer, for their God (and our God) is a God who rescues and restores those who return to him. He is the one who controls history, and he works to bring all things to the conclusion that he has planned.

---

3. Mark Boda, *Haggai, Zechariah,* NIV Application Commentary (Grand Rapids: Zondervan, 2004), 37.
4. C. Hassell Bullock, *An Introduction to the Old Testament Prophetic Books* (Chicago: Moody Press, 1986), 34.

» FURTHER READING «

Blenkinsopp, Joseph. *A History of Prophecy in Israel*. Revised Edition. Louisville: Westminster John Knox, 1996.

Bullock, C. Hassell. *An Introduction to the Old Testament Prophetic Books*. Chicago: Moody Press, 1986.

Hays, J. Daniel, J. Scott Duvall, and C. Marvin Pate. *Dictionary of Biblical Prophecy and End Times*. Grand Rapids: Zondervan, 2007.

Leclerc, Thomas L. *Introduction to the Prophets: Their Stories, Sayings, and Scrolls*. New York: Paulist Press, 2007.

Peterson, David L. *The Prophetic Literature: An Introduction*. Louisville: Westminster John Knox, 2002.

Sawyer, John F. A. *Prophecy and the Prophets of the Old Testament*. Oxford: Oxford University Press, 1987.

Walton, John H. *Ancient Near Eastern Thought and the Old Testament: Introducing the Conceptual World of the Hebrew Bible* (Grand Rapids: Baker, 2006).

» DISCUSSION QUESTIONS «

1. Discuss the differences between the Hebrew Tanak and our English Bibles in regard to how the prophetic books are arranged and where they are placed.

2. Explain each of the main terms used for prophets in the Old Testament.

3. Why was false prophecy such a problem in Israel and Judah?

4. How have views on authorship of the prophetic books changed during the last twenty years?

» WRITING ASSIGNMENTS «

1. Using a Bible that identifies the source of quotes for you in the footnotes, read through the gospel of Matthew and list all of the passages that quote directly from the prophetic books. Cite the Matthew text and the prophetic text it quotes. Example: Matthew 1:23 quotes from Isaiah 7:14.

2. Discuss the prohibitions of Deuteronomy 18:9–22. Which practices of Israel's neighbors were prohibited? Why?

3. Discuss the differences and similarities between prophecy in ancient Israel and prophecy in other nations of the Ancient Near East.

CHAPTER 2

The Prophets in History

"Surely the nations are like a drop in a bucket;
they are regarded as dust on the scales." (Isa. 40:15)

THE HISTORICAL OVERVIEW

The prophets that we are studying in this book lived during tumultuous times. Amos, the earliest prophet, preached during the reign of Jeroboam II, king of Israel (786–746 BC).[1] Malachi, the last prophet, probably ministered in the middle of the fifth century BC (ca. 450 BC). The rest of the prophets fall in between these two. Thus the prophets span about three hundred years, from around 750 BC to around 450 BC.

> During the time of the prophets, the history of the Ancient Near East was dominated by three successive empires: Assyrian, Babylonian, and Persian.

During this period, the history of the Ancient Near East was dominated by three successive empires: Assyrian, Babylonian, and Persian. All of these nations were located to the north of Israel and Judah in what are the modern countries of Iraq (Assyria, Babylonia) and Iran (Persia). In the other direction was Egypt (sometimes controlled by Cush, the nation to the south of Egypt), the southern world power. The prophetic era was characterized geopolitically by political intrigue, alliances, rebellions against the reigning superpowers, and,

---

1. In general, this book will follow the dating provided by John Bright, *A History of Israel*, 4th ed. (Philadelphia: Westminster/John Knox, 2000).

King Jehu of Israel bowing down and paying tribute to King Shalmaneser of Assyria, about 825 BC (from the Black Obelisk of Shalmaneser).

Todd Bolen/www.BiblePlaces.com

consequently, frequent invasions. Most of the Old Testament prophets delivered their messages in the context of a coming invasion by one of the dominant empires.

The Prophets and Associated Dominant Empires		
Assyrian Dominance (745 – 612 BC)	**Babylonian Dominance (612 – 539 BC)**	**Persian Dominance (539 – 336 BC)**
Amos	Jeremiah*	Daniel
Jonah	Zephaniah	Zechariah
Hosea	Habakkuk	Haggai
Isaiah	Ezekiel	Malachi
Micah	Daniel	
Nahum	Joel (?)	
Joel (?)		

*Jeremiah actually began his ministry in 626 BC, during the twilight years of the Assyrian Empire, but most of his book is to be understood in light of the rising Babylonian Empire. Also keep in mind that 612 BC (the fall of Nineveh) is an approximate date for the shift from Assyrian to Babylonian dominance. In reality, this shift took place over a number of years.

From Genesis to Amos

Let's put this in perspective by briefly reviewing the history of Israel up to the prophetic era. In Genesis 1 – 2 Yahweh creates the world and places mankind in a wonderful garden. Genesis 3 – 11 describes how people sin repeatedly, thus alienating themselves from Yahweh and from each other. This section presents the cosmic, worldwide story of sin and scattering (i.e., exile from the presence of Yahweh). Starting in Genesis 12, Yahweh begins to unfold his redemption plan, the answer to mankind's sinful behavior in Genesis 3 – 11. Yahweh makes a covenant with Abraham (see the further discussion in chapter 4 of this book), which is repeated to his descendants Isaac and Jacob. This covenant promises a land, descendants, and blessings both on the descendants and on the nations of the earth. At the end of Genesis, the twelve sons of Jacob have migrated to Egypt and are residing there.

> The covenant relationship was characterized by a three-part formula: "I will be your God; You will be my people; I will dwell in your midst."

When the book of Exodus opens, approximately four hundred years have passed, and the Israelites in Egypt have been forced into slavery and are being oppressed by the Pharaoh. Yahweh therefore raises up Moses to confront Pharaoh and to lead the people out of Egypt. Scholars disagree over the date of the exodus, opting either for 1446 BC or for around 1280 BC. Yahweh leads the Israelites out into the wilderness and enters into a covenant relationship with them. This covenant relationship is characterized by a three-part formula: "I will be your God; You will be my people; I will dwell in your midst." The latter half of Exodus describes the construction of the tabernacle. Since

Assyrian King List with eponyms.

Yahweh was coming to dwell in their midst, the tabernacle was needed to provide the proper place for him to reside and to meet with his people. Leviticus provides the instructions on how Israel was to approach and worship holy, awesome Yahweh now living in their midst. Numbers describes how Israel at first refused the Promised Land, resulting in forty years of wandering in the wilderness. Yahweh then takes the next generation back to the border of the Promised Land and restates the covenant (book of Deuteronomy) as the terms by which Israel can live in the land and be blessed. Israel then agrees to keep the laws of Deuteronomy. The central question that drives much of the rest of the Old Testament is this: Will Israel stay faithful to Yahweh and keep the book of Deuteronomy?

Yahweh then leads the people across the Jordan and into the Promised Land (book of Joshua). The first generation is faithful, conquering most of the land. However, the next generation starts to fall away, and the book of Judges chronicles the downward spiral of Israel as they digress morally and theologically. The end of Judges describes the terrible situation they end up in. Who will save them from the mess they are in? The book of Ruth

BC or BCE?

Throughout most of modern Western history, the universal system of dating was based on the birth of Christ. Thus we used BC (before Christ) and AD (*anno Domini,* which means "in the year of our Lord"). In recent years, primarily from within the fields of biblical studies and biblical archaeology, there has been a push to change these designations. During the last twenty years or so, these fields have tried to foster good working relationships between Christian scholars and scholars from other faiths, particularly those of the Jewish faith. The continued use of a dating system that referred to Christ was deemed offensive or inappropriate, and thus many scholars and scholarly publications began using the abbreviations BCE (before the Common Era) and CE (of the Common Era) in place of the traditional BC and AD. Many scholarly books and journal articles on the Bible and biblical archaeology over the last twenty years have followed this new terminology, and many journals and commentary series require their authors to follow the new convention. However, the practice has not spread outside of archaeology and biblical studies to any other fields to any significant degree. Furthermore, many Christians who write in the fields of biblical studies and biblical archaeology acknowledge that they write "as Christians" and thus want to retain the traditional convention of dating all of human history by the birth of their Lord. Evangelicals in particular have continued to prefer the traditional designations of BC and AD. Thus throughout this book we will stay with the traditional abbreviations BC and AD.

Obviously ancient peoples did not use modern calendars. So how do scholars know what year such-and-such king lived or what year such-and-such battle took place? There is a document from the Assyrian era called the Assyrian King List that lists the Assyrian kings in order. In this list the Assyrians also attached a unique name to each consecutive year. These names were based on the names of officials, called eponyms, and the Assyrians used these names to date the years of each king's accession. Thus we can tell exactly how many years it was from one Assyrian king to the next. Likewise Assyrian scribes dated other events by the use of these eponyms. The Assyrians mention a solar eclipse as occurring in one particular eponym. Modern astronomers have been able to pinpoint the precise date of that solar eclipse, June 15, 763 BC. By using that firm date and the Assyrian King List, scholars can determine accurate dates for most of Assyrian history. The Babylonians also produced king lists, which overlap with the Assyrian lists, so the Babylonian era can be dated fairly accurately as well. Numerous historical events that involve the Assyrians or the Babylonians are recorded in the Bible. Thus we are able to date those events fairly precisely. Since 1–2 Kings ties all of the Israelite and Judahite kings together by length of reign, scholars can start with Assyrian and Babylonian connections and then determine dates for all of the kings of Israel and Judah.

introduces David, who will be the "savior" who saves them from the terrible situation found at the end of Judges. The next books, 1–2 Samuel, are about David (who reigns from 1000 BC to 961 BC), including his rise to power as king and his restoration of the proper worship of Yahweh. David's son Solomon comes to the throne next (961 BC to 922 BC). Although Solomon does build a spectacular temple for Yahweh, the God of Israel, he also introduces and establishes the worship of numerous pagan gods into Israel, thus giving momentum to Israel's disastrous slide into idolatry. After Solomon dies, the nation splits into two kingdoms: the northern kingdom, Israel, and the southern kingdom, Judah. The northern kingdom immediately falls into idolatry, and the new king, Jeroboam, erects two golden calves at central worship centers to replace the worship of Yahweh in Jerusalem. For the next two hundred years or so, the two states (Israel and Judah) will exist side by side, often in hostility toward each other. Then Israel will be destroyed by the Assyrians (722 BC) and Judah will continue to survive for another 135 years until she falls to the Babylonians in 587/586 BC.

HISTORY OF THE PROPHETIC ERA

During the first half of the eighth century (i.e., the 700s BC) the Assyrians were experiencing a period of weakness. Under Jeroboam II (786–746 BC), Israel was expanding and enjoying a time of material prosperity (Amos will critique this). Israel was larger and more powerful than Judah to the south, and in the years following the death of Jeroboam, Israel (under King Pekah) and Syria (under King Rezin) allied together to attack the smaller Judah (under King Ahaz). This was the beginning of the Syro-Ephraimite war, and it formed the background for the beginning of Isaiah's ministry, especially as

Sennacherib's Prism. The Assyrian king boasts of conquering 46 cities in Canaan, but of Jerusalem he states, "(Hezekiah) I made a prisoner in Jerusalem like a bird in a cage. "

Left: Artist's reconstruction of the temple complex at Babylon. *Right:* Artist's reconstruction of the Ishtar Gate of Babylon.

seen in Isaiah 7–9. Micah prophesied during this time also. Meanwhile, Tiglath-pileser III, a new king, rose to power in Assyria, restored Assyria to military prominence, and began flexing the renewed Assyrian imperial muscles. King Ahaz of Judah, under attack from Syria and Israel, appealed to Tiglath-pileser III for help. The Assyrian king complied by pressuring Syria and Israel, subduing portions of their territory. This relieved Judah of the immediate threat but put her under Assyrian hegemony. Shalmaneser V, the next Assyrian king, soon crushed the rest of the northern kingdom Israel. In 722 BC he destroyed the capital city of Samaria and scattered the inhabitants of Israel. The northern kingdom Israel was gone.

> In 722 BC Shalmaneser V destroyed the capital city of Samaria and scattered the inhabitants of Israel. The northern kingdom Israel was gone.

Meanwhile, in the southern kingdom of Judah, Hezekiah (715 BC–687 BC) came to the throne. The new Assyrian king, Sennacherib, tried to expand his borders even further to the south, and in 701 BC he laid siege to Jerusalem. Isaiah, however, prophesied that Yahweh would deliver the city—and indeed, the angel of Yahweh struck down 185,000 men in the Assyrian camp. The Assyrian army quickly withdrew. This event is recorded in Isaiah 36–39 as well as in 2 Kings 18–19. The Assyrian kings, however, never admitted to any such catastrophic defeat in their annals. It is interesting to note, however, that Sennacherib never claimed to have actually conquered Jerusalem, only to having laid siege to it. In his annals, he put a positive political spin on the event, declaring, "As to Hezekiah, the Jew, he did not submit to

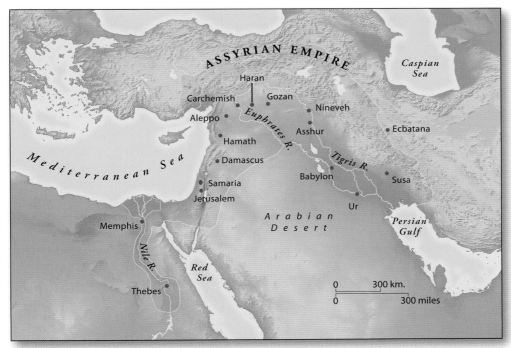

The Assyrian Empire in 700 BC.

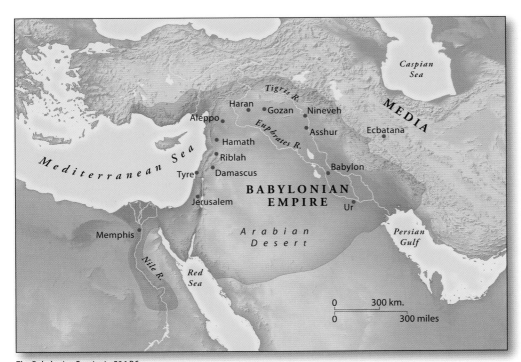

The Babylonian Empire in 586 BC.

my yoke, I laid siege to 46 of his strong cities, walled forts and to countless small villages in their vicinity and conquered them.... Himself I made a prisoner in Jerusalem, his royal residence, like a bird in a cage."[2]

Hezekiah's son Manasseh ruled over Judah next (687–642 BC). Manasseh became a loyal subject to Assyria, even fighting alongside the Assyrians in their campaign against Egypt in 667 BC. Theologically, Manasseh was one of the worst kings of Judah, and he facilitated the continuing slide away from Yahweh into idol worship. Manasseh was succeeded by his son Amon, who ruled for only two years before being assassinated. Manasseh's young son Josiah next came to the throne. Josiah was faithful to Yahweh and tried throughout his reign (640–609 BC) to rid the country of idolatry and to return the people to a true worship of Yahweh. Jeremiah began his long tenure as prophet during Josiah's reforms.

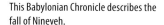

> Manasseh was one of the worst kings of Judah, and he facilitated the continuing slide away from Yahweh into idol worship.

Meanwhile, Assyria, plagued by internal strife and civil war, lost its grip on the region. The Egyptians quickly started to expand their influence in the south, and the Babylonians began challenging Assyria for control of Mesopotamia. In 612 BC, Nineveh, the capital of Assyria, fell to the Babylonians. The Assyrians formed an alliance with the Egyptians in a desperate attempt to stop the Babylonian juggernaut. The Egyptian king Neco II marched north from Egypt in 609 BC to assist the Assyrians in their stand against the expansion of the Babylonians. As Neco II passed through Judah, he was apparently opposed by King Josiah near the city of Megiddo. Neco II defeated the Judahites, and Josiah was killed. Judah now came under Egyptian control.

This Babylonian Chronicle describes the fall of Nineveh.

Todd Bolen/www.BiblePlaces.com

The Egyptians appointed Josiah's son Jehoahaz as king, but after only three months Neco II exiled Jehoahaz to Egypt and replaced him with Jehoahaz's brother Jehoiakim (609–598 BC). Jehoiakim was a disastrous king for Judah. He reversed all of the good religious reforms of Josiah, and he clashed frequently with the prophet Jeremiah over idolatry and social injustice. Politically, Jehoiakim remained a loyal vassal to Egypt until 605 BC, when the Babylonians crushed the Assyrian/Egyptian alliance at Carchemish. The Egyptians fled south for home, and the Babylonians, under King Nebuchadnezzar, marched into Palestine close on their heels. Jehoiakim switched sides, pledging fealty to Nebuchadnezzar, who now had control of the region. In 601 BC the Egyptians fought the Babylonians to a standstill at the Egyptian border. Nebuchadnezzar returned to Babylonia to reorganize his army. Interpreting this as a sign of Babylonian weakness, Jehoiakim switched his allegiance to the Egyptians and promptly rebelled against his Babylonian masters.

Nebuchadnezzar, however, quickly rebuilt his army and moved against the rebellious King Jehoiakim, arriving at the gates of Jerusalem in 598 BC. Judah's Egyptian allies pro-

---

2. James B. Prichard, ed., *Ancient Near Eastern Texts Relating to the Old Testament,* 3rd ed. (Princeton: Princeton University Press, 1969), 288.

vided no assistance. As the Babylonians were arriving, Jehoiakim died, probably assassinated by pro-Babylonian elements in Jerusalem. The new king, Jehoiakim's eighteen-year-old son, Jehoiachin, quickly surrendered to the Babylonians (597 BC), who deported the young king along with other leading citizens to Babylon. Included in this deportation was the prophet Ezekiel, a young man at the time. Jeremiah stayed in Jerusalem.

The Babylonians then installed Zedekiah, the brother of Jehoiakim, as the new "puppet" king. Like those before him (except Josiah), Zedekiah cared nothing about obeying the book of Deuteronomy or worshipping Yahweh alone. Not surprisingly, he and the prophet Jeremiah were in constant conflict. In 595 BC there was an uprising in Babylonia. Probably due to Egyptian instigation, Judah and her neighbors (Edom, Moab, Ammon, Tyre, and Sidon) began planning rebellion against their Babylonian masters. Ignoring the warnings of Jeremiah the prophet, Zedekiah rebelled. Nebuchadnezzar, however, had regained total control of Babylonia, and he soon marched south to punish his rebellious subjects.

> Jehoiakim reversed all of the good religious reforms of Josiah and clashed frequently with the prophet Jeremiah over idolatry and social injustice.

After conquering and destroying Judah's other fortress cities, the Babylonians arrived at Jerusalem and began a lengthy siege. This siege was interrupted briefly by the appearance of an Egyptian army, but Nebuchadnezzar quickly sent them scampering back into Egypt and resumed the siege. After two long years of siege, in 586 BC the Babylonians broke through the walls and captured Jerusalem. This time the Babylonians were furious at the rebellious Judahites, and they destroyed the city completely (as Jeremiah had warned). They killed thousands of Judah's inhabitants and took most of the survivors into exile to Babylon, leaving behind only the poor and those who had fled into the mountains. Jeremiah was also allowed to stay in Jerusalem, which was now in ruins.

The Babylonians appointed Gedaliah, who was not a member of the rebellious royal family, as governor. Before too long, however, some remnants of the Judahite army and nobility assassinated Gedaliah, thus challenging Babylonian control. When Nebuchadnezzar predictably responded, this faction fled in fear to Egypt, forcing Jeremiah to go with them.

> This time the Babylonians were furious at the rebellious Judahites, and they destroyed Jerusalem completely.

Nebuchadnezzar ruled Babylon and much of the Ancient Near East from 605 BC to 552 BC. After his death, however, Babylonian power began to wane, and soon it was eclipsed by the rising Persian empire (with the Medes as allies). In fact, the Persian king Cyrus captured Babylon in 539 BC with very little resistance. The Persians ruled over Palestine (what was once Judah and Israel) for the next two hundred years, and they were not driven out until Alexander the Great conquered the area in 333–332 BC.

The Persian king Cyrus, however, reversed the Babylonian policy of deportation, and in 538 BC he issued a decree stating that the Jews could return from their exile in Babylonia to their homeland. This era is thus frequently labeled the "postexilic" era. In several different waves down the generations that followed, under the leadership of Sheshbazzar,

Zerubbabel, Ezra, and Nehemiah, many of the Jews returned to Palestine and started rebuilding. The postexilic prophets Zechariah, Haggai, and Malachi prophesy in this context.

CONCLUSIONS

The Old Testament revolves around two parallel stories. One is the story of Genesis 3–11, a cosmic story of all humanity (the nations) scattered away from God and in need of salvation. The other story is that of Israel, who likewise sins and finds herself scattered and separated from God. The prophets bring these two stories together into one prophetic mega-story that involves both Israel and the nations. Thus the nations and the historical context surrounding the prophets are crucial elements in understanding the prophets. The focus of this book is on the "message of the prophets." Thus in this textbook we will spend more time focusing on the message rather than on the historical background. On the other hand, it is difficult to grasp the true message of the prophets without having a clear understanding of the complex geopolitical world in which they spoke. The two devastating and traumatic invasions of Israel and Judah by the Assyrians and then the Babylonians are especially crucial to understanding the preexilic prophets. Likewise, the Persian domination of the region following the collapse of the Babylonian empire forms an important backdrop for viewing the postexilic prophets.

> The two devastating and traumatic invasions of Israel and Judah by the Assyrians and then the Babylonians are especially crucial to understanding the preexilic prophets.

Other Historical Sources

The Assyrians, the Egyptians, and the Babylonians all produced historical-like literary texts during the OT prophetic period. Thousands of these documents have been found and translated. Some of these are administrative letters from provincial governors to the king. Many of them are royal annals, recounting the exploits of the king, especially military conquests. Occasionally, these annals contain references to biblical events. Scholars remind us, however, to be cautious when using this material. Often the royal annals were buried in the foundations of new temples. These annals were used to recount for the god the exploits of the king and the glory the king brought to that particular god. They were not necessarily used as historical records. Some other annals, however, were used as records, but they are notorious for their "political spin" and outright exaggeration — number of enemy soldiers killed, amount of gold taken, etc. Sometimes the Egyptian records conflict with the Assyrian and Babylonian records, and sometimes even the Assyrian records conflict with themselves. These sources are helpful to scholars for corroborating biblical events with non-biblical history; likewise these annals provide us with a wealth of historical background. But these sources are not always accurate and must be used with caution.

» FURTHER READING «

Blenkinsopp, Joseph. *A History of Prophecy in Israel*. Revised edition. Louisville: Westminster John Knox, 1996.

Bright, John. *A History of Israel*. 4th edition. Louisville: Westminster John Knox, 2000.

Chavalas, Mark W., and Lawson Younger Jr. *Mesopotamia and the Bible: Comparative Explorations*. Grand Rapids: Baker, 2002.

Provan, Iain, V. Philips Long, and Tremper Longman III. *A Biblical History of Israel*. Louisville: Westminster John Knox, 2003.

Sasson, Jack M., ed. *Civilizations of the Ancient Near East*. 4 vols. Peabody, MA: Hendrickson, 2000.

» DISCUSSION QUESTIONS «

1. Briefly retell the history of Israel/Judah from Abraham to the return of the exiles under Ezra, Nehemiah, and Zerubbabel.

2. Explain how historical dates in the Old Testament are determined.

3. Why is history important to our understanding of the prophets?

» WRITING ASSIGNMENTS «

1. Read 2 Kings and list all of the kings of Judah and Israel during the prophetic period. Identify which were "good kings" and which were "bad kings." Who were the three worst kings? Who were the three best kings?

2. Write a three-page report on the events that took place in Judah between 612 BC and 586 BC.

CHAPTER 3

The Literature of the Prophets

"The lion has roared—." (Amos 3:8)

THE GENRE OF THE PROPHETIC BOOKS

The Bible contains several different types of literature: gospels, epistles, narrative, and poetry, for example. Scholars use the term *genre* to refer to the type of literature one is dealing with. It is important for us as interpreters to be aware of the genre that we are studying because we cannot approach all types of biblical literature in the same way. Paul, for example, uses language differently in his epistles than the psalmist does. If we take a verse from Psalms and interpret it as if it came from Romans, we are likely to miss the author's intended meaning.

> The term *genre* simply refers to the type of literature one is dealing with.

What is the genre of the prophetic books? These books are made up primarily of oracles and visions from Yahweh, often delivered by the prophet in the form of short spoken or preached messages, usually proclaimed by the prophet to either Israel or Judah. The prophetic books also contain short narrative sections that sometimes include symbolic acts carried out by the prophet to illustrate Yahweh's message. Likewise, the prophetic literature also includes direct dialogues between Yahweh and his prophets. Much of this material is conveyed through colorful, poetic language, packed tightly with colorful wordplays and graphic figures of speech. The prophets can lift hearts with their beautiful praise of Yahweh, and they can also ridicule their skeptical opponents with scathing, sarcastic polemics.

Because of these features, the prophetic literature is perhaps the most difficult for us to understand of all the literary types in the Bible. It is challenging to find a genre in English literature that is similar to that found in the prophetic literature.

> There is little in the literature of our language and culture that resembles the prophetic literature of the Old Testament.

Think about it for a moment. We are familiar with narrative because we read stories all the time. Likewise, we are comfortable with psalms because we are familiar with hymns and choruses. The letters in the New Testament bear some similarities with modern letters, so we are not lost when confronted with the genre of letter. However, there is little in the literature of our language and culture that resembles the prophetic literature of the Old Testament. The world of the prophets can seem strange and baffling. Yet, even though we are not overly familiar with this type of literature, we can learn to recognize the elements of prophetic genre, and we can learn principles for interpreting it. Furthermore, there is perhaps a hint of genre similarity between Old Testament prophecy and some of our songs.

ANTHOLOGIES

The prophetic books are not essays organized around propositional statements and logical sequential argumentation. Neither are they stories driven by sequential time, action, and plot. While they are organized and logical, and while they do reflect plot (in the broadest sense), most of the prophetic books can probably best be categorized as *anthologies*. That is, most of the prophetic books are collections of material—oracles, sermons, dialogues, and short narrative episodes. In this sense they are similar in some regards to a modern anthology of a poet's life: poems, letters, stories, and so forth. Sometimes broad thematic unity is present, and occasionally a few short sections will be combined chronologically. Likewise, catchwords or "theme-words" will occasionally connect sections.

Yet because of this "collection" nature of the material, it is often quite difficult to develop a detailed outline of the prophetic books. Basic foundational themes (like judgment) can be used to unite very broad sections of text into units, but usually within that unit will be found short sections that don't really fit. For example, embedded in the midst of a large unit on judgment one may find a short oracle proclaiming deliverance and restoration. This doesn't mean that the prophets can not be analyzed or understood. Anthologies can be quite clear in their

An important feature to note about the prophets is that their books are primarily anthologies.

Bob Dylan and the Prophets

The Old Testament prophetic genre contains an unusual mixture of colorful poetry, powerful wordplay, and critique of the political and theological failures of the current Israelite/Judahite society, especially the ruling classes (monarchy, priesthood, court prophets, nobles, etc.). The closest thing to this genre in American culture is perhaps the protest songs of the 1960s, and, in particular, those of Bob Dylan (often called the "prophet of the sixties"). Of course, Dylan lacks the theological component, and he is not to be elevated to the status that the prophets deserve. Nonetheless, some of Dylan's songs bear points of similarity — highly figurative language used to deliver scathing polemical diatribes against the status quo of the society, and against the authority structures in particular. Like the prophets, Dylan also suggests that the consequences of failing to change will be judgment.

Consider, for example, a few lines from Dylan's "The Times They Are a-Changin'":

> Come gather 'round people, wherever you roam
> And admit that the water around you has grown;
> And accept it that soon you'll be drenched to the bone.
> If your time to you is worth savin',
> Then you'd better start swimmin' or you'll sink like a stone,
> For the times they are a'changin'.

Dylan uses the poetic imagery of a flood to paint a startling picture of what will happen if no change takes place. This is very similar to how the prophets use judgment imagery. Likewise, in the verses that follow, Dylan critiques the people of his day who exercise authority and influence: senators and congressmen (verse 2), writers (verse 3), and parents (verse 4). This critique is similar to the frequent warning and judgmental diatribes that the prophets

Bob Dylan, the "prophet of the sixties," gives us a genre that is similar to prophetic literature.

Associated Press

deliver against the king and his family, the court prophets, the priesthood, and the nobles as well as the rulers of the other powerful nations of the day. Hosea even uses a very similar flood imagery in his pronouncement of judgment: "Samaria and its king will float away like a twig on the surface of the waters" (Hos. 10:7).

message. It is just that the message will emerge differently than one derived from a narrative or a New Testament epistle, for example. For one thing, the prophets are quite repetitive; they do not mind saying exactly the same thing over and over to get the point across. In our study we will encounter several prophetic themes and messages that appear repeatedly throughout the material. Thus, throughout this book we will break each book down only into very broad units, usually based on thematic or structural considerations.

THE PROPHETS AND POETRY

As mentioned above, although the Old Testament prophets occasionally wrote in narrative (prose), they primarily wrote in poetry. Poetry is quite different than prose, and we will interpret the prophets better if we keep these differences in mind. Unlike Paul and much of the New Testament literature, the Old Testament prophets (through their poetic expression) appeal primarily to our emotions. Furthermore, they do not build complex grammatical arguments (as does Paul), but rather they use images to convey their meanings. They paint colorful pictures with words to express messages loaded with emotional impact. This doesn't mean that they ignore logic or argue illogically. It simply means that they focus on emotional more than on logical aspects. Likewise, Paul's letters are not devoid of emotion, but yet his focus is on reasoning.

> The Old Testament prophets primarily wrote in poetry.

Elements of Old Testament Poetry Used in Prophecy

Poetry in general, and Old Testament poetry in particular, is a form of art, and the aesthetics or artistic features of it are important to the authors. Of course the content or the message in the poetry is also important, even central, but the form of the text (in this case the poetic features) plays a critical role in communicating the intended meaning of the author. Thus if we want to understand the full impact of the prophetic message, we will need to appreciate the poetic aspects and understand how the Hebrew poetry is working.

Hebrew poetry is art, and as such it is not easy to define precisely. Furthermore, the prophets used narrative and dialogue in addition to poetry (and sometimes the dialogue is in poetry). There is not a clear line delineating the shift from prose to poetry. The primary characteristics of Hebrew poetry are (1) density (succinctness), (2) parallelism, (3) figurative imagery, and (4) high concentration of wordplay. Some Hebrew prose will not have any of these characteristics, and some Hebrew poetry will have high concentrations of all four, but often (especially in Jeremiah) we will also encounter texts that have some, but not all, of these characteristics. Are such texts poetry or prose? Scholars disagree. It is perhaps helpful to view the literature of the Old Testament on a spectrum. At one end of the spectrum is prose, containing little if any of the poetic characteristics. At the other end is poetry, containing high concentrations of all four characteristics. The more that a literary work reflects the four characteristics, the more it moves toward the poetry end of the spectrum.[1]

---

1. The concept of a spectrum is taken, with modification, from William W. Klein, Craig L. Blomberg, and Robert L. Hubbard Jr., *Introduction to Biblical Interpretation* (Dallas: Word Publishing, 1993), 216–17.

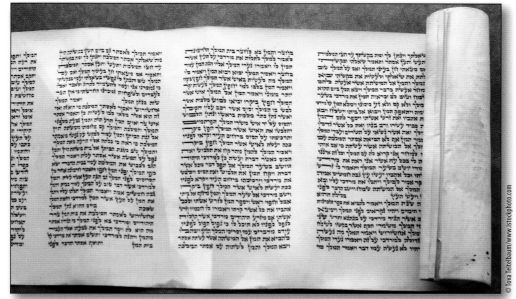

A Hebrew scroll.

The prophetic books contain literary texts all across the spectrum, but the majority of texts reflect all four characteristics and thus are very poetic. To help you detect these features and appreciate their poetic contribution, each is discussed in further detail below.

1. Density. Some scholars refer to this feature as succinctness or terseness. This simply means that poetry is the most compact of literary forms in regard to word usage. Poetry uses a minimum number of words, chosen carefully for their impact, power, and aesthetic qualities. Narrative texts in the Old Testament are characterized by fairly long, descriptive sentences, while the poetic texts in the prophets, on the other hand, are usually made up of short, compact lines of verse with few words.

2. Parallelism. One of the most obvious features of poetry in the prophets is that the text is structured around poetic lines of verse, rather than around sentences and paragraphs. So interpreters should train their eyes to read the poetic sections line by line rather than sentence by sentence. In addition, and most importantly, Hebrew poetic lines of text are usually grouped in units of two or three. Rather than expressing thoughts based on sentence structure, Hebrew poetry will group two (or occasionally three) lines of text together to convey each major thought. This type of structure is called *parallelism,* and it is one of the most common and most noticeable features of Hebrew poetry. For example, consider Isaiah 51:4:

Parallelism is the dominant structural characteristic of Old Testament poetry.

A¹ Listen to me, my people;
A² hear me, my nation:
B¹ The law will go out from me;
B² my justice will become a light to the nations.

Note how the first two lines ("listen to me, my people" and "hear me, my nation") are nearly synonymous. They go together to form one thought. Likewise the last two lines (regarding law and justice) also go together and form one main thought. Sometimes the verse notations will follow this pattern, and each verse will consist of two lines of text that yield one thought. Yet this varies. As seen above in Isaiah 51:4, often the verses in our English Bibles can contain four lines of poetic text, usually composed of two couplets, thus expressing two main thoughts. Such verse notations help us as we read because we need to interpret the text by reading each parallel construction together.

Sometimes the two lines of text will be very similar in meaning. On the other hand, the two lines can express opposite, or contrasting ideas. Yet most of the time the second line simply furthers the idea of the first line. Scholars have suggested that the best way to describe the relationship between two lines A^1 and A^2 is to understand it as "A^1 is so, and what's more, A^2." In this sense A^1 is a statement and A^2 is a "seconding" or addition to the statement.[2] The parallel connection is often related to word and phrase meanings, but the

2. James L. Kugel, *The Idea of Biblical Poetry* (New Haven: Yale University Press, 1981), 51; cited by James Limburg, "Psalms, Book of," *Anchor Bible Dictionary,* 5:529; Joel M. LeMon and Brent A. Strawn, "Parallelism," in *Dictionary of the Old Testament: Wisdom, Poetry and Writings,* ed. Tremper Longman III and Peter Enns (Downers Grove, IL: InterVarsity Press, 2008), 502–15.

The caves at Qumran. In these caves nearly 25,000 fragments were found from nearly 900 scrolls. These are commonly called the Dead Sea Scrolls. All of the prophetic books are represented, including portions of 21 scrolls of Isaiah.

William D. Mounce

connections can also be phonological (sound) or morphological (grammatical form), or any combination of these.[3] Yet these are merely the main categories that are observed frequently. There are numerous other ways that the parallel lines relate to each other. Keep in mind that we are dealing with poetry, so the attempt to categorize or classify too precisely runs counter to the nature of the genre.[4]

While parallelism is a central literary feature at the verse or line level of the text, it is important to note that the prophets will also use parallelism for larger units of text as well. That is, not only will line A^1 parallel line A^2, but strophes (several lines of text) can parallel other strophes, and stanzas (numerous lines of text) can parallel other stanzas.[5]

Photo Clara Amit, courtesy Israel Antiquities Authority

A fragment of I Enoch, a noncanonical apocalyptic book, in Aramaic (200 – 150 BC), part of the Dead Sea Scrolls.

Likewise, larger units in the prophetic books can be in parallelism as well, even if the units are prose. For example, the structure of Jonah reflects the following parallel units:

A¹ Jonah's commissioning (1:1 – 3)
　 B¹ Jonah and the pagan sailors (1:4 – 16)
　　 C¹ Jonah's pious, grateful prayer (1:17 – 2:10)
A² Jonah's recommissioning (3:1 – 3a)
　 B² Jonah and the pagan Ninevites (3:3b – 10)
　　 C² Jonah's angry resentful prayer (4:1 – 4)
　　　 D Yahweh's lesson for Jonah (4:5 – 11)[6]

In numerous cases the prophets will use a direct style of parallelism like that seen in the book of Jonah (A¹, B¹, C¹, etc. followed by A², B², C², etc.). On the other hand, the poets of the Old Testament, including the prophets, also liked to invert the parallelism, where the outer elements (lines, verses, strophes, or stanzas) parallel each other, and the inner elements parallel each other. The pattern for this would be A¹, B¹, C¹, D, C², B², A². Such a pattern is called a *chiasm,* and it is quite common in Hebrew poetry (and occasionally in Hebrew narrative). Note in this example that D falls in the middle and does not have a parallel unit. Often when the central element does not have a parallel companion, it serves as the focal point or the main idea of the chiasm.

For example, several scholars have noted the chiasmic structure in Amos 5:1 – 17:

3. J. P. Fokkelman, *Reading Biblical Poetry: An Introductory Guide,* trans. Ineke Smit (Louisville: Westminster John Knox, 2001), 29.

4. LeMon and Strawn, "Parallelism," 510 – 12.

5. Fokkelman, *Reading Biblical Poetry,* 30.

6. David A. Dorsey, *The Literary Structure of the Old Testament: A Commentary on Genesis-Malachi* (Grand Rapids: Baker, 1999), 17.

A¹   Current lamentation over fallen Israel (5:1–3)
   B¹   Call to repentance (5:4–6a) (words "seek" and "live"; seven verbs of exhortation)
      C¹   Condemnation of Israel's injustice (5:6b–7) (words "justice" and "righteousness")
         D   CENTER: Yahweh's power (5:8–9) (7 verbs)
      C²   Condemnation of Israel's injustice (5:10–13) (words "righteous" and "justice")
   B²   Call to repentance (5:14–15) (words "seek" and "live;"; seven verbs of exhortation)
A²   Coming lamentation (5:16–17)[7]

According to some scholars, another important feature of poetic structure is meter, which is related to rhythm. Hebrew poetry employs accented and unaccented syllables (along with occasional assonance and occasional rhyme or similar sounds) to create rhythm as well as to heighten the effect of the parallelism. However, scholars are divided over how to analyze meter and rhythm, and in recent years many scholars have concluded that Hebrew poetry simply does not employ meter at all.[8] Either way, since all of the meter is lost in the translation process, it is difficult if not impossible to note metrical aspects in the English translation.

3. Figurative Imagery. Another characteristic of Hebrew poetry in general and of the prophets in particular is the extensive use of *figures of speech*. The prophetic books are loaded with colorful, vivid figures of speech, a feature that makes this material interesting and engaging. The prophet Amos does not merely say "God is angry." Rather, he proclaims: "The lion has roared." Isaiah does not philosophically discuss how terrible sin is and how wonderful forgiveness is; he announces: "Though your sins are like scarlet, they shall be as white as snow." Jeremiah is disgusted with the nation's unfaithful attitude toward Yahweh and wants to convey some of the pain that Yahweh feels because Judah has left him for idols, so he frequently compares the nation of Judah to an unfaithful wife who has become a prostitute. "You have lived as a prostitute with many lovers," Jeremiah proclaims, referring figuratively to Judah's idolatry.

> A central feature of Hebrew poetry is the extensive use of *figures of speech*. The Old Testament prophets do not write essays; they paint pictures.

The Old Testament prophets do not write philosophical essays or theological tractates; they paint colorful pictures. Like master artists they use figures of speech, wordplay, and verbal nuances, along with structural elements, to paint the complex interacting shades of color that proclaim their message.

Since most English speakers and writers today use figures of speech and wordplay all the time, we are not strangers to this feature. In English, if someone takes a figure of speech literally, he or she will misunderstand what the speaker is trying to say. If someone says, "I'm so hungry I could eat a horse," they just mean that they are extremely hungry. If we take the figures of speech in the Bible literally, we will misunderstand the text as badly as thinking that the person could actually eat an entire horse. If we want to understand the Old Testa-

---

7. Ibid., 281; see also Robert B. Chisholm Jr., *Handbook on the Prophets* (Grand Rapids: Baker, 2002), 391–92.

8. Walter L. McConnell, "Meter," in Longman and Enns, *Dictionary of the Old Testament*, 472–76.

ment prophets, it is critical that we recognize figures of speech for what they really are and then interpret them accordingly.

On the other hand, we must not forget the connection between figurative language and literal reality. Figures of speech use figurative language to express literal realities. The speaker above does not actually believe that they could consume an entire horse, but recognizing this fact does not diminish the literal truth being communicated. The speaker is really hungry. That is the literal reality that the figurative language communicates. Our job as readers is to grapple with the figures of speech and to strive to grasp the literal reality as well as the emotion that the poets are conveying by their figurative language.

Types of Figures of Speech

Most of the figures of speech we will encounter in the prophetic books will fall into one of two main categories: figures involving *analogy,* and figures involving *substitution.* Usually we can spot figures of speech and come to a reasonably accurate understanding of the author's meaning by classifying it into one of these two main categories.

Figures of Speech Involving Analogy

Some figures of speech work by drawing analogies between two items that are not normally seen as similar. There are numerous ways of making these figurative analogies, and the prophets use a wide range of these subcategories of analogy in their figures of speech.

Top left: The prophets use figures of speech from real life in their own day and time. Almost all of them use the lion imagery. *Bottom left*: "Those who hope in Yahweh will renew their strength. They will soar on wings like eagles" (Isaiah 40:31). *Below*: "I myself will tend my sheep" (Ezekiel 34:15).

Apocalyptic Literature

Another literary genre that is closely associated with Old Testament prophecy is *apocalyptic*. Large portions of the book of Daniel and Zechariah, for example, differ significantly in literary style and somewhat in theological focus from other prophetic books and thus fall into the category of apocalyptic rather than prophecy. Typically, the genre of apocalyptic has been defined as "a genre of revelatory literature with a narrative framework, in which a revelation is mediated by an otherworldly being to a human recipient, disclosing a transcendent reality which is both temporal, insofar as it envisages eschatological salvation, and spatial insofar as it involves another supernatural world."[1] Although scholars differ to some degree on the details, in general the characteristics of apocalyptic literature can further be summarized into five basic components: (1) the use of highly graphic images and symbols, usually associated with visions; (2) the periodization of future world history; (3) an emphasis on God's sovereignty; (4) the use of angels and visions to reveal the future; and (5) the ultimate victory of God and God's people over the forces of evil.[2] Although some scholars maintain that apocalyptic developed out of prophecy after prophecy ceased, it is probably best to view apocalyptic as a "sub-genre" within the broader phenomenon of prophecy. This apocalyptic style occurs not only in the Old Testament books of Daniel and Zechariah but in numerous noncanonical Jewish works (1–2 Enoch, 4 Ezra, 2–3 Baruch, etc.) as well as in the New Testament book of Revelation.

1. John J. Collins, *The Apocalyptic Imagination: An Introduction to Jewish Apocalyptic Literature,* 2nd ed. (Grand Rapids: Eerdmans, 1998), 5.
2. Paul R. House, *Old Testament Theology* (Downers Grove, IL: InterVarsity Press, 1998), 498.

Analogy-related figures of speech include simile, metaphor, hypocatastasis, hyperbole, and personification or anthropomorphism.

Similes are common both in English and in the prophets. Similes bring two normally different entities into comparison by using the words *like* or *as* to make the comparison. For example, Isaiah writes, "Though your sins are *like* scarlet, they shall be as white *as* snow" (Isa. 1:18).

Metaphors are similar in that they also highlight a comparison or analogy between two normally different entities. Metaphors differ from similes in that metaphors make the analogy between entities by a direct statement without the use of *like* or *as*. For example, in Isaiah 42:6 Yahweh tells the Servant, "I will make you ... a light for the Gentiles." Note the difference between metaphor and simile. A simile would have said, "I will make you *like* a light for the Gentiles." Yet ultimately the difference in meaning between simile and metaphor is usually minimal; both are drawing analogies and making comparisons between two normally different entities. They draw the analogy in that a certain aspect of the two different entities is similar. The prophets tend to use metaphor more than simile.

Hypocatastasis (indirect analogy) is a little more complicated than simile or metaphor. It employs the analogy without directly telling the reader that a comparison is even being

> Similes bring two normally different entities into comparison by using the words *like* or *as* to make the comparison.

made. In using hypocatastasis the author assumes that the reader can make the comparison without explicitly being informed of the comparison. Thus hypocatastasis can be more subtle than metaphor or simile. If Yahweh's wrath is being compared to a storm, a simile usage might declare, "The wrath of Yahweh is like a storm." A metaphor would be similar, stating the analogy as, "the wrath of Yahweh is a storm." Hypocatastasis, on the other hand, omits the announcement that an analogy is being made and states directly, "See, the storm of Yahweh will burst out in wrath, a driving wind swirling down on the heads of the wicked" (Jer. 30:23).

Hyperbole is another common figure of speech. Hyperbole can be defined as a "conscious exaggeration for the sake of effect." That is, hyperbole intentionally exaggerates, usually with the intention of expressing strong feeling or emotion. "It advertises its lack of literal truth," making no pretense at all of being factual.[9]

The prophets use hyperbole frequently. They intentionally exaggerate in order to stress their deep emotion. For example, Jeremiah 14:17 states, "Let my eyes overflow with tears night and day without ceasing."

Personification is a figure of speech in which a human characteristic or feature is attributed to a nonhuman entity. For example, at the beginning of Isaiah, the prophet calls on the heavens and the earth as witnesses to Israel's unfaithfulness. The prophet addresses them like people, stating: "Hear, O heavens! Listen, O earth!"

When God is described with human features, or when the actions of God are described in terms that are normally associated with people rather than deity, the figure of speech being used is called *anthropomorphism*. This type of figurative language is fairly common throughout the Old Testament, and especially in the prophets. Thus Yahweh is described as having hands, arms, feet, a nose, breath, a voice, and ears. He walks, sits, hears, looks down, thinks, talks, remembers, gets angry, shouts, lives in a palace, prepares tables, anoints heads, builds houses, and pitches tents. He has a rod, staff, scepter, banner, garment, tent, throne, footstool, vineyard, field, chariot, shield, and sword. He is called a father, husband, king, and shepherd. One of the challenges of interpretation is determining when this kind of language is figurative ("his hand is upraised" Isa. 9:12, 17, 21; 10:4) and when it might be literal. Some characteristics are common to some extent for both Yahweh and for people (love, anger, compassion). But what about remembering or thinking? Pondering? Hurting? Feeling remorseful? In regard to Yahweh, are the terms anthropomorphic or literal? We will discuss the problem of literal versus figurative interpretation in more detail in chapter 5.

Figures of Speech Involving Substitution

There are several figures of speech that involve the concept of substitution. For example, *metonymy* is a figure of speech in which the author states the "effect" when he wants the reader to understand the "cause." This can also work in reverse, where the "cause" is stated when the "effect" is the point. The prophet Isaiah uses metonymy when he declares, "Every warrior's boot used in battle and every garment rolled in blood will be destined for

> *Hyperbole* is a "conscious exaggeration for the sake of effect."

---

9. Leland Ryken, *How to Read the Bible as Literature* (Grand Rapids: Zondervan, 1984), 99–100.

burning, will be fuel for the fire" (Isa. 9:5). The burning of old battle clothes is the stated *effect*. What he is really talking about is the peace that the coming Child will bring (9:6–7).

Synecdoche is another figure of speech that uses substitution. It works on the principle of representation. Rather than mentioning the intended entity itself, the prophets will often point to a representative part of that entity. In English, this would be equivalent to using the city of Washington, D.C., to represent the entire United States. The Old Testament prophets employ synecdoche when they use Ephraim (the largest northern tribe) or Samaria (the capital city) to refer to the northern kingdom Israel, and Jerusalem (the capital city) to refer to the southern kingdom of Judah. Synecdoche (representation) is used frequently by the prophets in other contexts as well. For instance, *bow, sword,* and *chariot* are often used to represent weapons of war or military power in general (Ps. 20:7; 44:6). In similar fashion, body parts such as bones or feet can be used to represent the entire person (Ps. 6:2; 31:10; 32:3; 40:2; 44:18; 122:2).

> The terms *bow, sword, and chariot* are used to represent weapons of war or military power in general.

Miscellaneous Figures of Speech

There are some figures of speech, however, that do not fall into either of the two main categories discussed above. Keep in mind that figurative imagery is artistic and aesthetic in nature, so it sometimes resists detailed categorization. Likewise, some figures of speech are incredibly complex or subtle. In addition, occasionally we do not have enough linguistic and semantic background information to understand what a particular Hebrew figure of speech means. Thus there will always be some figures of speech that will fall into an *undefined* or *miscellaneous* classification.

One of these miscellaneous figures of speech that the prophets use quite often is *irony* and its related cousin, *sarcasm*. A writer using irony will often say the exact opposite of what he really means. The ridiculousness of the statement gives the impact and stress that the writer intends. Often a sarcastic tone accompanies the use of irony. For example, Yahweh appears to be using sarcastic irony in Amos 4:4 where Yahweh in essence tells Israel to "go ahead and sin." Likewise, catch the sarcasm in Isaiah 41:22–23 as Yahweh mocks the idols with the ironic challenge: "Bring in your idols to tell us what is going to happen. Tell us what the former things were, so that we may consider them and know the final outcome. Or declare to us the things to come, tell us what the future holds, so we may know that you are gods. Do something, whether good or bad, so that we may be dismayed and filled with fear."

> The prophets love wordplay and use it frequently, especially in poetic texts.

4. Wordplay. Wordplay includes a wide range of features connected to words (semantic range; word association; rhyme, assonance, or other similar sound; etc). We use wordplay quite regularly in English, and we appreciate wordplay, especially when it is clever. For example, as he signed the Declaration of Independence, Ben Franklin is said to have quipped, "Let us all *hang together* or else we may all *hang separately*." Franklin was making a play on two very different possible meanings of the word *hang*.

Hebrew wordplay often functions in a similar manner, playing off of the possible semantic range of a word. In addition, many examples of Hebrew wordplay are developed around similar sounding words. For example, in Isaiah 5:7 the prophet describes the disappointment Yahweh feels when he comes to his vineyard (Israel). The wordplay revolves around the fact that the Hebrew word for justice (*mishpat*) is similar in sound to the word for bloodshed (*mishpach*), and the word for righteousness (*tsedakah*) is similar sounding to the word for cries of distress (*tse'akah*):

> And he [Yahweh] looked for justice (*mishpat*),
> But saw bloodshed (*mishpach*);
> for righteousness (*tsedakaha*),
> but heard cries of distress (*tse'akah*).[10]

The Old Testament prophets love wordplay and use it throughout the prophetic literature. As pointed out above, usually the word games will either play off of variant possible meanings of a word or else they will play off of sound similarities. Unfortunately, Hebrew wordplay rarely translates well into English, and if we are unable to read Hebrew, we will need commentators or other reference tools to help us spot and understand it. Yet the pages of the prophetic books are filled with wordplay; indeed, the high concentration of wordplay is one of the characteristics of the prophetic literature, especially in poetic prophetic texts.

---

10. Klein, Blomberg, and Hubbard, *Introduction to Biblical Interpretation*, 223.

» FURTHER READING «

Collins, John J. *The Apocalyptic Imagination: An Introduction to Jewish Apocalyptic Literature.* Grand Rapids: Eerdmans, 1998.

Dorsey, David A. *The Literary Structure of the Old Testament: A Commentary on Genesis-Malachi.* Grand Rapids: Baker, 1999.

Fokkelman, J. P. *Reading Biblical Poetry: An Introductory Guide.* Translated by Ineke Smit. Louisville: Westminster John Knox, 2001.

Grabbe, Lester L. and Robert D. Haak. *Knowing the End from the Beginning.* Journal for the Study of the Pseudepigrapha Supplement Series 46. London: T. & T. Clark, 2003.

Longman, Tremper III, and Peter Enns. *Dictionary of the Old Testament: Wisdom, Poetry & Writings.* Downers Grove, IL: InterVarsity, 2008.

Sandy, D. Brent. *Plowshares & Pruning Hooks: Rethinking the Language of Biblical Prophecy and Apocalyptic.* Downers Grove, IL and Leicester, England: InterVarsity Press, 2002.

Ryken, Leland, James C. Wilhoit, and Tremper Longman III. *Dictionary of Biblical Imagery.* Downers Grove, IL: InterVarsity Press, 1998.

1. Why does Yahweh himself speak so often in poetry in the prophetic literature?

2. What are the words of one of your favorite songs that really affects you or moves you the most? Why does it affect you so? Is it the music or the lyrics that move you?

3. How does apocalyptic literature differ from the rest of the prophetic literature?

» WRITING ASSIGNMENTS «

1. Discuss the figures of speech in the following passages: Isaiah 1:5, 6, 8, 18, and 21. In each verse identify the figures of speech and identify what category it falls into (simile, metaphor, hypoca-tastasis, hyperbole, personification/anthropomorphism, metonymy, synecdoche, or irony). Then explain what the figure of speech means and how it works.

2. Isaiah 51:1 – 6 is reproduced below with each line in each verse assigned a letter. For each verse, identify which lines go together to form the main thought and then explain what that thought is. You will have two or three lines together to form a thought; each verse will have two or three thoughts. For example, in 51:4, lines a. and b. go together. The thought is that Yahweh is calling on his people/nation to listen to him.

51:1
   a. Listen to me, you who pursue righteousness
   b. and who seek the LORD :
   c. Look to the rock from which you were cut
   d. and to the quarry from which you were hewn;

51:2
   a. look to Abraham, your father,
   b. and to Sarah, who gave you birth.
   c. When I called him he was but one,
   d. and I blessed him and made him many.

51:3
   a. The LORD will surely comfort Zion
   b. and will look with compassion on all her ruins;
   c. he will make her deserts like Eden,
   d. her wastelands like the garden of the LORD.
   e. Joy and gladness will be found in her,
   f. thanksgiving and the sound of singing.

51:4

    a. Listen to me, my people;

    b. hear me, my nation:

    c. The law will go out from me;

    d. my justice will become a light to the nations.

51:5

    a. My righteousness draws near speedily,

    b. my salvation is on the way,

    c. and my arm will bring justice to the nations.

    d. The islands will look to me

    e. and wait in hope for my arm.

51:6

    a. Lift up your eyes to the heavens,

    b. look at the earth beneath;

    c. the heavens will vanish like smoke,

    d. the earth will wear out like a garment

    e. and its inhabitants die like flies.

    f. But my salvation will last forever,

    g. my righteousness will never fail.

CHAPTER 4

The Message of the Prophets

"What does Yahweh require of you?
To act justly and to love mercy
    and to walk humbly with your God."

(Micah 6:8)

THE HISTORICAL AND THEOLOGICAL CONTEXT

The message of the prophets was not delivered in a vacuum. In chapter 2 we reviewed the tumultuous historical context in which the prophets lived. Their message is integrally connected to that context, and they cannot be properly understood apart from it. But the prophets also deliver the word of Yahweh in a particular context relating to the *theological* history of Israel. Thus placing the message of the prophets into the proper theological context is critical for understanding them properly. This is especially true as we endeavor to develop theology for today from the prophetic message.

> Placing the message of the prophets into the proper theological context is critical for understanding them properly.

As we discussed in chapter 2, the historical setting for the preexilic (and exilic) prophets is dominated by the two major powers that successively controlled the region, Assyria and Babylonia. During the exile, the Persians overran the Babylonians, and they play an important role in setting the historical context for the postexilic prophets. The two major devastating invasions, that by the Assyrians in 722 BC and that by the Babylonians in 587/586 BC, cast a huge shadow over the entire era. First and Second Kings recounts the tragic story of Israel's and Judah's continued rebellion against Yahweh and the terrible consequences that ensued, ending in the destruction of Jerusalem and exile to Babylonia. Historically, most of the prophets preach in one of these two contexts: just prior to the Assyrian invasion, which destroyed the northern kingdom, Israel; or just prior to the Babylonian invasion, which destroyed the southern kingdom, Judah.

Theologically the prophets proclaim the word of Yahweh in the context of the Mosaic covenant, primarily as defined by Deuteronomy. After Yahweh delivered the Israelites from Egypt and as he led them to the Promised Land, he entered into a covenant agreement with them, as spelled out in Deuteronomy. This defined the relationship Yahweh was to have with his people, and it spelled out clearly the terms by which the Israelites could live prosperously in the land under the blessing of Yahweh. As the people enter into the Promised Land (book of Joshua), the driving question is: Will they be obedient and keep the terms of the law as spelled out in Deuteronomy? The tragic answer recorded in Judges to 2 Kings is "no." In general, the Israelites abandon Yahweh to worship idols, and they also succumb to the low judicial and moral standards of their neighbors. The prophets deliver Yahweh's

Deuteronomy provides much of the theological context of the prophets. Portions of 32 different Deuteronomy scrolls were found with the Dead Sea Scrolls.

word in a situation of flagrant covenant violation and of almost total disregard for the book of Deuteronomy.

The message of the prophets, however, expands beyond Israel. As we saw earlier, the Scriptures open with two major story cycles. In the first story cycle, Genesis 3–11 presents the cosmic, worldwide story of sin and scattering (exile from the presence of Yahweh); Genesis 12:3 presents the hope of restoration (blessings for the scattered nations in Genesis 10–11). The other story runs from Genesis 12 to 2 Kings 25 and is about Israel. It parallels the first story and follows the same pattern of sin, exile, and promised restoration. The remarkable theological contribution of the prophets is that they wed these two stories together. Sin will result in judgment on both Israel/Judah and on the nations. Likewise, the prophets proclaim, the true picture of the future restoration is one in which Yahweh restores Israel and the nations to himself. Thus the prophets declare that the specific theological story of Israel will merge with the cosmic universal theological story of Genesis 3–11 into a spectacular restoration that will bring Israel and the nations together in a true worship of Yahweh. This new people of Yahweh will be led by a glorious and righteous messianic Davidic king who will fulfill the Abrahamic promises both for Israel and for the nations. They will enter into a new covenant and will be empowered and enlightened by the very indwelling presence of Yahweh's Spirit.

> Theologically the prophets proclaim their message from the context of the Mosaic covenant, primarily as defined in Deuteronomy.

> The prophetic picture of future restoration is one that restores Israel and the nations together to Yahweh.

THE BASIC PROPHETIC MESSAGE

The Standard Preexilic Prophets

The prophets included in this group are Isaiah, Jeremiah, Ezekiel, Hosea, Joel, Amos, Micah, Habakkuk, and Zephaniah. They are described as "preexilic" because their times are located prior to (or during) the destruction of Jerusalem and the exile of 586 BC. We call them standard because they all stress similar central themes. Because this group comprises a majority of the prophetic material, we have labeled this group as "standard" and the others as "nonstandard," although both groups reflect authoritative scripture. Although the "standard" prophetic books do reflect a large degree of diversity in many details, the central themes discussed below are common in most of them to various degrees.

Within the Mosaic covenant context (primarily defined by Deuteronomy) and within the historical context of the looming expansionistic world powers of Assyria and Babylonia, the message of the prophets can be summarized by the following three basic points:

1. You (Israel/Judah) have broken the covenant; you had better repent!
2. No repentance? Then judgment! Judgment will also come on the nations.
3. Yet there is hope beyond the judgment for a glorious future restoration both for Israel/Judah and for the nations.

1. Point 1 underscores how extensively Israel and Judah have violated the covenant. Indeed, the prophets accuse the people of shattering the covenant and abandoning Yahweh

himself. The prophets point to a litany of sins that Israel has committed and continues to commit, sins that were clearly delineated in the book of Deuteronomy. This is the central theme in Isaiah 1–2. Likewise, this theme runs throughout Jeremiah 1–29. These sins or "covenant violations" fall into three major categories, all of which are explicitly listed in Deuteronomy: idolatry, social injustice, and reliance on religious ritualism.

a. *Idolatry* challenged the very foundation of Yahweh's relationship with his people. At the heart of the covenant was the formula statement: "I will be your god; you will be my people." Yet, beginning with the golden calf episode in Exodus 32, Israel struggles continually with the temptation to embrace the religious beliefs and practices of her neighbors, particularly in the area of idolatry. During the prophetic era, this problem becomes especially acute. The northern kingdom, Israel, falls into idolatry immediately upon its separation from Judah by constructing golden calf idols at Bethel and Dan. Judah soon follows, sliding into serious syncretism (the mixing and blending of different religions). The other nations in the region all worship numerous gods, particularly Baal and his consort, Asherah. The royal court, the court prophets, and the priesthood of Judah add the worship of these gods alongside the worship of Yahweh. Thus they continue to maintain many of the rituals associated with worshiping Yahweh, but they also participate in the rituals and festivals of numerous pagan gods. The prophets preach continuously against such idolatry, calling on the people to repent and to return to worshiping Yahweh alone (e.g., Isa. 2:8–9, 18; Jer. 2:20–28; 10:1–16; Ezek. 8:1–18; Hos. 4:10–19; 8:5; Amos 5:26; 7:9; Mic. 1:5–7; Hab. 2:19–20; Zeph. 1:4–6).

In the book of Ezekiel, Yahweh finally reaches the limits of his patience. In Ezekiel 8 the Spirit takes Ezekiel on a tour of the temple in Jerusalem, pointing out to him the serious idolatry that has moved into the temple itself. Yahweh shows him several shocking things: an idol at the entrance to one of the temple gates, drawings and carvings of idols and unclean animals on the walls inside the temple, women burning incense to the Babylonian vegetation god Tammuz, and elders with their backs to the presence of Yahweh in the Holy of Holies, facing the east and worshiping the sun. Yahweh has had enough and declares, "This will drive me from my sanctuary." Ezekiel 10 then describes the actual departure of Yahweh from the temple. The departure has profound theological implications, for it alters significantly the covenant arrangement between Yahweh and his people defined in Deuteronomy. Indeed, some scholars view this event as signaling the end of the Mosaic covenant.

Idolatry was not simply a minor ritualistic shortcoming, but it was an abandonment of faith-

Left: Bronze figure of Baal. *Right:* The goddess Astarte.

Z. Radovan/www.BibleLandPictures.com

Doug Bookman/www.BiblePlaces.com

fulness to Yahweh. It struck at the heart of the relationship between Yahweh and his people. Throughout the Old Testament the covenant is often founded on the central covenant formula made by Yahweh: "I will be your God; you will be my people. I will dwell in your midst." When Israel turned to other gods, they were rejecting this relationship. Yahweh's departure from the temple (i.e., no longer dwelling in their midst) was an acknowledgment of that shattered relationship. The decision by Israel and Judah to forsake Yahweh to worship other gods had both legal and relational implications. Because they violated the legal covenant stipulations of Deuteronomy, judgment would follow. Yet the seriousness of this sin goes even deeper. Several of the prophets stress the emotional hurt that Yahweh feels at this rejection. For Yahweh the issue is not only legal but relational — the people he loves so much have forsaken him to worship other gods.

> Idolatry challenged the very foundation of Yahweh's relationship with his people.

The prophets preach continuously against idolatry. It is a central feature of most prophetic books and is usually introduced early in each prophetic book. In addition to chastising the people for embracing behavior that undermined their very relationship with Yahweh, the prophets also deliver scathing polemical diatribes against the idols. "Bring in your idols," Isaiah taunts, "to tell us what is going to happen. Tell us what the former things were ... or declare to us the things to come ... so that we might know that you are gods. Do something," the prophet challenges, "whether good or bad, so that we will be dismayed and filled with fear" (Isa. 41:22–24). Jeremiah also ridicules the idols, pointing out their impotence: "Like a scarecrow in a melon patch, their idols cannot speak; they must be carried because they cannot walk. Do not fear them; they can do no harm nor can they do any good" (Jer. 10:5).

b. The second major indictment made by the prophets against Israel and Judah is their participation in and support of *social injustice*. Yahweh wanted his people to worship him alone, but such worship also entailed treating each other with love and concern, especially in the area of justice. This was spelled out clearly in Deuteronomy, which bound Yahweh's people to both a vertical relationship (with him) and a horizontal relationship (with other people). Relationship with Yahweh demanded proper relationship with people. In the book of Deuteronomy, Yahweh clearly expresses his deep concern for social justice throughout the entire society. In particular, Yahweh demands that the weaker individuals in society be cared for and that justice be provided for them. Deuteronomy demanded fair treatment of workers (24:14ff.); justice in the court system (19:15–21); and special care for widows,

Left: The god Baal with lightning and mace, from Ugarit.
Right: A gold-plated idol of a Canaanite god from Ugarit.

Marie-Lan Nguyen/Wikimedia Commons

Erich Lessing/Art Resource, NY

orphans, foreigners, and the poor (10:17 – 19; 15:1 – 11; 24:17 – 22; 26:12 – 13). As Israel and Judah abandon their relationship with Yahweh, they likewise abandon any concern they may have had for the weaker members of the society. The prophets condemn this practice quite vigorously, treating social injustice as seriously as idolatry. The prophets also proclaim that the sacrifices the people offer to Yahweh are meaningless if those offering the sacrifices regularly practice social injustice.

This point is stressed in Isaiah 1, for example, when the prophet announces that Yahweh will hide his eyes and not listen to the people as they sacrifice because of their regular involvement in social injustice. In similar fashion, the prophet Jeremiah indicts the people on this charge, proclaiming, "'They do not plead the case of the fatherless to win it, they do not defend the rights of the poor. Should I not punish them for this?' declares Yahweh" (Jer. 5:28 – 29). Micah 6:7 – 8 echoes this theme, driving home the point that justice is more important to Yahweh than the ritual of sacrifice:

> [7]Will Yahweh be pleased with thousands of rams,
>   with ten thousand rivers of oil?
> Shall I offer my firstborn for my transgression,
>   the fruit of my body for the sin of my soul?
> [8]He has showed you, O man, what is good.
>   And what does Yahweh require of you?
> To act justly and to love mercy
>   and to walk humbly with your God.

The loss of concern and compassion for the weaker members of the society was a serious violation of the book of Deuteronomy, but it also indicated that the people of Israel and Judah had lost sight of what Yahweh desired from them in their relationship with him.

c. *Reliance on religious ritualism.* As the people of Israel and Judah, along with their power structures and religious institutions, added idol worship and social injustice to their

Israel: The Unfaithful, Adulterous Wife

Often people view sin merely as a violation of God's law. That is, sin is like a speeding ticket — you've broken the law, and now someone must pay the penalty. Yet this concept mistakenly assumes that no one suffers any emotional pain and that the sin does not damage any close relationships. Through the prophets, Yahweh puts sin (and especially idolatry) into a much more relational category. To aptly illustrate this, several of the prophets use the faithful husband/unfaithful wife image. In fact, this is perhaps the central imagery Yahweh uses to underscore the seriousness of idolatry. In this image we see that sin is not like a speeding ticket that merely violates a law code; it is more like adultery, which not only violates the marriage law code but also involves a betrayal of the relationship and creates emotional pain. The prostitute/unfaithful wife image runs throughout the prophets. In fact, it is one of the central images in Jeremiah, occurring numerous times. Ezekiel also uses this relational picture, developing the image in detail in Ezekiel 16. And poor Hosea lives out the heartbreaking drama of the symbolism in this image through his own life and marriage.

Limestone altars inside a sanctuary in the Israelite city of Arad. Yahweh calls for justice, not meaningless, hypocritical ritual.

day-to-day living, they developed the thinking that maintaining the rituals of worship before Yahweh in the temple would satisfy him and thus cover over their idolatry and social injustice. In effect, the nation substituted the practice of lifeless religious ritualism in place of a living relationship with Yahweh. Israel forgot that ritual is only the means to the relationship, not a substitute for relationship. They became so enamored with the formalized ritualistic practices that they missed the entire point of the ritual — to develop and enhance their relationship with Yahweh. They drew the illogical conclusion that they could ignore the demands of Deuteronomy as long as they carried out their ritual practice (which continued to become more and more syncretistic). They failed to grasp the true significance of having Yahweh's holy presence in their midst.

The prophets point out the hypocrisy in the people's reliance on ritual. Yahweh wants justice, and without it, the ritual is simply meaningless, even annoying to Yahweh. Micah states this clearly in 6:7 – 8 (quoted above). Likewise, in Isaiah 1:11 – 13a Yahweh asks, "The multitude of your sacrifices, what are they to me? . . . Who has asked this of you, this trampling of my courts? Stop bringing meaningless offerings!"

Not only sacrifice, but the entire spectrum of ritualistic worship comes under prophetic critique. Isaiah, for example, addresses the uselessness of fasting without a concern for social justice: "You cannot fast as you do today and expect your voice to be heard on high," Isaiah says (58:4). He then declares what it is that Yahweh really desires:

> Is this not the kind of fasting I have chosen:
>> to loose the chains of injustice
>> and untie the cords of the yoke,
> to set the oppressed free
>> and break every yoke?
> Is it not to share your food with the hungry
>> and to provide the poor wanderer with shelter—
> when you see the naked, to clothe him,
>> and not to turn away from your own flesh and blood? (Isa. 58:6–7)

Idolatry, social injustice, and reliance on religious ritualism are the major themes that comprise the foundational charges or indictments made by the prophets against Israel and Judah in Point 1 of the prophetic message: *You have broken the covenant; you had better repent.* Yet the prophets do much more than merely point out sin and the seriousness of the sin. The second component of Point 1 is a call to repentance. The prophets plead with the people and beg them to repent and return to Yahweh before it is too late. Amazingly, the call to repentance of Point 1 is often intermixed with the proclamation of judgment (Point 2). Frequently, the prophets state very clearly that judgment is imminent and cannot be stopped; indeed, sometimes they note that the judgment is underway. Yet at the same time the prophets continue to plead for repentance, promising that the judgment can be averted, even at this late hour, if only the people will repent and turn back to Yahweh. Jeremiah, the classic example of this tension, proclaims on the one hand that the Babylonian invasion is absolutely inevitable, but on the other hand, he pleads with the people to repent so that such destruction can be avoided.

2. Point 2 of the prophetic message is *No repentance? Then judgment! Judgment will also come on the nations.* Even though the prophets beg the people to repent and to turn back to Yahweh and the covenant, neither Israel nor Judah does. In fact, almost no one listens to the prophets. The consequences of such arrogant, rebellious obstinacy, the prophets declare over and over, are a most devastating judgment. In fact, descriptions of the coming judgment (Assyrian or Babylonian invasion) dominate many pages in the prophetic books (e.g., Isa. 5:26–30; 8:6–8; 22:1–19; Jer. 4:5–6:30; Ezek. 4:1–17; 21:1–32; Hos. 13:1–16; Joel 2:1–11; Amos 3:1–15). In addition, the prophets also turn to Israel and Judah's neighbors, and proclaim severe judgment on the surrounding nations as well (including Assyria and Babylonia) for their defiance of Yahweh and for the injustices they committed (Isa. 13:1–21:17; 23:1–18; 34:1–15; 46:1–47:15; Jer. 46:1–51:64; Ezek. 25:1–32:32; Joel 3:1–8; Amos 1:3–2:3; Obad. 1; Nah. 1:1–3:19; Zeph. 2:4–15).

One of the most serious features of the judgment that fell on Israel and Judah was the loss of the Promised Land. As stated clearly in the warnings of Deuteronomy, Yahweh drives Israel and Judah out of the Promised Land, thus throwing into question their entire covenant relationship with him.

3. Point 3 of the prophetic message looks to the future restoration. This point can be summarized as follows: *Yet there is hope beyond the judgment for a glorious future restoration*

both for Israel/Judah and for the nations. This future restoration, the prophets declare, is not merely a return to the status quo before the terrible destruction of Jerusalem. A major component of this theme is that the theological and relational picture of Yahweh's people in the future will be different … and better. There will be a new exodus (Isa. 11:10–16; 43:5–6, 16–21; Jer. 31:7–11), a new covenant (Jer. 31:31–34; Ezek. 37:24–28), and a new presence of Yahweh's indwelling spirit (Ezek. 36:26–27; 37:14; Joel 2:28–29). This new day will be characterized by forgiveness and peace. Relationship will overshadow ritual.

> The prophets proclaim that in the future there will be a new exodus (Isaiah), a new covenant (Jeremiah), and a new presence of Yahweh's indwelling spirit (Ezekiel and Joel).

This theme of future restoration includes all of the wonderful prophecies of Christ. The people have failed to keep the law and the Mosaic covenant; thus they experienced the judgment that Deuteronomy prescribed. Yet the prophets point to a glorious time of restoration and regathering after the destruction that will be characterized by peace and blessing brought about by a righteous Davidic king. In addition, this time of restoration will include the non-Jewish peoples (the Gentile nations), who will join into the true worship of Yahweh. The Coming King will reign with justice and righteousness (in contrast to the old kings). He will inaugurate a new and better covenant, one written on hearts instead of on stone. These future events, the prophets proclaim, are not determined by kings or world powers. Neither are they by chance. All of the unfolding events, the prophets proclaim boldly, both the judgment and the restoration, are part of Yahweh's grand plan. He is the one who determines the course of history. He is the Lord over all history.

This fulfillment unites the cosmic story of Genesis 3–11 with the national story of Israel (Genesis 12–2 Kings 25), bringing all of human history together to focus on the Messiah as the ultimate answer to the problem of sin and alienation (exile) from the presence of Yahweh.

The three main points discussed above reflect a synthesis of the main themes found in the preexilic prophets. Isaiah, Jeremiah, Ezekiel, Hosea, Micah, and Zephaniah present all three points repeatedly. The book of Amos, on the other hand, is concerned primarily with the broken covenant and the coming judgment (Points 1 and 2). Amos does not proclaim the future hope and restoration until the end of the book (Amos 9), and even there the theme is rather brief. In contrast, the book of Joel has little to say about the broken covenant (Point 1), apparently assuming that it was common knowledge. Joel plunges right into the theme of judgment (Point 2) and then looks to the theme of hope and future restoration (Point 3). As discussed later in this book (Part 3), many scholars are proposing that the twelve Minor Prophets be studied as a unit (the Book of the Twelve) rather than totally independent of each other. Taken as a group, the Minor Prophets reflect all three points.

The Non-standard Preexilic Prophets

Obadiah, Nahum, and Jonah are preexilic prophets, but they do not present the standard three-point message discussed above. Obadiah and Nahum do not follow the typical pattern because they preach only against foreign nations (Edom and Nineveh, respectively)

The Prophets and Social Injustice Today

The sin of social injustice is a central theme that occurs repeatedly throughout the Prophets. Yahweh expects his people to live justly and to stand for justice. He is extremely serious about this, and the prophets place the sin of social injustice right next to idolatry. As part of this concern for social justice, the prophets address a wide range of issues — judicial bribery, marketplace dishonesty, failure to pay just wages. However, perhaps the central concern of Yahweh reflected in the message of the prophets is abuse, oppression, or even the neglect of the underclass, whom the prophets identify as the widow, the orphan, and the alien or foreigner (sometimes the poor are included). This triad (widows, orphans, foreigners) is specifically mentioned eight times in Deuteronomy (10:18; 24:17, 19, 20, 21; 26:12, 13; 27:19). Part of the covenant relationship that Israel had with Yahweh was the command that they care for the underclass, those people who did not have enough political and economic clout in the society to fend for themselves. Deuteronomy required that Israel pay special attention to this group, providing them with justice in the courts as well as food and participation in the worship festivals. Yet as Israel and Judah abandoned their relationship with Yahweh, they quickly lost their motivation to care for the underclass. In general they tended to completely ignore the commands of Deuteronomy in regard to those in the society who were weak and unprotected. This is one of the major sins that the prophets focus on in their indictment of Israel and Judah.

This theme is so pervasive in the prophets that it simply cannot be ignored by Christian readers today. How should we interpret and apply this theme today? First of all, following standard evangelical interpretive method, we should seek to develop a universal principle from this theme. Such a principle might be as follows: *God is very concerned for those who are weak, either physically or socioeconomically. He expects his people, since he lives in their midst, to be actively helping and defending such people.* As a check, it is always helpful to take the universal principles developed from the Old Testament and review them in light of the New Testament. In this case, the New Testament does not alter the principle at all, but clearly it includes social justice in the call to discipleship. Jesus illustrates the Levitical commandment "Love your neighbor as yourself" with the story of the good Samaritan, indicating that those who would follow him must care for those in need even if, or *especially* if, the one in need is racially or culturally different from them.

The challenge for us is to live out this call for social justice in our day-to-day lives. The problem is that often Christians today let their culture, family, or even their political party define the issues and actions relating to social justice instead of the Scriptures.

We need to explore applications from within the context of the biblical principle. For example, a relevant question to ponder is, Who today does not have enough political and economic clout to get justice or food? Minorities? Illegal immigrants? The poor? The elderly? Children? Abused women? The unborn? We have not really complied with the biblical mandate until we recognize how serious this issue is to God and realize that, as in ancient Israel, God holds his people (us) responsible to care for those who do not have the political or economic power to care for themselves.

and not against Israel or Judah. Thus they are similar in that they preach judgment on the nations, but they do not contain the standard message delivered by the other prophets to Israel and Judah. These two prophets, however, do play a role in the overall prophetic message, especially due to their canonical location. They are part of the larger message of judgment on the foreign nations. Nahum, proclaiming judgment on Nineveh, qualifies the message of Jonah, where the Ninevites are saved (at least temporarily for that generation).

Jonah is very important to the basic prophetic message even though he also preaches against a foreign city (Nineveh) and not against Israel or Judah. Probably the best understanding of Jonah is that while the actual historical preached message was to the Ninevites, the literary message was directed to Jonah's own people. Therefore his story forms an indictment against Israel and Judah. In a literary sense, Jonah is a foil for the rest of the prophets. The repentance of the Ninevites stands in stark contrast to the obstinacy of the Israelites. What happens in Nineveh is what should have happened in Jerusalem but did not. For example, Jeremiah preaches in Jerusalem for decades and the response is only one of hostility. No one repents, from the greatest to the least of them. Jonah, by contrast, preaches a short, reluctant sermon in Nineveh (of all places!) and the entire city repents, from the greatest to the least. The book of Jonah underscores how inexcusable is the response of Israel and Judah to the prophetic warning.

> Nahum, proclaiming judgment on Nineveh, qualifies the message of Jonah.

THE POSTEXILIC PROPHETS AND DANIEL

Typically, Haggai, Zechariah, and Malachi are identified as the "postexilic" prophets because they delivered their messages after the return of the exiles to Jerusalem following the Babylonian/Persian exile. This terminology is strongly entrenched in the vocabulary of biblical studies. Such a terminology, however, reflects a historical (and geographical) situation and not necessarily the theological one. True, many Jews did return to Jerusalem and Palestine from Babylon and Persia after the terrible destruction of Jerusalem and the exile. However, this return hardly signaled the inauguration of the glorious restoration that had been prophesied by the preexilic prophets. Indeed, the theological reality was that the Jews of the world, both those in Palestine and those throughout the dispersion, had not experienced restoration and were, to some extent, still in the exile.

During the Persian era, some Jews were able to return to Jerusalem and begin to rebuild their community out of the ashes. Haggai, Zechariah, and Malachi addressed this discouraged and disillusioned community. As this "remnant" returned and began rebuilding Jerusalem and the temple, the question in the minds of the community would have been whether or not this was the restoration the earlier prophets had promised. These three prophets answer this question with a sobering negative.

Both Haggai and Zechariah open with a reference to the reign of Darius the Persian, indicating from the very beginning that national and political restoration had certainly not been experienced. The dream of a Davidic king ruling over a strong and independent Israel appears to be dim indeed. Haggai focuses on the reconstruction of the temple, which, despite its less-than-glorious construction, helped to galvanize the tattered Jewish remnant into a surviving religious community. At least it helped to keep the survivors focused on Yahweh and his promises. Yet in the book of Haggai, although Yahweh tells the people that he is with them, he does not come to fill the temple with his presence as he did so spectacularly in the time of Solomon. Instead, Yahweh points to the future, telling the Jewish inhabitants of the land that the coming of his glory to the temple still lies in the future (Hag. 2:6–9). As mentioned earlier, the presence of Yahweh left the temple as the Babylonians drew near (Ezekiel 10). Neither of the accounts of postexilic temple reconstruction in Ezra or in Haggai mentions the return of Yahweh's presence to the temple. This absence is a clear indication that this return to the Land did not result in a return to the blessings of life in the land promised in Deuteronomy. The old covenant arrangement was gone with the wind.

> Despite its less-than-glorious construction, the rebuilt temple helped to galvanize the tattered Jewish remnant into a surviving religious community.

The "postexilic" prophets look to the future restoration and strive to rebuild, but their message indicates that the return of a Jewish remnant to the Land in their lifetime was certainly not the true restoration that had been promised. These prophets saw their era as "preliminary and preparatory to complete renewal," which still lay in the future.[1] Both Zechariah and Malachi contain "a mixture of hope and disillusionment,"[2] underscoring the fact that the restoration remained part of the future. This is clearest in the book of Zechariah, where the wonderful and glorious "not yet" is mixed in with the depressing and difficult "now," thus pointing to an ultimate final victory still future.[3] In this sense, from a theological perspective, the people were still in exile. The restoration was still future, something to anticipate and hope for. Canonically, these three postexilic prophets bring the prophetic corpus to a close by restating the main prophetic message and continuing to direct the readers in hope forward to the promised coming of the Messiah.

> Both Zechariah and Malachi contain "a mixture of hope and disillusionment."

Also, although the Jews who returned to the land appear to have been cured of idolatry, the other two indictments of the preexilic prophets (social injustice and religious ritualism) resurface in the postexilic prophets. Both Zechariah and Malachi mention the issue of social justice for the widows, orphans, and foreigners (Zech. 7:8–10; Mal. 3:5). All three books testify to the rising problem of religious ritualism, in which maintaining the rituals begins to take priority over relationship with Yahweh and the administering of social justice.

This problem will continue to develop within Judaism even into the New Testament era, producing the legalistic Pharisaism that is part of the context of the Gospels.

The book of Zechariah also addresses the nations, merging them into the future picture in much the same way the preexilic prophets did. Thus Zechariah pronounces judgment on the nations due to their sin and rebellion, but he also proclaims hope for the conversion

---

1. Paul R. House, *Old Testament Theology* (Downers Grove, IL: InterVarsity Press, 1998), 383.
2. Donald E. Gowan, *Theology of the Prophetic Books: The Death and Resurrection of Israel* (Louisville: Westminster John Knox, 1998), 170, 178.
3. I. M. Duguid, "Zechariah," *New Dictionary of Biblical Theology*, ed. Brian S. Rosner et al. (Downers Grove, IL: InterVarsity Press, 2000), 258.

of the nations as well. The nations are included in his vision of the ultimate restoration in which all of Yahweh's people come to worship him (Zech. 2:11; 8:20–23; 14:16–19).[4]

The book of Daniel has been included in this section because both the context and the message of Daniel have points of similarity with that of the postexilic prophets. In the Hebrew canon Daniel is placed in the section known as the Writings, along with the wisdom books. Yet in the Christian canon the book of Daniel is located with the Prophets because of its future-looking prophecies. Some scholars suggests that these two different canonical locations reflect the two major theological "thrusts" of the book, one relating to wisdom and one relating to eschatology.[5] Daniel 1–6 is made up of narrative, relating how Daniel the Jew is able to remain faithful to God, living wisely even while under Babylonian and Persian rule. Daniel 7–12, however, focuses on visions of the future, including the restoration, and deals with all the nations of the world. Yet without doubt, as discussed in chapters 17 and 18, the first six chapters of Daniel also carry a message relating to world empires and thus connect integrally to the latter half of the book.

> All three postexilic books testify to the rising problem of religious ritualism.

The book of Daniel makes a clear connection with the central three-part message of the preexilic prophets. The confessional prayer in Daniel 9 reflects a strong continuity with the Deuteronomistic story. Daniel confesses the sin of Israel, acknowledging that their punishment of exile and foreign domination was due to their covenant violation. His prayer is similar to Nehemiah's (Neh. 1), and he prays for the restoration of the nation and of Jerusalem. Yet much of Daniel suggests that the ultimate restoration is still far off, and that in the meantime, the community of God will live under persecution.

Similar to the preexilic prophets, Daniel merges the story of Israel with the cosmic story of the nations begun in Genesis 1–11. The restoration of Israel is cast into the light of—indeed, apparently subordinated to—God's ultimate plan for all of human history.[6] The restoration of Israel is swallowed up by the larger theme of the kingdom of God. The covenant name Yahweh practically disappears from the book of Daniel to be replaced with names carrying more of a universal significance for the nations: God in heaven, God of gods, and God Most High. In Daniel 7, arguably the climax of the book, the messianic Son of Man comes into the presence of the Ancient of Days and is given power and authority, which evokes the worship of "all peoples, nations, and languages." This phrase is an allusion to Genesis 10–12 and shows that the fulfillment of the Abrahamic promise as a solution to the Genesis 3–11 problem will be carried out by the Son of Man in the eschatological future.

> Daniel suggests that the ultimate restoration is still far off, and that in the meantime, the community of God will live under persecution.

One of Daniel's major themes is that God is sovereign over all humankind and over all human kingdoms. Indeed, history moves forward toward the goal of establishing God's

---

4. Ibid., 259–60. See also Gowan, *Theology of the Prophetic Books,* 169.

5. John E. Goldingay, *Daniel,* Word Biblical Commentary (Dallas: Word, 1998), 333.

6. Goldingay writes, "The prophets concern themselves with international history insofar as it affects the history of Israel; Daniel is closer to having a philosophy of international history in itself" (*Daniel,* 331).

great kingdom. In the meantime, however, Daniel warns that for those still in the exile awaiting the restoration, persecution can be expected. Like Daniel, God's people should face this persecution by remaining faithful and trusting in the power and current presence of God, ever looking forward to the future coming of the Son of Man and the establishment of God's kingdom, the true and ultimate restoration.

» FURTHER READING «

Hays, J. Daniel. "The Prophets: Sin, Exile, and Restoration." In *The Story of Israel: A Biblical Theology*, C. Marvin Pate et al. Downers Grove, IL: InterVarsity Press, 2004, 88–103.

House, Paul R. *Old Testament Theology*. Downers Grove, IL: InterVarsity Press, 1998.

Robertson, O. Palmer. *The Christ of the Prophets*. Philadelphia: P & R Publishing, 2004.

Seitz, Christopher R. *Prophecy and Hermeneutics: Toward a New Introduction to the Prophets*. Studies in Theological Interpretation. Grand Rapids: Baker, 2007.

Sweeney, Marvin A. *The Prophetic Literature*. Interpreting Biblical Texts. Nashville: Abingdon Press, 2005.

Walton, John H., and Andrew E. Hill, *Old Testament Today: A Journey from Original Meaning to Contemporary Significance*. Grand Rapids: Zondervan, 2004, 228–85.

» DISCUSSION QUESTIONS «

1. What is the basic three-part message of the prophets? What are the three indictments?

2. For each of the three indictments the prophets make against Israel, give a contemporary application for today.

3. How does the book of Deuteronomy relate to the prophetic message?

1. Read carefully Leviticus 26 and Deuteronomy 28.

    a. For each chapter make a chart listing and comparing the blessings for obedience and the curses for disobedience. List them by categories (economic, political, personal/family) as shown below:

Category	Blessings	Curses
Economic		
Political		
Personal/family		

    b. Discuss the similarities and differences between the blessings and the curses of Leviticus 26 and Deuteronomy 28.

    c. Discuss how the message of the prophets relates to these two chapters.

2. One of the indictments that the prophets make against Israel and Judah is that they were trusting in religious ritual to cover over their failings regarding social injustice and idolatry. How does this apply to Christians in the church today?

CHAPTER 5

The Prophets and Biblical Eschatology

"Behold, I will create new heavens and a new earth."

(Isa. 65:17)

INTRODUCTION

Eschatology (from the Greek term *eschaton,* or "last") refers to the study of last things but extends to cover a broader biblical perspective concerning God's purpose and direction for history. In contrast to a cyclical view of history, Scripture reveals that God is moving history toward a future goal. As a result, eschatology deals not only with the end of history but also with the outworking of God's good and sovereign purposes for his creation. The biblical hope rests on God's covenant faithfulness to destroy evil, rescue his people, and restore his creation.

> Eschatology deals not only with the end of history but also with the outworking of God's good and sovereign purposes for his creation.

Throughout history, people have had different views of the future and of the concept of movement forward toward a future. Premodern society gave priority to the past, focusing their hopes and understanding on their forefathers. Modernity, springing up in Western cultures out of the rational and science-based emphasis of the Enlightenment, changed this perspective, giving priority to the future. Modernity produced a hope in human progress and in humanity's control of the future, often replacing religious-based hope with secular-based hope. Education and technology replaced grace and divine creation in the attempt to remove fear of the future. Through human achievement based on science, modernity believed that the future would always be better. With the end of modernity and the emergence of postmodernity, however, the belief that science and technology could guarantee a safe and better future all but collapsed. As in the premodern era, fear is back for many; the future is frightening rather than encouraging. This postmodern society is now focusing on the present and withdrawing from the bleak prospect of the future. The Western postmodern culture has lost faith in any kind of meta-narrative that gives hope for the future.[1]

The Bible, however, and the Old Testament prophets in particular, gives hope to such a disillusioned culture. In contrast to postmodernity, the Bible offers a meta-narrative with an ending. The prophets declare that history is moving toward a God-controlled end. This is the contemporary relevance of biblical eschatology and the message of the prophets regarding the future.

INTERPRETIVE CHALLENGES

As mentioned above, the prophets spend most of their time proclaiming the broken covenant and announcing the coming judgment. A smaller but very important part of the pro-

Zechariah 6:1 – 8 provides the background for the Four Horsemen in Revelation 6. This is an engraving by Albrecht Dürer from 1498, entitled "The Four Horsemen of the Apocalypse."

The Four Horsemen of the Apocalypse, Dürer, Albrecht (1471–1528)/Private Collection/The Bridgeman Art Library

---

1. Richard Bauckham and Trevor Hart, *Hope Against Hope: Christian Eschatology at the Turn of the Millennium* (Grand Rapids: Eerdmans, 1999), 1 – 25.

The Prophets and the End Times

Often the assumption is made that the term *prophecy* only refers to events of the end times. Based on this assumption, many people conclude that the prophets of the Old Testament are primarily concerned with predicting the end times. Yet this assumption is not accurate and requires some modification. For example, Fee and Stuart write: "Less than 2 percent of Old Testament prophecy is messianic. Less than 5 percent specifically describes the new-covenant age. Less than 1 percent concerns events yet to come in our time."[1] As discussed in chapter 4, most of the material in the prophetic books relates to the indictment of Israel/Judah for breaking the Mosaic covenant, the call to repentance, and the proclamation of severe judgment due to their refusal to repent (i.e., Points 1 and 2 of the standard prophetic message).

On the other hand, although the prophets devote many more pages to indictments and judgments in their own day, the sections on the coming future restoration are extremely important to us as New Testament believers. Indeed, the New Testament writers themselves interacted with the Old Testament prophets in this way. Thus Ronald Clements, for example, concludes, "Two things are immediately striking in this summary of Old Testament prophecy; the prophets are regarded as having proclaimed a unified message, and this message is regarded as one concerning the era of salvation which the New Testament writers now regard as having dawned."[2] Therefore, as we study the Old Testament prophets from a New Testament perspective, it is appropriate — to some degree — to give an unbalanced emphasis to the shorter sections in the prophets that deal with the future restoration and the coming messianic age.

---

1. Gordon D. Fee and Douglas Stuart, *How to Read the Bible for All Its Worth* (Grand Rapids: Zondervan, 2003), 182.
2. Ronald E. Clements, *Old Testament Prophecy: From Oracle to Canon* (Louisville: Westminster John Knox, 1996), 191 – 93.

phetic message deals with future restoration and the coming Messiah. One of the ironies that we as interpreters face is that the sections dealing with broken covenant and judgment are easier to interpret and understand than the sections dealing with the future (in which most New Testament believers are more interested). Indeed, there is much more unanimity among evangelical scholars regarding the judgment sections than regarding the future restoration sections.

> In contrast to post-modernity, the Bible offers a meta-narrative with an ending.

The main interpretive challenges for us regarding the predictive aspects of the Old Testament prophets can be grouped around six central issues: the land; the near view/far view phenomenon; conditional prophecy; figurative language; the relationship between Israel and the church; and the nature of the future kingdom.

1. *The Land.* Throughout the Old Testament one of the most important themes is that of "the Land." It is promised to Abraham, it plays a central role in the blessings of Deuteronomy, it is lost in 2 Kings due to disobedience, and yet it appears to be included in the prophetic promise of future restoration. In the New Testament, on the other hand, it disappears as a prophetic theme. What are we to make of the New Testament writers' omission of this central Old Testament theme? Is the Promised Land still implied as part of the kingdom Jesus proclaims even though it is not specifically mentioned? Or does

The Promised Land as seen from Mount Nebo, where Moses first saw it.

the New Testament completely spiritualize it? Evangelical scholars remain divided over how to understand the Old Testament theme of "the Land" in regard to the New Testament era.

2. *The near view/far view phenomenon.* When the prophets paint pictures of the future, they often don't appear to make chronological distinctions. For example, in a poetic picture of future judgment they may mix together into the same vision numerous future events, some from the immediate future and some from the far future. Thus, while they see clearly the imminent destruction of Israel or Judah by the Assyrians or Babylonians, they also see glimpses of destruction on other nations that may happen later. Indeed, this vision of judgment expands into "the day of Yahweh," which includes a future judgment on the entire world. The *near* judgment (Assyrian or Babylonian) is easy for us to identify historically, but the *far* judgment is much more difficult to define with precision.

> In the New Testament, the Land disappears as a prophetic theme.

In proclaiming the future restoration, the prophets will likewise often mix and merge several different events into one powerful poetic picture of restoration. In their depiction of the future restoration, the prophets can be referring to one, two, or all of the following historical events in the same text: (1) the return of the Jewish exiles to Israel under Ezra, Nehemiah, and Zerubbabel; (2) the first coming of Christ; or (3) the second coming of Christ. This poses a challenge for us as interpreters, because we often cannot tell if they are describing the "near future" or the "far future." That is, the prophets will often slide back and forth from describing events that will occur soon within their lifetimes (the near view) to events that will occur during the first advent of Christ (the far view) to events that are still future even for us (the even farther view).

This near view/far view feature of the prophets can perhaps best be understood through an analogy. If you stand on the flat prairie and look west toward the Rocky Mountains, you will see a view of overlapping mountains, similar to the sketch below:

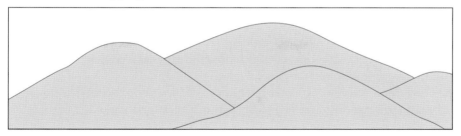

From a distance, the mountains in this view look to be two-dimensional; that is, they all appear to be in the same area and equidistant from us. The mountains in front and the mountains in back merge together into one flat picture with little distinguishable distance between them. Yet in reality the various mountains in our picture are rather far apart, with significant valleys between them.

The prophets' pictures of the future are analogous (to some degree) to the mountain range. The prophetic picture of the return of the exiles under Ezra, Nehemiah, and Zerubbabel is like the mountain we see in the foreground, while the events relating to the first and second comings of Christ parallel the mountains in back. To the prophets, these events are all part of the glorious future restoration. In addition, as we read through these texts

Typology

Related to the near view/far view phenomenon is a feature usually called *typology* (some scholars prefer a more general term like "foreshadowing"). A *type* can be defined as "a biblical event, person, or institution that serves as an example or pattern for other events, persons, or institutions." The Old Testament flows into the New Testament as part of a continuous salvation-history story. What is promised in the Old is fulfilled in the New.[1] This can be accomplished through prophetic word, which foretells the future, or through prophetic actions and events, which foreshadow the future. Both of these prophetic tools involve typology. Typology is therefore prophetic and is part of the promise-fulfillment scheme that connects the two Testaments.[2] Thus, besides describing "far view" events in the future, the prophets will also occasionally describe contemporary things in the "near view" (historical leaders and events from their day and time) that also typologically represent future events. The New Testament identifies numerous Old Testament passages that are fulfilled typologically.[3]

1. Douglas J. Moo, "The Problem of *Sensus Plenior*," in *Hermeneutics, Authority, and Canon*, ed. D. A. Carson and John D. Woodbridge (Grand Rapids: Zondervan, 1986), 195–96.
2. Not all evangelical scholars agree that such usage is "predictive" or truly "prophetic." See, for example, the discussion in William W. Klein, Craig L. Blomberg, and Robert L. Hubbard, *Introduction to Biblical Interpretation* (Dallas: Word Publishing, 1993), 130.
3. See the discussion in R. T. France, *Jesus and the Old Testament* (Downers Grove, IL: InterVarsity Press, 1971), 75–76; and G. K. Beale and D. A. Carson, eds., *Commentary on the New Testament Use of the Old Testament* (Grand Rapids: Baker, 2007), xxv.

we observe that the prophets sometimes seem to shift from one future event to another and then back again without giving us clear indication that they have done so.

In light of this phenomenon we should be cautious in our interpretation of the specific details of future events. We, of course, are interested in the historical details of future events, and we often desire to locate events along a clear historical timeline. Yet we need to keep the near view/far view mode of prophetic revelation in mind. The prophets may have intentionally blended these events together so that their readers would in fact focus more on the broader principles than on the details.

3. *Conditional Prophecy.* Another interpretive challenge we face is that the prophetic books occasionally appear to include conditions in their proclamations. Thus in Jeremiah 18:7–10, for example, Yahweh states:

> If at any time I announce that a nation or kingdom is to be uprooted, torn down and destroyed, and if that nation I warned repents of its evil, then I will relent and not inflict on it the disaster I had planned. And if at another time I announce that a nation or kingdom is to be built up and planted, and if it does evil in my sight and does not obey me, then I will reconsider the good I had intended to do for it.

In a text like this, Yahweh appears to be saying that what will actually happen depends on the response of the people to the prophetic word. Placing elements of conditionality on future events does not indicate uncertainty on God's part or undermine his sovereignty. In fact, if we read the text carefully, we realize that this conditionality is part of God's sovereign will and is related to his sovereign right to decide such things (Jer. 18:6). Such texts prevent us from distorting sovereignty and foreknowledge into fatalism and determinism.

> Yahweh seems to be saying that what will actually happen depends on the response of the people to the prophetic word.

Another example of conditional prophecy is in the book of Jonah. As Jonah arrives in Nineveh, he proclaims, "Forty more days and Nineveh will be destroyed." However, the people of Nineveh listen to the prophetic word and repent of their evil deeds. As a result of their repentance, Yahweh responds with compassion and cancels the prophesied destruction (Jonah 3:10), in accordance with the pattern described in Jeremiah 18:7–10. Thus, while Yahweh's prophetic word is powerful and always true, he remains free to exercise his sovereign choice and to modify the fulfillment of a prophetic word according to the response of people. The interpretive challenge for us is to discern which prophetic descriptions of the future are certain and unconditional and which ones are conditioned by the response of people.

4. *Figurative language.* Remember our important discussion of poetry and figurative language in chapter 3. The prophets use poetic language continuously, and one of the central features of their literature is the extensive use of figures of speech. They continue to use figurative language as they poetically describe the future restoration. The interpretive challenge for us is that it is often difficult to determine with precision whether the picture they paint of the future is a literal description or a figurative, symbolic one (or a mixture of both). As mentioned in our earlier discussion of figurative language, the prophets will use figures of speech to represent real historical future events, but such figures of speech do not

always portray these events in a literal manner. On the other hand, some prophetic pictures of the future are quite literal in their portrayal (i.e., Jesus was born in the literal town of Bethlehem, as prophesied by Micah 5:2). The challenge for us is to discern which is which.

To illustrate this problem, let's consider Isaiah 11:6:

> The wolf will live with the lamb,
>   the leopard will lie down with the goat,
> the calf and the lion and the yearling together;
>   and a little child will lead them.

Obviously, Isaiah is speaking of a future time that is characterized by peace, but is his portrayal of future peace a literal picture or a symbolic one? That is, are the "wolf" and the "lamb" used as figures of speech to represent traditional international military enemies? Does this passage prophesy of a future time when nations will no longer go to war against each other? Or is Isaiah's prophecy completely literal? In the coming messianic age, will wolves and lambs literally live together in peace? That is, does Isaiah prophesy the end of carnivores? What is the intent of Isaiah in this passage?

Is Isaiah 11:6 literal or figurative? Is it about the end of war or the end of carnivores?

Another challenging example is Isaiah 65:17 – 20. In 65:17 Yahweh declares that he will "create new heavens and a new earth." Then in 65:20 he adds the following:

> Never again will there be in it
>   an infant who lives but a few days,
>   or an old man who does not live out his years;
> he who dies at a hundred
>   will be thought a mere youth;
> he who fails to reach a hundred
>   will be considered accursed.

Should this passage be understood literally or figuratively? Is this passage prophesying that Yahweh will literally create a new physical earth? Do we take the entire passage literally? That is, will such a new creation be an earth in which people literally live quite long but still die? Or is it all symbolic? Or perhaps a mixture?

Evangelical scholars are divided over how to interpret texts like these. Even among scholars who hold the same evangelical presuppositions regarding the veracity of God's Word, there is often strong disagreement over how to interpret prophetic texts that use figurative language to describe future events. The disagreement emerges out of the basic approach one takes in answering two central questions. The first question is the broad one: How literal are the images that the prophets use to predict the future? That is, do we interpret the figures of speech in a literal sense or a symbolic sense? The second question, arising from the details of the first, grapples with a related issue and leads us to the fifth interpretive challenge.

5. *The relationship between Israel and the church.* The central question is, Does the New Testament church fulfill the Old Testament prophecies that refer to Israel? That is, does the church *replace* Israel in the promises of God? Or are Israel and the New Testament church totally separate? When the prophets declare that in the future Israel will be regathered and will dwell in peace in Jerusalem and will worship Yahweh there, are they speaking of literal fulfillment by believing Jews in Israel, or is this a symbolic/figurative reference to the New Testament church? Evangelical scholars are sharply divided over this issue.

> Does the New Testament church fulfill the Old Testament prophecies about Israel?

6. *The nature of the future kingdom.* The prophets paint a picture of a future kingdom with a Davidic king on the throne in Jerusalem. How does this kingdom promise relate to the first coming of Christ, when Jesus proclaimed that "the kingdom is at hand"? Are all aspects of the promised kingdom still in the future, or were some fulfilled by the first advent of Christ? Likewise, are some aspects being fulfilled now, in the church? You can see that several of these challenges are interrelated, stemming from the issue of figurative versus literal language.

Does the church replace Israel in prophetic fulfillment, or are they totally separate?

How does modern Israel fit into biblical prophecy?

INTERPRETIVE SYSTEMS

The issues introduced above and the debates stemming from them are lengthy and complex, and a complete discussion is beyond the scope of this book. However, a brief overview of how many evangelicals understand these issues is appropriate, and it will help give you perspective in your study of the prophetic books. Keep in mind that I am not trying to convince you of any particular theological position. However, regarding the eschatology of the Old Testament prophets, one's broad theological understanding of future events and of the relationship between the church and Israel usually determines one's methodological answer to the interpretive challenges above. This is not necessarily bad, for we should interpret individual passages within the context of the entire Bible.

> There are three basic systems for interpreting prophecy regarding the kingdom—amillennial, premillennial, and postmillennial.

The New Testament also has much to say about future events, providing us with numerous passages that address the nature of God's kingdom, the relationship between Israel and the church, the second coming of Christ, and the events of the end times. So our understanding of these New Testament teachings will necessarily influence the way we translate the expression of meaning for the Old Testament audience into an expression of meaning for the church today. Thus we are looking for an approach and an understanding of eschatology that combines the Old Testament prophets with the New Testament teaching on the end times into a coherent unity.

There are three basic systems for interpreting prophecy regarding the kingdom—amillennial, premillennial, and postmillennial (although few evangelicals today espouse postmillennialism). The terminology for the names of these systems is derived from Revelation 20:1–6, which refers to the thousand-year reign of the coming Righteous King. This thousand-year reign is called "the millennial kingdom." In general, the methodological issue that divides these systems pertains to how literally or how symbolically one takes future-related prophecies. Thus, in regard to how one interprets Old Testament prophecies about the future, premillennialists tend to stress a more literal interpretation, while amillennialists tend to stress a more symbolic or spiritualized understanding. Both views appeal to the New Testament for support. The issue of Israel and the church is likewise closely connected to the literal/symbolic approach that one takes. One taking a very literal approach such as a dispensational premillennialist (see below) would see a sharp distinction between Israel and the church, whereas one taking a symbolic or spiritualized approach (such as an amillennialist) maintains that the church has replaced Israel. Thus for the amillennialist the prophecies in the Old Testament about the future of Israel are fulfilled by the New Testament church.

> The methodological issue that divides these systems pertains to how literally or how symbolically one takes future-related prophecies.

Amillennialism

The prefix *a-* means "no," and thus this view maintains that there will not be a literal earthly reign of Christ after his coming. As mentioned above, this view stresses a symbolic or figurative approach to the interpretation of prophecies relating to the future rather than a more literal approach. Thus for amillennialists the "thousand years" mentioned in Revelation 20:1–6 does not refer to a literal kingdom here on earth but rather symbolizes the heavenly reign of Christ with Christians who have already died and gone to be with Christ. In the amillennial view, the return of Christ will come at the end of the age, followed immediately by a general resurrection, the last judgment, and the eternal state (John 5:28–29; Rom. 8:17–23; 1 Cor. 15:20–26; 2 Thess. 1:5–10; and 2 Peter 3:3–14). For amillennialists there will not be an earthly millennial kingdom.

> Amillennialists maintain that all of the future promises regarding Israel in the Old Testament prophets will be ultimately fulfilled by the church.

In regard to the Old Testament prophets, amillennialism differs from premillennialism especially concerning the nature of the future time of restoration during the messianic age. In regard to the restoration, the prophets frequently paint a picture of a restored Israel once again centered about Jerusalem, with the nations of the world streaming to Jerusalem to worship Yahweh along with restored Israel. Amillennialists will underscore the figurative nature of these texts and interpret them symbolically. Typically, amillennialists maintain that all of the future promises regarding Israel in the Old Testament prophets will ultimately be fulfilled by the church. They argue that all Old Testament prophecies referring to Israel and Judah either have already been fulfilled in Christ and the church at his first coming or will be fulfilled in the eternal state. They do not see any connection between modern Israel and Old Testament prophecies regarding Israel and Judah.

Premillennialism

The prefix *pre-* means "before." Thus premillennialism is the view that Christ will return "before" the millennial kingdom. The premillennial view takes the Old Testament prophecies about restored Israel as literally as possible, while still acknowledging the proper role of figures of speech. This view understands the "1000-year reign of Christ" as being a literal earthly kingdom established by Christ on the earth. Thus premillennialists maintain that most of the Old Testament prophecies portraying the restored kingdom of Israel/Judah find ultimate fulfillment during this period. After the millennium, Satan will lead a final rebellion of evil, only to be defeated in God's final victory, which includes final judgment and the eternal state. Interpreting the Old Testament prophets against this sequence of events, premillennialists usually see certain aspects of "the day of Yahweh" as finding fulfillment during the millennium, while other aspects will find ultimate fulfillment during those events that follow the millennium.

Premillennialists can be further classified into two major subgroups, divided over the issue of when Christ returns in relationship to the tribulation that precedes the millennium. Although this is a New Testament issue and not directly related to the Old Testament prophets, it is important to recognize the distinction between these two major branches of premillennialism. The view of the first subgroup is called "dispensational premillennialism." This view argues that Christ will rapture the church prior to the tribulation (pre-tribulation rapture). That is, Christ will first return for his church in a secret coming to remove his church from the terrible coming tribulation, and then, after the tribulation, he will come again visibly and publicly with his church and establish his millennial kingdom on earth. Dispensational premillennialists are themselves divided into two groups: classical dispensationalists and progressive dispensationalists.

The second main subgroup or viewpoint of premillennialism is called "historic premillennialism." The primary difference between historic premillennialism and dispensational premillennialism is that historic premillennialists maintain that Christ will not return until after the tribulation (posttribulation view) and that the church will endure the tribulation. Thus we have three subgroups of premillennialism: classic dispensational, progressive dispensational, and historic. Each subgroup is discussed in more detail below:

> There are three subgroups of premillennialism: classic dispensational, progressive dispensational, and historic.

1. *Classic dispensational premillennialism.* The term "dispensation" refers to the concept of an administration or management order (developed from the New Testament Greek word *oikonomia*, meaning "household management"). Dispensationalists maintain that God interacts differently with people throughout history during the different "dispensations" or "administrations" of biblical history. Of the three premillennial positions, the classic dispensational premillennial view is the most literal in its approach to Old Testament prophecy. Thus, classic dispensationalists often believe that as part of prophetic fulfillment, Israel as a nation will be literally restored according to the literal portrayal in the prophets, including such things as a restoration of the worship system and a rebuilt temple. Another characteristic of classic dispensational premillennialism is a sharp and clear distinction between Israel and the church. References in the prophetic books to Israel and Judah always mean literal Israel and should not be understood symbolically or in a spiritualized fashion. Thus the important New Covenant formulation in Jeremiah 31:31 – 33, for example, is made with literal Israel (as stated in Jer. 31:31) and not with the church.

2. *Progressive dispensational premillennialism.* Adherents of this view, which emerged toward the end of the twentieth century, still tend to view Old Testament prophecy in a literal manner, but they pay more attention to the role of figurative language and symbols than the classic dispensationalists tend to do. The central theological concept for the progressive movement holds the literal and figurative approaches in balance and maintains an "already-not yet" understanding of the kingdom. That is, they argue that Christ inaugurated the kingdom of God at his first coming (the "already") but that he will not consummate the kingdom or establish it fully until his second coming when he rules over his millennial kingdom (the "not yet"). As a result, believers today live in the tension between what God has "already" started and what he has "not yet" completed. Thus Old Testament prophecies regarding the future kingdom that will be restored to Israel can find partial fulfillment in the "already" phase, but ultimate fulfillment awaits the millennial kingdom.

> The central theological concept for the progressive dispensational movement is the "already-not yet" understanding of the kingdom.

There are two other important differences between progressive dispensationalists and classic dispensationalists. First, the progressives maintain that there is an "already" aspect of Davidic covenant fulfillment in Jesus (Psalm 110:1), in the sense that at his ascension he entered into heaven and began to reign. Second, while progressives still maintain a distinction between Israel and the church, they do not see this distinction as universally present in the Old Testament. That is, they see Israel and the church as "mostly separate" rather than totally separate. Progressive dispensationalists would argue that some Old Testament promises made to Israel are at least partially fulfilled in the church. On the other hand, progressive dispensationalists do agree with the classic dispensationalists that there will be a future restoration for national (literal) Israel (Romans 11).

3. *Historic premillennialism.* Many of the early church fathers believed that Christ would return to establish his millennial kingdom prior to the final judgment and establishment of the eternal state. Historic premillennialists derive their name by seeking to connect with this "historic" premillennial view. The historical premillennial view is similar to other premillennial views in that it maintains that Christ will return to earth to establish a literal millennial kingdom.

> Historic premillennialists fully embrace the "already-not yet" concept of the kingdom.

Historic premillennialism tends to be less literal in its understanding of Old Testament prophecy than the dispensational premillennial groups. Like the progressive dispensationalists, the historic premillennialists fully embrace the "already-not yet" concept of the kingdom, and this understanding drives much of their interpretation of prophecy. Unlike the dispensational views, however, the historical premillennial view does not make a sharp distinction between Israel and the church. Instead, historic premillennialists understand the church to be the fulfillment of the promises to Israel in the sense that the church is the "true Israel."

Although they are open to the possibility of many Jews converting to Christ at the end of the age, they do not believe that the literal nation Israel itself has a unique role in the unfolding plan of God for the future, as do the dispensationalists.

Postmillennialism

This view posits that due to the proclamation of the gospel, the majority of people will come to saving faith in this present age and thus usher in a "kingdom-like" time (the millennium) when righteousness, peace, and prosperity will reign. Thus Christ will return in glory *after* ("post" means "after") this millennial era. Postmillennialists do not interpret prophecies regarding the millennial kingdom in a literal sense, but rather they understand the millennial kingdom as a gradual development that includes all of church history from Christ's first advent until his return.

> Postmillennialism was very popular at the end of the nineteenth century and the beginning of the twentieth century.

Postmillennialism was very popular at the end of the nineteenth century and the beginning of the twentieth century. The social optimism of modernity was wedded to postmillennial theology, and world missions was connected to the spread of Western ("Christian") civilization in the belief that together they could bring the kingdom of Christ to earth. This social optimism about Western ("Christian") civilization died in the trenches of Europe during the First World War, when these "civilized Christian" nations killed each other by the hundreds of thousands. Consequentially, postmillennialism was largely abandoned by the mid-twentieth century. Although it does have its proponents, it is very much a minority view among evangelicals today.

CONCLUSIONS AND SUGGESTIONS

Although the postmillennial view is fairly rare today, the other four views are very strong within evangelicalism. Among evangelicals today, one can find large numbers of strong advocates for amillennialism, classic dispensational premillennialism, progressive dispensational premillennialism, and historical premillennialism. All four of these views are respected, defensible systems. The goal of this book is not to take one view or the other but to make you aware of the differences and the impact these views will have on interpreting the Old Testament prophets. We will struggle with the issues (figurative versus literal, Israel and the church, etc.) throughout our study of the prophets any time we ask about contemporary significance of the predictive passages. Some of you may be confused at this point: Which approach should you use?

> Postmillennialism had been largely abandoned by the mid-twentieth century.

A few suggested guidelines may be helpful. First, do not overlook the poetic aspect of prophecy. That is, do not allow your theological pre-understanding to ride roughshod over your appreciation and understanding of imagery and figures of speech. You should spend more time struggling to grasp the prophets' images than trying to fit the events they describe into some overall future time schedule. Yet keep in mind that grappling with the imagery and the figures of speech certainly does not suggest a negation of the literal reality behind the images. Jesus Christ came to earth as a literal, physical fulfillment of Old Testament prophetic imagery. The way in which he fulfilled prophecy in his first advent on earth is perhaps suggestive of how he may fulfill prophecy during his future coming.

Second, focus more on translating and applying the broader theological principles of the prophetic message than on trying to fit all the details into a system. The prophets soar like eagles, painting their images of the future with broad strokes. They appear to have little concern for presenting an organized, structured, detailed description of the end times.

> The prophets appear to have little concern for presenting an organized, structured, detailed description of the end times.

Third, do not forget the way the prophets use the *near view/far view*. The near and far future events are often intermingled.

Finally, be cautious against allowing your fixed theological understandings to dictate how you interpret a particular passage even before you begin to struggle with it. The correct balance is maintained as we allow the parts and the whole to inform each other. That is, we do bring our overall theological understanding with us into these predictive texts, but we also constantly seek to update and mature our overall theological understanding (the whole) precisely by our study of particular texts (the parts).

» FURTHER READING «

Bauckham, Richard, and Trevor Hart. *Hope Against Hope: Christian Eschatology at the Turn of the Millennium*. Grand Rapids: Eerdmans, 1999.

Beale, G. K., and D. A. Carson, eds. *Commentary on the New Testament Use of the Old Testament*. Grand Rapids: Baker, 2007.

Blaising, Craig A., and Darrell L. Bock. *Progressive Dispensationalism*. Grand Rapids: Baker, 2000.

Brower, Kent E., and Mark W. Elliott, eds. *Eschatology in Bible and Theology*. Downers Grove, IL: InterVarsity Press, 1997.

Dumbrell, William J. *The Search for Order: Biblical Eschatology in Focus*. Eugene, OR: Wipf and Stock Publishers, 2001.

Hays, J. Daniel, J. Scott Duvall, and C. Marvin Pate, *Dictionary of Biblical Prophecy and End Times*. Grand Rapids: Zondervan, 2007.

Moore, Russell D. *The Kingdom of Christ: The New Evangelical Perspective*. Wheaton, IL: Crossway, 2004.

Riddlebarger, Kim. *A Case for Amillennialism: Understanding the End Times*. Grand Rapids and Leicester, England: Baker and InterVarsity Press, 2003.

Walvoord, John F. *The Millennial Kingdom*. Grand Rapids: Zondervan, 1959.

» DISCUSSION QUESTIONS «

1. Explain the difference between amillennialism and premillennialism.

2. Isaiah 11:6 was used as an example in this chapter. How do you think that verse should be interpreted?

3. Which of the four systems that are popular among evangelicals (amillennialism, classic dispensational premillennialism, progressive dispensational premillennialism, historic premillennialism) do you prefer? Why?

4. How do you understand the relationship between the promises to Israel and the church today?

» WRITING ASSIGNMENTS «

1. Choose one of the main evangelical systems of eschatology (amillennialism, classic dispensational premillennialism, progressive dispensational premillennialism, historic premillennialism) and write a three-page paper describing your view. Use the bibliographic resources above as needed.

2. Discuss the differences between how an amillennialist and a classic dispensational premillennialist would interpret Isaiah 11:6.

PART 2

The Major Prophets

CHAPTER 6

Isaiah 1 — 6

"Yahweh takes his place in court...."

(Isa. 3:13)

OVERVIEW OF ISAIAH

Setting

Isaiah lives and proclaims his message in Jerusalem, the capital of Judah, during the Assyrian crisis. Isaiah 1:1 connects his message to the reigns of Uzziah, Jotham, Ahaz, and Hezekiah, all kings of Judah who reigned from 792 until 687 BC. Recall our discussion in chapter 2 of the Assyrian rise to power. During the reign of Ahaz (735–715 BC), Judah is

> Isaiah lives and proclaims his message in Jerusalem, the capital of Judah, during the Assyrian crisis.

threatened by the Syro-Ephraimite (Syria and Israel) alliance and turns to Assyria for help. Assyria destroys the northern kingdom Israel in 722 BC, and in 701 BC the Assyrian king Sennacherib attacks Jerusalem. The first 39 chapters of Isaiah are cast in this geopolitical setting. The second half of Isaiah (40–66), however, appears to be directed to those in the exile (i.e., after 586 BC) and under Persian domination (i.e., after 539 BC). So the geopolitical setting for the two halves of Isaiah appears to be different, and a shift in the book of Isaiah appears to take place between chapters 39 and 40. Isaiah 39 describes an event in the late eighth century, but Isaiah 40 contains words of comfort directed rather explicitly to the exiles in Babylon, thus addressing a situation that did not exist until after 586 BC. Also, the second half of Isaiah mentions the Persian king Cyrus specifically by name several times, even though Cyrus lived 150 years after the events of Isaiah 36–39.

For much of the twentieth century the standard, near-consensus view of nonevangelical Old Testament scholarship was that the present biblical form of Isaiah is made up of three separate works produced by three different authors (or groups) at three different stages of Israel's history. According to this view, Isaiah 1–39 was associated with the actual prophet Isaiah mentioned in Isaiah 1:1 and thus dated to the eighth century. Chapters 40–55 were the work of an anonymous prophet (or group of prophets) in the Babylonian exile. Usually this prophet and his work were called Deutero-Isaiah. Finally, chapters 56–66 were understood to be postexilic, produced by another anonymous prophet, generally referred to as Trito-Isaiah.

Evangelical Old Testament scholars often countered this view, noting the many unifying themes occurring across this supposed three-part division, themes that pointed to a unity of authorship. They also noted that the New Testament quoted from all three sections, always calling the author Isaiah. Finally, they noted that there was absolutely no textual evidence that the book of Isaiah had ever been in a three-part form.

Michelangelo's portrayal of Isaiah, in the Sistine Chapel.

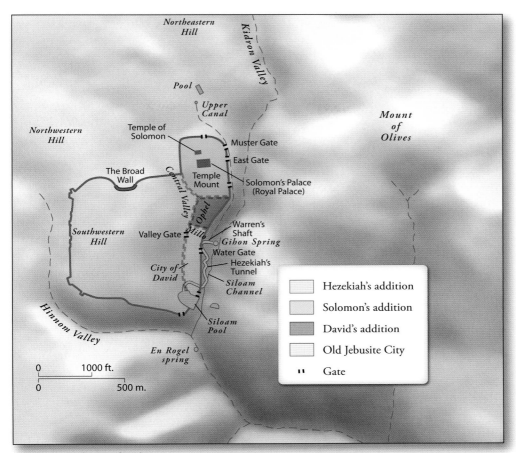

Jerusalem during the time of Isaiah.

Throughout the last half of the twentieth century, the majority of evangelical Old Testament scholars maintained that the eighth-century prophet Isaiah wrote the entire book. Yet this was not a consensus view, and there were always a minority, even within evangelicalism, that disagreed. This minority did not see any theological problem with assigning much of Isaiah 40–66 to a later writer or school of writers.

Recently, mainstream nonevangelical Old Testament scholarship has revised its view of Isaiah significantly. Literary studies on the book of Isaiah over the last twenty years have pointed out that not only are there numerous literary themes connecting the entire book together, but the actual literary structure of the book argues for unity. At the same time, the canonical approach was also gaining in popularity among Old Testament scholars, an approach that acknowledged development in the books of the Bible but nonetheless advocated studying the final form of the text for theological meaning. Thus, by the end of the twentieth century, the standard "Three-Isaiah" view had largely been abandoned (or at least revised significantly) by most nonevangelical Old

> Recently, mainstream nonevangelical Old Testament scholarship has revised its view of Isaiah significantly.

Testament scholars, especially those who specialized in the Prophets. Replacing it was the view that the book of Isaiah had developed over four centuries in numerous small stages, constantly being edited and integrated into a coherent literary unity. Sweeney, for example, writes, "Although chs. 1–39 clearly portray an 8th century historical setting much earlier than that of chs. 40–55 or 56–66, there is no evidence that chs. 1–39 ever constituted a distinct prophetic book separate from their present literary context in the book of Isaiah. Literary, exegetical, and thematic links between the various parts of the book demonstrate that, although Isaiah was composed over the course of some four centuries, it now constitutes a single literary entity."[1] This view is finding wide acceptance among nonevangelical Old Testament scholarship.

> The book of Isaiah *stresses* that Yahweh knows the future and will bring about his plan.

Evangelical Old Testament scholars, on the other hand, remain divided. A few, like McConville, tend to lean toward the view expressed above by Sweeney—that the book of Isaiah is a literary unity, but it was produced over a span of nearly four centuries.[2] Many others continue to maintain that the eighth-century prophet Isaiah wrote the entire book (with perhaps some very minor grammatical or syntactical editorial updating).[3] They note that the book of Isaiah *stresses* that Yahweh knows the future and will bring about his plan. The identification of Cyrus in advance is an illustration of Yahweh's ability to "know the end from the beginning" (Isa. 46:10). In regard to the question of why Isaiah would address the exiles, who were 150 years into the future, Chisholm suggests a helpful analogy. He says it is like an aging grandfather who writes a letter to his baby granddaughter to be opened on her wedding day. He knows he will probably not be around then, but wants to give her encouragement and advice at this critical time of her life.[4]

> The name Isaiah means "Yahweh is salvation."

Yet while disagreement exists between the nonevangelical academy and most scholars within evangelicalism on the actual production of the text, they both agree that the book is a literary and theological unity. Likewise, there is much agreement between the two groups in regard to the message and theology reflected in the book.

Throughout our discussions on Isaiah, we will refer to Isaiah as the author; that is, the prophet who delivered the message, both verbal and literary.

MESSAGE

The three-point standard preexilic prophetic message discussed in chapter 4 is a good synthesis of Isaiah:

---

1. Marvin A. Sweeney, *Isaiah 1–39: With an Introduction to Prophetic Literature,* Forms of the Old Testament Literature (Grand Rapids: Eerdmans, 1996), 41.

2. J. Gordon McConville, *Exploring the Old Testament: A Guide to the Prophets* (Downers Grove, IL: InterVarsity Press, 2002), 1–11.

3. See, for example, John N. Oswalt, *Isaiah,* NIV Application Commentary (Grand Rapids: Zondervan, 2003), 33–41; and Andrew E. Hill and John H. Walton, *A Survey of the Old Testament*, 3rd ed. (Grand Rapids: Zondervan, 2009), 520–22.

4. Robert B. Chisholm Jr., *Handbook on the Prophets* (Grand Rapids: Baker, 2002), 14.

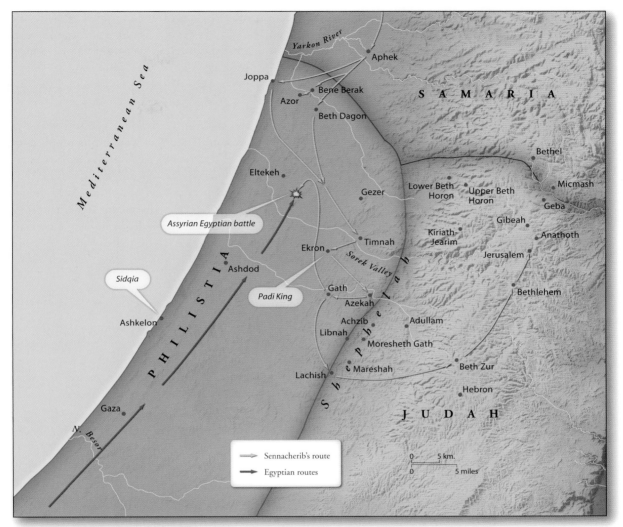

Sennacherib's campaign against Judah (701 BC).

1. You've broken the covenant (through idolatry, social injustice, religious ritualism), so repent!
2. No repentance? Then judgment! Judgment will also come on the nations.
3. Yet there is hope beyond the judgment for a glorious future restoration both for Judah/Israel and for the nations.

As mentioned earlier, the prophetic books are often difficult to outline in detail. However, in general, and with broad strokes, Isaiah can be broken down into three main parts:

1. Isaiah 1–39 focuses on judgment but also contains glimpses of deliverance.

2. Isaiah 40–55 focuses on deliverance and restoration through the Servant but also contains glimpses of judgment.

3. Isaiah 56–66 focuses on righteous living by Yahweh's true people/servants in the meantime.

Some of the most explicit messianic prophecies are found in Isaiah, and the New Testament quotes from Isaiah frequently.

Isaiah 1–39 likewise breaks down into three main units. Isaiah 1–12 stresses judgment (based on Yahweh's righteousness and justice) on Judah (but with strong promises of hope in Isaiah 9 and 11). Isaiah 13–35 focuses on Yahweh's righteousness established among the nations, primarily through judgment, demonstrating that Yahweh is supreme master over the nations of the world. Isaiah 36–39 is quite different from the first 35 chapters, for it is a narrative account of how Yahweh actually delivered Jerusalem and King Hezekiah from the Assyrians. The central question addressed to Judah running through these first 39 chapters is, Whom will you trust, Yahweh or the strength of mankind (i.e., alliances, military power)?

> Some of the most explicit messianic prophecies are found in Isaiah.

ISAIAH 1–3 — THE COVENANT LAWSUIT

Isaiah does not waste any time with lengthy introductions. Likewise, he puts off the account of his own prophetic calling until Isaiah 6. In chapters 1–3, right from the beginning, Isaiah launches into a scathing diatribe against the people of Judah for their repeated and blatant covenant violation (especially of Deuteronomy). Yahweh is seated in court, prepared to judge (3:13). Isaiah, like a prosecuting attorney, and with the voice of Yahweh himself, levels charge after charge against Judah.

In Isaiah 1:2 the prophet calls on heavens and earth to bear testimony. In Deuteronomy the heavens and earth were called upon to be witnesses to the covenant agreement that Yahweh and Israel agreed to keep (Deut. 4:25–26; 30:19; 31:28). Now, using the image

---

Isaiah's Place in the Canon

In the Hebrew Bible the book of Isaiah follows after 1–2 Kings. Thus, ironically, the opening warning chapters of Isaiah follow right after the fall and destruction of Jerusalem (2 Kings 25). In the canonical order of both the Hebrew Bible and our English Bibles, Isaiah introduces the literary prophetic books, laying out the major themes that will be followed, by and large, throughout the rest of the prophetic material. Isaiah connects directly into the story presented in the Historical Books (especially tied to 2 Kings) and into the covenant blessings and curses from the book of Deuteronomy. Isaiah also looks forward to the glorious restoration, and he provides numerous ties to the coming of Christ in the New Testament. Thus there is a sense in which Isaiah ties most of the Bible together into a coherent unified story.

of a court trial, Isaiah figuratively calls on heavens and earth as witnesses against the covenant violation of Judah.

In Isaiah 1:2–3 Yahweh states that he raised children (lit. "sons," referring to the people of Israel/Judah) but that they have rebelled against him. Worse than that, his children no longer even know him. In 1:3 the prophet declares that even a dumb donkey knows who feeds him and takes care of him, but the people of Israel/Judah, in contrast, no longer know or acknowledge their master. Isaiah 1:4 stresses the rupture of the relationship: "They have *forsaken* Yahweh," implying a broken relationship like a divorce; "they have *spurned* the Holy One of Israel," indicating that

An Israelite altar from Beersheba. In Isaiah 1, Yahweh asks for justice, not more sacrifices.

they despise Yahweh rather than love him; and "they have *turned their back* on him." Proper protocol and respect in the Ancient Near East required that people never turn their backs to the king. To do so was disrespectful and was considered a serious insult to the king's honor. Not only had Israel done all of these terrible things to rupture their special relationship with Yahweh, but they have been totally unresponsive to Yahweh's correction and discipline (1:5–6). Therefore, in 1:7–9 Isaiah describes the coming judgment—invasion, destruction of cities and fields, decimation of the population—the "curses" that were spelled out clearly in Deuteronomy 28 as punishment that would come upon Israel if they abandoned the covenant.

One of the major indictments made by the prophets is that of religious ritualism. Israel/Judah believed that they could ignore the righteous demands of Yahweh regarding true worship and righteous behavior if they simply continued to carry on the rituals of worshipping Yahweh (along with their worship of other gods). Through the prophets, Yahweh will repeatedly and clearly reject this notion. Isaiah 1:10–17 introduces this theme. In fact, Yahweh indicates that their "worship" activities are actually annoying to him and that he will no longer even listen to their prayers. Very often the people of Israel/Judah thought that their religious rituals would cover over their lack of righteous living, especially in the area of social justice. Yahweh rejects this: "Take your evil deeds [i.e., hypocritical worship and bloodshed] out of my sight! Stop doing wrong, learn to

> Isaiah launches into a scathing diatribe against the people of Judah for their repeated and blatant covenant violation (especially of Deuteronomy).

do right! Seek justice, encourage the oppressed. Defend the cause of the fatherless, plead the case of the widow" (1:17). This call for righteous living and standing for justice is repeated throughout the prophetic literature. Likewise, the call to defend the socioeconomically

Swords and Plowshares

At the time of Isaiah, iron was still fairly rare and quite valuable. Many peasant farmers were forced to plow with only wooden plowshares (i.e., plow points, the part that actually goes into the ground and turns the soil). A peasant farmer with a piece of iron could have it hammered into a plowshare, install it on the end of his plow, and then be able to plow much more land, especially in rocky areas. In the armies of the Ancient Near East, only the elite professional soldiers had iron swords; the peasants, who comprised a large portion of the armies, were often armed only with sticks and clubs. If a poor soldier came across a sword on the field of battle, it would be a huge acquisition for him. Likewise, when the campaign was over, this soldier could return home with his sword and convert it into an iron plow, becoming the envy of the community. It would be like returning home to the farm today with a brand-new John Deere tractor. Hammering a sword into a plowshare (the point of the plow) was a powerful and graphic way of illustrating the dawn of a peaceful era. The major emblematic tool of death and destruction was being converted into the major tool for peace and food production.

weak "underclass" (orphans, widows, foreigners, poor) is common and is a major expectation that Yahweh has for his people.

In Isaiah 1:18–20 Yahweh issues a last-minute plea for his people to be reasonable. Their sin could still be forgiven, he states, if they would only repent and change their ways. Isaiah seems to pause, waiting for the nation to repent, and then, hearing not a word of repentance, he continues in 1:21–31 to list out their many sins and declare the consequential coming judgment.

> The people of Israel/ Judah thought that their religious rituals would cover over their lack of social justice.

Isaiah 2:1–4 interrupts the proclamation of judgment with a brief promise of future hope. Isaiah introduces the concept that the "nations" (i.e., the peoples of the world) will be included in the wonderful time of restoration. Isaiah, along with several of the other prophets, frequently paints a picture of the nations of the world streaming to Jerusalem to worship Yahweh. Stressed in this text is the promise of peace, as Isaiah declares, "They will beat their swords into plowshares ..." (2:4). This passage is repeated practically verbatim in Micah 4:1–3.

Isaiah 3 continues the theme of judgment. The leaders are accused of plundering and crushing the poor (3:14–15), and their wealthy wives are indicted as well (3:16–26). Isaiah graphically describes the judgment on these women, contrasting their current fine clothes with the destitution that they will experience when the judgment comes.

ISAIAH 4 — THE BRANCH OF YAHWEH

Isaiah 4 interrupts the judgment with another brief look at restoration, centered on the appearance of the "Branch of Yahweh," a messianic image. Likewise, this passage promises a

Vineyards were common in Israel, and they came to symbolize the nation.

spectacular, powerful return of the presence of Yahweh, using the images from the time of the exodus (cloud by day, fire by night).

ISAIAH 5 — THE VINEYARD OF YAHWEH

Back in Isaiah 3:14, the prophet accuses the leaders of ruining Yahweh's vineyard.

A frequent image in the prophets is Israel represented as a vineyard. In Isaiah 5 the prophet develops this analogy in some detail. Yahweh plants a vineyard and then expects to find good fruit in it, but he only finds bad fruit (5:1 – 2). Therefore, he announces that he will remove the protective hedge around it, allowing it to be destroyed. This implies that Yahweh will no longer protect Israel from foreign invasion.

> A frequent image in the prophets is Israel represented as a vineyard.

NT Connection: Jesus and the Vineyard

Shortly before his arrest and crucifixion, Jesus enters the temple in Jerusalem and begins teaching. The chief priests, the teachers of the law, and the elders challenge his authority. Jesus then tells a parable about a vineyard and the vineyard's tenants (Matt. 21:33 – 46; Mark 12:1 – 12; Luke 20:9 – 19). Jesus clearly builds this parable on Isaiah 5, modifying it to fit even more specifically the situation he is facing. Read the account in Mark 12:1 – 12. How does Jesus' parable differ from the one in Isaiah 5? How is it similar? Why do the leaders in the temple think that Jesus is speaking against them? How does this relate to Isaiah 3:14?

One of the central repeated themes of Isaiah is that of justice and righteousness (1:21, 27; 5:7). Yahweh himself is characterized by justice and righteousness. He expects his people to live according to justice and righteousness, as spelled out clearly in Deuteronomy. At the end of the vineyard analogy in Isaiah 5, Isaiah makes a colorful but powerful wordplay on the Hebrew words for justice and righteousness. As mentioned in chapter 3, in Isaiah 5:7 the prophet declares that Yahweh looked for justice (*mishpat*), but instead saw bloodshed (*mishpach*). He looked for righteousness (*tsedakah*), but heard cries of distress (*tse'akah*).

> One of the central repeated themes of Isaiah is that of justice and righteousness.

The result? The rest of Isaiah 5 focuses on sin and the coming judgment. Isaiah proclaims "woe" (i.e., something bad is going to happen) on those who are frivolous, uncaring, unjust, evil drunkards: "Woe to those who call evil good and good evil.... Woe to those ... who acquit the guilty for a bribe, but deny justice to the innocent" (5:20–23). Connected to the woes are statements of consequential judgment such as: "Therefore, my people will go into exile ..." (5:13). Isaiah 5:26–30 then describes the coming foreign invasion.

ISAIAH 6 — THE CALL OF ISAIAH

In Jeremiah, the call of the prophet is placed prominently at the beginning of the book. In Isaiah, by contrast, the indictments of the covenant lawsuit and the coming judgment are presented first, for emphasis. Isaiah describes his call only later, here in Isaiah 6.

> Isaiah 6 is one of the few accounts in the Old Testament where someone has a direct encounter with Yahweh.

This passage is one of the few accounts in the Old Testament where someone actually has a direct encounter with Yahweh (see also Moses' encounter in Exod. 3:1–2 and Ezekiel's in Ezek. 1:3). These appearances of Yahweh are called theophanies, and they are always frightening and overwhelming. As readers we would like to be given more detailed information here. What exactly does Yahweh look like? Notice, however, that Isaiah only describes the peripheral features. He tells us that Yahweh is seated on the throne but only describes the bottom of Yahweh's robe and the creatures flying above him. He does not give us an actual description of Yahweh. Probably Isaiah is overwhelmed by Yahweh's majesty and splendor. Most likely he has his face down to the ground and is unable to lift up his eyes and look directly at Yah-

---

Seraphim and Cherubim

The seraphim (Hebrew plural of seraph) that fly around the throne in Isaiah's vision are very similar to the cherubim (Hebrew plural of cherub) described throughout the rest of the Old Testament, although the seraphim in Isaiah 6 have six wings, while cherubim generally have four. Likewise, the four living creatures around the throne in Revelation 4:6–8 and 5:8 are similar both to the cherubim in Ezekiel 1, 10 and the seraphim in Isaiah 6. These beings are usually associated with the throne or dwelling place of Yahweh.

weh. He describes the seraphim (lit. "the burning ones") who fly above the throne proclaiming Yahweh's glory and holiness. The seraphim extol the glory and holiness of Yahweh with such volume that the building itself is shaking, adding to Isaiah's trepidation. Likewise, the temple fills with smoke, probably to veil the glory of Yahweh and to protect Isaiah.

The passage progresses through four main movements. In 6:1–4 Isaiah encounters Yahweh on his throne in all his holiness and glory. In 6:5–7 Isaiah responds with fear and guilt, but Yahweh answers with cleansing and forgiveness. One of the seraphim actually touches Isaiah's mouth with a coal from the altar and then proclaims that Isaiah's mouth is now cleansed, thus preparing the way for Isaiah to proclaim the word of Yahweh. In 6:8 Isaiah now sees the issues of life clearly. Yahweh is sovereign, holy, and glorious. When Yahweh asks who will go on his behalf, Isaiah — probably still bowing to the ground before the throne of Yahweh, with the seraphim still thundering the glory of Yahweh — gives the only logical response, "Here am I. Send me."

A human-headed winged bull from the Assyrian palace of Sargon II (710 BC), contemporary to Isaiah. Throughout the Ancient Near East, winged composite creatures regularly guarded the entrance to temples and palaces.

In the concluding movement of this passage (6:9–13), Yahweh tells Isaiah what he is to do. He is to proclaim to the people that they will hear the truth but it will only harden their hearts and minds. In essence, Yahweh is telling Isaiah that most of his prophetic ministry will not lead people to repentance (even though he begs them to repent) but will cause them to defy the message and to entrench themselves even more resolutely in their opposition

Theophany

A theophany is a direct appearance of Yahweh. These appearances of Yahweh are fairly rare, and thus when they occur they carry unique significance. Usually theophanies happen at "watershed moments in the lives of individuals or the community." They often provide new (or more clear) direction for the relationship between Yahweh and his people. While the initial human response to these theophanies is often fear, Yahweh usually moves quickly to calm the fear, for his intended effect is usually connected to the delivery of the spoken word, usually a promise. Furthermore, the role of the actual personal appearance of Yahweh not only underscores the importance of the delivered message but also stresses the heightened personal relationship established between Yahweh and the one he reveals himself to.[1]

1. Terence E. Fretheim, *The Suffering of God: an Old Testament Perspective,* Overtures to Biblical Theology (Philadelphia: Fortress, 1984), 79–88.

The Most Quoted OT Passage

In Isaiah 6:9 – 10 Yahweh commands Isaiah to tell the people, "Be ever hearing, but never understanding." The New Testament quotes this passage more than any other Old Testament scripture (e.g., Matt. 13:14 – 15; Mark 4:10 – 12; Luke 8:10; John 12:39 – 41; Acts 28:26 – 27; Rom. 11:8). For Isaiah, the truth of his prophetic proclamation was going to cause people to become hardened against Yahweh and his prophet. In the New Testament, this passage underscores that when Jesus the Messiah actually comes and proclaims the fulfillment of the Old Testament prophets, the Jews once again do not respond to the truth but are hardened by it, even becoming hostile to the prophetic word and to the Messiah.

to Yahweh and his prophet. Thus, Isaiah's word will actually serve to harden many hearts and therefore seal the judgment coming against them. There is no neutral ground before the prophetic word of Yahweh. One either embraces it in total obedience ("Here am I, send me") or else one defies it and becomes hardened against it.

"How long will this go on?" Isaiah asks in 6:11. Yahweh's answer: "until the land is destroyed and the people exiled."

» FURTHER READING «

Childs, Brevard S. *Isaiah*. The Old Testament Library. Louisville: Westminster John Knox, 2001.
Oswalt, John N. *The Book of Isaiah: Chapters 1 – 39*. The New International Commentary on the Old Testament. Grand Rapids: Eerdmans, 1986.
Williamson, H. G. M. *Isaiah 1 – 5*. The International Critical Commentary. London and New York: T & T Clark, 2006.

» DISCUSSION QUESTIONS «

1. What are the main views held today regarding the authorship of Isaiah?

2. Why is Isaiah 1 – 3 called a "covenant lawsuit"?

3. Discuss the differences and similarities between the vineyard text in Isaiah 5 and the vineyard text in Mark 12:1–12.

4. Discuss the call of Isaiah in chapter 6. What does Yahweh call him to do? Why does Yahweh appear to Isaiah when he calls him?

» WRITING ASSIGNMENTS «

1. Compare the judgments pronounced on Israel in Isaiah 1–5 with the curses that Yahweh warns Israel about in Deuteronomy 28:15–68.

2. Discuss the theme of social injustice in Isaiah 1–6. Also discuss how this theme and these texts have application for Christians today.

3. Discuss the theme of the holiness of Yahweh in Isaiah 1–6. Which verses mention Yahweh's holiness, and what role does his holiness play in those texts?

CHAPTER 7

Isaiah 7 — 39

"For to us a child is born ... and he will be called
Wonderful Counselor, Mighty God, Everlasting Father,
Prince of Peace." (Isa. 9:6)

OVERVIEW OF ISAIAH 7–39

As mentioned in chapter 6, Isaiah 1–39 focuses on judgment but contains glimpses of future hope and restoration. Isaiah 1–12 deals with the situation in Judah, focusing on judgment but also containing several passages about future hope. Isaiah 7–12, the second half

> Isaiah 1–39 focuses on judgment but contains glimpses of future hope and restoration.

of that unit, continues this pattern. Next, Isaiah 13–35 demonstrates how Yahweh's justice and righteousness will be established among the powerful nations of the world, primarily through judgment. Isaiah 35, however, the final chapter in that unit, looks beyond the judgment to a time of peaceful restoration. Isaiah 36–39 then changes to a narrative style of writing and covers the events concerning King Hezekiah and the Assyrian siege of Jerusalem in 701 BC. This story demonstrates that Yahweh can be relied upon to deliver his people from even the most powerful adversaries.

ISAIAH 7–12 — THE COMING CHILD

The larger unit, Isaiah 1–12, opens and closes with references to Yahweh as the "Holy One of Israel" (1:4; 12:6), a central theme not only in this unit but throughout Isaiah. Likewise, in the opening declarations of judgment, the people are called "daughter of Zion" (1:8) and at the end, now in joyful restoration, they are called "people of Zion" (12:6). These two terms, "Holy One of Israel" and "Zion," serve as an *inclusio,* that is, they open and close the section.

The three successive chapters (Isaiah 7, 8, and 9) all share a common theme — the expectation and sign of a special child. Isaiah 7 is connected explicitly to the reign of Ahaz (735–715 BC) and the Syro-Ephraimite war that took place early in his reign. Yahweh, trying to encourage the wavering Ahaz to trust in him rather than in military alliances, invites Ahaz to ask for a sign that will prove Yahweh's power and faithfulness to deliver. The foolish Ahaz refuses. Yahweh decides to give him a sign anyway, albeit an unusual, ironic sign. A young woman (NIV, "virgin") will give birth to a child who will be called Immanuel (the meaning of the Hebrew word *Immanuel* is "God is with us"), and before this baby gets to be very old, the two threatening kings of Syria and Israel will be destroyed. However, because of Ahaz's lack of faith in Yahweh, this sign will also point to coming judgment on Judah (7:10–25).

In Isaiah 8 a child is indeed born, but this child is the son of Isaiah and is given the name Maher-Shalal-Hash-Baz ("quick to the plunder, swift to the spoil"). Once again the prediction is given that before this child gets very old, Syria (Damascus is the capital) and Israel (Samaria is the capital) will be destroyed (8:3–4). Many scholars maintain that this child is the immediate fulfillment of the prophecy regarding the child in Isaiah 7.

Yet the prophecy in 7:14 of a child called Immanuel does not

King Tiglath-pileser III developed Assyria into an expansionistic world power.

Zion

Early in biblical history the term *Zion* referred specifically to the bluff or mount in Jerusalem just south of the future temple site between the Kidron Valley and the Valley of Hinnom. The first use of the term is in 2 Samuel 5:7, describing David's conquest of Jerusalem from the Jebusites: "David captured the fortress of Zion, the City of David." After Solomon comes to the throne, he brings up the ark of the covenant from "Zion, the City of David" and places it in its new location in the temple, located just to the north. Throughout the rest of Scripture, the Temple Mount area will frequently be referred to as Zion, especially in Psalms and in the prophets.

The Old Testament prophets use Zion in both a literal and a metaphorical sense. They use the term in a literal sense to refer to the physical mountain ridge site where the temple was located. Metaphorically, the prophets use Zion to refer either to the temple itself, to the entire city of Jerusalem, or specifically to the inhabitants of Jerusalem. The phrase "daughter of Zion" is used frequently by the prophets in reference to the people living in Jerusalem.

The prophets often use the term Zion when they are describing the glorious future restoration and the associated reign of Yahweh. For example, Micah 4:7 proclaims, "Yahweh will rule over them in Mount Zion."

The New Testament writers draw extensively from the Old Testament prophets (as well as Psalms), so it is no surprise to find them using the term Zion in a manner similar to the prophets. Thus Matthew 21:5, for example, uses the phrase "Daughter of Zion" to refer to the inhabitants of Jerusalem (quoting Zech. 9:9). Yet the New Testament broadens the prophets' metaphorical usage of Zion to some extent to include allusions to the "heavenly Jerusalem." Thus in Hebrew 12:22 the writer states: "But you have come to Mount Zion, to the heavenly Jerusalem, the city of the living God." In similar fashion, Revelation 14:1 depicts Jesus Christ (the Lamb) as standing on "Mount Zion."

---

appear to be a simple prophecy fulfilled in its entirety by the child in 8:3–4. This kind of prophecy is often referred to as typology, which is related to the "near view/far view" phenomenon discussed in chapter 5. The "near view" child, born to Isaiah, does fulfill the prophecy in a short-term sense. However, in the texts that follow, Isaiah indicates that there are aspects of this prophetic child that have not yet been fulfilled, but will be in the future.

Thus in 8:8 Isaiah refers to the land of Judah as "your land, O Immanuel," indicating that Immanuel is something greater than the child born in 8:3. The term Immanuel is likewise used at the end of 8:10, indicating that "God with us" will be the cause of the defeat of the hostile nations. Then in Isaiah 9:6 the prophet speaks of a child again, only now the child is connected to the messianic hope of a great coming Davidic king. Isaiah refers to this child as "Wonderful Counselor, Mighty God, Everlasting Father, Prince of Peace." This Coming One is presented as one who fulfills the Davidic covenant of 2 Samuel 7. Once again justice and righteousness are the high standards by which this coming kingdom is defined (Isa. 9:7). By the end of Isaiah 9:7, the child first mentioned in 7:14 as a sign to Ahaz has merged into a spectacular

> The three successive chapters (Isaiah 7, 8, and 9) all share a common theme — the expectation and sign of a special child.

dramatic personality with divine attributes that will bring about restoration based on the promises to David. So while a child born back in the eighth century BC fulfilled part of this prophecy (the sign to Ahaz), that child was but a type or foreshadowing of the ultimate fulfillment that took place in Jesus Christ. Without hesitation, the New Testament clearly identifies Jesus as the fulfillment of this prophecy. Yet even then, some of the consummate fulfillment regarding the establishment of the described kingdom lies in the future (at least from a premillennial view).

Isaiah 9:8 – 10:34 returns to the theme of judgment. The statement "Yet for all this, his anger is not turned away, his hand is still upraised" is repeated four times (9:12, 17, 21; 10:4). Once again, social injustice against the poor, the oppressed, widows, and orphans is cited as part of the serious sin problem. Yet in numerous places in Isaiah the prophet declares that a remnant will survive the coming judgment. That is, as severe as the disobedience was, and as severe as the resultant punishment will be, there will always be a remnant of the people of God. Isaiah 10:20 – 22 is one of those texts, frequent in Isaiah, that points to the remnant, small as it might be.

> Isaiah indicates that there are aspects of this prophetic child that have not yet been fulfilled, but will be in the future.

Isaiah 11, however, returns to the promise of a Davidic king that was introduced in 9:2 – 7. David's father was Jesse, and this passage refers to the Coming One as a "shoot" or "branch" coming from the "stump" of Jesse (11:1, 10). This Coming One will be empowered by the Spirit of Yahweh (11:2), and in contrast to the existing rulers, he will judge the needy and the poor with righteousness and justice. This stress on righteousness and justice will be repeated over and over throughout Isaiah. In addition, this coming king will bring about a time of unparalleled peace. Isaiah paints a colorful picture of this situation: "The wolf will live with the lamb, the leopard will lie down with the goat" (11:6 – 8). As introduced in chapter 5 of this book, interpreters today

---

NT Connection: The Virgin Birth

Because some liberal scholars in the twentieth century denied the virgin birth of Christ, the translation and interpretation of Isaiah 7:14 became a hotly debated and sensitive issue. As evangelicals, we certainly affirm the miraculous virgin birth of our Lord Jesus Christ. But the actual prophecy in Isaiah 7:14 is not simplistic, and as already discussed, it is intertwined into typology and the near view/far view phenomenon. Here, briefly, is the issue. The Hebrew word used in Isaiah 7:14 is 'almah, which generally refers to a young woman. The Hebrew word does not carry specific connotations of virginity other than the fact that most young women, if unmarried, were virgins. However, years later, when Isaiah was translated into Greek (called the Septuagint), the Greek word used in this passage was parthenos, which does explicitly refer to a virgin. Matthew, who was familiar with both the Hebrew form of Isaiah and the Greek translation, declares that Jesus fulfills this passage by his virgin birth and his identity as Immanuel, "God with us" (Matt. 1:23).

are faced with a challenge when trying to determine whether to take passages like this as literal predictions or as figurative. Premillennial dispensationalists will understand this passage to be fulfilled literally in the thousand-year kingdom that Christ will establish here on earth. That is, part of the coming kingdom is a restoration of the natural world, and peace will be so pervasive as to extend to nature. Amillennialists, on the other hand, will understand this passage to be figurative, speaking of peace in general that Christ brings as he establishes his kingdom within the people of his church.

> The Coming One will be empowered by the Spirit of Yahweh and will judge the needy and the poor with righteousness and justice.

Another highly significant element of Isaiah 11 is the connection between the coming "Root of Jesse" and the nations. When this wonderful Davidic king comes and establishes his kingdom, it will not be just for the remnant of Israel and Judah (note that they are reunited in 11:13), but for all of the nations of the world (11:10–12).

ISAIAH 13–23 — JUDGMENT ON THE NATIONS

The prophet Isaiah lived in tumultuous times. Early in his ministry Judah had to contend with the Syro-Ephraimite alliance. Then for the next forty years the region was dominated by Assyria, and the times were characterized by political intrigue, alliances, rebellions, and invasions. Isaiah 13–23 is made up of oracles concerning the many nations involved in the political intrigue of the region. While most of these oracles are judgment oracles directed against each specific nation (note, however, that Isaiah 18:1–7, dealing with Cush, and 20:1–6, dealing with Egypt and Cush, are different in form and content), the real target audience for Isaiah is probably the people and leaders of Judah. He is warning them not to get involved in alliances with these nations. He is proclaiming that Yahweh's people should

---

The Remnant

A prominent theme occurring throughout the prophets is that of the *remnant*. The concept of remnant is broad and fairly fluid, but the basic idea at the heart of "remnant theology" is that even at the time of the most appalling apostasy and during the terrible judgment and destruction that follows, Yahweh continues to maintain a small faithful group that he delivers and blesses.

The remnant theme surfaces in several places in the Old Testament. For example, when Elijah complains to Yahweh that he is the only faithful one left, Yahweh corrects him by pointing out that he has maintained a remnant of 7,000 faithful ones in the midst of national apostasy (1 Kings 19:10–18).

Although the remnant theme occurs frequently throughout the Old Testament, it is the prophetic literature that develops the theme most extensively. In fact, the prophets will use the Hebrew word for remnant over one hundred times. The prophets proclaim the coming terrible judgment on Israel and Judah as well as the future hope and restoration beyond the judgment. In this context the prophets announce that many will be destroyed in the judgment, but not all. A remnant will survive through which Yahweh will work to bless and to restore. Typically, the remnant refers to those who actually go into exile but who continue to have hope for returning to the Land. Frequently, the prophets will associate the return and the reestablishment of the remnant in the Land with the inauguration of the messianic age.

An artist's depiction of a royal procession going through the Ishtar Gate into Babylon. Isaiah prophesied the end of Babylon (Isaiah 13–14) and the restoration of Israel.

trust in Yahweh, for he is the ruler and judge of all, including the political powers of the day.

This unit deals with the following nations:

Babylon (13:1–14:23)
Assyria (14:24–27)
Philistia (14:28–32)
Moab (15:1–16:14)
Damascus (17:1–11)
General summary concerning the nations (17:12–14)
Cush (18:1–7)
Egypt (19:1–25)
Egypt/Cush (20:1–6)
Babylon (21:1–10)
Dumah (21:11–12)
Arabia (21:13–17)
Jerusalem (22:1–25)
Tyre (23:1–18)

Oracles against the nations, like these in Isaiah, occur frequently in the prophets, demonstrating that Yahweh is the Lord and Master of all creation. The point of these oracles is usually that Yahweh's people need not fear the world powers or rely on them for protection, but should instead trust in him.

In some theological circles, a few verses from the oracle against Babylon (13:1–14:23) are pulled out of their context and viewed as describing the fall of Satan from heaven. They point to Isaiah 14:12: "How you have fallen from heaven, O morning star, son of the dawn! You have been cast down to the earth, you who once laid low the nations!" This view was fueled by the King James Version, which translated the Hebrew word for morning star (lit. "shining one") as "Lucifer." However, both the KJV translation and the connection to Satan in this passage are unwarranted and have been universally rejected by Old Testament scholarship. The context is clearly one of judgment on Babylon. The rest of this unit (13:1–14:23) makes little sense when applied to Satan.

> Yahweh's people need not fear the world powers.

Likewise, doing so violates the context of the larger unit (Isaiah 13–23). The language used in 14:12 is figurative, not literal. The background for this image (the fallen star) is that of pagan mythology from the religious and literary world of the surrounding region. A minor god in the pagan pantheon (called by the same term, "shining one") rebelled against the supreme god and was thrown down to the underworld. Isaiah's text is a parody on this theme, mocking the king of Babylon and his prideful arrogance and comparing him to this minor god who was thrown down into the underworld.

Although most of this unit deals with judgment, there are glimpses of hope and deliverance, even for the nations. Indeed, Isaiah's vision of the future kingdom includes the foreign nations. For most of Isaiah's ministry, the two major superpowers were Assyria to

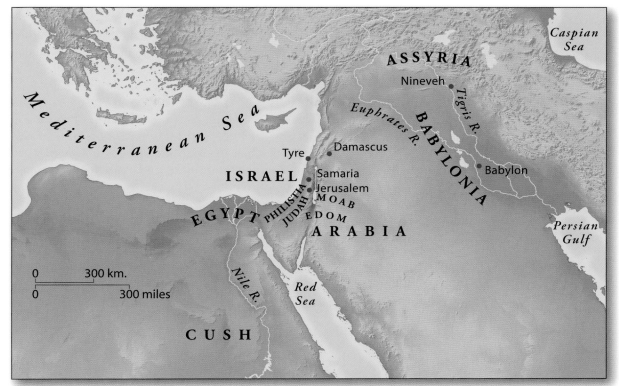

The nations the prophet included in his oracles (Isaiah 13 – 23).

the north and Egypt/Cush to the south (the black African nation of Cush ruled over Egypt throughout most of Isaiah's life). In Isaiah 19:23–25 the prophet describes a future highway from Assyria to Egypt that allows the two antagonistic superpowers to join together with Israel in peaceful worship of Yahweh, who blesses them and calls Egypt "my people" and Assyria "my handiwork."

> In Isaiah 13–23 Yahweh judges not only the nations but all of creation.

ISAIAH 24–27—YAHWEH'S JUDGMENT ON THE WORLD

This unit functions as a conclusion to Isaiah 13–23, for here Yahweh judges not only the nations but all of creation. He is God over all heaven and earth. Because this unit contains some apocalyptic imagery and because it resembles the book of Revelation in some respects, earlier scholars often called it "The Isaiah Apocalypse" (see the discussion of apocalyptic literature in chapter 3). In more recent years, scholars have concluded that this unit is simply eschatological and does not really contain many apocalyptic characteristics. In this sense, these chapters form the conclusion to Isaiah 13–23 without any change in genre.[1]

---

1. John N. Oswalt, *Isaiah,* NIV Application Commentary (Grand Rapids: Zondervan, 2003), 440; J. Gordon McConville, *Exploring the Old Testament: A Guide to the Prophets* (Downers Grove, IL: InterVarsity Press, 2002), 19.

ISAIAH 28–35 — JUDGMENT FOLLOWED BY DELIVERANCE

This section of Isaiah contains a mix of judgment proclamations and deliverance promises. Isaiah 28–32 emphasizes judgment, first on Israel (called Ephraim in 28:1) and on Judah (Jerusalem is called Ariel in 29:1). Isaiah 29:13 stresses Jerusalem's reliance on religious ritualism ("these people honor me with their lips, but their hearts are far from me"). Jesus quotes this passage as applicable to the Jews of his day (Matt. 15:8–9; Mark 7:6–7), implying judgment on Jerusalem as Isaiah 29 proclaims. Next the foolishness of trusting in human allies (such as Egypt) is underscored (30:1–5; 31:1–3), a situation that is played out in narrative texts a few chapters later in Isaiah 36–37. Also scattered throughout Isaiah 28–32, however, are promises of deliverance and future restoration. Isaiah 32, for example, once again points to justice and righteousness as primary characteristics of the coming king (32:1–2, 15–20).

As is common in many prophetic texts, judgment on the nations follows close on the heels of judgment on Israel and Judah. Judgment on Assyria, predicted in 31:8–9, is expanded in Isaiah 33. Using Edom as a representative, Isaiah 34 then announces judgment on the nations. Isaiah 35, however, standing at the end of the unit, is a wonderful picture of deliverance in the future kingdom of peace, when the blind will see and the lame will walk (35:5–6) and Yahweh's redeemed ones will enter Zion with singing and joy (35:9–10).

ISAIAH 36–39 — HEZEKIAH AND THE ASSYRIANS

Chapters 36–39 are in narrative form, and they deal with King Hezekiah and the Assyrian invasion and siege of Jerusalem in 701 BC. The events in this unit parallel those described in 2 Kings 18:17–20:19. Isaiah describes the Assyrian siege of Jerusalem. He predicts victory for Judah and urges Hezekiah to stand firm in trusting Yahweh. Yet Isaiah also adds that Yahweh's promised deliverance is "for my sake and for the sake of David" (37:35), continuing the frequent prophetic theme that deliverance often stems from Yahweh's covenant with David. In 37:36–38 Yahweh miraculously defeats the Assyrians, and the Assyrian king, Sennacherib, is later assassinated. Isaiah 38 recounts Hezekiah's illness, miraculous recovery, and prayer of thanksgiving.

Hezekiah's Tunnel. To strengthen the defense of Jerusalem, Hezekiah had a 1,750-foot tunnel constructed to bring water inside the walls.

In Isaiah 39, however, Hezekiah entertains an envoy from Babylon and even shows the envoy all of his wealth. Isaiah, knowing that the Babylonians will be the ones in the future who will completely destroy Jerusalem and exile the people, rebukes Hezekiah for his foolishness. Thus, as Isaiah 1–39 comes to a close, Yahweh has delivered Hezekiah and Jerusalem from the Assyrians, but the growing danger of Babylon is introduced, providing a

Sennacherib, king of Assyria, watches as the booty from the captured Judahite city of Lachish is paraded before him (701 BC).

fitting introduction to the next unit (Isaiah 40–55), which addresses the future exiles in Babylon.

One of the rather unique aspects of this unit is that in general the king and the people listen to Yahweh's prophet Isaiah. Thus the destruction of Jerusalem is averted. This positive response to the prophet is in stark contrast to what will happen in the book of Jeremiah, where no one—king, priests, prophets, nobles, or people—will listen to Yahweh's prophetic messenger, thus ensuring the destruction of Judah and Jerusalem. It is also interesting to note that in the Hebrew canon the books of Isaiah and Jeremiah follow immediately after 2 Kings, which ends with the destruction of Jerusalem and the exile. Isaiah 37–39 shows what could have happened if the people and the king had but listened to Yahweh's prophet and obeyed.

» FURTHER READING «

Childs, Brevard S. *Isaiah.* The Old Testament Library. Louisville: Westminster John Knox, 2001.
Oswalt, John N. *The Book of Isaiah: Chapters 1–39.* The New International Commentary on the Old Testament. Grand Rapids: Eerdmans, 1986.
Sweeney, Marvin A. *Isaiah 1–39.* Forms of the Old Testament Literature. Grand Rapids: Eerdmans, 1996.

» DISCUSSION QUESTIONS «

1. Discuss the role of the "child" in Isaiah 7.

2. Why has Isaiah 14:1–23 been understood by some as referring to the fall of Satan? Why is this interpretation doubtful? Who is Isaiah 13:1–14:23 talking about?

3. Discuss the messianic aspects of Isaiah 9:1–7.

» WRITING ASSIGNMENTS «

1. Choose either the amillennial or premillennial view and discuss the meaning of Isaiah 11:6–9 from that viewpoint.

2. Discuss the theme of the justice and righteousness of Yahweh in Isaiah 7–39.

3. Discuss and critique the actions of Hezekiah in Isaiah 36–39.

CHAPTER 8

Isaiah 40—55

"We all, like sheep, have gone astray,

each of us has turned to his own way;

and Yahweh has laid on him

the iniquity of us all." (Isa. 53:6)

CHARACTERISTICS OF ISAIAH 40–66

Although we will discuss Isaiah 40–55 and Isaiah 56–66 in separate chapters, the two sections are related and need to be introduced briefly as a unit. As discussed in the overview of Isaiah in chapter 6, the second half of Isaiah (chapters 40–66) is a bit different from the first half. Here are some of the characteristics of Isaiah 40–66:

> The primary people whom Isaiah addresses are those in the exile.

1. The primary people whom Isaiah addresses are those in the exile.
2. No specific historical events are mentioned, and there are no words addressed to specific kings or individuals (like Ahaz, Hezekiah, Sennacherib, etc., as in Isaiah 1–39).
3. "Fear not!" is a major theme, often accompanied with words of comfort.
4. Israel is still being charged with covenant violation, as in Isaiah 1–39.
5. Salvation is promised (as in Isaiah 1–39) both in the near sense and in the far sense, often expressed in terms of a "new exodus," one that even includes Gentiles.
6. Yahweh refers to his people in personal, intimate terms.
7. Yahweh is praised for his many awesome attributes (holiness, sovereignty, power, control of history, etc.).
8. As in Isaiah 1–39, there are strong polemics against the idols and the nations.
9. Cyrus (king of Persia) is presented as Yahweh's instrument for judgment (on Babylon) and for deliverance (for Israel).

The Great Scroll of Isaiah (1QIsaᵃ), one of the best preserved of the Dead Sea Scrolls, is almost totally intact.

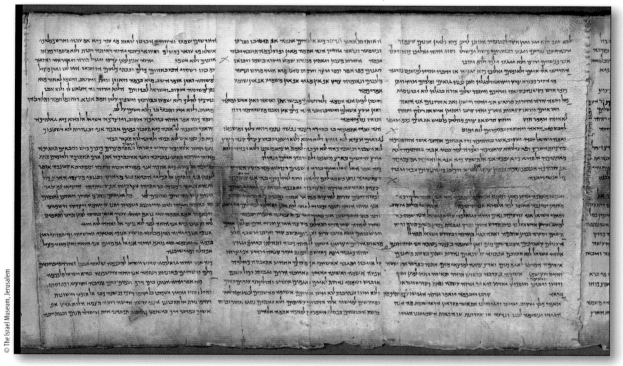

10. Deliverance focuses on the role of the Servant, presented in four Servant Songs (42:1–9; 49:1–13; 50:4–11; 52:13–53:12). Uniquely, the coming Servant will bring salvation through suffering.[1]

OVERVIEW OF ISAIAH 40–55

While Isaiah 1–39 focuses on the first two points of the prophetic message (broken covenant and judgment), Isaiah 40–55 centers on the third point—future hope and restoration for Israel and the nations. At the heart of this section is Yahweh's saving grace.

ISAIAH 40—BE COMFORTED AND SOAR LIKE AN EAGLE

Just as Isaiah 1 introduces 1–39, so Isaiah 40 introduces 40–66. Furthermore, these two introductory chapters are related through the use of many similar words, themes, and images. Terminology from Isaiah 1 that refers to sin and judgment reappear in Isaiah 40, but in the context of comfort and restoration. In effect, while in chapter 1 the punishments prophesied have already taken place, chapter 40 shifts the focus toward the glorious restoration.

> While in chapter 1 the punishments prophesied have already taken place, chapter 40 shifts the focus toward the glorious restoration.

In essence, Isaiah 40 serves not only as introduction but also as a summary of many of the major themes of 40–66. In 40:1–2 comfort is proclaimed to Jerusalem, and an end to her punishment is announced. Next the prophet orders that preparations be made, for the glory of Yahweh is coming and will be revealed to all (40:3–5). This is in accordance with the word of Yahweh, which stands firm forever, unlike frail humanity, which perishes quickly (40:6–8). After the preparation and in accordance with his word, sovereign Yahweh comes, combining strong, victorious power with kind, gentle compassion (40:9–11). This is beyond our understanding because mere mortals cannot comprehend Yahweh or his plans (40:12–14). All of the nations that have caused so much consternation and suffering for Yahweh's people are nothing before him; indeed, they are like drops in a bucket (40:15–17). Yahweh, on the other hand, is everything, the supreme all-powerful being. The idols cannot compare to him, for they are like the nations—nothing (40:18–26). Therefore, and in conclusion, Yahweh's people should not despair, but rather soar like eagles (40:27–31).

> The nations are like drops in a bucket.

---

1. These characteristics have been developed from those suggested by Claus Westermann, *Isaiah 40–66*, Old Testament Library (Philadelphia: Westminster, 1969), 11–21.

ISAIAH 41:1–44:23—FEAR NOT, FOR I AM WITH YOU

Isaiah 41 continues the theme of Yahweh's power over the nations and the idols. Yahweh declares that he is the one who will raise up Cyrus to subdue many of the nations. Although Cyrus is not specifically named yet, later passages make clear that Isaiah is referring to Cyrus in 41:2–3 and in 41:25. Likewise, this chapter includes comforting words for the Israelites (41:8–10), words that will be repeated frequently in the chapters to come. Yahweh reminds them that they are very special ("my servant, whom I have chosen, seed of Abraham"). In Isaiah 41:10 Yahweh exhorts his people not to fear, because he is with them. This is a statement of Yahweh's powerful and empowering presence, a major theme in the prophets—and, indeed, throughout the entire Old Testament.

> **Yahweh exhorts his people not to fear, because he is with them.**

As mentioned above, Isaiah 40–55 contains four passages that focus on a very unique and special Servant of Yahweh (42:1–7; 49:1–6; 50:4–10; 52:13–53:12). These passages are filled with messianic references, and the New Testament frequently

---

The New Exodus

The exodus is without doubt one of the most significant theological events in the Old Testament. Yahweh miraculously and powerfully delivers his people from slavery in Egypt. He leads them through the Red Sea, across the desert, through the Jordan River, and victoriously into the Promised Land, defeating all nations who dared to oppose them. In the Old Testament the exodus event becomes the paradigm or model of what salvation is all about. In a sense, one could say that the exodus is to the Old Testament as the cross is to the New Testament.

The prophets draw heavily from the events of the exodus, frequently using the images associated with that great deliverance. Occasionally, the prophets will describe the coming judgment in terms of an exodus reversal, that is, a reversal of their great salvation history (e.g., Jeremiah 41–43). But most frequently, the prophets use the imagery of the exodus to describe the coming messianic age. When the prophets proclaim the coming glorious restoration, they will often describe it poetically and figuratively in terms of a great New Exodus. Isaiah, in particular, speaks colorfully of a coming time when Yahweh will once again gather his shattered people, deliver them from their oppressors, and lead them into the Promised Land. In this New Exodus, Yahweh will dry up waters and rivers to allow his people to cross safely (Isa. 11:15; 19:5; 43:2), just as he had led Israel through the Red Sea and the Jordan River in the first exodus.

A striking development in the prophets' exodus imagery, however, is that they proclaim quite clearly that the New Exodus will be even more glorious than the original exodus. For example, in the original exodus, Yahweh gathered up the Hebrew slaves from Egypt, but in the New Exodus, he now includes the lame, the blind, and other weak people (Mic. 4:6–7; Isa. 40:11; 42:16; Jer. 31:8). In the New Exodus these regathered people will come not only from Egypt but from all nations, north, south, east, and west (Isa. 43:5–6). In addition, the New Exodus will not be limited to the deliverance of Israel, but it will extend to the nations as well, including even Israel's old adversary, Egypt herself (Isa. 11:10–16; 19:19–25). The New Testament continues this theme, identifying Jesus as the one who brings about the New Exodus prophesied by the Old Testament prophets.

NT Connection: Jesus Quietly Withdraws

In Matthew 12:15 – 16 Jesus withdraws from the crowd, warning those who followed him and have been healed to be quiet about who he is. Matthew cites this quiet withdrawal of Jesus as a fulfillment of Isaiah 42:1 – 4 (Matt. 12:17 – 21).

connects Jesus to these Servant Songs. Isaiah 42:1 – 7, the first Servant Song, stresses that this coming Servant will have the Spirit of Yahweh and will establish justice on the earth for all the nations (note the repetition of *justice* in 42:1, 3, and 4). Uniquely, though, and in contrast to most conquerors, the Servant will be quiet and meek (42:2 – 3). Yahweh reminds the audience that he is the creator of all life (42:5) and also the one who proclaims what is going to happen before it happens (42:9). Yahweh tells the Servant that he has called him in righteousness and will make him a "covenant for the people and a light for the Gentiles [or nations], to open eyes that are blind, to free captives from prison and to release from the dungeon those who sit in darkness" (42:6 – 7). Thus the Servant is presented as one who will be a mediator of a (new?) covenant as well as the one who delivers the nations and opens their eyes to the truth.

Isaiah 43:1 – 7 once again encourages the people in exile to "fear not!" In this passage Yahweh stresses the close, intimate relationship he has with his people. Because he has created them, redeemed them, and called them by name, they belong to him (43:1). He also refers to them as sons and daughters and tells them how precious they are to him and how he loves them (43:4 – 6). In 43:5 Yahweh repeats, "Fear not, for I am with you," comforting them with his powerful presence.

Isaiah 40 – 55 contains four passages that focus on a very unique and special Servant of Yahweh.

In Isaiah 43:14 – 21 Yahweh promises deliverance from the Babylonians. In 43:16 – 17 he alludes to the exodus event, which was perhaps the central salvation event in Israel's history so far. Yet Yahweh states in 43:18 – 19 that the "new thing" he is doing (the deliverance and restoration brought about by the Servant and proclaimed throughout Isaiah) will overshadow the "former things" (even the exodus!).

Isaiah 44:1 – 6 repeats again, "Do not be afraid!" Yahweh promises a time of refreshing that culminates in his pouring out his Spirit on the people of Israel (44:3). As the prophets look forward to the new, better reestablished relationship with Yahweh, one of the spectacular new features mentioned by Isaiah, Joel, and Ezekiel is the gift of Yahweh's Spirit to people. Joel 2:28 – 29 and Ezekiel 36:26 – 27 expound on this phenomenon in more detail than Isaiah does, but all three passages point to the future outpouring of Yahweh's Spirit that was fulfilled in the New Testament at Pentecost (Acts 2).

Isaiah 44:6 – 20 is a polemic against the idols. The prophet's tone is sarcastic, and his diatribe is filled with ironic humor. A man cuts down a tree. Half of the tree he puts in the fire to warm himself, and half of the tree he uses to fashion an idol to which he bows down to worship (44:14 – 17). Isaiah proclaims that to worship and to trust in such idols is ridiculous.

The tomb of Cyrus, King of Persia.

ISAIAH 44:24–48:22—CYRUS

As discussed in chapter 2, Cyrus came to the throne of Persia in 559 BC, and in 539 BC he conquered the Babylonian Empire, thus controlling the Jewish exiles that were in Babylon. In 538 BC he issued a decree that allowed the Jewish exiles to return home.

Earlier in Isaiah, the prophet referred to Cyrus simply as "the one from the north" or "the one from the east" (the Persian Empire stretched far enough across Mesopotamia that it was both to the east and to the north). Several times Isaiah refers to Cyrus explicitly by name (44:28; 45:1, 13) and a few times implicitly and unnamed (46:11; 48:14–15). As a demonstration of his ability to control history, predict the future, and bring events into being that had been foretold, Yahweh raises up Cyrus to judge Babylon. Yahweh thus stresses his incomparability. The idol gods, even those of Babylon, cannot do this (Isaiah 46). In fact, through Cyrus, Babylon will fall (Isaiah 47).

In Isaiah 48 Yahweh calls upon Israel to pay attention and to acknowledge that the idols simply cannot compare with him and his actions in history. Then Yahweh orders the Israelites to "leave Babylon," thus announcing the end of the exile (48:20).

ISAIAH 49–55—THE SERVANT AND ZION

This unit contains three of the four Servant Songs (49:1–6; 50:4–10; 52:13–53:12). Although in Isaiah 44–45 Cyrus, king of Persia, was to play a leading role in Yahweh's unfolding plan, now the future focus moves beyond Cyrus (who fades away) to the Servant of Yahweh. The Servant will be the crucial character in bringing about the future restoration and all of the "new things" that Yahweh has planned. The other major theme in this unit is the restoration and renewal of Zion (Jerusalem). These two themes — the Servant and the restored Zion — intertwine throughout this unit.

Isaiah 49:1 – 6 contains the second Servant Song. In 49:1 – 4 the Servant describes his calling from Yahweh. Next he describes his mission (49:5 – 6). Yahweh has given the Servant a twofold task: the restoration of Israel, and salvation for the nations (Gentiles). Once again, the Servant is proclaimed to be "a light for the Gentiles [nations]."

Using imagery from the exodus and implying a comparison between the coming Servant and Moses, Isaiah 49:8 – 12 once again describes the coming restoration of Israel. Isaiah 49:13 calls for shouts of joy and singing in response to the glorious

> The Servant will be the crucial character in bringing about the future restoration and all of the "new things" that Yahweh has planned.

A map of the Babylonian Empire in the early 6th century BC. Isaiah prophesies the fall of Babylon.

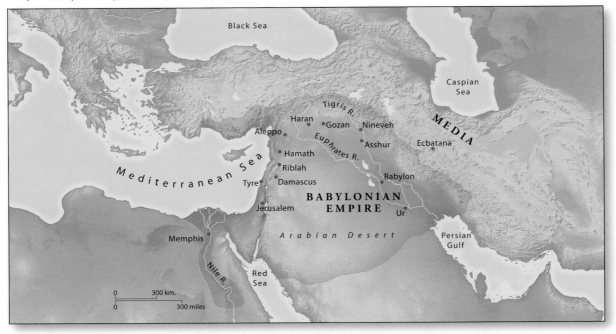

salvation of Yahweh, a theme running throughout the prophets. The personified Zion cries out in the next section (49:14–50:3) that Yahweh has forsaken her, but Yahweh answers with intimate compassionate words of reassurance that the restoration will truly happen.

The third Servant Song appears in 50:4–9. In this song the Servant declares his trust in Yahweh during difficult times of persecution and ridicule. The following section (Isa. 50:10–52:12) centers again on the restoration of Zion (Jerusalem). Numerous earlier themes reappear: New Exodus motifs, justice and righteousness, comfort for Jerusalem, Yahweh as powerful creator, the eternal nature of Yahweh's salvation in contrast to humanity's temporary nature, judgment on the oppressors, and joy and singing in response to Yahweh's salvation.

> The Servant declares his trust in Yahweh during difficult times of persecution and ridicule.

The final and climactic Servant Song appears in Isaiah 52:13–53:12. Some scholars have dubbed this passage "the high-water mark of Old Testament prophecy." Without doubt, this passage is the most famous of the Servant Songs because of its strong messianic prophecies and the many aspects of this text that were fulfilled during the crucifixion of Jesus Christ.

Like many other poetic units of prophetic literature, this one has clear structural features. There are five main stanzas, each consisting of three verses (52:13–15; 53:1–3, 4–6, 7–9, 10–12). The first and the fifth stanzas—the opening and the closing of the unit—describe the exaltation of the Servant. This is in strong contrast to the middle three stanzas, which detail the humiliation and suffering of the Servant. Indeed, this contrast is one of the central themes of the poem. Interconnected with this is the irony

---

Who Is the Servant of Yahweh?

Throughout history there has been much discussion about the identity of the Servant of Yahweh. Recall the puzzlement of the Ethiopian eunuch in Acts 8:32–34 regarding the identity of the Servant in the fourth Servant Song (Isa. 52:13–53:12). The Ethiopian asks of Philip, "Who is the prophet talking about, himself or someone else?"

This is a valid question because Isaiah presents us with some confusing data. Several times Isaiah refers to the people Israel (or Jacob) as Yahweh's servant (41:8; 44:1; 49:3; implied in 42:18–22). In these texts the term "Servant" seems to have a corporate sense. On the other hand, many of the texts in the Servant Songs clearly refer to the Servant as an individual (e.g., 49:5–6).

Apparently, the people of Israel had been called to be Yahweh's servant; that is, ones who should obey him and carry out his plan. But in this they failed. The Coming One (i.e., Jesus the Messiah), on the other hand, will be the true or ideal "Israel" in the sense that he will be and do all that Israel failed to be and do. Thus, in response to the Ethiopian's question, Philip "began with that very passage of Scripture and told him the good news about Jesus" (Acts 8:35). The New Testament clearly identifies Jesus as the Servant who fulfills the tasks assigned to the Servant in Isaiah.

Mount Zion today.

of the peoples' misperception of the Servant. Their negative view of him is contrasted with the reality of who he is and what he really will do for them.[2]

In Isaiah 52:13–15 Yahweh speaks, declaring that although the Servant was "disfigured" and people were horrified by his appearance, nonetheless he will be exalted above kings. The second half of 52:15 expresses a certain puzzlement that later finds clarification ("what they have not heard, they will understand"). The startling reality explained in the rest of the passage is that no one ever expected that one so lowly and persecuted could ever be so exalted as to sit on the very throne of Yahweh, having played the crucial role in Yahweh's great deliverance. In the Gospels, the humble origins of Jesus (from Nazareth and Galilee) frequently led many Jews to doubt that he could be God's great deliverer.

Isaiah is most likely the speaker of the next three stanzas (53:1–3, 4–6, 7–9). He seems to speak from a time when the suffering of the

> Who would expect that one so lowly and persecuted could ever be so exalted as to sit on the very throne of Yahweh?

2. John Oswalt, *The Book of Isaiah: Chapters 40–66,* New International Commentary on the Old Testament (Grand Rapids: Eerdmans, 1998), 376.

"How beautiful on the mountains are the feet of those who bring good news" (Isa. 52:7).

Servant has been completed but before the actual coming exaltation takes place. Picking up on the contrast of the previous section, Isaiah likewise underscores the contrast between the obscure origins of the Servant ("like a tender shoot, a root out of dry ground") and the role he will play as the "arm of Yahweh." "Arm" is a figure of speech that usually refers to great conquering military power (Isa. 40:10; 48:14; 51:5, 9; 52:10; 63:5–6). Not only were the Servant's origins obscure, the prophet proclaims, but there was nothing majestic about him to attract followers. Most monarchs of the day dressed in elaborate, beautiful clothes and rode spectacular, powerful horses in order to impress the people. This Servant did not come in this fashion. Ironically, he was a "man of sorrows, and familiar with suffering," and thus he was rejected and despised. How could this one be an exalted conqueror?

Isaiah 53:4–6 proclaims the greatest irony in history. The very one who was despised and persecuted was the one who would bear their suffering and sorrows (the Hebrew words translated as "infirmities" and "sorrows" in 53:4a are identical to those translated as "suffering" and "sorrows" in 53:3a) and provide them with peace and forgiveness. The significance of this passage cannot be overstressed. Isaiah points to one of the most important theological truths of Scripture—one that is not fully explained until the New Testament but that is at the

"We all, like sheep, have gone astray" (Isa. 53:6).

very heart of Christianity: The coming Servant (i.e., the Messiah) will suffer and die as a substitute for those who have sinned. The irony of 53:6 is incredible. "We all," Isaiah states, "like sheep, have gone astray." Sheep have a propensity to wander off, but remember that sheep are also the primary animal of sacrifice! Isaiah seems to be saying that we are the sheep, but that the Servant will be the one who dies in our place. This suffering and death of the Servant will bring peace (with God), forgiveness, righteousness (see 53:11), and healing (in a figurative sense).

> The coming Servant will suffer and die as a substitute for those who have sinned.

The suffering of the Servant, Isaiah explains, will lead to his death, described in 53:7 – 9. The Servant is innocent, but he goes quietly and willingly to his death in obedience to Yahweh's will (53:10 – 11). In fact, Yahweh breaks in to speak in 53:11, announcing that "my righteous servant will justify [Heb. 'cause to be righteous,' i.e., acquit] many." Then in 53:12, Yahweh speaks of the Servant's final exaltation because of his obedient death.

Much of Jesus' life and death as portrayed in the Gospels can be read as a fulfillment of the fourth Servant Song.

The discussion in Isaiah 54 returns to the bright future of Zion. Isaiah uses the marriage analogy, an image frequently employed by the prophets. Zion is the bride, and Yahweh is the husband. She is barren and distraught, but her husband will take her back; she will have many children, and she will know peace.

A Bedouin tent. Isaiah 54:2 uses the imagery of stretching out the cords and enlarging the tent to represent restoration.

© Steven Allan/www.istockphoto.com

"Come, all you who are thirsty, come to the waters" (Isa. 55:1). The Spring of Banias forms the headwaters of the Jordan River.

Isaiah 55 calls the weary, hungry, and thirsty exiles to a great feast. This is the figurative imagery used of the great restoration that is coming. This restoration, this great feast, is a result of the new everlasting covenant, based on the Davidic covenant of 2 Samuel 7, that Yahweh will inaugurate (55:3). Sinners are called upon to repent and be saved (55:7). This is astonishing, but Yahweh reminds them that his ways and his understanding are above the ways and understanding of people (55:8–9). Yahweh's word is powerful and effective (55:11), leading to the great deliverance that produces joy within his people (55:12).

» FURTHER READING «

Childs, Brevard S. *Isaiah*. The Old Testament Library. Louisville: Westminster John Knox, 2001.

Goldingay, John, and David Payne. *Isaiah 40–55*. International Critical Commentary. 2 vols. London and New York: T. & T. Clark, 2006.

Oswalt, John N. *The Book of Isaiah: Chapters 40–66*. New International Commentary on the Old Testament. Grand Rapids: Eerdmans, 1998.

Smith, Gary V. *Isaiah 40–66*. New American Commentary. Nashville: Broadman & Holman, 2009.

Westermann, Claus. *Isaiah 40–66*. The Old Testament Library. Philadelphia: Westminster Press, 1969.

» DISCUSSION QUESTIONS «

1. Isaiah frequently ridicules the worship of idols and the fact that people who worship idols are putting their trust in something that they themselves created out of wood or stone. Discuss things that people today trust in that are really their own creations.

2. Discuss the irony in Isaiah of referring to the coming deliverer as both Davidic king and suffering servant. How does Jesus fulfill both of these seemingly contradictory images?

» WRITING ASSIGNMENTS «

1. Isaiah 42:7 states that the Servant of Yahweh will open eyes that are blind. Discuss how Jesus fulfills this, both literally and symbolically. Be sure to address how the literal healing of blind people often symbolized "seeing" the truth. Look particularly at Mark 8:14–30 and John 9.

2. Discuss how the historical details (the arrest, trial, beatings, crucifixion) and the theological significance (substitutionary atonement) of Jesus fulfills specific verses of the fourth Servant Song (Isa. 52:13–53:12).

CHAPTER 9

Isaiah 56 — 66

"Maintain justice, and do what is right,

for my salvation is close at hand." (Isa. 56:1)

OVERVIEW OF ISAIAH 56−66

Isaiah 1−39 stresses points one and two of the prophetic message: (1) You've broken the covenant. Repent! and (2) No repentance? Then judgment is coming. Isaiah 40−55 then stresses the final point: (3) There is hope beyond the judgment for a glorious, future restoration, both for Israel/Judah and for the nations. Isaiah 56−66, on the other hand, calls on Yahweh's people to live righteously in the meantime. The previous section (Isaiah 40−55) focuses on Yahweh's grace. The Servant will bear the sin of those who do not deserve it, and Yahweh will restore his people based on his grace, not on their merit or on their piety. Isaiah 56−66 then points out that although salvation is based on grace, Yahweh, the Righteous One, calls on his people to live righteously and to worship authentically. Thus this section condemns false, hypocritical worship—remember that the third prophetic indictment is religious ritualism! It also underscores that mere genealogical membership in physical Israel does not automatically make one a "servant of Yahweh"; rather, the "servants of Yahweh" are those who choose to follow Yahweh authentically and to live righteous lives as he graciously empowers them.[1] This empowerment is critical because one of the repeated points in this section of Isaiah is that the people cannot live righteously in their own strength, but they can if they trust in Yahweh's empowerment. Finally, as Yahweh's servants live out righteous lives in his service, they are also to keep their eyes on the future promises—that glorious time when Yahweh will restore all of creation and make a "new heavens and earth" (Isaiah 65).

> Isaiah gives hope for the future but also calls on Yahweh's people to live righteously in the meantime.

ISAIAH 56−59—ISRAEL'S INABILITY TO LIVE RIGHTEOUSLY

Isaiah 56:1−8 introduces the unit, opening with the familiar call to justice and righteousness. This passage quickly takes an unusual turn, however, as Yahweh declares that love and true worship define his new servants, not bloodlines or genealogy. Eunuchs and foreigners who love Yahweh and serve him faithfully are included among the true worshippers of Yahweh. These people enter into close relationship with him, for they are declared to be pleasing to him, their worship is accepted by him, and they are allowed close access to him (his presence).

In contrast to those "outsiders" (the eunuchs and foreigners) who worship Yahweh correctly, the next passage (Isaiah 56:9−57:13) focuses on the failure of Israel's leaders (the supposed "insiders") to live righteously and to worship Yahweh faithfully. Greedy for gain and blind to justice and righteousness, they become idol worshippers and fall under Yahweh's judgment, as Isaiah declared so clearly in Isaiah 1−39. As the prophets regularly proclaim, however, Yahweh is always ready to respond to any who come to him with a humble spirit of repentance (57:14−21).

Throughout Isaiah we are presented with numerous insights into the character of Yahweh himself. Isaiah 57:15 is one of those texts where Yahweh makes an explicit statement about himself:

---

1. John Oswalt, *The Book of Isaiah: Chapters 40−66,* New International Commentary on the Old Testament (Grand Rapids: Eerdmans, 1998), 452−53.

For this is what the high and lofty One says—
he who lives forever, whose name is holy;
"I live in a high and holy place,
but also with him who is contrite and lowly in spirit,
to revive the spirit of the lowly
and to revive the heart of the contrite...."

This is one of those remarkable biblical texts that unites God's transcendence (his otherness, his holiness, all that is beyond us) and his immanence (how he relates intimately to his people). Yahweh declares that he dwells in a lofty and holy place (beyond the grasp of humanity) but that at the same time he also dwells with broken, fragile people to revive and to restore them.

As we have mentioned several times, throughout the prophetic books the prophets repeatedly charge Israel/Judah with three basic indictments: idolatry, lack of social justice, and reliance on religious ritual rather than true relationship. Isaiah 57 addresses idolatry. Isaiah 58 combines the last two (social justice, religious ritualism) in a scathing critique

> Yahweh is always ready to respond to any who come to him with a humble spirit of repentance.

NT Connection: "A House of Prayer for All Nations"

As Yahweh discusses his close relationship with eunuchs and foreigners (traditional outcasts) based on their true worship (Isa. 56:1–8), he declares, "My house will be called a house of prayer for all nations" (56:7), a radical concept for many Jews but one that was actually introduced by Solomon at the dedication of the temple (1 Kings 8:41–43). Jesus quotes Isaiah 56:7 as he cleanses the temple of the market and the moneychangers (Matt. 21:12–13; Mark 11:15–19; Luke 19:45–48). Apparently, the market area was set up in the Courtyard of the Gentiles, the one area where foreigners could come and worship. In essence, Jesus (as the messianic king with rights over the temple, and as the returned presence of God) pronounces judgment on those who were currently running the temple, for they had turned it into something other than what God desired. Note that the verses that follow Isaiah 56:7 proclaim condemnation on Israel's leaders because of self-centered greed, the same thing driving the leaders of the temple in Jesus' day.

A model of the temple in the time of Jesus, showing the Courtyard of the Gentiles, where Jesus cited Isaiah 56:7: "My house will be called a house of prayer for all nations."

Courtesy of www.HolyLandPhotos.org

of the people's attempt to be pious through the practice of fasting: "'We have humbled ourselves and we have fasted,' they declare to Yahweh. 'Why haven't you noticed?'" (58:3). Yahweh answers by pointing out that while they were fasting they were also exploiting their workers and that their fasts usually ended up in quarreling and fighting (58:3–4). Yahweh states that the fast he wants is not just a one-day exhibit of hypocritical humility. He then declares,

> Is not this the kind of fasting I have chosen:
> to loose the chains of injustice
> and untie the cords of the yoke,
> to set the oppressed free
> and break every yoke?
> Is it not to share your food with the hungry
> and to provide the poor wanderer with shelter? (58:6–7)

Once again Yahweh teaches that what he wants is relationship and not merely religious ritual. Part of a true relationship with Yahweh is living righteously in an authentic manner (because he is righteous). A critical aspect of this just and righteous lifestyle is a deep concern for other people. It is very important to Yahweh that his people be concerned for social justice, especially for the poor, the orphan, the widow, and the foreigner—those who are at the bottom of the socioeconomic power structure. Likewise, Yahweh repeatedly stresses that religious ritual does not cover up unethical behavior and social injustice. In fact, those who ignore social injustice and yet feel smug and pious due to their religious practices are annoying to Yahweh.

Isaiah 59:1–15 continues a similar theme—the preponderance of sin and the accompanying total absence of justice in the society. Indeed, the central theme throughout this unit (Isaiah 56–59) is Israel's inability to live righteously, and 59:1–15 encapsulates the problem. The final passage in this unit, however, presents the solution: the strong right arm of Yahweh will come in power and deliver his people victoriously (59:16–21). Yet note that this text has shifted focus somewhat from earlier passages on deliverance. Military imagery is used for the deliverance, but the traditional invading foes (Assyria, Babylonia, etc.) are not mentioned. The enemy here in Isaiah 56–59 is sin, and Yahweh promises to come in power and victory, defeating sin.[2] Integral to this deliverance is the promise of a covenant in which Yahweh's Spirit will

In Isaiah 56–59 the enemy is no longer portrayed as the Assyrians (shown below) or the Babylonians, but as sin.

Caryn Reeder

---

2. Ibid., 527.

Light

Because light plays such a profound role in daily human life, it is no surprise that the Bible frequently uses light as a theological concept. Light can be used in a figurative sense to represent knowledge of the truth or to portray the divine enlightenment that allows one to see or comprehend the truth. In the Old Testament, light is often associated with concepts of true justice and true righteousness. Yet light is also used in contexts of God's presence and the power that comes from it, especially in regard to his powerful acts of creation. Thus light and life are often closely related. Recall that at creation (Genesis 1), light was the first thing God created, followed soon by the creation of life. In addition, in both the Old Testament and the New Testament, light is frequently associated with the glory of God, another aspect of his presence. Darkness, in contrast, implies not only ignorance and foolishness but also judgment, involving the loss of God's presence and consequently death itself.

Oil lamps from the time of Isaiah. Light is a central theme in Isaiah.

The prophets in general, and Isaiah in particular, use the image of light frequently. Isaiah describes the coming messianic age with the image of light replacing darkness: "The people walking in darkness have seen a great light" (Isa. 9:2). In later texts Yahweh declares to the Servant, "I will also make you a light to the nations [Gentiles], that you may bring my salvation to the ends of the earth" (Isa. 49:6; 42:6). Clearly, Isaiah is using the image of light and the phrase "light to the nations" to mean more than mere enlightenment or knowledge; he is referring to all that is involved in the salvation of the Gentiles (God's presence, power, knowledge, etc.). Near the end of the book, Isaiah describes the coming kingdom as characterized by the dazzling light of Yahweh's presence, "The sun will no more be your light by day, nor will the brightness of the moon shine on you, for Yahweh will be your everlasting light" (Isa. 60:19).

In the New Testament Jesus is identified as the one who fulfills Isaiah's prophecies about the "light to the nations/Gentiles." This is proclaimed by Simeon early in Luke when baby Jesus is brought to the temple (Luke 2:32). In Acts 13:47, in response to Jewish rejection, Paul redirects the gospel to the Gentiles and quotes Isaiah 49:6, "I have made you a light to the Gentiles, that you may bring salvation to the ends of the earth." John 1 identifies Jesus as the light repeatedly (John 1:4, 5, 8, 9), connecting Christ to the major Old Testament themes regarding Yahweh and light: creative power, enlightenment, and presence. Isaiah's "light to the nations" theme reaches its ultimate fulfillment at the end of the book of Revelation. Compiling several images and texts from Isaiah (especially Isa. 60:19), Revelation 21:23 – 24 describes the New Jerusalem, saying, "The city does not need the sun or the moon to shine on it, for the glory of God gives it light, and the Lamb is its lamp. The nations [Gentiles] will walk by its light."

empower his people to speak (59:21), presumably so they can proclaim Yahweh's glory and righteousness to the nations.

ISAIAH 60–62—FUTURE SALVATION

Point three of the standard prophetic message is a promise of hope and future restoration. Isaiah 60–62 is basically an extensive development of that theme. It is filled with passages describing Israel's future salvation and the blessings that will be on Yahweh's people. Numerous themes introduced earlier in Isaiah are repeated here: Yahweh will deliver his people and exalt them; he will give them light, share his glory with them, comfort and raise up the oppressed and brokenhearted, draw the nations to him, and bless all who come to him.

> Isaiah 60–62 is filled with passages describing Israel's future salvation and the blessings that will be on Yahweh's people.

ISAIAH 63–66—A CALL TO ETHICAL LIVING

It is significant that the book of Isaiah does not end by focusing on the theme of Israel's glorious restoration and future blessing as presented in Isaiah 60–62, but instead it closes by focusing on the theme of ethical behavior. Isaiah 63–66 includes a picture of the coming eschatological future (new heaven and new earth), but the stress is on obedience to Yahweh in the present. This theme of "obedience and just behavior now while waiting expectantly for the glorious future" is one that is continued throughout the prophetic books and into the New Testament.

Ruins of the triple gate at Megiddo. Gates were a critical part of a city's defenses. Isaiah proclaims that in the restoration the city gates will always stand open, a sign of peace (Isa. 60:11).

NT Connection: Isaiah 61 and Jesus in the Synagogue

During the opening days of his public ministry, Jesus enters into the synagogue in Nazareth on the Sabbath. Invited to read the Scriptures, he is handed the scroll of Isaiah. Turning to Isaiah 61, he reads aloud from verses 1 and 2: "The Spirit of the Lord is on me, because he has anointed me to preach good news to the poor. He has sent me to proclaim freedom for the prisoners and recovery of sight for the blind, to release the oppressed, to proclaim the year of the Lord's favor." After sitting down, Jesus explains the significance of this text by stating, "Today this scripture is fulfilled in your hearing" (Luke 4:18 – 19). Thus, from the inauguration of his ministry, Jesus clearly identifies himself as the One whose coming Isaiah had promised..

A particular distinctive of the Messiah that Isaiah stresses and that Jesus identifies with is the concept of comfort and help for the poor and brokenhearted. When John the Baptist sends his disciples to question Jesus about his identity, Jesus responds by stating, "The blind receive sight, the lame walk, those who have leprosy are cured, the deaf hear, the dead are raised, and the good news is preached to the poor" (Luke 7:22). Jesus' answer draws from a number of Isaian passages (29:18 – 19; 35:5 – 6; 42:18; 43:8; 61:1) and underscores his identity with Isaiah's messiah and with the ministry that Isaiah describes for the Messiah. Throughout the prophetic material, and in Isaiah particularly, the care and concern for the sick, wounded, imprisoned, and poor that the Coming One brings is closely interconnected with the theme of justice (Isa. 61:1 – 8), a connection readers often overlook when reading the Gospels. Compare Jesus' declaration regarding justice in Luke 18:6 – 8 with his statements a few verses later to the rich ruler, "Sell everything you have and give to the poor." This theme continues on into Luke 19:1 – 10, where Zacchaeus the tax collector makes restitution and gives to the poor.

In this regard, Isaiah 63 – 66 is similar to Isaiah 56 – 59. Structurally, the two units are similar in their themes, but the order of the themes is inverted. Isaiah 56 – 59 opens with a picture of foreign converts (56:1 – 8) and ends with a description of the Divine Warrior (59:15 – 21). The final section of Isaiah, on the other hand, begins with the Divine Warrior (63:1 – 6) and ends with the gathering of foreign converts to worship Yahweh (66:18 – 24).[3]

As mentioned, this unit starts with the coming of the Divine Warrior, who is bringing judgment on his enemies (63:1 – 6). The central image is that of a winepress where grapes are crushed to make wine. Yahweh states that he has been trampling the hostile enemy nations like grapes in a winepress, even splattering the red (blood-like) juice on his garments. This imagery of winepress and the grapes of wrath is used again of God's judgment in Revelation 14.

> The book of Isaiah closes by focusing on the theme of ethical behavior.

Isaiah 63:7 – 64:12 is a sorrowful prayer (lament) where the prophet speaks on behalf of Yahweh's sinful people. He reviews the history of Yahweh's faithfulness to Israel, pointing especially to the exodus (63:11 – 14). He pleads for deliverance, asking Yahweh to "rend the heavens and come down" (64:1), a text alluded to in the New Testament in connection with the baptism of Christ (Mark 1:10).

---

3. Ibid., 593.

In Isaiah, Yahweh promises his people that one day he will usher in a new creation — "Behold, I will create new heavens and a new earth. The former things will not be remembered, nor will they come to mind" (Isa. 65:17; cf. 66:22). The goodness of Yahweh's original creation described in Genesis 1 – 2 had been marred by Satan and by humanity (Genesis 3 – 11); indeed, sin had produced death. The prophets proclaim that the disobedience of God's chosen people Israel and their total rejection of Yahweh and his covenant parallel this sin, spoiling the creation itself. Thus, as Isaiah looks to the coming messianic age, he describes a vision of a "new heaven and new earth."

The New Testament continues to develop this theme. Romans 8:18 – 25 declares that God is working to free his creation from bondage and to reverse the curse of sin. Drawing from Isaiah, Revelation 21 – 22 describes the future cosmic restoration of the creation as a "new heaven and new earth"; thus, the final home of the righteous will be new and different, excluding some elements familiar to those living in the present age, such as the sea (Rev. 21:1); crying, mourning, pain, and death (Rev. 21:4); anything impure, including unrighteous or wicked people (Rev. 21:8, 27; 22:15); a man-made temple (Rev. 21:22); natural lights (sun and moon) or night (Rev. 21:23 – 24; 22:5); and the curse of sin (Rev. 22:3).

Yahweh responds in the final section (65:1 – 66:24), pointing out that although he has revealed himself to this people, they have persisted in sin and disobedience, trusting in their hypocritical religious rituals instead of true faith and worship. The first unit (65:1 – 16) stresses disobedience and judgment, but the unit following immediately afterward contains a wonderful promise of peace and hope as Yahweh describes his coming "new creation" (65:17 – 25). Indeed, throughout the final section of Isaiah the themes of judgment and hope alternate back and forth, just as they did in earlier sections. Yahweh is reminding them that inclusion in the future restoration is neither automatic nor based on Israelite lineage. Yes, it will be by his power and his righteousness that the glorious future time will come into being, but nonetheless, the people are called to live humbly, faithfully, and righteously before Yahweh. Also, once again the exaltedness of Yahweh is contrasted with the fact that it is the humble and contrite one who has access to him (66:1 – 2), not the hypocrite trusting in rituals (66:3 – 4).

> The people are called to live humbly, faithfully, and righteously before Yahweh.

The final section of Isaiah (66:15 – 24) draws the entire unit (Isaiah 56 – 66) as well as the book as a whole to a close by restating several prominent themes. Some people, both Israelites and Gentiles, will continue to sin against Yahweh and thus will experience judgment. On the other hand, both Israelites and Gentiles who trust and obey Yahweh will be gathered together and brought into his presence to worship him and experience his glory.

» FURTHER READING «

Beale, G. K., and D. A. Carson, eds. *Commentary on the New Testament Use of the Old Testament.* Grand Rapids: Baker, 2007.

Childs, Brevard S. *Isaiah.* The Old Testament Library. Louisville: Westminster John Knox, 2001.

Oswalt, John N. *The Book of Isaiah: Chapters 40–66.* New International Commentary on the Old Testament. Grand Rapids: Eerdmans, 1998.

Smith, Gary V. *Isaiah 40–66.* New American Commentary. Nashville: Broadman & Holman, 2009.

Westermann, Claus. *Isaiah 40–66.* The Old Testament Library. Philadelphia: Westminster Press, 1969.

» DISCUSSION QUESTIONS «

1. Discuss the meaning of Isaiah 58 for the church today. That is, evaluate the religious rituals of your church and whether or not these are reflective of true righteous living. How does our view of piety or obedient Christian living relate to how we treat the less fortunate? How does our worship of God relate to our care for others?

2. What does the New Testament add to the discussion above regarding true worship and care for others?

3. What does Isaiah 57:19 teach us about God?

» WRITING ASSIGNMENTS «

1. Trace the theme of light throughout Isaiah. Use a concordance to locate the passages that contain "light." Be sure to discuss the theological meaning of the term as it is used.

2. Discuss the main message (central themes) in the book of Isaiah.

3. Write a 2–3 page paper on the biblical theme of "the new heavens and new earth."

4. Trace the theme of "justice" throughout Isaiah 56–66.

CHAPTER 10

Jeremiah 1 — 10

"If you really change your ways ... and deal with each other justly ... and if you do not follow other gods ... then I will let you live in this place." (Jer. 7:5–7)

OVERVIEW OF JEREMIAH

Setting

Isaiah lives and prophesies in Jerusalem during the time of Assyrian expansion and domination. Although Jeremiah also lives and preaches in Jerusalem, his ministry takes place during the time of the Babylonian empire. Perhaps more than any other prophet, Jeremiah repeatedly ties his message firmly into historical events. He begins his ministry in 627 BC during the reign of Josiah (the last good king of Judah), and he prophesies throughout the reigns of Jehoahaz, Jehoiakim, Jehoiachin, and Zedekiah. Most of Jeremiah's confrontations and conflicts are with Jehoiakim and Zedekiah. Jeremiah experiences the terrible siege and destruction of Jerusalem in 587/586 BC. He continues to prophesy to those who remain in Judah under the governor, Gedaliah, after the destruction and exile, but then he is forced to go to Egypt with those Jews who are fleeing from Babylonian wrath for foolishly assassinating Gedaliah. For a review of this time period, reread chapter 2, "The Prophets in History," especially the part from King Manasseh's reign in Judah (687–642 BC) to the fall of Jerusalem (587–586 BC). This history provides important background material for understanding the message of Jeremiah.

> Jeremiah's ministry takes place during the time of the Babylonian empire.

Although the spoken messages of Jeremiah and the events portrayed in the book take place just before and after the fall of Jerusalem, the final compilation of the book probably took place a short time later. Jeremiah 1:2–3 describes the duration of Jeremiah's ministry, which continues into the time "when the people of Jerusalem went into exile." This reveals to us the final point of view of the book. While Jeremiah's preached verbal message was "Repent! The Babylonians are coming!" the written final form of the message is probably targeted at the people in exile, providing an explanation for the tragedy: "Look at what happened because you didn't repent and trust in Yahweh!" Moreover, the fall of Jerusalem and the Babylonian exile exonerated Jeremiah, proving him to be the true prophet of Yahweh with the true word of Yahweh for his people, thus adding great weight to his promise of future restoration and blessing.

Message

The three-point standard preexilic prophetic message discussed in chapter 4 is an excellent synthesis of Jeremiah. Thus Jeremiah's message can be summarized as follows:

1. You (Judah) have broken the covenant; you had better repent!
2. No repentance? Then judgment! Judgment will also come on the nations.
3. Yet there is hope beyond the judgment for a glorious future restoration both for Israel/Judah and for the nations.

Like many of the other prophets, Jeremiah focuses on the three central indictments that underscore how seriously Judah has broken the covenant. These indictments (sins or infractions against the covenant) are idolatry, social injustice, and religious ritualism. These three will surface time and time again in Jeremiah. Furthermore, like most of the other prophets, Jeremiah draws heavily from the book of Deuteronomy.

The book of Jeremiah provides more insight into the prophet himself than does any other prophetic book. We are provided with glimpses into his internal fears and struggles through a series of "laments" or "confessions." Because of his "lamenting," scholars have often labeled Jeremiah "the weeping prophet." However, it may be more appropriate to call him the "Dirty Harry" of the Old Testament. As in the case of policeman Harry Callahan in the old Clint Eastwood movies, Jeremiah is given a very tough job that no one else would want. Throughout the book, Jeremiah is engaged in serious (and dangerous) conflict with the political powers in Jerusalem — the king, the king's prophets, the nobles, and the priests.

> The book of Jeremiah provides more insight into the prophet himself than does any other prophetic book.

The Nature of the Book of Jeremiah

Ironically, even though the book of Jeremiah has numerous references to kings and other historical events, only Jeremiah 37 – 44 is in chronological order. The rest of the book hops back and forth from one king to another. The structure and order seem to be based on thematic elements or even on word repetitions rather than chronological sequence. Also, in general, Jeremiah is like an anthology, a collection of poetic oracles and proclamations, narrative events, and dialogues. It is very difficult if not impossible to outline the book in detail, and often the connection between literary units is unclear. However, the overall message as discussed above is very clear, and Jeremiah repeats the three indictments (idolatry, social injustice, religious ritualism) and the three main points (broken covenant, judgment, restoration) over and over. Likewise, while tight logical connections between small sections are not always discernible, the book can be broken down into larger sections that are unified by broad, general themes:

Jeremiah 1 – 29 — The Broken Covenant and Imminent Judgment
Jeremiah 30 – 33 — Restoration and the New Covenant
Jeremiah 34 – 45 — The Final Days of Jerusalem and Judah
Jeremiah 46 – 51 — Oracles Against the Nations
Jeremiah 52 — Postscript

> Like most of the other prophets, Jeremiah draws heavily from the book of Deuteronomy.

An interesting problem in the book of Jeremiah is the textual issue. The Old Testament portion of our English Bibles is largely translated from Hebrew manuscripts that are referred to as the Masoretic Text (MT). Prior to the discovery of the Dead Sea Scrolls in 1948, the earliest MT manuscript of Jeremiah dated to around AD 900. Another important ancient manuscript is the Septuagint, often referred to as the LXX. The LXX is a Greek translation made from the Hebrew Old Testament around 200 – 150 BC. The LXX was the primary Old Testament used by the early church until the fourth and fifth centuries AD. In Jeremiah, the MT and the LXX differ in several significant ways. First of all, the LXX is one-eighth shorter than the MT; that is, numerous passages and phrases in the MT are missing from the LXX. Significant passages that are in the MT but not in the LXX include Jeremiah 33:14 – 26; 39:4 – 13; 51:44b – 49a; and 52:27b – 30. In addition, some verses have a different word order or vary slightly in the words included. Furthermore, in the LXX, the text of Jeremiah 46 – 51 (the oracles against the nations) does not follow after Jeremiah 45, but follows Jeremiah 25:13, and before Jeremiah 26.

For much of the twentieth century it was thought that the MT was a better reflection of the original than the LXX. However, when the Dead Sea Scrolls were discovered, one of the ancient Hebrew fragments of Jeremiah reflected the reading of the LXX rather than the MT, suggesting that the LXX was an accurate translation of an ancient Hebrew text that was older than the MT. Some other fragments, however, followed the MT.

> The Septuagint version of Jeremiah is one-eighth shorter than that in the Masoretic Text.

Scholars disagree as to how we should view these differences. Some argue that the MT is the superior text and thus it should be followed. On the other hand, some argue that the LXX reflects an earlier tradition and thus is superior to the MT. Others suggest that perhaps two different editions of Jeremiah were composed, one in Babylon (the basis of the MT) and one in Egypt (the basis of the LXX). Thus both editions could be viewed as the inspired word of God.[1] At any rate, while the textual differences are significant, there are no significant theological differences between the two versions, and the central message of Jeremiah is clear in both traditions.

Another unique feature of Jeremiah is the detail given in regard to its writing. Unlike the other prophetic books, the book of Jeremiah mentions several times the actual writing down of the prophet's words onto a scroll. For example, Jeremiah 36:4, 28, 32 indicates that Jeremiah dictated a fairly large portion of the book to Baruch (his colleague and scribe), who wrote the material down. Based on the time references given in the text, the scroll mentioned in Jeremiah 36:32 may have included most of Jeremiah 1–25. At the end of Jeremiah 36:32 are the words: "And many similar words were added to them," indicating an expansion of the scroll that Jehoiakim had burned in Jeremiah 36:20–26. But even if one concludes that Jeremiah was responsible for the writing and composition of the book, it is improbable that he wrote the last chapter. At the end of Jeremiah 51 the text reads, "The words of Jeremiah end here." So the book itself indicates that someone other than Jeremiah wrote Jeremiah 52.

> The book of Jeremiah mentions the actual writing of Jeremiah's prophecies onto a scroll.

JEREMIAH 1 — YAHWEH CALLS A RELUCTANT PROPHET

Unlike Isaiah, the book of Jeremiah starts with the prophet's divine call. Significant aspects of Jeremiah's call include the following: (1) Yahweh is the one who calls; (2) Yahweh chose him for this task before he was even born; (3) the call centers on the proclamation of the word of Yahweh; (4) Yahweh will empower the young Jeremiah to speak this word; (5) opposition, even persecution, is promised; and (6) Yahweh promises his empowering presence ("I am with you"). There is no "health and wealth" promise in Jeremiah's call.

In Jeremiah 1:9–10 Yahweh informs the young prophet that he has been appointed "over nations and kingdoms to uproot and tear down, to destroy and overthrow." This im-

---

1. See the discussion by J. Daniel Hays, "Jeremiah, the Septuagint, the Dead Sea Scrolls, and Inerrancy: Just What Exactly Do We Mean by the 'Original Autographs'?" in Vincent Bacote, et al., *Evangelicals and Scripture: Tradition, Authority and Hermeneutics* (Downers Grove, IL: InterVarsity Press, 2004), 133–49.

Jeremiah sees an almond tree like this one. The Hebrew word for "almond tree" sounds similar to the Hebrew word for "watching."

agery will occur frequently in Jeremiah, especially in the first 29 chapters, for they focus on judgment. However, Yahweh also promises Jeremiah that by the power of his word he will "build and plant," the opposite images of "uproot and tear down." The figurative imagery of building and planting will also be used frequently throughout the book of Jeremiah, especially in restoration passages such as Jeremiah 30–33.

Yahweh then shows Jeremiah two significant visions (1:11–14). First the prophet sees an almond tree. The Hebrew word for "almond tree" (*shākēd*) sounds very similar to the Hebrew word for "watching" (*shōkēd*). The vision of the almond tree (*shākēd*) indicates that Yahweh is certainly watching (*shōkēd*) to be sure that his word is indeed fulfilled. Thus Yahweh declares the certainty of his prophetic word. Then Jeremiah sees a vision of a boiling pot, tilted away from the north, apparently about to tumble over and spill boiling water over the area to the south of it. This is a reference to the coming Babylonian invasion. Yahweh then declares, "Their kings will come and set up their thrones in the entrance of the gates of Jerusalem" (1:15), stating very clearly from the beginning that Jerusalem will fall to the Babylonians.

> There is no "health and wealth" promise in Jeremiah's call.

JEREMIAH 2 — THE INDICTMENTS AGAINST JUDAH

Jeremiah 2 presents the formal indictments against Judah; that is, Jeremiah immediately proclaims the central sins of Judah. In this chapter the sin that is stressed is idolatry, although social injustice is mentioned briefly at the end. While there are formal, legal aspects of covenant violation, this chapter stresses the personal, intimate injury against Yahweh that Judah has inflicted through their idolatrous behavior. Three times Yahweh declares that they have "forsaken" him (2:13, 17, 19). Throughout this chapter, as well as throughout the book, Jeremiah uses the common prophetic motif of Judah/Israel as the unfaithful, adulterous wife and Yahweh as the wronged husband. Chasing after foreign gods is paralleled to a wife having adulterous affairs with other men. Yahweh recalls the good days at the beginning of the "marriage" (i.e., during the exodus) (2:2), and how he loved them and blessed them. "What fault did your fathers find in me?" Yahweh asks (2:5), seemingly puzzled at why Israel should abandon him after all the good things he has done for them. Yahweh's criticism of Israel's unfaithfulness is scathing in this chapter. In 2:24 he compares them to a wild female donkey in heat.

> Jeremiah 2 stresses the personal, intimate injury against Yahweh that Judah has inflicted through their idolatrous behavior.

JEREMIAH 3:1–4:4 — THE CALL TO REPENTANCE

Throughout this unit Yahweh repeatedly calls on the people to turn back to him (3:12, 14, 22; 4:1). Moving beyond the image of the adulterous wife, in 3:2–5 Yahweh states that Israel has become like a hardened prostitute who no longer blushes with shame at her actions. That is, Israel no longer even acknowledges her sin as sin. "Acknowledge your guilt," Yahweh pleads with his people (3:13).

In 3:6–11 Jeremiah describes Israel and Judah as two sisters. The older sister (Israel) committed adultery and was sent away (i.e., conquered by the Assyrians). Therefore, certainly the younger sister Judah should take heed and learn from the mistakes of her sister. But of course she doesn't. Ezekiel will use this same analogy and even develop it further.

Shūv! Shūv! Shūv!

The Hebrew word *shūv* is one of Jeremiah's favorite words, occurring more than one hundred times in the book. Theologically, it lies at the heart of his message. The basic meaning of *shūv* is "to turn." However, it can mean "to turn to," "to turn back," or "to turn away." Thus Jeremiah uses *shūv* as his central word for "repent" (i.e., a turning away from sin and a turning to Yahweh). On the other hand, Jeremiah also uses *shūv* for turning away from Yahweh. So *shūv* can refer either to true repentance or to apostasy. Jeremiah is fond of wordplay, and he employs the multiple meanings possible for this word in numerous ways. In Jeremiah 3:1–4:4 (the call to repentance) *shūv* occurs eleven times. In Hebrew, Jeremiah 3:22 only has five words, and three of the words are forms of *shūv*. The English text reads, "Return, faithless people; I will cure you of backsliding." If we are allowed to mix the Hebrew and English word forms a bit, the text would literally read, "*Shūv*, sons of *shūv*ing, I will cure you of your *shūv*ings." Likewise, note the repeated use of *shūv* in Jeremiah 8:4b–5: "When a man turns away [*shūv*] does he not return [*shūv*]? Why then have these people turned away [*shūv*]? Why does Jerusalem always turn away [*shūv*]? They cling to deceit; they refuse to return [*shūv*]." Both the proclamation of apostasy (turning away from Yahweh) and the call to repentance (turning to Yahweh) are central themes in Jeremiah, and they both center on the word *shūv*.

In the midst of this call to repentance is a glimpse of the future restoration (Jer. 3:14–18). Yahweh describes a time when the ark of the covenant (the symbol of the old Mosaic covenant) will be gone and not even missed anymore. As the book of Isaiah also describes, this future time will be characterized by the presence of Yahweh in Jerusalem and by the gathering of the nations there to worship him.

JEREMIAH 4:4–6:30 — INEVITABLE AND TERRIBLE JUDGMENT

The prophet Jeremiah charges the nation with serious sin in Jeremiah 2 and then calls on them to repent in Jeremiah 3. Judah, however, is obstinate and rebellious, refusing even to acknowledge her sin, much less to repent and turn back to Yahweh. Thus in Jeremiah 4:4–6:30 the prophet describes the horrific judgment that is coming — an invasion by the Babylonian army. The alarm trumpets are sounded and signals sent. Everyone is fleeing to fortified cities before the invaders (4:5–6). The

> Judah is obstinate and rebellious, refusing even to acknowledge her sin, much less to repent and turn back to Yahweh.

Elephantine Island, located on the Nile River in Egypt. A significant Jewish settlement was here during the Persian Era.

Todd Bolen/www.BiblePlaces.com

During the exodus, Yahweh gave instructions to Moses regarding how to build the ark of the covenant (Exodus 25). The ark was a rectangular box (approx. 4' x 2½' x 2½'), covered with gold inside and out. On top of the ark was a golden cover, shaped into the "mercy seat," with gold cherubim on either side. The ark of the covenant played a critical role in the early history of Israel; indeed, it was the focal point for the very presence of Yahweh, and it was thus also associated with Yahweh's great power. The ark was an integral part of the Holy of Holies, first in the tabernacle and later in the temple.

In Jeremiah 3:16, the prophet Jeremiah makes the audacious proclamation that in the future the ark of the covenant will cease to exist. What's more, Jeremiah announces, no one will even miss it, and a replacement will not be built. As Jeremiah predicts, due to the continued apostasy of Judah and Jerusalem, the Babylonians eventually conquer Judah and destroy Jerusalem completely. No mention is made in Jeremiah or in 2 Kings about the fate of the ark as Jerusalem falls to the Babylonians. In all likelihood the Babylonian army melted the ark down and carried the gold back to Babylon along with the other treasures they captured.[1]

> Yahweh describes a time when the ark of the covenant will be gone but not even missed anymore.

However, numerous legends, rumors, and speculations about what actually happened to the ark have emerged and have continued to circulate for centuries. One dubious Jewish tradition postulates that Jeremiah himself took the ark of the covenant and secreted it beneath the Temple Mount just before the Babylonians captured Jerusalem. Most Old Testament scholars find this to be quite unlikely.

Another account of what happened comes from Ethiopia. According to national folk legend, the Queen of Sheba, who ruled the area now known as Ethiopia, visited King Solomon in Jerusalem and later gave birth to Solomon's son. When he grew older, the son, named Menilek, visited Jerusalem to see Solomon, but then stole the ark of the covenant from the temple and carried it back to his home. The Ethiopian Orthodox Church claims that the ark remains to this day in a special, guarded church in the ancient city of Aksum (which was the center of Menilek's kingdom and the seat of the Aksumite dynasty for many years). Unfortunately for scholars, church authorities will not let outsiders enter the supposed resting place of the ark.

The major problem with this account is that the details of the story do not accord well with history. King Solomon's reign in Israel predates the Aksumite kingdom of Menilek by about one thousand years. Thus it is highly unlikely that Solomon was Menilek's father. On the other hand, the Ethiopian legend cannot be totally dismissed. The Ethiopian Orthodox Church does apparently have *something* in that guarded church in Aksum that is very, very old and yet related to the ark in some way. In addition, the religious festivals of the Ethiopian Orthodox Church incorporate models of the ark into their ritual processions, a tradition that can be traced back hundreds of years. How did such a custom get started? Why does the ark of the covenant play such an important and significant role in the Ethiopian Orthodox

---

1. K. A. Kitchen, "Ark of the Covenant," in *New Bible Dictionary,* 3rd ed., ed. I. H. Marshall et al. (Downers Grove, IL: InterVarsity Press, 1996), 81.

Church when no other branch of Christianity uses it in such a manner?

One explanation that has been offered relates to a Jewish colony in Upper Egypt. Near the beginning of the sixth century BC, Jewish mercenaries were hired by the Egyptians to build and defend a fortress on the island of Elephantine in the Nile. A Jewish community thus grew up around this fortress in Upper Egypt. However, after around two hundred years, this Jewish community disappeared from history. During the twentieth century, archaeological excavations on the island of Elephantine discovered the ruins of the settlement that these Jewish mercenaries had built, including what appears to be the ruins of a model of the Jewish temple in Jerusalem. Some scholars have suggested that if these Jews in Egypt built a model of the temple, then they probably also built a model of

An artist's rendition of the ark of the covenant.

the ark of the covenant to place in the temple. What happened to these Jewish settlers? No one knows for certain, but some scholars have posited that these Jewish mercenaries may have migrated east into Ethiopia and settled there, carrying their replica of the ark with them. This theory at least provides a plausible explanation of how the Jewish ark of the covenant came to be so central to the festivals and worship ceremonies of the Ethiopian Orthodox Church. If this explanation is correct, the Ethiopians have a very old (and significant) religious box in Aksum, but not the original ark of the covenant.

As mentioned above, however, the most probable fate of the ark is that it was captured and destroyed by the Babylonians. Whatever really happened to the ark of the covenant, it did indeed disappear, in accordance with Jeremiah's prophecy.

The point that Jeremiah is stressing in Jeremiah 3:16 is that in the future the presence of Yahweh will no longer be located in the temple; thus the ark of the covenant will no longer have a central role to play. Highlighting the irony of Jeremiah's prophecy is the fact that the inhabitants of Jerusalem were superstitiously relying on the ark of the covenant to magically protect them from the Babylonians. Jeremiah tells them that the ark itself will soon disappear (and not be needed in the new covenant era). The fulfillment of Jeremiah's prophecy begins with the disappearance of the ark after the Babylonians capture Jerusalem. Ultimately, Jeremiah's prophecy finds fulfillment in the New Testament era when God's presence dwells within each believer through the Holy Spirit rather than in the temple around the ark. As Jeremiah predicted, God's people today have God's presence dwelling directly within them through the Holy Spirit, and they have direct access to God through Jesus Christ. Thus no one even misses the ark.

Babylonians come rapidly, with swift horses and chariots (4:13). The enemy comes from the north and moves south across Israel and Judah toward Jerusalem (4:15; from Dan in the far north to Ephraim in the middle, etc.). In Jeremiah 4:19–21 the prophet seems to actually see the coming destruction and all of the terrible things that will happen.

> Throughout Jeremiah, wounds and sickness will be used figuratively for sin, with healing used as a symbol for forgiveness and restoration.

In Jeremiah 5:1, Yahweh challenges Jeremiah to search the streets of Jerusalem and find even one person who is honest and who seeks the truth. Find one, Yahweh states, and Jerusalem will be forgiven. This is an obvious allusion to Genesis 18:16–33, where Abraham negotiates with Yahweh over how many righteous people need to be in Sodom to avert the judgment. There Abraham argues God down to ten people. Here Yahweh suggests that Jerusalem does not have *any*, making the startling suggestion that Jerusalem is worse than Sodom and certainly worthy of the imminent judgment. In 5:3–5 Jeremiah searches among the poor and among the leaders, but comes up empty-handed.

An Assyrian relief depicting the king in his chariot. The prophets refer frequently to the chariots of the invaders (e.g., Jer. 4:13).

When Jesus finds the market and moneychangers in the temple, he quotes directly from Jeremiah 7:11, stating that they have made the temple into a "den of robbers" (Matt. 21:13; Mark 11:17; Luke 19:46). The irony of Jeremiah 7 is that the robbers come to the temple for safety (a den of robbers would be a safe resting place, their hideout). They come right before the holy and powerful presence of Yahweh, the very one they have offended, and the one who is bringing punishment on them. The judgment context of Jeremiah 7 is an important background to understanding Jesus' comment. He is implying the same thing that Jeremiah states clearly — the sin and disobedience in Jerusalem will lead to its destruction. For Jeremiah's audience, this occurred in 587/586 BC, and for Jesus' audience this occurred in AD 70, when the Romans destroyed Jerusalem and the temple.

Other significant themes appear in this unit. The concept of the "remnant" is introduced into Jeremiah as Yahweh states that he will not destroy everyone in the judgment (5:10, 18). The charge of social injustice is made, especially against the wealthy and the leaders (5:26–31). Likewise, in light of their profound sin, Yahweh dismisses their religious rituals (6:19–20).

Another motif introduced in this section is that of sickness and healing (6:7, 14). Wounds and sickness will be used figuratively for sin throughout Jeremiah (and the other prophets), with healing used as a symbol for forgiveness and restoration. Another common theme introduced here is that the theological leaders of Judah (court prophets and priests) declare that Jeremiah is wrong about the judgment. Everything is all right, they counter: the people are not really sinning. These leaders continually predict peace, while Jeremiah predicts death and destruction (6:13–15).

JEREMIAH 7–10—FALSE RELIGION AND ITS PUNISHMENT

Jeremiah 7–10 focuses on the particularly serious sin of idolatry within Jerusalem. Coupled with this is Yahweh's rejection of their syncretistic religious rituals. In 7:1–15 Jeremiah delivers a message in the temple (called the "Temple Sermon"). The actual results of this sermon are chronicled in Jeremiah 26. If they will really change their ways, Jeremiah tells them, and if they will truly care for the orphans, widows, and foreigners, and if they will abandon their idolatry, then Yahweh will avert the coming judgment and they can stay in Jerusalem (7:2–11). The people, however, continue to break the Ten Commandments habitually, especially in regard to idolatry (7:9), and then they have the audacity to come to the temple expecting Yahweh to give them safety. Yahweh responds with incredulity. Look at what happened to Shiloh, Yahweh points out, where the tabernacle once was housed. Just as Shiloh was destroyed, so will be Jerusalem (7:12–15).

Jeremiah 7:30–34 describes what is perhaps the most horrific and disgusting sin of Jerusalem. The prophets often mention the abhorrent worship of Molech and Chemesh, usually adding a comment such as "those detestable gods of the

A Canaanite idol, perhaps Chemesh, associated with the Moabites and Ammonites and often associated with child sacrifice.

Ammonites and Moabites." What was particularly abhorrent about worshipping these idols was that it required child sacrifice. At the time of Jeremiah, the people of Jerusalem had built "high places" (sacrificial sites) at which they sacrificed their children, in the Valley of Ben Hinnom, which was right outside the walls of Jerusalem! Yahweh declares that in the coming judgment this valley will be filled with the dead bodies of those who have perpetrated such terrible sins (7:30–34).

Throughout Jeremiah 7, Yahweh underscores that the people have not listened to him or obeyed him (the same word in Hebrew is used for both nuances). Jeremiah 8 focuses on

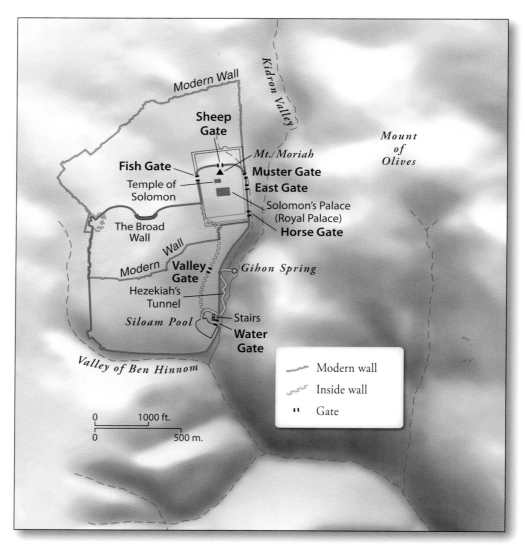

The people had built "high places" in the Valley of Ben Hinnom, where they practiced child sacrifice right outside the walls of Jerusalem.

The ruins of ancient Shiloh. Yahweh said that if he could destroy Shiloh because of her wickedness, then he could likewise destroy Jerusalem (Jer. 7:12 – 15).

the lies and deceit that they have been listening to instead, all of which will lead them astray. One of the main motifs in Jeremiah 9 is wailing, a phenomenon in the ancient world that normally accompanied tragedies (like a horrific invasion). The message of Jeremiah 8:4 – 9:25 appears to connect these two themes, stating that because the nation has foolishly listened to lies rather than to the voice of Yahweh, what they will hear next is wailing, the sound of judgment.

Jeremiah 10:1 – 16 sounds very much like Isaiah. Yahweh ridicules the idols and those who worship them. The idols are "like a scarecrow in a melon patch," Yahweh declares. They can't walk or talk; thus they can't help you or hurt you either (10:5). Yahweh, on the other hand, is the all-powerful, all-wise creator of heaven and earth with control over all the nations and all creation (10:6 – 15). His judgment and his wrath are to be feared, not those of the idols.

> Because the people of Judah have foolishly listened to lies rather than to the voice of Yahweh, what they will hear next is wailing, the sound of judgment.

A Canaanite god, perhaps El.

» FURTHER READING «

Clements, R. E. *Jeremiah*. Interpretation. Atlanta: John Knox Press, 1988.

Craigie, Peter C., Page H. Kelley, and Joel F. Drinkard Jr. *Jeremiah 1–25*. Word Biblical Commentary. Dallas: Word Books, 1991.

Dearman, J. Andrew. *Jeremiah/Lamentations*. NIV Application Commentary. Grand Rapids: Zondervan, 2002.

Hays, J. Daniel. "Jeremiah, the Septuagint, the Dead Sea Scrolls, and Inerrancy: Just What Exactly Do We Mean by the 'Original Autographs'?" In Vincent Bacote et al., *Evangelicals and Scripture: Tradition, Authority and Hermeneutics*. Downers Grove, IL: InterVarsity, 2004.

Fretheim, Terence E. *Jeremiah*. Smith & Helwys Bible Commentary. Macon, GA: Smyth & Helwys, 2002.

Holladay, William L. *Jeremiah*, Vol. 1. Hermeneia. Philadelphia: Fortress Press, 1986.

Longman, Tremper. *Jeremiah, Lamentations*. New International Biblical Commentary. Peabody, MA: Hendrickson, 2008.

McConville, J. Gordon. *Judgment and Promise: An Interpretation of the Book of Jeremiah*. Winona Lake, IN and Leicester, UK: Eisenbrauns and Apollos, 1993.

McKane, William. *Jeremiah*, Vol. 1. International Critical Commentary. Edinburgh and New York: T. & T. Clark, 1986.

Thompson, J. A. *The Book of Jeremiah*. The New International Commentary on the Old Testament. Grand Rapids: Eerdmans, 1980.

» DISCUSSION QUESTIONS «

1. Discuss the relevance of Jeremiah 6:13–15 for the church today.

2. What are the differences between the text of Jeremiah in the Septuagint and in the Masoretic Text?

3. Discuss the meaning of Jeremiah 9:23–24 in its relation to the prophetic message. How do kindness, justice, and righteousness relate to the prophetic message? How does this passage relate to today?

1. Compare and contrast the call of Jeremiah with the call of Isaiah (Isaiah 6). Include a discussion of what kind of success and what kind of opposition Yahweh promises each of them. What relevance does this have for being called into ministry today?

2. Read 4:5 – 31. (a) Discuss the sequence of events and identify the invader that Jeremiah sees in: 4:5 – 6; 4:13 – 17; and 4:29. (b) Describe the actions of the individual in 4:30. How is her response to the invasion different from those in 4:29? Explain the reason for her approach to the invaders. What happens to her (4:31)? (c) Which other scripture passage is Jeremiah referring to in 4:23? What is the point of 4:23?

3. Read 5:1 – 5. Which patriarchal story is the background for 5:1? Briefly compare and contrast that story with the situation Jeremiah addresses. What are the charges that Jeremiah makes in 5:26 – 31? Who are the charges against?

4. Trace the theme regarding the leaders (especially the king, priests, prophets) of Judah in Jeremiah 1 – 10.

CHAPTER 11

Jeremiah 11—29

"Both the house of Israel and the house of Judah
have broken the covenant I made with their forefathers.
Therefore ... I will bring on them a disaster
they cannot escape." (Jer. 11:10—11)

OVERVIEW OF JEREMIAH 11–29

Recall from our earlier discussions that Jeremiah 1–29 focuses primarily on the broken covenant and the consequential imminent judgment, with a few brief glimpses of future restoration scattered throughout. As mentioned earlier, Jeremiah is notoriously difficult to outline, and not surprisingly, there is no consensus regarding the organization and structure of Jeremiah 11–29. However, one of the major repeated motifs running throughout Jeremiah 11–29 relates to Jeremiah's conflict with the kings of Judah and their court prophets who oppose Jeremiah and prophesy lies in the name of Yahweh. Likewise, closely related to this conflict are the repeated passages of judgment on the institutions of Judah, particularly the monarchy and the false prophets who serve the king. For convenience, this section will be divided into two parts (Jeremiah 11–20; Jeremiah 21–29), but these divisions and the associated subtitles are somewhat arbitrary. Numerous aspects of the two themes mentioned above appear in both of these sections.

> Jeremiah 1–29 focuses primarily on the broken covenant and the consequential imminent judgment.

JEREMIAH 11–20 — THE BROKEN COVENANT AND YAHWEH'S PROPHET IN CONFLICT

Jeremiah 11:1–17 once again stresses that Judah has broken the Mosaic covenant. This section is tightly connected to Deuteronomy 28, which warned of the consequences of disobeying Yahweh and ignoring the covenant. The Hebrew word *shema*, "hear," repeated

Michelangelo's portrayal of Jeremiah the Prophet (Sistine Chapel, AD 1508–1512).

The Prophet Jeremiah, Buonarroti, Michelangelo (1475-1564)/Vatican Museums and Galleries, Vatican City, Italy/The Bridgeman Art Library

numerous times throughout this section, is usually translated as "listen" or "obey" (11:2, 3, 4, 6, 7, 8, 10, 11, 14). Yahweh declares that since Israel and Judah have not "listened to" (obeyed) Yahweh's word (the Mosaic covenant, i.e., the words of Deuteronomy), Yahweh will no longer "listen" (hear) their cries when disaster falls upon them (i.e., the coming Babylonian invasion). In fact, Yahweh tells Jeremiah not to intercede for them because he will no longer listen; the time for listening is over, and the time for judgment has come. In 11:10 Yahweh states explicitly that Israel and Judah have broken the covenant. The Hebrew word translated as "broken" does not carry a mere connotation of "to violate" as when we break the law today, say, by speeding; it implies breaking the relationship, as in an annulment. It is the same word used in 14:21 when Jeremiah pleads with Yahweh not to break the covenant. Clearly, there is no danger of Yahweh "violating the rules," but rather the threat is of Yahweh ending the covenant relationship defined in Deuteronomy. In Jeremiah 11 Yahweh declares that Israel and Judah have broken (ended) the Mosaic covenant, thus setting up the need

Jeremiah Mourns the Destruction of Jerusalem (Rembrandt, AD 1630).

for a "new" covenant, as presented in Jeremiah 31. It is because of the broken covenant that Yahweh will no longer listen to their cries or allow Jeremiah to intercede for them (11:11–12, 14).

In Jeremiah 11:18–23, men from Anathoth, Jeremiah's hometown, plot to kill him. In the very next passage (12:1–4), Jeremiah responds with a "complaint" or "lament," imploring Yahweh to get on with it and administer justice to the evil ones right now. Yahweh answers Jeremiah with a mild rebuke in 12:5–6, in essence telling Jeremiah that he can't start giving up already; things are going to get much, much worse.

Yahweh shares an object lesson in Jeremiah 13:1–11, a section written in prose instead of poetry. He tells Jeremiah to buy a linen belt and then to hide it in the rocks. After a while, Yahweh tells Jeremiah to go back and retrieve it. Of course, by that time the fine linen belt is ruined. "In the same way," Yahweh explains, "I will ruin the pride of Judah and the great pride of Jerusalem" (13:9).

Israel and Judah have shattered the relationship based on the Mosaic covenant.

Jeremiah 14:1–15:9 deals with the intercessory role of the prophet. Both Moses (Exodus 32) and Samuel (1 Sam. 7:9) interceded on behalf of the people and averted Yahweh's wrath.

> These other prophets "are prophesying to you false visions, divinations, idolatries and the delusions of their own minds."

Could Jeremiah do the same? The unit opens with a lament concerning a terrible drought that was gripping the land (14:1–6). Droughts were one of the judgments included in the warnings of Deuteronomy 28. In Jeremiah 14:7–9 the prophet cries out on behalf of the people, "You are among us, O Yahweh, and we bear your name; do not forsake us!" Yahweh answers in 14:11, "Do not pray for the well-being of this people." Jeremiah points out that all of the other prophets are proclaiming peace instead of destruction (14:13), implying, perhaps, that the people are not to be blamed since they have been deceived. Yahweh responds by declaring that these other prophets "are prophesying to you false visions, divinations, idolatries and the delusions of their own minds" (14:14). These prophets, Yahweh continues, who prophesy that "no sword or famine will touch this land," will themselves "perish by the sword and famine" (14:14–18). Jeremiah cries out again on behalf of the people: "For the sake of your name do not despise us.... Remember your covenant with us and do not break it" (14:21). But in essence, as Yahweh had pointed out back in Jeremiah 11, the covenant has already been broken and annulled by Israel and Judah. So in Jeremiah 15:1 Yahweh tells Jeremiah that even if Moses or Samuel pleaded with him he would not listen and the people would be driven away from his presence anyway.

Throughout the book of Jeremiah, Yahweh reminds the people that their sinful and disobedient behavior is something that has been going on for a long time; it is not something that just recently started happening. In 15:4 Yahweh declares that he "will make them abhorrent to all the kingdoms of the earth" (cf. Deut. 28:37) because of what Manasseh, son of Hezekiah king of Judah did in Jerusalem. Recall from chapter 2 ("The Prophets in History") that Manasseh was the grandfather of Josiah. He was one of the worst kings of Judah's history, especially regarding idolatry and shedding innocent blood (see 2 Kings 21 for a description of his terrible acts). Josiah tries to reverse the

Yahweh compares Judah to a thriving olive tree, but he is about to strip the branches and set the tree on fire (Jer. 11:16).

© Benoit Rousseau/www.istockphoto.com

evil acts of Manasseh (2 Kings 23:26) but isn't able to change the negative momentum of the people toward idolatry and other sinful behavior.

Frustrated with his inability to effect any change in the people perhaps, and no doubt weary of the many schemes and plots against him, Jeremiah complains again, "Alas, my mother, that you gave me birth, a man with whom the whole land strives and contends! I have neither lent nor borrowed, yet everyone curses me" (15:10). Yahweh promises him deliverance (15:11), but Jeremiah complains again of his misery in 15:15–18. This time he goes too far, actually accusing Yahweh of having deceived him (15:18). Yahweh answers with a stern rebuke: "If you repent, I will restore you that you may serve me; if you utter worthy, not worthless words, you will be my spokesman. Let this people turn to you, but you must not turn to them" (15:19).

To symbolize the terrible time of destruction and suffering that is coming, Yahweh prohibits Jeremiah from marrying (16:2). Likewise, to underscore that there will be very little comfort during this time of suffering, Yahweh tells Jeremiah not to attend any funerals (16:5). In fact, Yahweh declares, don't go to any house where there is feasting and celebration, for "I will bring an end to the sounds of joy and gladness and to the voices of bride and bridegroom in this place" (16:9). Jeremiah will predict the end of this sorrowful situation when he looks to the future time of restoration in Jeremiah 30–33. Likewise, as discussed later, Jesus specifically reverses these curses by attending numerous feasts and by keeping the wedding celebration alive by changing water into wine.

Jeremiah 17:5–13 reads much like one of the psalms, expressing the general wisdom of trusting in Yahweh. "Cursed is the one who trusts in man.... But blessed is the man who trusts in Yahweh" (17:5, 7). This is followed by a positive "confession" made by Jeremiah, expressing his confidence and trust in Yahweh: "Save me and I will be saved, for you are the one I praise" (17:14).

One of the ironies (and theological tensions) of the book of Jeremiah is that Yahweh continually intertwines the message of inevitable judgment with calls to repentance in order to avert the (inevitable?) judgment. In 18:1–12 Yahweh takes Jeremiah to a potter's house to watch the potter at his wheel.

> "Alas, my mother, that you gave me birth, a man with whom the whole land strives and contends! I have neither lent nor borrowed, yet everyone curses me."

> To symbolize the terrible time of destruction and suffering that is coming, Yahweh prohibits Jeremiah from marrying.

"Like clay in the hand of a potter, so are you in my hand, O house of Israel" (Jer. 18:6).

© Carlos Martinez/www.istockphoto.com

"I will smash this nation and this city just as this potter's jar is smashed" (Jer. 19:11).

When one of the pots becomes marred, the potter simply reforms it into another pot. Yahweh declares that he is like the potter, with the power to reshape nations based on their response and whether or not they repent of their sin.

In Jeremiah 19 Yahweh uses the pottery symbol again. This time, however, the pot has hardened and cannot be reshaped. Yahweh tells Jeremiah to buy a clay pot and go to the Valley of Ben Hinnom near the Potsherd Gate. Recall that this particular valley just outside Jerusalem was the center of numerous shrines for the worshipping of false gods. This was also the site of altars for child sacrifice, the worship associated with the gods Chemesh and Molech. Jeremiah is told to smash the pot and say, "This is what Yahweh Almighty says: 'I will smash this nation and this city just as this potter's jar is smashed and cannot be repaired.'"

Throughout his ministry, Jeremiah faces opposition and persecution. Jeremiah 20:1–6 chronicles one of these events. A priest named Pashhur, the chief officer in the temple, responds to Jeremiah's preaching by having him beaten and placed in the "stocks" (this Hebrew word is uncertain; probably it refers to a small dungeon-like cell). When Jeremiah is released, he announces judgment on Pashhur, changing the priest's name to Magor-Missabib, which means "terror on every side" (see also Jer. 6:25; 20:10; 46:5; 49:29). This episode is followed by Jeremiah's last "confession" (20:7–18), in which the prophet mixes praise and trust in Yahweh (20:11–13) with depressing statements of discouragement (20:14–18) such as "Why did I ever come out of the womb to see trouble and sorrow and to end my days in shame?" Jeremiah lives in a real world with dangerous people. He obediently continues to deliver Yahweh's message to the people of Jerusalem even though they reject the message, attacking him instead of repenting of their sin. Jeremiah is quite honest both with Yahweh and with the readers of the book regarding how difficult it was for him.

JEREMIAH 21–29 — JUDGMENT ON JUDAH'S INSTITUTIONS

Jeremiah 21 takes us to a setting around 589–588 BC when the Babylonians have actually started their southern campaign to squelch the rebellion there among the smaller states (including Judah). King Zedekiah sends two officials to Jeremiah to ask him to inquire of Yahweh about the Babylonian king Nebuchadnezzar's invasion. They want to know if Yahweh will deliver them miraculously as he did in the past (21:1–3). After all of Jeremiah's preaching, this question is rather absurd, and Jeremiah delivers a sobering answer from Yahweh. Not only will Yahweh not deliver them, Jeremiah declares, but Yahweh says, "I myself will fight against you ... in anger and fury and great wrath" (21:5).

The Mesha Stele ("the Moabite Stone") in which Mesha, king of Moab, praises his god Chemesh for enabling him to defeat Israel (mid-ninth century BC).

With the Babylonian army besieging Jerusalem, Yahweh gives Jeremiah a message that will get the prophet in considerable trouble (his arrest because of this message is described in 38:1–6). The message from Yahweh is this: "Whoever stays in this city will die by the sword, famine or plague. But whoever goes out and surrenders to the Babylonians who are besieging you will live" (21:9). Thus, while the leaders of Jerusalem are trying to rally the troops to stand strong against the Babylonian siege, Jeremiah proclaims that resistance is useless because Yahweh himself has raised up the Babylonians to destroy Jerusalem. The best one can do is to accept the will of Yahweh and surrender. That act of faith will lead to one's survival.

> Jeremiah delivers a scathing criticism against Jehoiakim for failing to deliver justice to the weak ones in the society and for shedding innocent blood.

In Jeremiah 7, the prophet preached the "Temple Sermon." Here in Jeremiah 22, he preaches the "Palace Sermon." Although several kings are mentioned (along with the officials), the main king that Jeremiah confronts in this sermon is Jehoiakim, the king who rebels against Babylonia but who dies just before they arrive to punish him in 598 BC. So Jeremiah 22 predates Jeremiah 21 by around ten years. The main issue is social injustice, and Jeremiah delivers a scathing criticism against Jehoiakim in this chapter for failing to deliver justice to the weak ones in the society (orphans, widows, foreigners, poor) and for shedding innocent blood. Jeremiah draws a strong contrast between Jehoiakim, who builds his palace without paying a fair wage (22:13–14), and Jehoiakim's father, Josiah, the good king who defended the cause of the poor and needy (22:15–16).

Jeremiah 23 continues this theme. "Woe to the shepherds who are destroying and scattering the sheep of my pasture," Yahweh declares in 23:1, referring to the leaders of Judah, and in particular probably to Jehoiakim (and others) from the previous chapter. However, following this criticism is a forward-looking promise as Yahweh declares that he himself will gather the scattered flock (23:3). Furthermore, Yahweh declares that he will raise up a righteous "Branch" from the lineage of David (23:5) who will do what is just and right (in contrast to the current rulers). This text is messianic, looking forward to the coming of a righteous Davidic King and Shepherd. The shepherd motif is used to describe the coming Messiah several times in Jeremiah as well as in the rest of the prophetic literature (especially Ezekiel) and in the New Testament. The rest of the chapter (Jer. 23:9–40) deals once again with false prophets and the serious judgment coming on those who falsely claim to speak the words of Yahweh.

> The future promise lies with the remnant that goes into exile.

Jeremiah 24 looks beyond the fall of Jerusalem (587/586 BC) to consider the two groups of Jews that survive. Zedekiah and his officials, along with those who are able to slip through the hands of the Babylonians and stay in the land, are compared to rotten figs that cannot be eaten. Those who go into exile, on the other hand, are compared to good figs. The point that Yahweh is making is that the future promise lies with the remnant that goes into exile.

In Jeremiah 25 Yahweh repeats the frequent charge that the people are not listening to him or to his prophets (25:1–7). Thus Yahweh is raising up Nebuchadnezzar to destroy

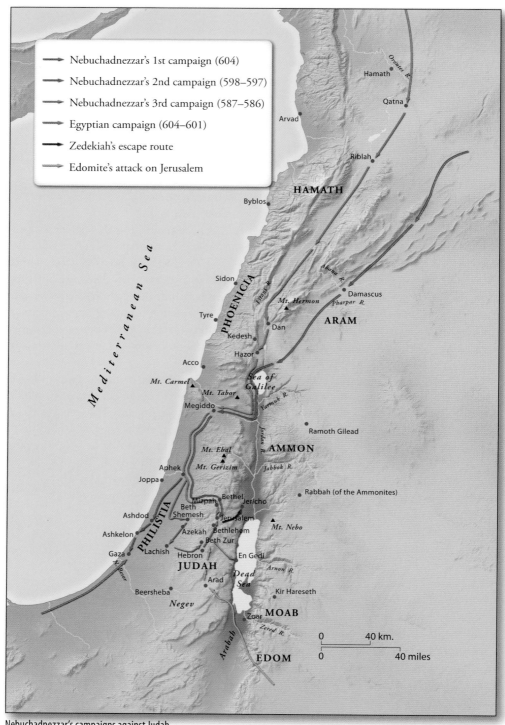

Legend:

→ Nebuchadnezzar's 1st campaign (604)
→ Nebuchadnezzar's 2nd campaign (598–597)
→ Nebuchadnezzar's 3rd campaign (587–586)
→ Egyptian campaign (604–601)
→ Zedekiah's escape route
→ Edomite's attack on Jerusalem

Nebuchadnezzar's campaigns against Judah.

the land. The joyful sounds of bride and bridegroom will end, and the people of Judah will serve Babylon seventy years. In Jeremiah 25:15–38 Yahweh proclaims judgment on the nations, listing out most of the nations addressed in Jeremiah 46–51.

Jeremiah 26–29 centers on Jeremiah's controversies with the false prophets of the court. In Jeremiah 26 we see the results of the "Temple Sermon" (Jeremiah 7) — the priests, the prophets, and the people seize Jeremiah with the intention of killing him because of

Jeremiah's Seventy Years of Exile

In Jeremiah 25:11 the prophet declares: "This whole country will become a desolate wasteland, and these nations will serve the king of Babylon seventy years." Later, after the first wave of exiles has been taken to Babylon, Jeremiah writes them a letter, stating: "This is what Yahweh says, 'When seventy years are completed for Babylon, I will come to you and fulfill my gracious promise to bring you back to this place'" (Jer. 29:10). Other biblical writers mention Jeremiah's seventy years as well. Daniel, for example, refers to these statements by Jeremiah (Dan. 9:2). In 2 Chronicles 36:21, Jeremiah's seventy years is cited, and an explanation added: "The land enjoyed its Sabbath rests; all the time of its desolation it rested, until the seventy years were completed in fulfillment of the word of the LORD spoken by Jeremiah."

Jeremiah appears to be using "seventy years" to refer to the length of time that Israel would be in exile as well as for the time that Babylon would be in power. In 2 Chronicles 36:22 the end point of the seventy years is apparently identified with the Decree of Cyrus (538 BC) that permitted the exiles to return to their land. Thus it is challenging to identify with certainty which historical events begin and end Jeremiah's seventy years. The following chronologies have been suggested:

1. From the fall of Nineveh (i.e., the rise of Babylon) (612 BC) to the fall of Babylon (539 BC) equals 73 years.
2. From the fall of Nineveh (i.e., the rise of Babylon) (612 BC) to the Decree of Cyrus (538 BC) equals 74 years.
3. From the victory of the Babylonians over the Assyrians at the battle of Carchemish (605 BC) to the fall of Babylon (539 BC) equals 66 years.
4. From the victory of the Babylonians over the Assyrians at the battle of Carchemish (605 BC) to the Decree of Cyrus (538 BC) equals 67 years.
5. From the fall of Jerusalem and the beginning of the exile (587/586 BC) to the reconstruction of the temple (520–515 BC) equals 70+/- years.[1]

Although there is no firm consensus, many scholars understand Jeremiah's use of "seventy years" to be a figurative or approximate period of time basically referring to a lifetime. Thus, when he tells the exiles in his letter that they will not return to their country for seventy years (Jer. 29:10), Jeremiah's main point seems to be that few if any of those adults in exile will live to see the return because seventy years is a lifetime. Yet seventy years also serves as a good approximation, both for the time the Babylonian Empire endured, and for the time of the exile, brought to an end by the Decree of Cyrus.

1. From J. Daniel Hays, J. Scott Duvall, and C. Marvin Pate, *Dictionary of Biblical Prophecy and End Times* (Grand Rapids: Zondervan, 2007), 427–28.

his prophecies against Jerusalem (26:7–11). Jeremiah, however, is defended by some of the elders of the land (i.e., people who are not from Jerusalem), who point out that the prophet Micah also preached against Jerusalem, and no one punished him for that. Thus Jeremiah escapes with his life (26:24).

> The priests, the prophets, and the people seize Jeremiah with the intention of killing him because of his prophecies against Jerusalem.

In Jeremiah 27–28 Jeremiah has a run-in with the false prophet Hananiah. King Zedekiah had been scheming with the neighboring countries, trying to convince them to rebel with him against Babylon. Zedekiah brings envoys from these countries to Jerusalem, apparently to plan the rebellion. Yahweh, however, instructs Jeremiah to make a wooden yoke and to place it on his neck, symbolizing for these envoys the subservience their nations should show to Nebuchadnezzar instead of rebellion (27:1–7). Hananiah, however, tries to counter Jeremiah, proclaiming that the exiles of 598 BC will return within two years (28:2–4). Hananiah then takes Jeremiah's yoke and breaks it, claiming that Yahweh has declared that he will break the yoke of Nebuchadnezzar (28:10–11). Yahweh responds by sending word through Jeremiah that Hananiah has broken a wooden yoke but that they (Jerusalem and the surrounding nations) will receive instead an iron yoke from Nebuchadnezzar (28:12–14). In addition, Yahweh declares that Hananiah will die within the year. The false prophet dies two months later (28:17), underscoring the fate of those who oppose the true prophet of Yahweh.

Jehoiakim rebelled against Nebuchadnezzar, but was probably murdered just as the Babylonian army arrived (598 BC). The city surrendered and the new young king, Jehoiachin, and most of the nobility were carried off to Babylonia (the first exile). In the years that followed, many false prophets proclaimed that these exiles would be returning home soon. Jeremiah, however, writes those exiles a letter, preserved for us in 29:4–23. Jeremiah tells them to settle down, marry, build houses, and plant crops because they are going to be there for seventy years (29:5–6, 10). Shemaiah, one of the leaders in the exile, writes back to the chief priest in Jerusalem, complaining about Jeremiah's letter and urging that Jeremiah be arrested and stopped (29:24–28). The chief priest, however, ignores this request, and Jeremiah 1–29 ends with Yahweh pronouncing judgment on Shemaiah.

> Jeremiah tells the exiles to settle down, marry, build houses, and plant crops because they are going to be there for seventy years (a lifetime).

» FURTHER READING «

Clements, R. E. *Jeremiah*. Interpretation. Atlanta: John Knox Press, 1988.

Craigie, Peter C., Page H. Kelley, and Joel F. Drinkard Jr. *Jeremiah 1 – 25*. Word Biblical Commentary. Dallas: Word Books, 1991.

Dearman, J. Andrew. *Jeremiah/Lamentations*. NIV Application Commentary. Grand Rapids: Zondervan, 2002.

Fretheim, Terence E. *Jeremiah*. Smith & Helwys Bible Commentary. Macon, GA: Smyth & Helwys, 2002.

Holladay, William L. *Jeremiah*, Vol. 1. Hermeneia. Philadelphia: Fortress Press, 1986.

Longman, Tremper. *Jeremiah, Lamentations*. New International Biblical Commentary. Peabody, MA: Hendrickson, 2008.

McConville, J. Gordon. *Judgment and Promise: An Interpretation of the Book of Jeremiah*. Winona Lake, IN and Leicester, England: Eisenbrauns and Apollos, 1993.

McKane, William. *Jeremiah*, Vol. 1. International Critical Commentary. Edinburgh and New York: T. & T. Clark, 1986.

Thompson, J. A. *The Book of Jeremiah*. The New International Commentary on the Old Testament. Grand Rapids: Eerdmans, 1980.

» DISCUSSION QUESTIONS «

1. What does Jeremiah specifically mean in 11:10 when he declares that Israel and Judah have "broken the covenant"?

2. What is the point of the linen belt episode in Jeremiah 13:1 – 11?

3. What does Yahweh say about the court prophets in 14:14 – 16?

» WRITING ASSIGNMENTS «

1. The Hebrew word *shema* can be translated as "hear" or (as NIV does frequently) as "obey." Trace this word through Jeremiah 11:1 – 14 by noting when the English words "hear" or "obey" are used. Explain the irony and theology conveyed by the usage of this word in Jeremiah 11.

2. What three things does Yahweh prohibit for Jeremiah in 16:1 – 9? Why does Yahweh do this?

3. Using Jeremiah 18:1 – 12 as a basis, explain the concept of conditional prophecy.

4. Discuss Jeremiah's conflict with the false prophets in Jeremiah 11 – 23.

5. In what ways does Jesus Christ fulfill the prophecies of Jeremiah 23:1 – 6?

CHAPTER 12

Jeremiah 30—33

> " 'The time is coming,' declares the LORD, 'when I will make a new covenant with the house of Israel and with the house of Judah.' " (Jer. 31:31)

THE BOOK OF CONSOLATION—AN OVERVIEW

While Jeremiah 1–29 focuses primarily on judgment (with glimpses of restoration), Jeremiah 30–33 stresses restoration (with a few brief reminders of judgment). Because these four chapters deal extensively with the themes of hope, restoration, and the new covenant, many scholars refer to this unit as "the Book of Consolation." These chapters are similar in style to Isaiah 40–66. However, Jeremiah's great contribution to our understanding of messianic prophecy and how the New Testament relates to the Old Testament is that he explicitly describes a coming glorious "new" covenant (Jer. 31:31–34) that will replace the old one that Israel/Judah has shattered and annulled (Jer. 11:10). In fact, in Jeremiah 30–33 Yahweh takes all of the major judgment images of Jeremiah 1–29 (incurable sickness, scattering, no weddings or joy, etc.) and changes them into restoration images (healing, regathering, joyful singing by brides, etc.).

> Jeremiah's great contribution to our understanding of messianic prophecy and how the New Testament relates to the Old Testament is that he explicitly describes a coming glorious "new" covenant.

Several interesting aspects of Jeremiah 30–33 are important to note. Unlike much of the rest of Jeremiah, chapters 30 and 31 contain no historical dates or ties to the reign of a king. This absence of dates or specific historical ties gives these first two chapters a certain timelessness. Also, in chapters 30–33 Jeremiah does not connect the future restoration to the downfall of Babylon. Instead, the restoration is tied theologically to the fulfillment of both the Abrahamic and the Davidic covenants—that is, the new covenant and the associated blessings of restoration come as a fulfillment of those prior covenants (which are not broken).

These chapters are characterized by several other general features. The verbal authority of Yahweh is invoked fifty-nine times ("the word of Yahweh," "declares Yahweh," "Yahweh spoke," etc.). While this feature is present throughout Jeremiah, particularly in the poetic sections, the frequency and intensity of these references appears to increase in the Book of Consolation, stressing the authority and emphasis of this section.

Several themes relating to the coming messianic restoration run throughout the Book of Consolation. A prominent theme encountered in the opening verses and continued throughout is the promise of restoration for both Judah and Israel in a reunified nation (Jer. 30:3, 10; 31:5–6, 8–9, 20, 27; 32:27; 33:7). The northern kingdom is referred to as Israel, Samaria, and Ephraim. The term "Israel," while sometimes employed in reference to the northern kingdom, is also used as a reference to the united nation (Jer. 30:10; 31:1–2), thus reflecting a future time of unity. This theme of regathering is a continuation of the concept introduced in Jeremiah 3:18 and 23:8.

Closely related to the regathering motif is the theme of the restored Land. Jeremiah strongly implies that Israel and Judah lost their right to the Land of Promise because of disobedience. Thus the exile, as judgment, carried a special theological significance. The tradition of the Land was deeply rooted in the patriarchal traditions, and Jeremiah makes many allusions to the Abrahamic promises in association with the Land. The future glorious

Judgment Themes	Restoration Themes (Reversal Of Judgment)			
Jer 1-29	**Jer 30**	**Jer 31**	**Jer 32**	**Jer 33**
Jerusalem destroyed	The city rebuilt 30:18	Jerusalem rebuilt 31:38-40		
Population diminished	Population increased 30:19			Countless as the stars 33:22
Exile and scattering	Returned to the land 30:3	Gathered, returned to the land 31:6, 10, 17, 23	Gathered from the lands where they were banished 32:37	Returned to the land 33:7
Incurable sickness and wounds	Healing 30:17			Health and healing 33:6
No joy (no singing or celebrating; no weddings)	Songs and the sound of rejoicing 30:19	Joyful singing and dancing 31:4, 7, 12, 13		Joy and praise in worship 33:9 Joyful sound of weddings 33:11
Broken Mosaic Covenant (broken relationship)	"You will be my people, and I will be your God" 30:22	New Covenant 31:31-33	"They will be my people, and I will be their God" 32:38 Everlasting covenant 32:40	Covenant with David and with Levites 33:21
Harlot image		Virgin Israel 31:4, 21		
Destroyed and desolate fields		Fruitful fields with abundant food 31:5, 12, 14	Fields once again bought and sold 32:43-44	Restored pastures 33:12-13
Bad leaders (shepherds)	David the king 30:9 Good leader 30:21			Davidic king 33:15, 17
Foreign domination	End of foreign domination 30:8			
Judgment on sin		Forgiveness 31:34		Cleansing and forgiveness of sin 33:8
Terror and fear	Peace, security, no fear 30:10		Live in safety 32:37	Peace and security 33:6 Peace 33:9
Loss of Yahweh's presence	"I am with you" 30:11			

The Judgments of Jeremiah 1-29 Are Reversed in Jeremiah 30-33

return will thus be to "the land given to the fathers" (Jer. 30:3) and will be characterized by prosperity (Jer. 31:12; 32:42) and an increase of descendants (Jer. 30:19; 33:22).

In this section of Jeremiah, the Land in a general sense often narrows to a specific picture of Zion, "the city built on a hill." The destroyed city of Jerusalem will be rebuilt, and this time it will honor Yahweh (Jer. 30:18; 31:12, 23; 33:9). In contrast to many of the other prophets (like Isaiah), Jeremiah does not portray the city as the center of Gentile pilgrimage, nor does he allude to any rebuilding of the temple itself.

> The time of restoration will be characterized by joy and joyful gatherings, in contrast to the sorrowful times of judgment presented earlier in Jeremiah.

This time of restoration will be further characterized by joy and joyful gatherings, in contrast to the sorrowful times of judgment presented earlier in Jeremiah, which were marked by an absence of joy and excluded joyful gatherings such as weddings. The new era will be characterized by songs of thanksgiving and the sound of rejoicing (Jer. 30:19), the dancing of maidens (31:13), and the sound of the wedding feast (33:11).

INTERPRETIVE CHALLENGES

In chapter 5, "The Prophets and Biblical Eschatology," we discussed some of the interpretive challenges we face in the prophetic books. These challenges are particularly acute in future-looking passages, where we as Christians are trying to determine how these prophecies are to be fulfilled. Since Jeremiah 30–33 focuses extensively on the coming kingdom and the new covenant, we will encounter these interpretive problems frequently in this section. Clearly, Jesus inaugurates Jeremiah's new covenant at the Last Supper ("This cup is the new covenant in my blood," Luke 22:20), but are all aspects of Jeremiah 30–33 fulfilled during the first advent of Christ? Is the new covenant limited to Israel and Judah (Jer. 31:31), or is it a covenant with the church? How are the promises about the Land to be fulfilled? We are faced with the same questions we raised in chapter 5. How much of the glorious restoration of Jeremiah 30–33 was fulfilled in the "near view" (return under Ezra, Nehemiah; first advent of Christ), and how much awaits the "far view" (second coming of Christ)? Or is some of it being fulfilled now, during the church age? Related to this, how do we interpret the symbolic and figurative imagery?

> How are the promises about the Land to be fulfilled?

Likewise, as we discussed in chapter 5, evangelical scholars split on how to answer these questions and how to interpret Jeremiah 30–33. Classic dispensationalists will take a fairly literal approach, arguing that the new covenant was made only with Israel but that the Gentile church enjoys the benefits of that covenant. Likewise, they will see a literal fulfillment of the regathering images taking place in the land of Israel during the millennial kingdom. Amillennialists will interpret these texts more symbolically and figuratively, understanding that the church has replaced Israel and thus the new covenant is made with the church. Amillennialists therefore argue that the regathering images are fulfilled figuratively by the church. Progressive dispensational and historic premillennial views will fall somewhere in the middle.

JEREMIAH 30 — "I WILL RESTORE YOU TO HEALTH AND HEAL YOUR WOUNDS"

In Jeremiah 30:2 Yahweh tells Jeremiah to write down all the words he speaks. Then he declares that "the days are coming when I will bring my people Israel and Judah back from captivity and restore them to the land I gave their forefathers to possess." Recall our discussion of *shūv* in chapter 10. In Jeremiah 30:3, Yahweh uses the word *shūv* twice as he promises to return his people to the Land. In 30:8–9 Yahweh promises to "break the yoke" of foreign domination (remember the yoke image and confrontation in Jer. 27:2; 28:2, 10–14) and to establish a Davidic king. He also promises peace and security (30:10–11). Note that in the postexilic times of Haggai, Ezra, and Nehemiah, although Israel was to some extent regathered back to the Land, they were not free from foreign domination. This reality is stressed in those books by their constant reference to the ruling Persian monarchs.

"I will restore you to health and heal your wounds."

In 30:12–17 Jeremiah revisits the incurable wound/sickness image, restating that there is no remedy or healing available (humanly speaking). "But," Yahweh declares in 30:17, "I will restore you to health and heal your wounds." This follows the theme of reversing the curses of Jeremiah 1–29 (see fig. 12.1). Likewise, 30:18–21 describes the reconstruction of Jerusalem, now filled with sounds of singing and rejoicing. The number of people will increase (fulfilling the Abrahamic covenant) rather than decrease, and they will have one of their own rule over them instead of foreigners.

The Last Supper by Leonardo Da Vinci (1498). Jesus announces at the Last Supper that his death inaugurates the new covenant.

The Last Supper, Leonardo da Vinci (1452-1519)/Santa Maria della Grazie, Milan, Italy/The Bridgeman Art Library

At the heart of Yahweh's covenant relationship with Israel was the formulaic statement: "I will be your God; you will be my people." This formula defines the relationship between Yahweh and his covenant people throughout the Old Testament. When Israel/Judah breaks (annuls) the covenant, they lose the benefits of this relationship (Jeremiah 11). Now, as part of the great restoration, Yahweh once again defines the relationship in the same terms: "I will be your God; you will be my people." This statement is also repeated in various forms throughout Jeremiah 30–33 (31:1, 33; 32:38).

JEREMIAH 31 — THE NEW COVENANT

Jeremiah 31 continues the focus on the glorious future restoration. Like Isaiah, Jeremiah often uses imagery and terminology from the exodus to describe the regathering, thus implying a sort of New Exodus (Jer. 31:2, 8). As throughout the rest of 30–33, Jeremiah 31 contains numerous texts that reverse the judgment images of 1–29.

> The prophets frequently use Ephraim to represent the entire northern kingdom.

Whereas throughout Jeremiah 1–29, for example, Israel/Judah is described as an unfaithful wife and a hardened, shameless prostitute, Jeremiah 31:4 and 31:21 refer to the nation as "O Virgin Israel." The transformation from a hardened prostitute to a young, pure virgin is a powerful image of the change that Yahweh's salvation can bring. The image continues in 31:4 as Yahweh declares that the young virgin maidens will dance and make joyful music, in contrast to the end of joyful music proclaimed as part of the judgment in Jeremiah 1–29. Indeed, joy at the wonderful salvation and restoration of Yahweh is a major theme in this chapter (31:4, 7, 12, 13).

Throughout this chapter there are frequent references to Ephraim (31:6, 9, 20). Recall that Ephraim was the largest of the ten northern tribes that became Israel. The prophets frequently use Ephraim to represent the entire northern kingdom. In Jeremiah this is perhaps surprising, because the northern kingdom was destroyed by the Assyrians more than a hundred years earlier, and Israel as a political entity had practically ceased to exist. As Yahweh speaks of restoration, however, he speaks not only of returning the exiles from Judah (the Babylonian exile) but also of regathering the scattered exiles from the Assyrian invasion. Thus the new covenant is declared to be with both Judah and Israel (Jer. 31:31).

Jeremiah 31:27–28 recalls the initial commission that Yahweh gave Jeremiah at his calling (1:10–12), including the wordplay between "almond" and "watching." Here in 31:28 Yahweh states, "Just as I watched over them to uproot and tear down, and to overthrow, destroy and bring disaster, so I will watch over them to build and to plant."

Next Jeremiah cites a popular proverb, "The fathers have eaten sour grapes, and the children's teeth are set on edge" (31:29). This proverb reflected the

A traditional depiction of the Ten Commandments. Yahweh states that the new covenant will be written on hearts, not stone.

Herod, the Babies in Bethlehem, and Rachel Weeping for Her Children

In Jeremiah 31:15 Yahweh says, "A voice is heard in Ramah, mourning and great weeping, Rachel weeping for her children…." Rachel was one of the matriarchs of Israel, the wife of Jacob (renamed Israel) and the mother of Joseph and Benjamin. Joseph, remember, is the father of Ephraim and Manasseh. So the tribes of Benjamin, Ephraim, and Manasseh were, figuratively speaking, her children, and in a figurative sense she was the mother of all Israel. In Jeremiah 31:15 Yahweh appears to be describing the scene soon after the horrific destruction of Jerusalem by the Babylonian army. Thousands of people are killed, and most of those who remain are being carried off into exile. Jeremiah 40:1 seems to indicate that Ramah, a village just to the north of Jerusalem, was the staging area from which the shattered exiles began their trek to Babylon. Thus, with thousands dead and Jerusalem in ruins as the tattered, beaten Judahites began their long trip into exile, Rachel, the "mother" of Israel, is said to be weeping.

There was a tradition in Israel that Rachel was buried near Bethlehem (south of Jerusalem). Even today the tomb of Rachel is traditionally identified with a structure in Bethlehem. In Matthew 2, therefore, after Herod the Great murders all of the children in Bethlehem in an attempt to kill the baby Jesus, no doubt a loud sound of weeping was heard. Matthew, who knew of the traditional burial site of Rachel near Bethlehem, connects the incident to Jeremiah 31:15 and identifies this time of weeping as a fulfillment of that passage, implying figuratively that Rachel was crying out from her tomb. Equally important for understanding Matthew's use of Jeremiah is to note the context of Jeremiah 31:15. In Jeremiah 31, Yahweh describes the sound of weeping due to the destruction and exile (31:15), but he goes on to say that the weeping will be ended, declaring, "So there is hope for your future…. Your children will return" (31:17). In the deepest time of heartbreak and sorrow in Jeremiah's time, Yahweh reminds them that something new and glorious is coming. Likewise, Matthew is implying that, in the midst of

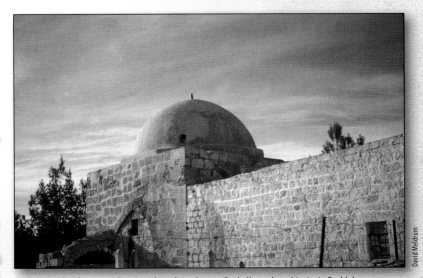

Rachel's Tomb. A long-standing Jewish tradition locates Rachel's tomb at this site in Bethlehem.

David Meldrum

this terrible time of wailing, as the hostile king Herod kills the innocent babies of Bethlehem, something new and glorious will emerge out of the tragedy. His use of Jeremiah 31:15 implies the entire context of Jeremiah 31, including the new covenant. As Jesus ushers in the glorious coming kingdom, the sound of weeping will be replaced with joyful singing.

idea of corporate punishment—Israel and Judah in exile will continue to suffer for the sins of their fathers. Jeremiah himself implies as much in 15:4 and 32:18 (see also Exod. 20:4–6). Yahweh, however, declares that a change is coming. This passage introduces the coming new covenant. In those coming days, Yahweh states, this proverb will fall out of use, for the new covenant will shift from a national, corporate focus to an individual focus. Ezekiel will also quote this proverb and discuss the change in focus (Ezek. 18:2). The message to Jeremiah's audience is that they should not despair or become fatalistic because of their parents' sin and the judgment that resulted. Yahweh will give each of them the opportunity to respond individually and to be saved individually.

> This "new covenant" will not be like the old one Yahweh made with their fathers.

The new covenant is presented in Jeremiah 31:31–34 against the background of the broken covenant in Jeremiah 11. This "new covenant," Yahweh declares, will not be like the old one he made with their fathers (the Mosaic covenant) because they broke (annulled) that covenant (31:32). The new covenant will be characterized by an internal change, for this covenant will be written on their hearts rather than written on stone, and the law will be placed within each person (31:33–34). Recall that in the Hebrew of the Old Testament the term "heart" usually refers to one's "seat of volition." That is, one's heart is where one makes decisions, especially whether to follow Yahweh in obedience or not.

The other great characteristic of the new covenant is that because of this new covenant, Yahweh will forgive sins. There is no mention of sacrifice here. Forgiveness is cited as one of the important blessings that accompany the new covenant.

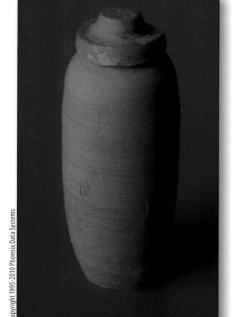

In Jeremiah 32:14 the prophet puts the deed (scroll) for the land he purchased into a clay jar like this, in order to store it for a long time.

Jesus states clearly that his death inaugurates the promised new covenant of Jeremiah (Matt. 26:28; Mark 14:24; Luke 22:20; 1 Cor. 11:23–26). Likewise, the book of Hebrews cites Jeremiah 31:31–34 directly, and then for three chapters discusses the implications of the new covenant (the end of the old obsolete covenant, the end of the Jewish sacrificial system because of Christ's ultimate sacrifice, etc.). Thus Jeremiah's new covenant is foundational for our understanding of how Christ fulfills the Old Testament promises. The new covenant that Jesus inaugurates ushers in the beginning of the glorious time of restoration that the prophets predicted.

JEREMIAH 32—DURING THE SIEGE, HOPE FOR THE FUTURE

Unlike 30 and 31, Jeremiah 32 is written in prose and is placed in a clear historical time setting. During the Babylonian siege of Jerusalem (588–586 BC) Jeremiah had been placed under house arrest because of his negative preaching against King Zedekiah and his prediction that the city would fall to the Babylonians (32:1–5). While Jeremiah is under house arrest, one of his relatives from Anathoth (not far from Jerusalem) comes to see if he would buy one of the family fields. Leviticus 25:25–31 specifies that land could be sold within the family but not outside the family. Note the irony here—no one in Judah has been paying much attention to the Law in all other regards. Also recall that it was men from Anathoth who were plotting to kill Jeremiah earlier (11:21). Furthermore, from an economic viewpoint, it would be very unwise to buy land during a siege, especially if the Babylonians were to win (as Jeremiah predicted). However, Yahweh tells Jeremiah to buy this land as a symbol of faith in the future time of restoration. Yahweh states that "houses, fields and vineyards will again be bought in this land" (32:15).

> Yahweh tells Jeremiah to buy this land as a symbolic sign of faith in the future time of restoration.

Jeremiah obeys and buys the field. However, he is a bit confused about the wisdom of it, and he voices his concern in a prayer to Yahweh (32:16–25). Yahweh answers in 32:26–44. He states that Jerusalem and Judah will most certainly be destroyed by the Babylonians. Yet in the future, Yahweh declares, he will restore them to this land. He promises to make a new covenant with them (32:40) and he restates the basic covenant formula: "They will be my people, and I will be their God" (32:38).

JEREMIAH 33—RESTORATION THROUGH THE DAVIDIC KING

While Jeremiah is still under house arrest, Yahweh comes to him again with a message of hope regarding the future restoration. First he reiterates that Jerusalem will indeed be destroyed (33:1–5). However, Yahweh then turns to the future and describes the glorious time of restoration. "I will heal my people" Yahweh declares, "and let them enjoy abundant peace and security" (33:6). Significantly, Yahweh speaks of cleansing them from sin and forgiving them for their rebellion (33:8), thus continuing to connect forgiveness of sin with the coming restoration. Joyful sounds such as wedding celebrations and the worship of Yahweh will be heard again in Jerusalem and throughout Judah (33:11). Likewise, sheep and shepherds will once again be common across the countryside, a sign of peaceful prosperity (33:12–13).

The promise of sheep and shepherds provides a transitional link to the repeated promise of a Davidic king (33:14–26). Although Jeremiah 33:14–26 does not appear in the Septuagint (LXX), and although some scholars may therefore doubt its authenticity, these verses primarily repeat the same promise of a Davidic king that was made in Jeremiah 23:5–6, which is nearly identical to 33:15–16. Throughout Jeremiah and indeed the rest of the prophetic literature, judgment will be proclaimed against God's people because of violations of the Mosaic covenant found in Deuteronomy, but restoration will be proclaimed in fulfillment of the covenants with Abraham and, especially, King David.

» FURTHER READING «

Clements, R. E. *Jeremiah*. Interpretation. Atlanta: John Knox Press, 1988.

Dearman, J. Andrew. *Jeremiah/Lamentations*. NIV Application Commentary. Grand Rapids: Zondervan, 2002.

Fretheim, Terence E. *Jeremiah*. Smith & Helwys Bible Commentary. Macon, GA: Smyth & Helwys, 2002.

Holladay, William L. *Jeremiah*, Vol. 2. Hermeneia. Philadelphia: Fortress Press, 1989.

Longman, Tremper. *Jeremiah, Lamentations*. New International Biblical Commentary. Peabody, MA: Hendrickson, 2008.

McConville, J. Gordon. *Judgment and Promise: An Interpretation of the Book of Jeremiah*. Winona Lake, IN and Leicester, England: Eisenbrauns and Apollos, 1993.

McKane, William. *Jeremiah*, Vol. 2. International Critical Commentary. Edinburgh and New York: T. & T. Clark, 1996.

Thompson, J. A. *The Book of Jeremiah*. The New International Commentary on the Old Testament. Grand Rapids: Eerdmans, 1980.

» DISCUSSION QUESTIONS «

1. Why was a *new* covenant needed?

2. What are the similarities and differences between the new covenant of Jeremiah 31:31 – 34 and the "old" covenant seen in Deuteronomy?

3. What does Jeremiah question Yahweh about in 32:24 – 25? How does Yahweh answer in 32:26 – 27? What does God's answer teach us today about God?

» WRITING ASSIGNMENTS «

1. Reread Jeremiah 31:31 – 34 and Jeremiah 11:9 – 14. Why was a *new* covenant needed? Next compare and contrast the new covenant described by Jeremiah in chapter 31 with the Mosaic covenant of Exodus and Deuteronomy. (Stay in the OT on this question; discuss the new covenant as described by Jeremiah and not as described in the New Testament). Finally, read Luke 22:20; Mark 14:24; Matthew 26:28; 1 Corinthians 11:25; and especially Hebrews 8:6 – 9:28. Discuss how the New Testament adds to our understanding of the new covenant.

2. Discuss the meaning and the usage of the phrase "I will be your God; you will be my people." Check the following passages (Exod. 6:7; Lev. 26:12; Deut. 27:9; Jer. 7:23; 11:4; 30:22; 31:1; 31:33).

3. Discuss the use of the wedding image in Jeremiah 7:34; 16:9; 25:10; 33:11. Then discuss the ways that the New Testament uses the wedding image.

CHAPTER 13

Jeremiah 34 — 52, Lamentations

"The Babylonians set fire to the royal palace
and the houses of the people and broke
down the walls of Jerusalem." (Jer. 39:8)

JEREMIAH 34–36—SLAVES AND SCROLLS

Jeremiah 34:8–22 chronicles an episode that takes place during the reign of Zedekiah. The king and the wealthy citizens had forced a large number of people into slavery, probably through various unjust actions. Furthermore, they had ignored the injunctions of their law that Hebrew slaves be freed every seven years (Exod. 21:2–6; Deut. 15:12–18). When the Babylonian army arrives to attack Jerusalem, King Zedekiah announces that all of the slaves in Jerusalem are to be freed, and this proclamation is ratified in a formal covenant. Zedekiah probably did this in the hopes that these former slaves would then become committed to defending Jerusalem. However, after the Babylonian siege of Jerusalem gets underway, the Egyptian army marches out to help the Judahites, and the Babylonians withdraw from their siege against Jerusalem to deal with the Egyptians.

> When the Babylonian army arrives to attack Jerusalem, King Zedekiah announces that all of the slaves in Jerusalem are to be freed.

When this happens, Zedekiah and the other former slave owners change their minds and re-enslave their former slaves. Yahweh is angered at these unjust actions, and he therefore proclaims "freedom" for the inhabitants of Jerusalem—"freedom to fall by the sword, plague and famine" (34:17).

In contrast, Jeremiah 35 recounts the example of the faithful Recabites. The Recabites were a tribe from the southern desert region of Judah who had come to Jerusalem for political/military protection. A unique custom of theirs was that they did not drink wine. Their forefathers had given them this commandment, and they had remained faithful to it through the years. Yahweh points out the stark contrast between the Recabites and the Judahites in Jerusalem. The Recabites continue to obey their forefathers, while the Judahites have completely abandoned the commandments handed down to them by their forefathers.

Jeremiah 36 goes back to the fourth year of Jehoiakim (605 BC). Yahweh tells Jeremiah to take a scroll and write down all of the words he has spoken to him up until this time. Yahweh expresses hope that the people will hear these words and repent (36:3). So Jeremiah calls Baruch (his assistant and scribe) to write down all of these words (36:1–4). Jeremiah then sends Baruch to read this document at the temple for all the people to hear. Several officials hear about the scroll and ask for a private reading. Thus Baruch reads it a second time, just for the officials (36:11–15). The officials, quite alarmed at the words, encourage Baruch and Jeremiah to hide, and they then report on this scroll

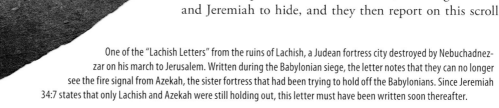

One of the "Lachish Letters" from the ruins of Lachish, a Judean fortress city destroyed by Nebuchadnezzar on his march to Jerusalem. Written during the Babylonian siege, the letter notes that they can no longer see the fire signal from Azekah, the sister fortress that had been trying to hold off the Babylonians. Since Jeremiah 34:7 states that only Lachish and Azekah were still holding out, this letter must have been written soon thereafter.

to Jehoiakim. The king orders that the scroll be brought to the palace and read aloud to him and his officials. Rather than responding to its message with fear and alarm, King Jehoiakim instead burns the scroll, piece by piece, as it is read (36:20–26) and then sends men to arrest Jeremiah and Baruch (whom Yahweh has hidden). This action underscores the sin and disobedience of Jehoiakim, who not only ignores the prophetic spoken word of Yahweh but also thinks so lightly of Yahweh that he assumes he can destroy Yahweh's written word and thus change the prophecy. Yahweh, however, reiterates the coming judgment on Jehoiakim (36:30–31). Yahweh then commands Jeremiah and Baruch to write the words again on another scroll.

JEREMIAH 37–45 — THE FINAL DAYS OF JERUSALEM

Jeremiah 37–45 describes the final days of Jerusalem. Unlike most of the rest of Jeremiah, these chapters are in chronological order. Jeremiah 37:2 sums up the tragic response of King Zedekiah and the people to Jeremiah's words: "Neither he [Zedekiah] nor his attendants nor the people of the land paid any attention to the words Yahweh had spoken through Jeremiah the prophet." As Jeremiah had

A model of an Egyptian scribe. Scribes were highly esteemed in the Ancient Near East. Baruch, the scribe of Jeremiah, plays a critical role in the book.

Baruch the Scribe

Baruch son of Neriah was a scribe and close associate of Jeremiah who played an important role in the life of Jeremiah and in the composition of the book of Jeremiah. Jeremiah 36:4–8 indicates that Baruch wrote down what appears to be the first compositional written unit of Jeremiah. Many scholars believe that this scroll contained much of Jeremiah 1:1–25:13 (note the reference to "this book" in 25:13). Baruch reads this scroll in the temple and then hides with Jeremiah to avoid Jehoiakim's wrath. Baruch then rewrites the scroll that Jehoiakim destroyed. Jeremiah 36:32 concludes with "And many similar words were added to them," implying that Baruch incorporated additional words into this work through the following years (probably producing the rest of the book of Jeremiah).

Jeremiah 45 presents a message of encouragement from Yahweh to Baruch after he wrote the scroll. With the king trying to kill him, Baruch probably needed encouragement. Yahweh tells him, "Wherever you go I will let you escape with your life" (45:5). Baruch does survive the destruction of Jerusalem, and he remains behind in Jerusalem with Jeremiah when the Babylonians take most of the Hebrews off to Babylon in exile. In fact, he gets blamed for inciting Jeremiah to prophesy against fleeing to Egypt after those left in the land murder Gedaliah (43:3). Baruch stays with Jeremiah, and they travel together to Egypt, against their will (43:6).

Baruch ("blessed") is a shortened version of the name Berechiah ("Yahweh blesses"). Archaeologists have discovered a seal impression in a royal archive from the time of Jeremiah that reads, "Belonging to Berekiah, son of Neriah, the scribe." It is very likely that this was the seal of Baruch, son of Neriah, who was the friend and scribe of Jeremiah.[1]

An impression from the seal of "Baruch, son of Neriah, the scribe."

1. Nahman Avigad, "Jerameel and Baruch: King's Son and Scribe," *Biblical Archaeologist* 42.2 (Spring 1979): 114–18.

predicted, due to Judah's covenant violation and her refusal to repent, the Babylonians invaded, and in 588–587 BC Nebuchadnezzar laid siege to Jerusalem.

Early in the siege the Egyptian army approaches and the Babylonians withdraw from Jerusalem to deal with the Egyptians (37:5). Jeremiah takes this opportunity and tries to leave Jerusalem to visit the field in Anathoth that he had purchased earlier (Jer. 32:1–15). The guards at the gate think he is deserting to the Babylonians, so they beat him and imprison him (37:11–16). Ironically, Zedekiah then sends a messenger to Jeremiah to ask if he has a word from Yahweh.

> Where are your prophets who prophesied to you, "The king of Babylon will not attack you or this land"?

Jeremiah tells King Zedekiah that the king will be handed over to the Babylonians. Then, somewhat exasperated, Jeremiah asks, "What crime have I committed against you or your officials or this people, that you have put me in prison? Where are your prophets who prophesied to you, 'The king of Babylon will not attack you or this land'?" (37:18–19). Zedekiah then orders that Jeremiah be placed in the courtyard of the guard and given bread to eat as long as the bread holds out (37:21).

Even while in the courtyard of the guard, however, Jeremiah continues to preach to the inhabitants of Jerusalem that it is futile to resist Nebuchadnezzar because Yahweh has raised him up to judge Judah. This message is extremely unpopular with the Hebrew officials who are engaged in the defense of Jerusalem. They accuse Jeremiah before King Zedekiah, who promptly decrees that these officials can do with Jeremiah as they please. With royal permission, they seize Jeremiah and lower him into a mud-bottomed cistern, ostensibly to let him die there (38:1–6). In essence, the entire nation has rejected Yahweh's prophet and his message. No one from Judah intercedes for Jeremiah.

> Ebedmelech the Cushite boldly intercedes for Yahweh's prophet, securing permission from the king to rescue Jeremiah from the cistern.

Help for Jeremiah comes from an unlikely source. A foreigner called "Ebedmelech the Cushite" boldly intercedes for Yahweh's prophet, securing permission from the king to rescue Jeremiah from the cistern. This action probably saves Jeremiah's life (Jer. 38:7–13).

From his house arrest in the courtyard of the guard, Jeremiah continues to advise Zedekiah to surrender to the Babylonians, but Zedekiah, fearing his own people more than the Babylonians or Yahweh, does not heed his message (38:17–28). Consequently, Jerusalem finally falls to the Babylonians (39:1–2). Zedekiah flees, but the Babylonians catch him near Jericho (39:4–5). The Babylonians kill all of the nobles (those who had opposed Jeremiah and tried to kill him), as well as the sons of Zedekiah. After Zedekiah watches his sons die, the Babylonians blind him and carry him to Babylon in shackles.

The Babylonians, however, treat Jeremiah with respect, allowing him to choose whether to go to Babylon or to stay in Judah (39:11–14; 40:1–6). Jeremiah opts to stay in Jerusalem. Ebedmelech also survives. Jeremiah 39:15–18 adds an important postscript to his story. Prior to the fall of Jerusalem Yahweh spoke to Jeremiah, promising that Ebedmelech would survive the destruction of Jerusalem. The reason for this, Yahweh stated, was that

Who Was Ebedmelech?

Ebedmelech the Cushite is an interesting character. First of all, note that he is called "the Cushite" four different times (38:7, 10, 12; 39:16), apparently indicating that this identification is important. The kingdom of Cush was located along the Nile just to the south of Egypt. It was an African kingdom; Jeremiah refers to the black skin of the Cushites when he cites a proverb about them in 13:23.

Throughout its history, Cush was closely connected to Egypt. Although Cush had ruled over Egypt for part of the eighth and seventh centuries BC, by the time of Jeremiah neither country controlled the other. On the other hand, Cush and Egypt were still closely interrelated economically, culturally, and militarily. Cushites had a reputation for being good soldiers, and they often served as mercenaries in armies throughout the Ancient Near East. This was true especially in Egypt, where Cushites regularly served in Egyptian armies. In addition, it is important to keep in mind that Egypt was the major military ally of Judah in Zedekiah's rebellion against Babylonia. Thus the most likely explanation for what a Cushite is doing in Jerusalem during the Babylonian siege of Jeremiah's day is that he is there in a military capacity and is perhaps connected to the Egyptian army.[1]

The portrayal of a Cushite mercenary from a Greek vase (550 – 525 BC).

The meaning of Ebedmelech's name ("servant of a king") has generated interesting discussions. Older commentators often assumed that "servant of a king" implied that Ebedmelech was a slave, but this conclusion is highly unlikely. Slave status does not fit well with the details of the story. If he were a slave, would he have been able to approach King Zedekiah and severely criticize the king's actions? And would Zedekiah have agreed with a slave and acquiesced to his request? Unlikely. Furthermore, it is doubtful that the name Ebedmelech actually has anything to do with the notion of a slave or personal servant. Although the term "servant" (*ebed*) by itself carried the nuance of servant or slave-like status, the specific phrase "servant of a king" is used in quite different contexts and carried no implications of slavery. On the contrary, the phrase "servant of the king" or "servant of such-and-such king" appears numerous times on Israelite and Judahite seals from this era in reference to high-ranking officials.

Thus the most plausible explanation for Ebedmelech's name, nationality, and presence in Jerusalem is that he is some type of military officer. He may have been leading a contingent of Cushite soldiers. His connection with Zedekiah suggests that perhaps he was in charge of the palace bodyguards. He may also have been an important representative of the Egyptian army, like a modern-day military attaché. If he held this position, it would explain how he could have ready access to the king and why Zedekiah gave in to his requests so easily. Jerusalem was under siege by Nebuchadnezzar and the powerful Babylonian army; Zedekiah could hardly afford to offend the Egyptians and the Cushites, his only significant remaining military allies.[2]

---

1. J. Daniel Hays, "From the Land of the Bow: Black Soldiers in the Ancient Near East," *Bible Review* 14 (1998): 28 – 33, 50 – 51.
2. See the extended discussion of Ebedmelech in J. Daniel Hays, *From Every People and Nation: A Biblical Theology of Race,* New Studies in Biblical Theology (Downers Grove, IL: InterVarsity Press, 2003), 130 – 38.

The Irony of Ending at Jericho

That Zedekiah was captured near Jericho is a tragic irony (Jer. 39:5). Jericho, remember, was where the great and glorious conquest of the Promised Land began. In essence, the conquest began with the destruction of Jericho, as Joshua led the Hebrews victoriously into the Land. This story ends with the destruction of Jerusalem, with the king being captured near Jericho as he tried to flee, and with the Hebrews led out of the Promised Land in defeat into exile.

Ebedmelech "trusted" in Yahweh. At a time when the entire Hebrew nation is being judged because of disobedience and covenant violation, a Black Cushite is delivered because of his faith. Indeed, Ebedmelech is specifically contrasted with Zedekiah. Yahweh did for Ebedmelech exactly what he would not do for Zedekiah—save him from the Babylonians. Ebedmelech thus becomes the representative of an important remnant—the remnant of faith.

The Babylonians appoint Gedaliah as governor over Judah and what is left of Jerusalem and then return victoriously to Babylon with most of the Jews as captive exiles. Initially, those who stay behind do well, harvesting a good crop the first year (40:7–12). However, Jeremiah 41–43 describes the disastrous actions of some of those remaining in the land. Ishmael, an officer from the Judahite royal family, gathers some men and foolishly assassinates Gedaliah the governor and the small remaining Babylonian garrison (41:3). Johanan and a group of Judahite army officers loyal to Babylon respond by attacking Ishmael, but the assassin escapes to Ammon (41:11–15). Fearing Babylonian reprisals, Johanan and his group conclude that they must flee to Egypt. Jeremiah vigorously opposes this action, declaring, "O remnant of Judah, Yahweh has told you, 'Do not go to Egypt!'" (42:19). However, these leaders and the people ignore Jeremiah once again, and "they entered Egypt in disobedience to Yahweh," even forcing Jeremiah to go with them (43:6–7).

> Ebedmelech becomes the representative of an important remnant— the remnant of faith.

Note the continued irony as the salvation history story of Israel goes into reverse. Yahweh had saved Israel out of Egypt, defeated enemies along the way, destroyed Jericho for them, and then given them the Promised Land, where he would be their God and bless them. Yet they then rejected Yahweh, lost the blessings, and were defeated first by the Assyrians and then by the Babylonians, who destroyed Jerusalem and then captured the king near Jericho. Finally, those Jews who remained in the land reject the good promises that Yahweh gives them through Jeremiah, and they return full circle to Egypt.

> Note the continued irony as the salvation history story of Israel goes into reverse.

Jeremiah 44 describes the unthinkable. After the Hebrews from Judah arrive in Egypt, they immediately return to worshiping the Queen of Heaven, a female astral goddess. Jeremiah had earlier preached against worshiping this particular goddess (Jer. 7:18). So even after the terrible judgment by the Babylonians, these Hebrews have not learned the lesson. They fall back into idolatry and thus Jeremiah pronounces judgment on them (44:24–30).

The British Museum has over 100,000 clay tablets written in cuneiform, most from the Assyrian and Babylonian eras. In the summer of 2007, a scholar translating some of these tablets discovered a tablet that was a receipt for an offering given to a temple in Babylon. The one who gave the gift was Nebo-Sarsekim, the chief officer (or eunuch), and the time was in the tenth year of Nebuchadnezzar. This same individual with exactly the same title is mentioned by Jeremiah as one of Nebuchadnezzar's officials who took their seats in the gates of Jerusalem after it fell (Jer. 39:3).

This tablet, dating from 595 BC, is a receipt for a gold donation to a Babylonian temple by a certain Nebo-Sarsekim, "chief of the officials," undoubtedly the same person mentioned in Jeremiah 39:3.

The story of Israel will continue with the exiles who went to Babylon, but the story of Jeremiah ends in Egypt, where Jeremiah and Baruch apparently lived out their final years.

JEREMIAH 46–51—ORACLES AGAINST THE NATIONS

Many of the prophets deliver messages of judgment not only against Israel and Judah but also against the surrounding nations. Jeremiah also delivers an extensive series of oracles of judgment against several nations. These judgments are often based on the nations' violent actions against Judah, especially their complicity in the Babylonian invasion. However, judgment is also rendered for other sins as well—idolatry, violence, and arrogance, among others. Sometimes, particularly in Jeremiah 46–51, no specific reason is stated—merely judgment. Apparently, the reasons were understood. The nations that Jeremiah pronounces judgment upon are Egypt, Philistia, Moab, Ammon, Edom, Damascus, Kedar and Hazor (Arab tribes), Elam, and especially, Babylon.

> Jeremiah delivers oracles of judgment against several nations.

One interesting aspect of these oracles is that some of the nations will be judged and yet will survive and continue as nations, while some of them will be judged and will completely disappear. Judgment will come on Egypt (46:1–25), but Egypt will not be destroyed completely and will have a future (46:26). Recall that Isaiah prophesied a time when the Egyptians would worship Yahweh (Isa. 19:23–25). On the other hand, no hope is given for the Philistines (Jeremiah 47). As history shows, Nebuchadnezzar put an end to the Philistines, who disappear from history, leaving only their name on the region; Palestine. Moab, Ammon, and Edom were the small nations to the immediate east and southeast of Judah. Jeremiah prophesies judgment on these kingdoms

(Jer. 48–49:22). Moab and Ammon will still have a future (48:47; 49:6), but no hope for the future of Edom is presented. Obadiah also prophesies against Edom, and portions of Obadiah are very similar to Jeremiah's oracle against Edom (49:7–22). Jeremiah's oracle against Damascus (the capital of Syria/Aram) is brief, and the future beyond the immediate defeat is not mentioned (49:23–27). The Arab tribes are represented by Hazor (different from the city Hazor in Galilee) and Kedar, and Jeremiah prophesies that Nebuchadnezzar will defeat them, leaving Hazor uninhabited (49:28–33). Elam, far to the east, will also be destroyed but will be restored in the future (49:39). Jeremiah then presents a lengthy oracle against Babylon (Jer. 50–51), the real focus of this "judgment against the nations" unit.

> Yahweh has not abandoned the Israelites to the winds of history.

Yahweh raised up the Babylonians to judge the disobedient Hebrews in Judah. Yet Jeremiah declares that Yahweh has not abandoned the Israelites to the winds of history. In the future he will restore them. Likewise, the Babylonians will come under judgment for all of their sin and violence. Indeed, Cyrus the Persian captures Babylon without much of a struggle in 539 BC, and the city (and empire) quickly fade from prominence and then disappear from history. Jeremiah 46–51 ends with the statement, "The words of Jeremiah end here," indicating, perhaps, that Jeremiah 52 is an added postscript, not to be attributed to Jeremiah.

The nations included in Jeremiah's "Oracle against the Nations" (Jeremiah 46–51).

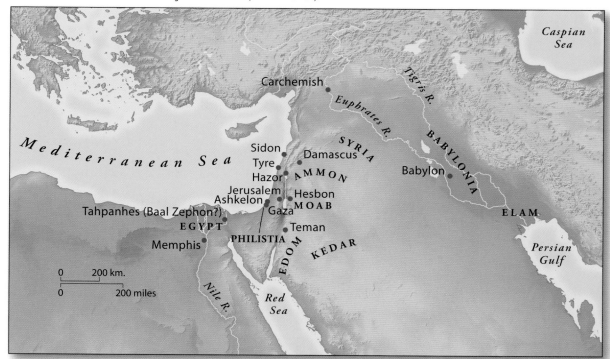

A relief figure in colorful ceramic of a serpent/dragon on the Ishtar Gate of Babylon. Speaking of Nebuchadnezzar, Jeremiah says, "Like a serpent he has swallowed us" (Jer. 51:34).

JEREMIAH 52 — THE FALL OF JERUSALEM DESCRIBED AGAIN

Jeremiah 52 repeats much of the material that was in Jeremiah 39 (and in 2 Kings 25) regarding the fall of Jerusalem. It adds a few more details that Jeremiah 39 omits, such as the release of Jehoiachin and his relative well-being in Babylon. Jehoiachin, remember, was the young man who succeeded Jehoiakim as king just as the Babylonians arrived in 598 BC. He surrendered to the Babylonians instead of fighting them as Zedekiah did in defiance of Yahweh's word. Therefore, Jehoiachin survived, leaving the end of the book of Jeremiah with a glimmer of hope tied to the remnant still alive in Babylon.

LAMENTATIONS — THE AGONIZED CRY OVER FALLEN JERUSALEM

Setting

A lament is a sad, agony-filled song often sung at funerals. The genre that is closest to this in our time is perhaps the blues. The book of Lamentations is a collection of five laments that graphically and poetically express shock and deep pain over the destruction and devastation of Jerusalem after it fell to the Babylonians in 586 BC.

> The book of Lamentations is a collection of five laments that graphically and poetically express shock and deep pain over the destruction and devastation of Jerusalem.

In the Septuagint (the ancient Greek translation of the Old Testament), Lamentations is associated with Jeremiah, who is even identified as the author. In the Hebrew Bible, however, Lamentations is not included with the prophets or associated with Jeremiah in any way, but is placed in the section called Writings. It is part of a smaller five-book unit called the *Megilloth* ("scrolls"), along with Song of Songs, Ruth, Ecclesiastes, and Esther. In Jewish tradition, each of these books was read liturgically on a specific feast day. Lamentations was read on the "Ninth of Ab," which commemorated the destruction of the temple. Christian Bibles, however, have traditionally followed the Septuagint, placing Lamentations after Jeremiah, and thus including it as part of the prophetic message.

> The poet of Lamentations will rise briefly above his agonized cry from the ashes to reaffirm the faithfulness of Yahweh and to pray for the restoration.

Message

Lamentations is a tragic, mournful cry, expressing grief over the fall of Jerusalem and the associated rupture of covenant fellowship with Yahweh. Read in its canonical location in our Bibles, close on the heels of Jeremiah, it also serves as a vindication of Jeremiah's message and his conflict with the false prophets and the kings of Judah. Jeremiah, of course, was right. He was the true prophet of Yahweh. Jerusalem ignored the warnings he spoke from Yahweh and now the temple is gone, the monarchy is gone, the city lies in ashes, and the people are scattered. Yet in keeping with the prophetic message, the poet of Lamentations will rise briefly above his agonized cry from the ashes to reaffirm the faithfulness of Yahweh and to pray for the restoration.

Each of the five chapters in Lamentations is a separate poem. The first four poems are "acrostics." An acrostic is a poetic form in which each successive verse begins with the next letter of the alphabet. The Hebrew alphabet has 22 letters. Lamentations 1 has 22 verses. Each verse has three poetic lines, but the first letter of the first line of each verse starts with the next letter of the Hebrew alphabet. Lamentations 2 follows the same pattern. Lamentations 3 is slightly different. Each letter of the alphabet starts off three consecutive verses of one line each, yielding a total of 66 verses. Lamentations 4 returns to the pattern of chapters 1 and 2 but with two lines per verse instead of three. Lamentations 5 is not an acrostic, but it does have 22 lines of text and 22 verses, matching the number of letters in the alphabet. The purpose of

Lamentations 3:1 – 15 in the Hebrew Bible. Remember that Hebrew reads from right to left. Note that the first three verses all start with the same letter. This is א (aleph), the first letter in the Hebrew alphabet. Likewise, the next three verses (3:4 – 6) all start with ב (beth), the second letter, and so forth.

this highly structured poetic style may have been to assist in memorization, but more likely it contributed to the overall meaning of the book. Using the total range of the alphabet implied a complete expression of grief and repentance.[1]

The opening lines of Lamentations capture the main point of the book: "How deserted lies the city, once so full of people!" (Lam. 1:1). Lamentations 1 describes the mournful weeping over destroyed Jerusalem. Throughout this chapter there are frequent statements that Jerusalem weeps and that there is no one to comfort her (1:2, 9, 16, 17, 21). Remember that Isaiah 40 starts out with "Comfort, comfort my people," indicating that part of the future restoration would be a time of comfort. But in Lamentations 1, comfort has not yet come. Likewise, this chapter contains a repeated confession of sin.

> Using the total range of the alphabet implied a complete expression of grief and repentance.

Lamentations 2 focuses on Yahweh's wrath, recounting the terrible destruction he brought on rebellious Jerusalem. Lamentations 3 opens with a long lament describing the terrible things that the writer has endured (3:1 – 20). Yet the author is not totally overwhelmed by despair, and in 3:21 – 26 he expresses his faith in Yahweh's great love (*hesed*). Indeed, the writer proclaims, Yahweh's great compassions are "new every morning; great is his faithfulness." Based on trust in Yahweh, Lamentations 3:40 – 42 exhorts the exiles to repent and confess their sins, thus pointing to a way forward. But the writer then returns to his lament in 3:48 – 54, followed by a call for Yahweh to exact vengeance on Judah's enemies (3:55 – 66).

The Western Wall of the Temple Mount in Jerusalem, often called the "Wailing Wall." Jews today often read from Lamentations when they are here.

Lamentations 4 returns to the terrible situation in Jerusalem, graphically retelling the horrific story of the destruction of the city and clearly framing this destruction as an outpouring of Yahweh's great wrath. Lamentations 4:9 – 10 (starvation in the city and eating one's children) alludes directly to the warnings of Deuteronomy 28:54 – 57 and perhaps functions ironically to show the horrific consequence of Jerusalem's refusal to heed Jeremiah's strong condemnation of child sacrifice (Jer. 7:30 – 33).

Lamentations 5 opens with a continuing description of the terrible situation for the survivors. In 5:7 the writer acknowledges the sin of previous generations, "Our fathers sinned and are no more, and we bear their punishment." Acknowledging that the terrible judgment was deserved, the writer recognizes that Yahweh is sovereign and has the power to restore them (5:19 – 22). In language similar to Jeremiah's, Lamentation 5:21 uses *shūv* (return, restore, repent) twice, and thus Lamentations ends with a humble call to Yahweh to restore and return his people to a relationship with him.

---

1. C. Hassell Bullock, *An Introduction to the Prophetic Books,* 2nd ed. (Chicago: Moody Press, 2007), 321.

» FURTHER READING «

Clements, R. E. *Jeremiah*. Interpretation. Atlanta: John Knox Press, 1988.

Dearman, J. Andrew. *Jeremiah/Lamentations*. NIV Application Commentary. Grand Rapids: Zondervan, 2002.

Fretheim, Terence E. *Jeremiah*. Smith & Helwys Bible Commentary. Macon, GA: Smyth & Helwys, 2002.

Hays, J. Daniel. *From Every People and Nation: A Biblical Theology of Race*. New Studies in Biblical Theology. Downers Grove, IL: InterVarsity, 2003, 130–38.

Holladay, William L. *Jeremiah,* Vol. 2. Hermeneia. Philadelphia: Fortress Press, 1989.

Huey, F. B., Jr. *Jeremiah/Lamentations*. New American Commentary. Nashville: Broadman and Holman, 1993.

Longman, Tremper. *Jeremiah, Lamentations*. New International Biblical Commentary. Peabody, MA: Hendrickson, 2008.

McConville, J. Gordon. *Judgment and Promise: An Interpretation of the Book of Jeremiah*. Winona Lake, IN and Leicester, England: Eisenbrauns and Apollos, 1993.

McKane, William. *Jeremiah,* Vol. 2. International Critical Commentary. Edinburgh and New York: T. & T. Clark, 1996.

Thompson, J. A. *The Book of Jeremiah*. The New International Commentary on the Old Testament. Grand Rapids: Eerdmans, 1980.

» DISCUSSION QUESTIONS «

1. What role does the story of the Recabites (Jeremiah 35) play in Jeremiah?

2. What is the significance of the story of Ebedmelech (Jeremiah 38–39)?

3. Why does Jehoiakim burn Jeremiah's scroll (Jeremiah 36)? What does Jeremiah then prophesy about this king (36:30–31)?

4. What is the role of the book of Lamentations in the overall prophetic message?

1. Choose one of the following motifs in Jeremiah and write a 3–4 page paper explaining how this theme contributes to Jeremiah's message: (a) wailing, weeping, and rejoicing; (b) social ethics; (c) wounds, sickness, and healing; (d) water, springs, deserts, and well-watered trees; (e) the land and its inheritance; (f) the exodus; (g) patriotism. Use the last paragraph to relate the meaning of this motif to us today.

2. Write a 3–4 page paper on the life of Jeremiah.

CHAPTER 14

Ezekiel 1 — 16

> "Do you see what they are doing—the utterly detestable things the house of Israel is doing here, things that will drive me far from my sanctuary?" (Ezek. 8:6)

OVERVIEW OF EZEKIEL

Setting

Jehoiakim, the king of Judah, rebels against the Babylonians, and in 598 BC the Babylonian army arrives to quell the rebellion. Jehoiakim dies (apparently assassinated), and young Jehoiachin becomes king. He quickly surrenders and in 597 BC is taken into captivity along with 10,000 other exiles. Included in this first exile of 597 BC is the young priest Ezekiel. In 593 BC, Yahweh calls the young Ezekiel to be his prophet (Ezek. 1:2). Ezekiel's primary audience is the Hebrew exiles in Babylon, who are struggling to make sense of their exile and the world events that have shattered their lives. Part of Ezekiel's ministry takes place between the two exiles; that is, he preaches some of his messages after the first exile of 597 BC but before the terrible destruction of Jerusalem in 587/586 BC. The fall of Jerusalem and the terrible destruction that followed is perhaps the central historical event in the book of Ezekiel. Remember, however, that he is in Babylon when it happens.

> Ezekiel's primary audience is the Hebrew exiles in Babylon, who are struggling to make sense of their exile and the world events that have shattered their lives.

Message

Ezekiel's message is similar to the standard three-part message of the preexilic prophets discussed in chapter 4 and seen throughout Isaiah and Jeremiah. Thus Ezekiel also declares the following: (1) You (Judah) have broken the covenant; you had better repent! (2) No repentance? Then judgment! Judgment will also come on the nations. (3) Yet there is hope beyond the judgment for a glorious, future restoration, both for Israel/Judah and for the nations. Of course, after a few years of Ezekiel's prophetic ministry, Jerusalem is actually destroyed, so Ezekiel's message of judgment on Judah and Jerusalem shifts somewhat from future warning to present explanation.

Within that three-part message, however, Ezekiel focuses on two related themes throughout the book. First, he stresses *the sovereignty and glory of Yahweh*. The Israelites may be in exile, but Yahweh is still in control of history, and he is moving events along according to his sovereignty and his glory. Connected to this theme is the repeated phrase "I am Yahweh" along with associated variations of this phrase such as the clause "that you may know that I am Yahweh" (which occurs 70 times in Ezekiel). Yahweh declares quite clearly that everyone will know that he is Yahweh—the sinful ones through the judgment they receive, and the believing, repentant ones through the blessings and restoration they will experience.

> Ezekiel stresses the sovereignty and glory of Yahweh. "That you may know that I am Yahweh" occurs 70 times in Ezekiel.

Thus the sovereignty of Yahweh is related to the main prophetic points of sin/judgment and restoration/blessing.

The second major theme of Ezekiel is the *presence of Yahweh*. At the heart of the covenant was the promise, "I will be with you/I will live in your midst." Yahweh's powerful presence was with Moses and Israel when they came out of Egypt, appeared in the pillar of fire and the cloud that led them in the wilderness, and then took up residence in the tabernacle. When the temple was built by Solomon, the presence of Yahweh came and filled it. From then on the powerful presence of Yahweh was associated with the temple. It was arguably the most significant blessing that Israel had while dwelling in the Land. When Yahweh departs from the temple (Ezek. 8–10), Israel loses that powerful presence and the wonderful blessings that accompanied it. The latter chapters of Ezekiel, however, describe a time of glorious restoration, centering on a description of the new temple, which is characterized by the presence of Yahweh. This is highlighted by the final statement of the book, "And the name of the city from that time on will be 'Yahweh is there'" (Ezek. 48:35).

The second major theme of Ezekiel is the presence of Yahweh.

Ezekiel can be divided into three main units: Ezekiel 1–24 emphasizes judgment and the destruction of Jerusalem, but with glimpses of deliverance and restoration; Ezekiel 25–32 contains oracles against the nations; and Ezekiel 33–48 looks to the future glorious restoration, focusing especially on the future new temple and the renewed presence of Yahweh.

Most of the preexilic prophets rely heavily on Deuteronomy for their message of covenant violation and judgment. Ezekiel is a priest, and he focuses on "priestly" concerns more that the other prophets do (even though Jeremiah is also from a priestly family). Thus it is not surprising that Ezekiel relies on Leviticus more than Deuteronomy, in contrast to the other prophets.

Raphael's interpretation of Ezekiel's vision, entitled *The Vision of Ezekiel* (1516).

EZEKIEL 1–3—EZEKIEL'S ENCOUNTER WITH THE GLORY OF YAHWEH

Recall that Isaiah's encounter with Yahweh and his commission to be a prophet came while he was in the temple (Isaiah 6). That made sense, for the presence of Yahweh was located in the temple. Like Isaiah, Ezekiel also encounters Yahweh seated on his throne. Unlike Isaiah, however, Ezekiel is not in the temple. He is in exile by a river in Babylon. This is highly significant, for Yahweh is demonstrating that his powerful presence and the throne he rules from is not tied to the temple in Jerusalem but is mobile and free to move throughout the world at his good pleasure. Uniting Ezekiel 1–3 (the prophet's encounter with Yahweh) is the theme "the glory of Yahweh" (1:28; 3:12, 23).

In Ezekiel 1:4–28 the prophet describes this encounter. Like Isaiah, he gives more details about the throne/chariot and the creatures that serve Yahweh than

about Yahweh himself. Like Isaiah, Ezekiel is probably limited in how well he can look directly at the glory of Yahweh.

Ezekiel sees four living creatures, which he later identifies as cherubim (10:20), coming out of a windstorm filled with lightning and bright light. Each creature has four faces and four wings, bright as fire and flying back and forth with the rapidity of lightning (1:4–14). Beside each one is a wheel (i.e., the four wheels of a wagon or four-wheeled chariot), and the wheels are quite unique in that they can go freely and quickly in any direction (unlike typical chariots of the day that had fixed axles and required a very large turning radius). The uniqueness of this throne-vehicle is that it is completely mobile. It can go up or down, backward, forward, left or right, in an instant — like lightning itself. Above the wheels and the cherubim is a spectacular throne on which sits someone who looks like a man but whose brightness is overwhelming. This, Ezekiel explains, is the "likeness of the glory of Yahweh" (1:25–28).

This "vision" or theophany conveys several important theological truths to Ezekiel. As in the theophany of Isaiah 6, the glory and holiness of Yahweh is revealed. Yes, many of the people of Jerusalem are in exile and under the rule of the Babylonians. Yes, the presence of Yahweh is about to leave the temple in Jerusalem, and the city is about to be destroyed. However, the glory and holiness of Yahweh is above all of this. His powerful presence, his throne, and his rule is not limited to the temple in Jerusalem. He is here now, with Ezekiel in Babylonia, to empower him to deliver Yahweh's word to his people.

Marie-Lan Nguyen/Wikimedia Commons

The cherubim Ezekiel sees have both animal and human features. This was not unusual to people in the Ancient Near East. This human-headed bull with wings guarded the entrance to the palace of the Assyrian King Sargon II (about 710 BC).

In Ezekiel 2:1–3:15 Yahweh commissions Ezekiel to be his prophet. As with Jeremiah and Isaiah, Yahweh warns him that the people are rebellious and probably won't listen to him (2:3–8). Yahweh gives Ezekiel a scroll to eat, symbolizing that the word of Yahweh — words "of lament and mourning and woe" — is now within the prophet, and he should now declare it (2:9–3:9).

Unlike Isaiah and Jeremiah, Yahweh calls Ezekiel by the title "son of man" (lit. "son of Adam"), probably stressing his humanness and his frailty (in contrast to the cherubim and Yahweh), and reminding everyone of Yahweh's creation. Then in 2:2 the Spirit (Hebrew *ruah,* lit. "wind," "spirit," or "breath") comes into "the son of Adam" (Ezekiel) and lifts him to his feet. This

Cherubim, Seraphim, and the Four Living Creatures

In Ezekiel's opening vision of the throne of Yahweh, he describes "four living creatures" hovering around the throne (1:4–21). Ezekiel 10:1–2 once again describes the throne along with the same creatures, but in this text the creatures are specifically called "cherubim" (plural of "cherub" in Hebrew). Scholars are uncertain as to the original meaning of the word, but most connect the term to a word that means "gatekeeper" or to one meaning "intercessor."

In these two passages Ezekiel provides us with quite an extensive description of these cherubim. They have the basic form of a human, but each of them also has four wings and four faces — a face of a man, a lion, an ox, and an eagle. The point of having four wings and four faces seems to be their total mobility. That is, their wings and faces allow them to fly in any direction without having to turn (Ezek. 10:11). This extensive mobility of the cherubim and of Yahweh's throne is in contrast to the fixed golden cherubim above the ark of the covenant in the temple. Ezekiel 10:12 states that the entire bodies of the cherubim were covered with eyes, perhaps emphasizing how extensively and completely God and his royal attendants see the entire world. Underscoring the powerful presence of Yahweh, the cherubim are closely associated with bright fire and lightning (Ezek. 1:5, 7, 13, 14; 10:2, 6, 7).

Cherubim first appear in Scripture in Genesis 3:24, when Yahweh appoints them to guard the entrance to the garden of Eden and to prevent banished humankind from returning to the Tree of Life. In this context the garden of Eden functions as an archetypal temple; that is, it was the meeting place between the presence of Yahweh and his people. Thus one of the basic functions of cherubim seems to be guarding the entrances to the places where Yahweh meets with people. This understanding accords well with Exodus 25:18–22, where Yahweh instructs Moses and the Israelites to construct golden cherubim on either side of the mercy seat on the ark of the covenant. Yahweh identifies this location as the place where he would "meet" with Moses (Exod. 25:22). Yahweh also directs the Israelites to incorporate pictures of cherubim into the decorations of the tabernacle (Exod. 26:1, 31). Later, Yahweh likewise incorporates cherubim imagery into the décor of the Solomonic temple (1 Kings 6:23–29; 7:29, 36; 8:6–7; 2 Chron. 3:14). In Isaiah 37:16 King Hezekiah prays to Yahweh in the temple, describing him as "enthroned between the cherubim." Likewise, Psalm 18:10 alludes to Yahweh as flying on the wings of the cherubim. Recall that Isaiah 6 refers to seraphim (lit. "burning ones") flying around the throne of Yahweh. These seraphim appear to be quite similar to the cherubim discussed above, but the seraphim have six wings instead of four, as the cherubim have.

In the New Testament, we find "four living creatures" around the throne in Revelation 4:6–8 and 5:8. These "living creatures" have similarities to both the cherubim in Ezekiel and the seraphim of Isaiah 6. These four creatures are "covered with eyes" (Rev. 4:6, 8; cf. Ezek. 1:18; 10:12). They are described as being "like" a lion, ox, man, and eagle (Rev. 4:7; cf. Ezek. 1:10), thus, as in Ezekiel, the living creatures are angelic but have features that represent earthly creatures, probably representative of all of God's creation. Like Isaiah's seraphim, each of the four living creatures in Revelation has "six wings" (Rev. 4:8; cf. Isa. 6:2). The overall message that is conveyed by the four living creatures in Revelation 4 is similar to that projected by the cherubim of Ezekiel and the seraphim of Isaiah — the presence of God is holy, powerful, and eternal, sovereign over all creation and worthy of worship.

In the *Chronicles of Narnia* series by C. S. Lewis, the lion Aslan (representing Jesus) uses the term "sons and daughters of Adam" to address the children. In all probability, Lewis draws this terminology from the book of Ezekiel, where "son of Adam" is Yahweh's favorite term for Ezekiel.

is suggestively similar to Genesis 2:7, where Yahweh breathes into the first Adam and gives him life. The Spirit (apparently the Spirit of Yahweh, i.e., the Holy Spirit) plays a major role in Ezekiel 2–3, repeatedly lifting Ezekiel up (2:2; 3:12, 14, 24), and then speaking to him at the end (3:24–27).

In the final episode of Ezekiel's commission, Yahweh underscores how important it is for Ezekiel to declare Yahweh's word and to call the people to repentance (3:16–27).

EZEKIEL 4–7 — OBJECT LESSONS AND MORE JUDGMENT

In Ezekiel 4 Yahweh tells Ezekiel to build a model of Jerusalem under siege. He is to lie next to it for 390 days (for the sin of Israel) and then 40 days (for the sin of Judah). This is to be a sign or an object lesson to the people. Likewise, in Ezekiel 5, the prophet shaves his head and beard, and then divides the hair into thirds. One third he burns inside the city (presumably the model he made in Ezekiel 4), one third he strikes with the sword outside the city, and one third he lets the wind scatter. This represents the fate of the inhabitants of Jerusalem when the terrible judgment comes. Ezekiel 6–7 continues by highlighting once again the sin of idolatry and the resulting judgment about to descend upon Jerusalem.

A Canaanite shrine at Megiddo. The prophets preached against these "high places" (Ezek. 6:3).

William D. Mounce

EZEKIEL 8–11 — YAHWEH LEAVES JERUSALEM

The events in Ezekiel 8–11 take place in 592 BC, five years before the fall of Jerusalem and the destruction of the temple by the Babylonians. The Spirit of Yahweh takes Ezekiel by the hair, lifts him up, and takes him "in visions of God" to the temple in Jerusalem, where the presence of Yahweh (the "glory of God") still resides (8:3–4). Yahweh shows him four terrible things in the temple: (1) a pagan idol in the entrance to the north gate, near the altar (8:5–6); (2) images of unclean, detestable animals as well as idols painted all over the walls of the temple, and seventy elders of Israel burning incense to these idols (inside the temple!) (8:7–12); (3) in the entrance to the north gate, women engaged in the ritualistic ceremony of mourning for Tammuz, a Mesopotamian "vegetation" god who dies every winter (8:13–15); and (4) in the "inner court," close to the very presence of Yahweh, twenty-five men (perhaps priests?), bowing down to the sun with their backs to the temple. In the Ancient Near East turning one's back toward his king or his god was an insult. Right in front of Yahweh, these men had turned their backs and were bowing down to the sun in the east, that is, worshipping a sun god (8:16).

A relief portraying Nabonidus, king of Babylon, praying to the moon, the sun, and Venus.

These four events are shocking, highlighting just how bad the idolatry had become in Jerusalem. In Ezekiel 8:17, Yahweh asks, "Is it a trivial matter for the house of Judah to do the detestable things they are doing here?" He declares in 8:6 that these things "will drive me far from my sanctuary." The sin of Judah in Jerusalem, and particularly in the temple itself, has multiplied to the point that the presence and holiness of Yahweh can no longer remain there.

As Ezekiel's vision continues, the glory/presence of Yahweh moves from the inner Holy of Holies to the doorway (threshold). Yahweh sends a man throughout the city to place

The figure in the center of this cylinder seal is probably the god Tammuz (called Dumuzi by the Sumerians).

a mark on the foreheads of all who are faithful and who are grieving over the detestable things in the temple. These are the ones who would survive, because in the vision Yahweh next sends armed men throughout the temple and the city to kill everyone else, thus symbolizing the coming judgment (9:1 – 11).

Ezekiel watches as the glory of Yahweh departs from the temple and leaves Jerusalem.

In Ezekiel 10 the prophet sees the same cherubim, wheels, and glory of Yahweh that he saw in Ezekiel 1 now at the doorway (threshold) of the temple. The glory of Yahweh then departs from there, stopping temporarily over the east gate to the temple (10:1 – 22). In 11:23 Ezekiel watches as the glory of Yahweh, the cherubim, and the wheels depart from the entrance to the temple and leave Jerusalem, stopping over the mountains to the east. Ezekiel is then carried back to Babylonia to tell the exiles of his vision.

EZEKIEL 12 — A SKIT SYMBOLIZING THE EXILE

In Ezekiel 12 Yahweh tells Ezekiel to act out an "exile" scene. He is to pack up his belongings and walk out of the city like he is going into exile. This is a sign for those back in Jerusalem that they will soon go into exile.

EZEKIEL 13 — FALSE PROPHETS

Ezekiel encounters the same kind of false prophets and confronts the same kind of false prophecies as did Jeremiah. This chapter proclaims judgment on those who claim to be prophets but who declare false and lying visions. They proclaim "peace" when judgment and exile are coming. Yahweh states that this is like putting whitewash over a flimsy wall that is about to fall over. Although the whitewash covers it for a moment, Yahweh declares

Yahweh's Departure from the Temple — and His Return

The departure of Yahweh from the temple is one of the most significant events in Ezekiel, and it carries tremendous theological implications. At the heart of the Mosaic covenant was the three-part formula statement by Yahweh: (1) I will be your God; (2) You will be my people; and (3) I will dwell in your midst. Yahweh's departure implies an end to this arrangement. He no longer dwells in their midst — at least not in Jerusalem or in the Promised Land. An interesting side note is that after the exile, when the people return to Palestine and Jerusalem and rebuild the temple, there is no mention of the presence of Yahweh returning to dwell in the temple. That is, there is no indication that things have returned to the preexile status. All indications are that Yahweh's presence does not dwell in the rebuilt postexilic temple as it did in the old temple. In fact, the biblical story indicates that Yahweh's presence does not return to the temple until Jesus walks in through the gates. Ironically, when that happens, what does Christ find? Moneychangers and scoundrels, but no true worshippers. The situation that Christ encounters in the temple is similar to that in Jeremiah's and Ezekiel's day. As do Jeremiah and Ezekiel, Jesus pronounces judgment on the temple and the city of Jerusalem, which is destroyed by the Romans in AD 70.

that he is sending a torrential rain to wash away the whitewash. Continuing with this metaphor, Yahweh declares, "I will spend my wrath against the wall and against those who covered it with whitewash. I will say to you, 'The wall is gone and so are those who whitewashed it'" (13:15). In 13:1 – 16 Yahweh speaks against the false prophecy of men, and in 13:17 – 19 he speaks against women who prophesy falsely.

EZEKIEL 14 – 15 — JUDGMENT ON JERUSALEM

Ezekiel 14 is similar to portions of Isaiah and Jeremiah. The prophet chastises Israel for her idolatry and warns of imminent judgment if there is no repentance. Ezekiel 15 then compares Jerusalem to a useless burnt branch of a vine. There is no fruit on it, but it is not good for anything else either (compare Jesus' use of the vine image in John 15).

> Ezekiel encounters the same kind of false prophets and confronts the same kind of false prophecies as did Jeremiah.

EZEKIEL 16 — JERUSALEM THE PROSTITUTE

Recall that Jeremiah uses the unfaithful wife/harlot imagery frequently; in fact, most of the prophets use that image. Ezekiel devotes this entire chapter to that image, going into quite some detail (and he will use this analogy again in chapter 23). In the extended metaphor of this chapter, Yahweh states that Jerusalem's ancestry and birth were in the land of the Canaanites and that her father was an Amorite and her mother a Hittite (underscoring her future pagan tendencies) (16:1 – 5). Yahweh found the newborn baby (Jerusalem) abandoned in a field, rescued her, and nourished her until she had grown into a beautiful young woman. In this analogy, Yahweh (the generous husband) takes her in and marries her, providing for her and blessing her with wonderful gifts (16:8 – 14). Jerusalem, however, rejects him and becomes a prostitute, offering herself to whoever comes by — the Egyptians, the Assyrians, and the Babylonians (16:15 – 34). She even practices child sacrifice (16:20 – 22), a terrible sin in Jerusalem that Jeremiah also mentions often. Therefore, Yahweh declares, judgment is coming! Continuing the analogy, Yahweh states that her older sister was Samaria (Israel to the north, destroyed in 722 BC) and her younger sister was Sodom (the epitome of sin and degradation) (16:44 – 52). Even so, miraculously, Yahweh points beyond the terrible betrayal and consequential judgment to the time of restoration when he will establish an "everlasting covenant" with her (16:59 – 63).

» FURTHER READING «

Allen, Leslie C. *Ezekiel 1 – 19*. Word Biblical Commentary. Dallas: Word Books, 1994.

Block, Daniel I. *The Book of Ezekiel: Chapters 1 – 24*. The New International Commentary on the Old Testament. Grand Rapids: Eerdmans, 1997.

Duguid, Iain M. *Ezekiel*. The NIV Application Commentary. Grand Rapids: Zondervan, 1999.

» DISCUSSION QUESTIONS «

1. Are the four living creatures of Ezekiel 1 real beings that we will see around the throne in heaven? Or are they part of a vision that has symbolic meaning but not really a picture of reality?

2. Why does Yahweh call Ezekiel "son of Adam"?

3. What is the significance of Yahweh's departure from the temple in Ezekiel 10? What causes him to leave? (see Ezekiel 8).

» WRITING ASSIGNMENTS «

1. Describe and discuss the things that Ezekiel is shown in the temple in Ezekiel 8.

2. Compare and contrast Ezekiel's harlot analogy in Ezekiel 16:1 – 43 with Jeremiah's in Jeremiah 2:1 – 3, 32 – 33; 3:1 – 4, 19 – 20.

3. Compare and contrast Ezekiel's four creatures in Ezekiel 1 and 10 with the four living creatures in Revelation 4.

CHAPTER 15

Ezekiel 17 — 32

"Then they will know that I am Yahweh."

(Ezek. 28:23, 24, 26; 29:6, 16, 21; 32:15)

OVERVIEW OF EZEKIEL 17–32

Recall that Ezekiel 1–24 deals primarily with judgment on Jerusalem. In this chapter we will first finish this large unit by discussing Ezekiel 17–24, which climaxes with the death of Ezekiel's wife (24:18) and the simultaneous fall (death) of Jerusalem. Then we will turn to a new unit, Ezekiel 25–32, composed of judgment on Judah's neighbors, that is, "oracles against the nations," similar to Isaiah 13–23 and Jeremiah 46–51.

Comparison of Isaiah, Jeremiah, and Ezekiel	
Judgment on Judah/Jerusalem	Isaiah 1–12; Jeremiah 1–29; Ezekiel 1–24
Oracles against the nations	Isaiah 13–23; Jeremiah 46–51; Ezekiel 25–32
Future restoration	Isaiah 40–55; Jeremiah 30–33; Ezekiel 33–48

EZEKIEL 17–24—JUDGMENT AND THE FALL OF JERUSALEM

Ezekiel 17 employs an analogy of two eagles and a vine to pronounce judgment on King Zedekiah, who had rebelled against Nebuchadnezzar and the Babylonians, turning to Egypt for help. Yahweh declares, "I will bring him to Babylon and execute judgment upon him there because he was unfaithful to me" (17:20). On the other hand, this chapter concludes with a brief promise of restoration (17:22–24).

"Do I take any pleasure in the death of the wicked?" declares the Lord Yahweh. "Rather, am I not pleased when they turn from their ways and live?" (Ezek. 18:23).

In Ezekiel 18 Yahweh quotes a popular proverb, "The fathers eat sour grapes, and the children's teeth are set on edge" (18:2). In Jeremiah Yahweh quotes this proverb in the context of the new covenant (Jer. 31:29), probably implying that the new covenant signaled a shift in emphasis from corporate responsibility to individual responsibility. In Ezekiel, the exiles in Babylon had probably concluded that their fate was set; they were being punished for what their fathers did and there was nothing they could do about it. In Ezekiel 18:4 Yahweh challenges this notion and states, "The soul who sins is the one who will die" (18:4). Yahweh repeats this statement in 18:20. Yahweh also gives several "case studies" to illustrate his point. If a man lives righteously and keeps Yahweh's laws, he will live (18:5–9). But if that same man has a violent, sinful son who ignores the laws of Yahweh, he will die (18:10–13). On the other hand, if the sinful son then has a son who turns from his father's sinful ways, he will live; he does not have to die for the sin of his father (18:14–20). Yahweh underscores that he does not delight in punishing the wicked; he would much prefer for them to repent (18:23). Yahweh's point seems to be directed to those exiles in Babylon who felt that how they lived had no relevance to their fate because they were being punished for the sins of their fathers. Yahweh sums up his message by exhorting them to repent and live obediently. Part of this new life, as Ezekiel explains later, is that they will then receive a "new heart and a new spirit" (18:30–32).

Ezekiel 19 is technically a funeral dirge or lament for the final kings of Judah. In reality, the poem is a parody, sarcastically ridiculing the rulers, especially the final kings of Judah. Note, for example, that Ezekiel calls them "princes" instead of "kings" (19:1).

Yahweh next reviews the sad, negative history of Israel (Ezekiel 20). Recall that in Jeremiah, Yahweh reflects on the early days of their relationship as the honeymoon of the marriage, setting up the outrage Yahweh feels when his "bride" later abandons him. In Ezekiel 20, by contrast, Yahweh dispenses with this analogy and declares quite pointedly that Israel was sinful and idolatrous from the beginning.

The Assyrian King Ashurbanipal uses a traditional sword to kill a lion. Ezekiel 21 focuses on the sword of Yahweh.

Ezekiel 21 reminds the leaders and inhabitants of Jerusalem that it is Yahweh himself who will fight against them. The main theme in this chapter is the "sword of Yahweh." Indeed, the word "sword" occurs 19 times in this chapter (89 times total in Ezekiel!). But Yahweh makes a startling identification — it is Babylonian King Nebuchadnezzar's sword that will carry out the judgment of Yahweh (21:19).

The terrible sins of Jerusalem and her leaders are reviewed in Ezekiel 22: killing innocent people (22:2–3, 6); idolatry (22:4); social injustice, that is, oppressing the foreigners, widows, and orphans (22:7); sexual sins (22:9–11); and economic sins (22:12). All of the various leaders are also included in this indictment: princes (i.e., kings and nobility) (22:25), priests (22:26), officials (22:27), and prophets (22:28). Finally, the "people of the land" are also included as participating in the social injustice being committed (22:29). It is at this point that Yahweh declares, "I looked for a man among them who would build up the wall and stand before me in the gap on behalf of the land so I would not have to destroy it, but I found none" (22:30). The entire leadership of Jerusalem had collapsed and fallen into serious sin. Jeremiah, remember, also makes this discovery as he searches the streets of Jerusalem looking for just one who is righteous (Jer. 5:1–6).

"I, Yahweh have spoken. The time has come for me to act" (Ezek. 24:14).

In Ezekiel 23 Yahweh returns to the analogy introduced in Ezekiel 16 — the sinful behavior of the two prostitute sisters, Samaria (capital of the northern kingdom Israel) and Jerusalem (capital of the southern kingdom Judah).

Ezekiel 24 brings the large unit of judgment (Ezekiel 1–24) to a conclusion, centering on the fall of Jerusalem. Judgment has been preached for several years (Ezekiel 1–23),

The ruins of Samaria, capital of Israel, destroyed by the Assyrians in 722 BC. Ezekiel's extended analogy of Ezekiel 16 and 23 describes Samaria as Judah's older promiscuous sister, ultimately destroyed by her lovers (the Assyrians).

but the people in Jerusalem and throughout Judah have not repented. As Yahweh states dramatically in 24:14, "The time has come for me to act." In 24:2 Yahweh tells Ezekiel that Nebuchadnezzar has begun the siege of Jerusalem. Recall from our study of Jeremiah that Yahweh told Jeremiah not to marry because as part of the coming judgment there would be an end to joyful celebrations like marriages. Apparently, Ezekiel was already married, for in 24:18 his wife dies, a real death that symbolized the death of Jerusalem. As Ezekiel's wife dies, so does Yahweh's "wife," Jerusalem. Yahweh tells Ezekiel not to weep or lament. Indeed, the implication is that Yahweh closes Ezekiel's mouth so that he cannot talk. Yahweh informs Ezekiel that he will hear the news of the fall from a fugitive, at which time his mouth will be opened (24:25–27). This does in fact happen, just as Yahweh foretells (33:21–22).

> Ultimately, everyone will know Yahweh, either through his judgment or through his restoration and blessing.

The sober concluding words of Ezekiel 1–24 is the familiar phase, "and they will know that I am Yahweh" (24:27). Ultimately, everyone will know Yahweh, either through his judgment (Ezekiel 1–24) or through his restoration and blessing (Ezekiel 33–44). People cannot turn their backs on him and ignore him as the elders were doing in the temple in Ezekiel 8:16.

EZEKIEL 25–32—JUDGMENT ON THE NEIGHBORING NATIONS

This section of Ezekiel contains judgment oracles directed at Judah's seven hostile neighbors. Ammon, Moab, and Edom, the three nations to the east and southeast, are addressed first. Then Yahweh addresses Philistia to the west and Tyre and Sidon to the north. Finally, Yahweh turns to Egypt, the nation to the south. Brief oracles will be presented against Ammon, Moab, Edom, Philistia, and Sidon, while rather lengthy oracles of judgment are made against Tyre and Egypt. Perhaps the reason for this focus is that Tyre and Egypt were the only two nations in the region still holding out against the Babylonians when Jerusalem fell. Throughout these oracles Yahweh repeats numerous times, "Then they [or you] will know that I am Yahweh."

> Tyre was the religious center of Baal worship and the major maritime power in the Mediterranean, thus the most powerful opponent of the Babylonians in the region.

Ammon (the modern country of Jordan—note that the capital of Jordan is still called Amman), Moab, and Edom are mentioned first. Their complicity in the destruction of Judah is cited as one of the reasons for judgment on them (compare Jeremiah's words in Jeremiah 48–49). They were minor powers in the region. Philistia likewise decreased in power throughout the Assyrian years and was now overshadowed by the power and influence of the city-state of Tyre. At the time of Ezekiel, Tyre, the religious center of Baal worship, was also the major maritime power in the Mediterranean and the most powerful opponent of the Babylonians in the region.

After Jerusalem falls, Tyre frustrates the Babylonians by holding out for another thirteen years. Thus it is no surprise that Ezekiel spends three full chapters (26–28) on this city. Ezekiel 26 declares that nations will rise up against Tyre and that her walls will become a bare rock, a place to spread nets. Even though Nebuchadnezzar doesn't actually capture the island fortress, he does capture and destroy the mainland fortress and city, thus fulfilling portions of Ezekiel 26. Alexander the Great will eventually destroy the island fortress, thus fulfilling much of this prophecy as well.

Ezekiel 27:1–24 describes Tyre's powerful maritime fleet and her economic wealth that resulted from this control of Mediterranean sea trade. In keeping with prophetic literary style, much of this chapter is poetic, coming in the form of a lament. For example, the opening lines describe the beauty of Tyre's many ships:

> You say, O Tyre,
> "I am perfect in beauty."
> Your domain was on the high seas;
> your builders brought your beauty to perfection.
> They made all your timbers
> of pine trees from Senir.

In Ezekiel 27:25–36, however, the description shifts to the poetic picture of an east wind storm that sinks the great fleet, thus ruining Tyre. This imagery is probably symbolic of the coming defeat and destruction.

Ezekiel 28 aims the judgment oracle directly at the king of Tyre. As king of one of the most powerful cities of the ancient world, sitting on the throne in an impregnable island fortress, commanding the largest fleet in the Mediterranean, and ruling over a large colonial empire that stretched across the Mediterranean, this king was understandably arrogant and proud. "I sit on the throne of a god in the heart of the seas" is probably a reference to his island fortress, but the king of Tyre goes beyond that to actually claim to be a god. Yet Yahweh declares that even though this king was lofty and powerful, adorned with unimaginable wealth, and given spectacular privilege, yet he will be judged and brought down because of his pride and his violent acts.

> Ezekiel 28 aims the judgment oracle directly at the king of Tyre.

The poetic imagery of this chapter has caused problems for some interpreters throughout church history. References like "you were in Eden" (28:13); "you were anointed as a guardian cherub" (28:14); "You were on the holy mount of God" [some translators prefer "god"] (28:14); and "I threw you to the earth" (28:17) have led some to take this passage as a description of Satan's fall from heaven. However, note that the context of these three chapters clearly refers to the actual king of Tyre. Much of the poetic imagery is drawn from the religious imagery of Canaanite mythology; indeed, many scholars maintain that this chapter spoofs Canaanite mythology. Likewise, cherubs are very common

Ruins of Tyre from the Roman era.

decorative creatures on recently discovered ivory artifacts from Tyre, indicating that cherubs played an important role in their religious mythology (the old Canaanite mythology). Notice also that the garden of Eden is used in other biblical texts as well, clearly in a figurative and not a literal sense (cf. Ezek. 31:9, where Assyria is called a tree that was the envy of the trees in the garden of Eden). Likewise the image of throwing someone from heaven to earth (28:17) is used in Lamentations 2:1 to describe Yahweh's judgment on Jerusalem carried out by the Babylonians. Most conclusive, however, is the context. This passage falls within a typical "oracles against the nations" prophetic unit. Furthermore, the surrounding text clearly identifies the recipient of this oracle as the king of Tyre. One of the reasons for

Tyre: Master of the Mediterranean

Tyre was a city on the Mediterranean coast to the north of Israel. In addition to two good harbors, this city also had two fortresses, one located on the mainland, and one on an island just offshore and across from the mainland city. Toward the end of the ninth century BC, Tyre became the leading maritime (naval and shipping) power in the Mediterranean Sea, a position she maintained at the time of Ezekiel. In 815/814 BC the people of Tyre (often called Phoenicians) founded a colony at Carthage in the western Mediterranean on the North African coast. Carthage became the center for Tyre's colonial empire in the Mediterranean. When Nebuchadnezzar defeated the Egyptians at Carchemish in 605 BC, the Egyptians withdrew from the region, retreating to Egypt. Tyre then became the major and most powerful foe of Babylon in the region. Although Tyre itself was but a city, its economic and military power (primarily from her control of the Mediterranean) in fact dwarfed that of Judah and Jerusalem. After Jerusalem fell, Nebuchadnezzar laid siege to Tyre. However, the powerful city had a strong offshore island fortress, a colonial empire, and total control of the seas. Thus Nebuchadnezzar's 13-year siege was unable to break the city. This is mentioned in Ezekiel 29:17 – 20. Nebuchadnezzar, however, finally negotiated a settlement whereby Tyre acknowledged his rule and paid tribute, but was not destroyed.

It was Alexander the Great who finally conquered and destroyed Tyre in 332 BC, actually fulfilling the prophecy of Ezekiel 26:3 – 5. Alexander, facing the same impregnable island fortress that Nebuchadnezzar had failed to capture, razed the mainland portion of Tyre to the ground and dumped the rubble in the ocean to build a causeway out to the island. This causeway, half a mile long and 200 – 300 yards wide, is still visible today. Tyre was rebuilt during the Roman era and continued to play an important role in the region during the New Testament era (siding with the Romans in the Jewish revolt of AD 66 – 70).

A model of a sixth-century Mediterranean ship similar to ones used in the fleet of Tyre.

Z. Radovan/www.BibleLandPictures.com

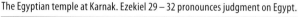

> Old Testament scholars are virtually unanimous in rejecting the interpretation that sees the fall of Satan in Ezekiel 28.

the king's "fall" was the violence associated with his widespread trade (28:16). How could this refer to the fall of Satan before humankind was even created? Old Testament scholars are virtually unanimous in rejecting the interpretation that sees the fall of Satan in Ezekiel 28. The passage is clearly an oracle against the powerful king of Tyre, who at the time was still holding out against Nebuchadnezzar, king of Babylon.

Ezekiel 29 – 32 shifts the focus to Egypt, specifically addressing Pharaoh, king of Egypt (29:1 – 6). In fact, Yahweh declares that since Nebuchadnezzar and his army fought so hard against Tyre yet came up empty, Yahweh would deliver Egypt to him instead (29:17 – 20). The next several chapters (Ezekiel 30 – 32) describe the terrible judgment coming upon Egypt.

The Egyptian temple at Karnak. Ezekiel 29 – 32 pronounces judgment on Egypt.

© Dmitriy Filippov/www.istockphoto.com

» FURTHER READING «

Allen, Leslie C. *Ezekiel 1–19*. Word Biblical Commentary. Dallas: Word Books, 1994.

_____. *Ezekiel 20–48*. Word Biblical Commentary. Dallas: Word Books, 1990.

Block, Daniel I. *The Book of Ezekiel: Chapters 1–24*. The New International Commentary on the Old Testament. Grand Rapids: Eerdmans, 1997.

_____. *The Book of Ezekiel: Chapters 25–48*. The New International Commentary on the Old Testament. Grand Rapids: Eerdmans, 1998.

Duguid, Iain M. *Ezekiel*. The NIV Application Commentary. Grand Rapids: Zondervan, 1999.

» DISCUSSION QUESTIONS «

1. In Ezekiel 20:32 Yahweh notes that the Israelites are saying, "We want to be like the nations, the peoples of the world, who serve wood and stone." In what way do Christians today long to "be like the peoples of the world"? What is it that the people of the world serve today that is attractive to some Christians?

2. In what sense do children suffer for the sins of their parents today? In light of this, how should Ezekiel 18 be understood for today?

3. In the context of Ezekiel 22, what does the phrase "stand … in the gap" (22:30) mean?

» WRITING ASSIGNMENTS «

1. In Ezekiel 28 the king of Tyre is called a cherub. What is the king of Egypt described as in 29:1–6? Also, note that the book of Exodus is the other biblical book that uses the phrase "I am Yahweh" or "that they may know that I am Yahweh" numerous times, as Ezekiel does. Discuss the irony in the comparison between Exodus 5:2 and Ezekiel 29:6.

2. Discuss the use of the phrase "that they may know that I am Yahweh" and similar phrases in Ezekiel 28:23, 24, 26; 29:6, 16, 21; 32:15. What application do these passages have for today?

3. Discuss the practice of child sacrifice (Ezek. 16:20; 20:31; 23:37, 39) in Judah.

CHAPTER 16

Ezekiel 33 — 48

"And the name of the city from that time on will be: Yahweh is there." (Ezek. 48:35)

OVERVIEW OF EZEKIEL 33–48

Remember the three-part message of the prophets: (1) You've broken the covenant. Repent! (2) No repentance? Then judgment (both on Israel/Judah and on the nations); and (3) Yet there is hope beyond the judgment for a glorious restoration. Ezekiel 1–24 focused on the first two points in regard to Judah/Jerusalem, and in Ezekiel 24 Jerusalem falls. Ezekiel 25–32 applied the judgment theme to the surrounding nations. This section (25–32) is a little like a parenthesis, interrupting the smooth flow from Ezekiel 24 to Ezekiel 33 (a transition chapter). In the final unit (Ezekiel 34–48), after the fall of Jerusalem, Yahweh points to the future, stressing the final point of the prophetic message—future hope and restoration. Because Israel and Judah rebelled against Yahweh and the covenant he gave them, his presence left the temple (Ezekiel 8–10).

> Yahweh promises a (new) covenant in which he will put his Spirit within his people.

Both Jerusalem and the temple have been destroyed. In this final unit, Yahweh now reverses many of these judgment events. New life and restoration becomes the focus. Yahweh promises a (new) covenant in which he will put his Spirit within his people. A Davidic king will come to shepherd the people in justice and peace. Finally, the last chapters (40–48) describe a spectacular future temple. The glory of Yahweh (as seen by Ezekiel in his opening vision in Ezekiel 1) returns to the temple and the presence of Yahweh then dwells there with his people—indeed, "Yahweh is there" becomes the name of the new city.

EZEKIEL 33—THE FALL OF JERUSALEM AND THE TRANSITION TO RESTORATION

Ezekiel 33 functions somewhat like a transition, carrying the message from judgment into the hope of Ezekiel 34. Yahweh declares that the people have sinned repeatedly and thus deserve judgment, but he also states that such judgment is not fixed or fatalistic. As in the book of Jeremiah, throughout the book of Ezekiel Yahweh and his prophet continue to call for repentance because true repentance will avert the judgment. Yahweh restates the truth that he takes no pleasure in judging the wicked and would much prefer them to repent and be saved (33:11).

> Yahweh and his prophet continue to call for repentance because true repentance will avert the judgment.

Ezekiel 33:21 picks up right after Ezekiel 24:26–27. In that text Yahweh told Ezekiel to expect a survivor to come from Jerusalem to report on the fall (24:26). In 33:21 a survivor does come and report. In 24:27 Yahweh states that this report will remove Ezekiel's inability to speak. Indeed, 33:22 records that Yahweh opened the mouth of his prophet. The implication is that Ezekiel will now be able to proclaim the coming future restoration. However, first Yahweh continues to deal with the people who are with Ezekiel in exile in Babylonia. Yahweh notes their hypocritical attitude: "With their mouths they express devotion, but their hearts are greedy for unjust gain" (33:31).

EZEKIEL 34—YAHWEH THE SHEPHERD

Ezekiel 34 introduces the larger unit on restoration. This entire chapter uses the shepherding image as the major motif. In 34:1–10 Yahweh declares that Israel's current shepherds (i.e., leaders) are greedy and selfish, and have not cared for the weak or sick. Remember that Jeremiah and Ezekiel both devote much of their prophetic message to criticizing the ineffectual, rebellious, and arrogant leadership of Israel/Judah. Yahweh underscores how terrible these leaders have been and then declares that he will rescue the people *from them* (34:10). Yahweh then promises that he himself will come to shepherd his flock. In contrast to these bad shepherds, Yahweh will shepherd with justice and will care for the weak (34:11–16). An interesting transition takes place in 34:23–24 as Yahweh—who has been saying that he will be the new shepherd—suddenly states that he will raise up a Davidic king to be the shepherd. This enigmatic mix of shepherds (is the shepherd Yahweh or a Davidic king?) becomes clear in the New Testament when Jesus claims to be the "Good Shepherd" (John 10).

> Yahweh promises that he himself will come to shepherd his flock.

Likewise, closely connected to the promise of a Davidic king as shepherd is the promise of a (new) covenant (34:25). Ezekiel calls it a "covenant of peace" rather than a "new covenant" as Jeremiah did, but the implications are certainly that this "covenant of peace" is part of the same new, wonderful time of blessing that Jeremiah proclaimed with the "new covenant." The foundational covenant formula language ("I will be your god; you will be my people; I will dwell in your midst") dominates Ezekiel 34:25–31.

Jesus draws from Ezekiel 34 for his shepherd imagery.

Shepherds were common in the Ancient Near East and were associated with the care and protection of their flocks; therefore, it was quite common for kings and the scribes in the service of these kings to employ shepherd imagery in extolling the king and underscoring his great care for his people. The Old Testament is thus not unique in using shepherd imagery to refer to the kings and other leaders of Israel and Judah. The prophets use the shepherd metaphor quite frequently, both in regard to good kings (and other good leaders) and to bad kings (and other bad leaders). The good shepherds are those who are just, righteous, and faithful, while the bad shepherds are those who are unjust, self-seeking, lazy, and unfaithful. Leaders of Israel and Judah that are frequently included in the bad shepherd category are the king, priests, nobility, and false prophets. Typically accompanying the "bad shepherd" critique are warnings and pronouncements of judgment (Jer. 10:21; 12:10; 23:1–2; Ezek. 34:1–10; Zech. 11:17), often expressed directly by Yahweh himself. Thus Yahweh declares in Jeremiah 23:1, "Woe to the shepherds who are destroying and scattering the sheep of my pasture!" Yahweh orders Ezekiel: "Prophesy against the shepherds of Israel … Woe to the shepherds of Israel who only take care of themselves! Should not shepherds take care of the flock?" (Ezek. 34:2).

One of the new and better aspects of the coming messianic era that Yahweh promises through the prophets will be the end to Israel's corrupt and selfish leadership and the establishment of a Davidic king who will rule justly and righteously. This coming righteous, just, and caring leader is often described with typical shepherd imagery. This imagery is especially appropriate because it combines strong, powerful protection of the flock with self-sacrifice and compassionate, tender care. Micah 5:4 declares that this coming ruler will shepherd the flock in the strength of Yahweh, providing true peace. In some passages Yahweh himself is the one who shepherds the flock (e.g., Isa. 40:10–11; Ezek. 34:11–16).

As we turn to the New Testament, we see strong echoes of the Old Testament prophetic use of shepherd imagery. In John 10:11 and 10:14 Jesus identifies himself with the shepherd prophecies by proclaiming, "I am the good shepherd." There is little doubt that Jesus is drawing from Ezekiel 34 with this statement. In John 10 Jesus delivers a detailed homily contrasting thieves and robbers (the bad leaders) with himself, the good shepherd who cares for and protects the sheep. The analogy is very similar to that found in Ezekiel 34. The New Testament frequently presents Jesus as the one who fulfills the Old Testament prophetic promises of the coming righteous shepherd. Indeed, all of the great virtues that the prophets assign to the coming shepherd are reflected in Christ. The book of Revelation continues the shepherd imagery, stating ironically that Jesus is both the Lamb and the shepherd, "For the Lamb at the center of the throne will be their shepherd" (7:17).

EZEKIEL 35–36 — EDOM, THE NATIONS, AND CLEANSING FOR YAHWEH'S PEOPLE

Ezekiel has already delivered a brief oracle against Edom (25:12–14). In Ezekiel 35 Edom is probably symbolic or representative of the nations in general (note the use of "wild animals" to represent the nations in 34:28). Ezekiel 36 is closely connected. In this chapter Yahweh states that Israel has "defiled" the Land itself by her sin. Likewise, as Israel was scattered among the nations, she became "unclean" and also profaned the name of Yahweh. For restoration to proceed, cleansing is needed, and Yahweh addresses the issue of cleansing in 36:24–38. Yahweh declares that he himself will cleanse them. Furthermore, he will give them a "new heart," and he will put his Spirit in them (36:26–27). It will be the Spirit of Yahweh that enables them to live obediently (36:27). Thus one of the significant additions that Ezekiel contributes to the prophetic picture of the future restoration is an introduction to the strengthening and empowering role the Spirit will play. Note also that the giving of the Spirit is closely connected to the theme of Yahweh's presence, a connection made clear in the New Testament as the presence of God in the temple is replaced with the presence of God in each believer's life (a "temple" of sorts) through the indwelling Spirit.

> Edom is probably symbolic or representative of the nations in general.

EZEKIEL 37 — NEW LIFE FOR THOSE WHO ARE REALLY, REALLY DEAD

In Ezekiel 37 Yahweh takes the prophet to a valley of dry bones, probably an old battlefield where the slain soldiers were left on the field where they fell. After years of scavenger animals, decay, and the bleaching action of the sun, all that now remains are bleached white bones scattered across the field. The point is that these people are really, really dead. Yahweh, however, tells Ezekiel to prophesy to the bones, telling them that Yahweh will breathe life into them. This chapter contains an extended wordplay, for one Hebrew word (*rūah*) can mean "breath," "wind," or "spirit," and all three meanings are used in this chapter. In fact, this word occurs ten times in Ezekiel 37, including four occurrences in one verse (37:9).

The meaning of this chapter is tied to Ezekiel's message of hope for the future restoration. If Yahweh can bring life back to those dead, dried, scattered bones, then he can bring life back to anyone, including scattered, defeated Israel. Playing a central role in this return to life is the empowering presence of Yahweh's Spirit (37:14), connecting this chapter back to the promise of Yahweh's Spirit in 36:27. Likewise, in Ezekiel 37:26 Yahweh promises a covenant of peace — an eternal covenant. He also restates the covenant formula ("I will be your God; you will be my people") several times.

The Edomites were replaced by the Nabateans, who built the spectacular rock-city of Petra.

EZEKIEL 38–39 — A FUTURE INVASION

In contrast to the covenant of peace promised in 37:26, Ezekiel 38–39 appears to describe a future battle that takes place after the return and restoration (note that in 38:11 Israel is at rest, living peacefully and unsuspecting). Apparently, in regard to the nations, there is more to be said that will take place in the far future. In Ezekiel 38 the prophet describes a coalition of nations that attacks peaceful Israel. There are seven nations from the north,

Who Is Gog, and Where in the World Is Magog?

The word of Yahweh comes to Ezekiel in chapters 38 and 39, telling him to prophesy against Gog: "Son of man, set your face against Gog, of the land of Magog, the chief prince of Meshech and Tubal; prophesy against him" (Ezek. 38:2). Who or what is Gog? Several scholars suggest that during the time of Ezekiel the names Gog and Magog were associated with the land of Lydia in Anatolia (modern Turkey). On the other hand, evidence for this understanding is meager. The evidence is much clearer in regard to Meshech and Tubal, those regions that Gog is said to rule over. The names Meshech and Tubal occur in Assyrian literature several times, associated fairly clearly with groups in Anatolia (modern Turkey). Ezekiel 38:5 – 6 lists five more nations, bringing the number of nations in the eschatological alliance that Gog leads to seven. These seven nations are from areas associated with the north, south, east, and west; thus, this list of nations appears to represent a worldwide alliance against Israel.

Gog and Magog appear again in Revelation 20:7 – 8: "When the thousand years are over, Satan will be released from his prison and will go out to deceive the nations in the four corners of the earth — Gog and Magog — to gather them for battle." In this passage Gog and Magog seem to symbolize nations from around the world. Many scholars propose that Gog and his alliance in Ezekiel 38 are functioning in a similar fashion. That is, this alliance symbolizes worldwide opposition and not necessarily specific nations.

On the other hand, throughout history numerous attempts have been made to identify Gog with a specific historical entity. Because there is a certain amount of ambiguity surrounding his identity, writers throughout the ages have been quite imaginative, frequently identifying Gog with hostile groups contemporary with them. For example, writers have identified Gog with the Goths (fourth century), the Arabs (seventh century), or the Mongols (thirteenth century). Gog has also been identified with various Roman emperors, popes, or the Turks.[1]

This line of interpretation is extremely questionable, for these writers apparently strive to identify Gog with whatever contemporary hostile nation or leader can possibly be connected by whatever means possible, even employing the flimsiest of evidence. In this tradition the Scofield Reference Bible, published in the early twentieth century, identifies Meshech and Tubal as the Russian cities of Moscow and Tobolsk, thus concluding that Gog must refer to Russia. Several "pop prophecy" writers continue to advocate this understanding even today. Almost all evangelical Old Testament scholars today dismiss this understanding, however, noting that the terms in this text (e.g., *rosh*, Hebrew for "chief" or "head"; 38:2) have absolutely nothing to do with modern Russia. Likewise, the only thing connecting Meshech to Moscow is that they both start with the letter "M," rather dubious and fanciful evidence (perhaps it means Minneapolis? Or Memphis?) that is unrelated to serious biblical exegesis.

---

1. Iain M. Duguid, *Ezekiel,* NIV Application Commentary (Grand Rapids: Zondervan, 1999), 452.

south, east, and west (a "perfect coalition"); thus, it is likely that these specific nations are representative or symbolic of a large future coalition of nations.

As Assyria and Babylonia had attacked Israel in the past, so a "perfect coalition" of nations will also attack Israel in the future, but this time Yahweh intervenes and defeats them. No longer will Yahweh's people experience shame and defeat, for Yahweh will demonstrate his glory through them and pour out his Spirit on them (39:25–29).

Ezekiel 38–39 plays an important role in the end times events as understood by many popular prophecy writers. Many of them argue that these chapters describe an imminent (from today's point of view) invasion of Israel that will be carried out by modern Russia and her Muslim allies. Although these chapters have several interpretive difficulties, most Old Testament scholars (dispensationalists and non-dispensationalist alike) maintain that this passage has nothing to do with modern Russia (or Islam). In fact, most scholars tend to lean toward a view that understands this chapter as a symbolic, figurative picture of hostility by Israel's worldwide enemies (i.e., attacks by seven nations from the four corners of the earth symbolizes a worldwide opposition). Of course, as mentioned throughout this book, scholars differ on their interpretation of the prophetic use of "Israel," some maintaining that these references are literal, referring to a literal restored Israel in the physical land of Palestine, and some see the references as figurative references to the church, which replaces Israel (see the discussion in chapter 5).

> In Ezekiel 38 the prophet describes a coalition of nations that attacks peaceful Israel.

EZEKIEL 40–48 — THE NEW TEMPLE AND THE PRESENCE OF YAHWEH

In Ezekiel 40–48 the prophet brings his book to a climactic close by describing in detail the new temple of the future. As stressed over and over again in the earlier chapters of Ezekiel, sin and covenant disobedience have destroyed the relationship between Yahweh and his people, causing the presence of Yahweh to depart from the temple in Jerusalem (Ezekiel 8–10), which was then totally destroyed. Yet in contrast, Ezekiel 40–48 describes a new and spectacular temple, along with the personnel, supplies, and storerooms — everything needed to operate it. In Ezekiel 43:1–12 the prophet sees Yahweh return to the temple, dramatically proclaiming that "the glory of Yahweh filled the temple" (43:5).

Ezekiel 47:1–12 describes a river flowing out of the temple. This description is similar in several respects to that of

> In Ezekiel 40–48 the prophet brings his book to a climactic close by describing in detail the new temple of the future.

A surveyor in ancient Egypt with measuring cord in hand.

Werner Forman Archive

The plan of Ezekiel's temple.

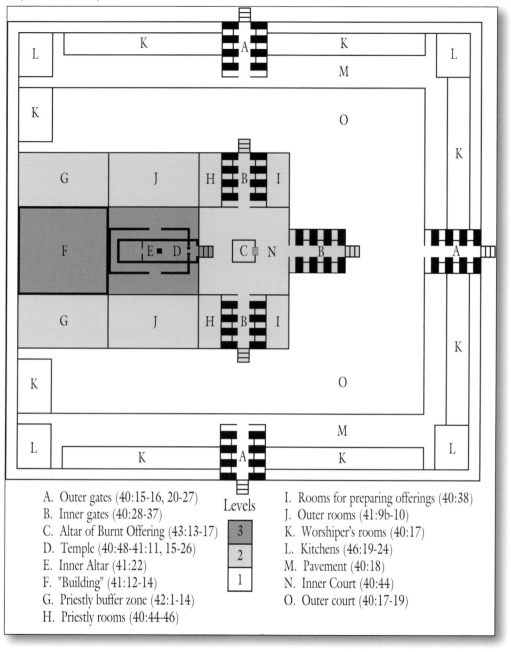

A. Outer gates (40:15-16, 20-27)
B. Inner gates (40:28-37)
C. Altar of Burnt Offering (43:13-17)
D. Temple (40:48-41:11, 15-26)
E. Inner Altar (41:22)
F. "Building" (41:12-14)
G. Priestly buffer zone (42:1-14)
H. Priestly rooms (40:44-46)

Levels

3
2
1

I. Rooms for preparing offerings (40:38)
J. Outer rooms (41:9b-10)
K. Worshiper's rooms (40:17)
L. Kitchens (46:19-24)
M. Pavement (40:18)
N. Inner Court (40:44)
O. Outer court (40:17-19)

NT Connection: The New Temple

The loss of the temple in 587/586 BC is devastating to the religious life and faith of Israel, for the temple is the focal point of Yahweh's presence. Thus, as the prophets speak of the future time of restoration, included in the wonderful prophecies of the glorious restoration are visions of a "new temple." Ezekiel is the primary prophet that develops the "new temple" theme, but other prophets mention it as well (see Isa. 56:7; 66:18–21; Hag. 2:9; Zech. 14:16–21).

The New Testament makes numerous allusions as well as direct connections to the concept of a new temple. John states that the "Word (Jesus) became flesh and lived (lit. 'tabernacled') among us" (John 1:14). Throughout the Gospels, many of the things that Jesus did are related to the Old Testament prophets' words in regard to the temple. In a manner reminiscent of the prophets, Jesus clearly predicts the destruction of the temple (Mark 11:12–25; 13:1–2). In Mark 14:57–58 and John 2:19–22, Jesus refers to replacing the destroyed physical temple with a temple "not made with hands," an allusion to himself. Jesus prophesies that he himself will be the new temple that replaces the old material temple as the embodiment of God's presence.

In Acts and in the Pauline letters, the imagery of the new temple is applied to the church. God now places his Spirit (presence) into believers; thus, the new church becomes the location for the presence of God previously located in the temple (Joel 2:28–29; Acts 2:1–4). Along these same lines, Paul tells the young church, "You yourselves are God's temple" since "God's Spirit lives in you" (1 Cor. 3:16; 2 Cor. 6:16; Eph. 2:21–22).

The book of Revelation makes several references to God's people serving him in the temple (Rev. 3:12; 7:9, 14–15). Likewise, Revelation 21:2–3 connects the New Jerusalem to the most basic Old Testament covenant language regarding God's presence, "Now the dwelling of God is with men, and he will live with them."

At the end of Revelation, however, John declares, "I did not see a temple in the city" (21:22). This is rather surprising at first, but John continues by explaining, "because the Lord God Almighty and the Lamb are its temple."[1]

---

1. J. Daniel Hays, J. Scott Duvall, and C. Marvin Pate, *Dictionary of Biblical Prophecy and End Times* (Grand Rapids: Zondervan, 2007), 312–13.

Revelation 22:1–3. This river, flowing out of the temple and getting deeper as it travels, gives life to everything along its banks (Ezek. 47:1–12). As mentioned earlier, the book of Ezekiel ends on a most important note—the presence of Yahweh, "And the name of the city from that time on will be: Yahweh is there." Thus, as Ezekiel looks to the future ultimate restoration and blessing, he is underscoring how important the presence of Yahweh will be in that scheme.

As in many other portions of prophetic literature that describe Israel's restoration, interpreters take differing views on Ezekiel 40–48. Some argue that it describes a literal temple that will be built in Jerusalem and used during the literal 1000-year reign of Christ. Others suggest that the focus of the passage may be on that future millennial temple but that it also has allusions and connections to the final new city of Jerusalem in Revelation

Courtesy of www.HolyLandPhotos.org

A model of the temple in the time of Jesus. Like the OT prophets, the NT writers speak of the end of the earthly temple, to be replaced with something much greater — the presence of God (Rev. 21 – 22).

21 – 22. They underscore the prophets' tendency to merge future pictures from differing time periods together into one vision. Still others maintain that Ezekiel 40 – 48 is almost totally symbolic and is thus fulfilled primarily in Christ (the new temple) and yet perhaps also pointing to the heavenly city in Revelation 21 – 22.

» FURTHER READING «

Beale, Greg K. *The Temple and the Church's Mission: A Biblical Theology of the Dwelling Place of God.* New Studies in Biblical Theology, ed. D. A. Carson. Downers Grove, IL: InterVarsity, 2004.

Block, Daniel I. *The Book of Ezekiel: Chapters 25 – 48.* New International Commentary on the Old Testament. Grand Rapids: Eerdmans, 1998.

Chisholm, Robert B. *Handbook on the Prophets.* Grand Rapids: Baker, 2002, 275 – 86.

Duguid, Iain M. *Ezekiel.* NIV Application Commentary. Grand Rapids: Zondervan, 1999.

1. How does Ezekiel 37 give encouragement to those today who feel they have no hope?

2. Do you think the temple described by Ezekiel in 40 – 48 is a real, literal temple or a symbolic one?

3. What is the significance for today of the presence of Yahweh theme that is stressed so much in Ezekiel?

» WRITING ASSIGNMENTS «

1. Read Ezekiel 34 and answer the following:

   A. What is the situation of Israel and Judah when Ezekiel prophesies this? (Note 33:21 as well as the introduction to Ezekiel.) Who are the "bad" shepherds, and what does Yahweh accuse them of? What specific things will Yahweh do when he comes as the shepherd? Is the promise in this message meant to be fulfilled in the future or in the time when Ezekiel delivers it?

   B. Compare Psalm 23 with Ezekiel 34. Does Psalm 23 reflect a present or future situation? Do the two passages differ on this perspective? Why?

   C. Read the following passages and compare them with Ezekiel 34:

   > John 10:1 – 18
   > Matt. 9:35 – 36
   > Matt. 10:6 – 8
   > Matt. 18:12 – 14
   > Matt. 25:31 – 33
   > 1 Peter 5:1 – 4

   D. If you were to preach Ezekiel 34 today, the sermon might fall into two main parts. Part 1 would explain the passage as it applied to Ezekiel's audience. Essentially this is what you did in answering A above. Part 2 would then involve applying these same points to today's audience. Answer the four questions of A above in the context of preaching this to today's audience. Identify (a) our situation, (b) the "bad" shepherds and their impact on us and our scattering, (c) the identity of the good shepherd and what he offers to do for us, and (d) whether this promise is future or present.

2. Compare and contrast the temple and the river in Ezekiel 47:1 – 12 with that in Revelation 21 – 22.

CHAPTER 17

Daniel 1 — 6

"His kingdom will not be destroyed, his dominion will never end. He rescues and he saves; he performs signs and wonders in the heavens and on the earth."

(Dan. 6:26b – 27a)

OVERVIEW OF DANIEL

Setting

The book of Daniel contains several historical superscriptions, indicating that the events and prophecies in the book spanned much of the sixth century BC. Daniel 1:1 dates the beginning of the book to the third year of Jehoiakim (605 BC). Nebuchadnezzar has defeated the Egyptians at Carchemish and has then moved south into Palestine, besieging Jerusalem, an event not mentioned in 2 Kings or in Jeremiah. Jehoiakim quickly surrenders, and Nebuchadnezzar carries away some items from the temple as well as some of the noble youth.[1] Daniel is one of the young men of the upper class who are carried off to Babylon to be trained in Babylonian administration. In this sense he is among the first group of exiles to be taken from Jerusalem to Babylonia. He continues to work for the Babylonian kings throughout the remaining years of the Babylonian empire, witnessing the nearly total destruction and exile of Judah and Jerusalem. The book of Daniel continues into the Persian era, with the last historical reference in the book tied to the third year of King Cyrus of Persia (i.e., 537 BC). The book of Daniel is thus similar

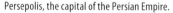

The book of Daniel is similar in setting to Ezekiel, taking place in Babylonia and addressing the disheartened and disillusioned remnant of Israel.

---

1. For a good discussion of the historical problems associated with Daniel 1:1–2, see Tremper Longman III, *Daniel,* NIV Application Commentary (Grand Rapids: Zondervan, 1999), 43–45.

Persepolis, the capital of the Persian Empire.

© Stefan Baum/www.istockphoto.com

In the three-part division of the Hebrew canon, Daniel is located in the Writings (between Esther and Ezra) instead of in the prophets. Thus, in early Jewish tradition, Daniel was often connected to the wisdom tradition, and the material in Daniel was used for instruction in wise living. In the Septuagint, however, and followed by most Christian Bibles, the book of Daniel is located with the prophets, following Ezekiel and preceding the Book of the Twelve. Matthew 24:15 refers to Daniel as a prophet, and Christian tradition has generally followed that connection and interpreted Daniel as a prophetic figure, placing him in the prophetic tradition.

The Septuagint version of Daniel also contains several additions that are not in the Hebrew text and thus have not been included in Protestant Bibles. Catholic editions of the Bible, on the other hand, have retained these additions as well as other texts from the Apocrypha. These additions to Daniel are four texts referred to as the Prayer of Azariah, the Song of the Three Jews, Susanna, and Bel and the Dragon.

in setting to Ezekiel, taking place in Babylonia and addressing the disheartened and disillusioned remnant of Israel.

Scholars are divided over many of the issues relating to the setting of Daniel (date, authorship, audience, etc.). Most evangelical scholars conclude that the book of Daniel is historical and that the prophecies do indeed come from the sixth century BC.[2] That will be the view expressed in this book. A few evangelicals, along with nonevangelical scholarship, date most, if not all, of the book to the second century BC.[3]

Message

Daniel is part of the prophetic tradition, but his central focus does not follow the three-part message followed by the other prophetic books we have studied. Even though the latter half of Daniel is difficult to interpret with certainty, the central message of Daniel is unmistakable: God is sovereign and rules over all people and kingdoms even though it does not always look that way. Although the Babylonians (and then the Persians) seem to control the world, Daniel proclaims that Yahweh is still very much in control and is moving to bring history itself to his divinely directed culmination. Thus there is much more to history than is often apparent on the surface. In the meantime, the true and faithful followers of God can expect to suffer, but they can endure the suffering in the knowledge that God will ultimately bring history to a climax centered on the establishment of his kingdom.[4]

Structurally, Daniel is traditionally broken down into two parts. Daniel 1–6 is made up of stories about the life of Daniel and his Jewish compatriots in the royal courts of Babylon. Daniel 7–12, on the other hand, is made up of Daniel's prophecies about world empires. The genre of the first half (1–6) is narrative, and the stories are fairly easy to follow. However, the genre of the second half (7–12) is primarily apocalyptic (see the discussion

---

2. See, for example, Longman, *Daniel.*

3. See, for example, John E. Goldingay, *Daniel,* Word Biblical Commentary (Dallas: Word Books, 1989).

4. Joyce G. Baldwin, "Daniel, Theology of," in *New International Dictionary of Old Testament Theology and Exegesis,* ed. Willem A. VanGemeren (Grand Rapids: Zondervan, 1997), 4:502–503.

of this genre in chapter 3), and therefore not as straightforward or easy to interpret. Yet, although the genre shifts dramatically between Daniel 6 and 7, numerous aspects unite the book and/or suggest other possible ways of viewing the structure.

If one reads the text in the original languages, one is struck by the fact that part of the book of Daniel is written in Hebrew and part in Aramaic (the official court language of the Babylonians). Linguistically, the breakdown is as follows:

Daniel 1:1–2:4a	Hebrew
Daniel 2:4b–7:28	Aramaic
Daniel 8:1–12:13	Hebrew

Within the Aramaic section, Nebuchadnezzar's vision of four world empires in Daniel 2 is paralleled by Daniel's vision of four world empires in Daniel 7, suggesting a structural connection between the two chapters. Joyce Baldwin suggests that the Aramaic section (Daniel 2–7) is structured in a chiastic fashion, as follows:

A[1] Four empires and God's coming kingdom (ch. 2)

    B[1] Trial by fire and God's deliverance (ch. 3)

        C[1] A king warned, chastised and delivered (ch. 4)

        C[2] A king warned, defiant and deposed (ch. 5)

    B[2] Trial in the lions' den and God's deliverance (ch. 6)

A[2] Four empires and God's everlasting kingdom (ch. 7)[5]

Although there have been attempts to organize the entire book as a chiastic structure with the major break between Daniel 5 and 6,[6] this proposal has not found wide acceptance. Rather, most scholars continue to see the major break between Daniel 6 and 7, acknowledging at the same time that there are parallel themes and numerous connections across the break. The central theme of Daniel 1–6 is God demonstrating that he is more powerful than the monarchs of Babylon and Persia. Daniel 7–12 focuses on God's plan for the future in regard to world kingdoms and especially in regard to his kingdom. Across the entire book each chapter forms a coherent unit, with the three final chapters (10–12) combining to form the concluding unit.

> The central theme of Daniel 1–6 is God demonstrating that he is more powerful than the monarchs of Babylon and Persia.

DANIEL 1 — DANIEL AND THE BABYLONIAN CAFETERIA

Daniel 1 tells how Daniel and three other young Hebrew men were taken to Babylon and placed in a special school to be trained in Babylonian language and literature. Apparently this training was to prepare these men to enter into government service, filling some of the many administrative positions in the extensive Babylonian Empire. Daniel and his three

---

5. Ibid., "Daniel," 4:499–500.
6. D. W. Gooding, "The Literary Structure of the Book of Daniel and Its Implications," *Tyndale Bulletin* 32 (1981): 43–79.

friends are given Babylonian names and immersed in Babylonian education. They are given expensive food from the king's court. Young Daniel and his friends, however, stay faithful to God and to the law of Moses, refusing to eat this defiled food. Perhaps this food violated the dietary laws of the Torah, but more probably the food and drink at the royal court was regularly part of offerings to the Babylonian gods. God honors these young men, causing the official in charge of them to be favorable toward them. God also gives them understanding and knowledge so that they excel in this school beyond the others. In addition, Daniel is able to understand dreams and visions. Note the similarity between Daniel (in Babylon) and Joseph (in Egypt; Genesis 37, 39–45). Both young men stay faithful in a foreign country and God enables both to interpret the troubling dream of a king when no one else can.

The Ishtar Gate from Babylon, reconstructed in the Pergamum Museum in Berlin.

Daniel 1:21 states that Daniel thus stayed in the administrative service throughout the remaining years of the Babylonian Empire until the first year of Cyrus the Persian. Thus the text quietly mentions the one who will conquer the Babylonians, who have captured these faithful Hebrew young men.

Through this simple opening story about diet, Daniel 1 introduces the main theme of the book. Daniel and his young friends are in a difficult situation that pressures them to compromise their faith in God. They remain faithful, however, and God works in their lives to protect and bless them within the Babylonian administration. Thus they become models for the exiles and for later Hebrews who find themselves under foreign domination.

Young Daniel and his friends stay faithful to God and to the law of Moses.

DANIEL 2—A DREAM ABOUT WORLD EMPIRES

In Daniel 2 Nebuchadnezzar, king of the Babylonians, has a troubling dream. He calls in the court professionals (magicians, enchanters, sorcerers, and "astrologers," lit. "Chaldeans") to interpret the dream for him, but he refuses to tell them the dream, thinking that if they really know the true meaning of the dream they should be able to determine by divine power what the dream was about. They are unable to do this, and thus Nebuchadnezzar decides to kill all of the men in this category, that is, those who were educated and were trained in interpreting dreams and prophesying the future. Keep in mind that these were the same people who, like Daniel, were also trained in literature and administration. Thus Daniel and his friends fall under the same decree.

Daniel, however, prays to God, and God reveals the dream of Nebuchadnezzar to him. Daniel then goes to the king and explains the dream and its meaning to him. The dream is

Names for God in the Book of Daniel

One of the differences between Daniel and the rest of the prophetic books is that while all of the other prophetic books use the name Yahweh regularly as their main name and reference to God, the book of Daniel has a preference for Elohim ("God"). As mentioned earlier, Yahweh is generally used in contexts of his covenant relationship with people, primarily Israel. Thus the name Yahweh predominates throughout the prophetic literature, both in the prayers and addresses of the prophets and in the narrative descriptive texts. Daniel, however, is focusing on world empires rather than on Israel, so he shows a preference for references to God that reflect God's relationship to and sovereignty over the entire world. Thus in Daniel terms like "God of heaven," "the great God," and "God of gods" are the common references to God. However, in the great confessional prayer of Daniel 9, especially in the context of Jeremiah the prophet and the history of Israel (9:2), Daniel repeatedly refers to "Yahweh my God" or to "Yahweh our God," indicating that concepts of covenant are not entirely absent from the book.

of a large statue built of differing materials. The head is gold, the chest and arms are silver, the belly and thighs are bronze, the legs are iron, and the feet are a mixture of iron and clay. A rock comes and smashes the statue to pieces.

Daniel explains to Nebuchadnezzar that the dream is about successive world kingdoms. The head of gold represents Nebuchadnezzar and the Babylonian Empire. The silver represents the next empire (probably the Persians), and so forth, until at the end God himself comes (the rock) and destroys the human kingdoms and establishes his own eternal kingdom. These four kingdoms of Daniel 2 are similar to the four kingdoms in Daniel's vision in Daniel 7. In the following chapter, we will discuss the differing interpretations regarding which kingdoms in history are being represented by these visions. It is important

> Daniel explains to Nebuchadnezzar that the dream is about successive world kingdoms.

to note that in Daniel 2 God reveals the future through a dream to the pagan King Nebuchadnezzar. However, Nebuchadnezzar can only understand the truth of the dream when it is interpreted by the divinely empowered Daniel. The point of the dream looks to the future, reminding everyone that in spite of all its spectacular glory, the Babylonian Empire is temporary and will not last. Likewise, the empires that follow diminish in glory (gold to silver to bronze to iron to iron mixed with clay) and are finally destroyed by God, who is stronger and more powerful than all of them. He will then establish his kingdom.

After Daniel explains the dream to Nebuchadnezzar, the king declares, "Surely your God is the God of gods and the Lord of kings" (2:47). Nebuchadnezzar then appoints Daniel and his three friends to significant administrative positions.

DANIEL 3 — THE FIERY FURNACE

Daniel 3 recounts the well-known story of Nebuchadnezzar's attempt to execute Daniel's three friends, Shadrach, Meshach, and Abednego, in a raging fire. The chapter deals with the difficult problem of idolatry during the exile. How were the Hebrew exiles to resist worshipping idols when their captors insisted on it? Daniel's three friends provide the model of faithfulness to God and resistance to pagan idolatry.

Nebuchadnezzar constructs a huge new idol of gold and orders everyone to bow down and worship it. Shadrach, Meshach, and Abednego (their Babylonian names) refuse to worship this idol, even at the specific direct order of the Babylonian king accompanied by a direct threat of execution. Indeed, Nebuchadnezzar threatens to throw them into the furnace (probably a kiln for making glazed bricks, for which Babylon was famous). Ironically, he asks, "Then what god will be able to rescue you from my hand?" (3:15).

When the king looks into the fire, he sees them unbound, unharmed, and walking around in the fire, accompanied by a fourth person, one who "looks like a son of the gods."

Nebuchadnezzar orders his men to throw the three young Hebrews into the raging hot furnace, but when the king looks into the fire, he sees them unbound, unharmed, and walking around in the fire, accompanied by a fourth person, one who "looks like a son of the gods" (3:25). Nebuchadnezzar orders them released from the fire and proclaims, "Praise be to the God of Shadrach, Meshach and Abednego, who has sent his angel and rescued his servants!" (3:28).

Note the irony of the passage. First of all, Nebuchadnezzar, who had asked sarcastically, "What god will be able to rescue you?" answers his own question with the proclamation, "Praise be to the God of Shadrach, Meshach and Abednego, who has sent his angel and rescued his servants." Note also the reversal in regard to who is worshipping whom. The three Hebrew men refuse to acknowledge or worship Nebuchadnezzar's god, and in contrast the king ends up praising (worshipping and acknowledging) their God.

There is also another important ironic theological statement regarding the power of Nebuchadnezzar over the Hebrews. Nebuchadnezzar, King of the Babylonians, was the one who destroyed Jerusalem, executed thousands of Jews, and then burned Jerusalem to the ground, destroying it completely. Yet in this episode, he is unable to kill three young Hebrew men in his own backyard. The power of Yahweh is not restricted, and Yahweh operates freely throughout the world, even in the royal courtyards of Babylon itself. This demonstration of Yahweh's protective power also shows that Nebuchadnezzar and the gods of Babylon did not succeed in conquering Jerusalem because they are more powerful than Yahweh, the God of Israel. The God of Israel can defy Nebuchadnezzar and rescue his people whenever he chooses, even in the heart of Babylon itself. Jerusalem did not fall because God was unable to defend it; it fell because of covenant violation. Indeed, God himself brought on the Babylonians (the message of Jeremiah and Ezekiel).

Nebuchadnezzar, the one who burned Jerusalem to the ground, is unable to kill three young Hebrew men in his own backyard.

One wonders if Shadrach, Meshach, and Abednego were familiar with Isaiah 43:2–3, "When you walk through the fire, you will not be burned; the flames will not set you ablaze. For I am Yahweh your God, the Holy One of Israel, your Savior." Likewise, while the specific identity of the fourth person in the furnace is not given (in 3:28 Nebuchadnezzar seems to suggest it is an angel; note also the mention of the angels Gabriel and Michael later in the book), the event points to the frequent prophetic theme that promises Yahweh's empowering presence.

DANIEL 4—NEBUCHADNEZZAR'S VISION OF A TREE

Daniel 4 reflects a slightly different literary genre than Daniel 1–3, for it is in the form of a decree or document of Nebuchadnezzar. Most of the account is in first person, although 4:19–33 is in third person. The chapter opens and closes with Nebuchadnezzar praising God and acknowledging God's great power.

Daniel 3 had demonstrated that God could deliver his people out of the hand of Nebuchadnezzar, even right in Babylon. Daniel 4 takes the power and sovereignty of God a big step further, for in this chapter God demands that Nebuchadnezzar, the most powerful man in the world, humble himself and acknowledge that God has sovereign control over all things.

> God demands that Nebuchadnezzar, the most powerful man in the world, humble himself and acknowledge that God has sovereign control over all things.

Nebuchadnezzar has a dream concerning a great tree that is cut down, leaving its stump exposed to the rain. Daniel alone is able to interpret the dream, informing the king that, unfortunately, the tree represents him, the king. If he

Belshazzar's Feast by Rembrandt (1635).

remains arrogant, refuses to acknowledge the total sovereignty of God, and continues to oppress people, he will become mad like an animal and live in the field. Nebuchadnezzar's dream does indeed come true, and he falls into insanity, living in the fields and eating grass. Finally, God returns him to sanity, at which point he humbly acknowledges the sovereignty of God.

DANIEL 5 — THE FALL OF BABYLON

The setting for Daniel 5 is 539 BC, the year the Persian king Cyrus conquered Babylon. By this time Daniel is an old man and Nebuchadnezzar is dead. Nabonidus, the current king, has left the throne to reside in Arabia, and his son and co-regent, Belshazzar, now rules Babylon.

> That very night Babylon falls to the Medo-Persian alliance and Darius the Mede.

Belshazzar throws a party and uses the sacred gold and silver goblets that had been taken from the temple in Jerusalem by Nebuchadnezzar, thus defiling the vessels. In addition, while drinking from the temple goblets, he and his guests praise their idols (5:4). At that point Belshazzar suddenly sees a hand, writing on the wall. Once again, only Daniel is able to interpret the vision. Through several intricate uses of wordplay, Daniel interprets the vision to mean that Belshazzar's kingdom will be given to the Medes and the Persians. That very night Babylon falls to the Medo-Persian alliance and Darius the Mede. This is not King Darius I (Darius the Great), a Persian king who comes to the throne later, but probably a reference to either Cyrus himself or to his general, who actually captured the city and killed Belshazzar. Darius was a common name among the Persians.

DANIEL 6 — DANIEL IN THE LIONS' DEN

Daniel 6 follows Daniel 5 chronologically and occurs during the Persian reign. The king is still called Darius (probably either Cyrus or a general appointed by him to serve as king over Babylon). Daniel is one of the most powerful administrators in the Persian Empire, and other administrators, jealous of Daniel's success, plot against him. Since Daniel's character is unassailable, these enemies of Daniel's resort to trickery, convincing the king to decree that no one can pray to any other god or man except the king. Daniel, of course, continues to pray to his God and is thus accused and convicted of violating the decree. The punishment is to be thrown into a den of lions. The king, sympathetic to Daniel and regretful of his decree, says to Daniel as they throw him to the lions, "May your God, whom you serve continually, rescue you" (6:16). The king anxiously returns the next morning and calls out, "Daniel, servant of the living God, has your God, whom you serve continually,

Kings in Mesopotamia often kept lions to use for lion hunts, as this panel from Assyria shows.

Werner Forman Archive/The British Museum

Daniel in the Lions' Den by J. B. Pratt (late 19th century).

been able to rescue you from the lions?" (6:20). From among the lions Daniel answers, "My God sent his angel, and he shut the mouths of the lions" (6:21). Rather than decreasing the power and influence of Daniel as his enemies hoped, this event actually increased Daniel's power and prosperity, and his enemies were thrown to the lions.

> From among the lions Daniel answers, "My God sent his angel, and he shut the mouths of the lions."

Note that throughout the Ancient Near East (and in the Old Testament as well) lions are often symbolic of monarchs. Thus it is probable that the lions surrounding Daniel in the lions' den, although real, also represent the nations and empires of the world. God sends his angels to rescue his faithful people from among the hostile nations.

Darius then issues a decree, which in fact sums up Daniel 1–6 very well:

"People must fear and reverence the God of Daniel. For he is the living God and he endures forever; his kingdom will not be destroyed, his dominion will never end. He rescues and he saves; he performs signs and wonders in the heavens and on the earth" (6:26–27).

» FURTHER READING «

For general exegetical help, see the following:

Baldwin, Joyce G. *Daniel*. Tyndale Old Testament Commentaries. Downers Grove, IL: InterVarsity, 1978.

Goldingay, John E. *Daniel*. Word Biblical Commentary. Dallas: Word Books, 1989.

Longman III, Tremper. *Daniel*. NIV Application Commentary. Grand Rapids: Zondervan, 1999.

For discussions on the historical problems in Daniel, see the following:

Archer, Gleason L. "Daniel." In *Expositor's Bible Commentary*, ed. Frank E. Gaebelein. Grand Rapids: Zondervan, 1985, 12–26.

Beaulieu, Paul-Alain, *The Reign of Nabonidus, King of Babylon 556–539 B.C.* New Haven: Yale University Press, 1990.

Bullock, C. Hassell. *An Introduction to the Old Testament Prophetic Books*. Chicago: Moody Press, 1986, 281–88.

Harrison, R. K. *Introduction to the Old Testament*. Grand Rapids: Eerdmans, 1969, 1106–34.

Yamauchi, Edwin M. "The Archaeological Background of Daniel: Archaeological Backgrounds of the Exilic and Post-Exilic Era, Part 1." *Bibliotheca Sacra* 137 (1980): 3–16.

» DISCUSSION QUESTIONS «

1. Discuss practical applications for today from Daniel 1 and 2.

2. Discuss practical applications for today from Daniel 3 and 6.

3. Is Nebuchadnezzar a true follower of the "God of Daniel"?

» WRITING ASSIGNMENTS «

1. Compare and contrast Daniel 4 with Daniel 5.

2. Compare and contrast Daniel with Joseph.

3. Trace the theme of pride/humility through Daniel 1–6.

4. Using the resources listed above, explain the issues regarding the authorship and date of Daniel.

CHAPTER 18

Daniel 7 – 12

"One like a son of man … was given authority, glory and sovereign power; all peoples, nations and men of every language worshiped him." (Dan. 7:13 – 14)

OVERVIEW OF DANIEL 7–12

As mentioned in chapter 17, the book of Daniel is about the sovereignty of God. In spite of how things might look because of powerful kingdoms like Babylon or Persia, God is still in control of history and will bring down his enemies and establish his own kingdom. Daniel 7–12 continues to develop this theme. In this part of the book, writes Longman, "we move from the present circumstances of God's people in captivity to their ultimate liberation. We move from human evil, evident also in the scope of chapters 7–12, to the perverse spiritual forces that stand behind them. We move from deliverance out of a burning furnace and a lions' den to salvation from the power of death itself (ch. 12)!"[1]

APOCALYPTIC: THE GENRE OF DANIEL 7–12

Daniel 7–12 contains some strange and bizarre imagery that is quite different from the imagery normally used by the other prophets. Likewise, Daniel appears to focus more on God's ultimate resolution of cosmic problems than on Israel's restoration. These are features of the literary genre referred to as "apocalyptic" (discussed in chapter 3).

> Daniel appears to focus more on God's ultimate resolution of cosmic problems than on Israel's restoration.

Although all prophetic literature uses images, figures of speech, and poetic language, in apocalyptic literature the language is characterized by a high degree of visionary symbolism, often appearing quite bizarre to the modern reader. The closest parallel to apocalyptic symbology that we have in contemporary literature is political cartoons. In American political cartoons, for example, the eagle represents America, the dragon is used to symbolize China, Britain is often a lion, and Russia a bear. The U.S. government is symbolized by a bearded old man with a red, white, and blue striped hat (Uncle Sam). Just as we recognize these symbols today, so the ancient readers of Daniel probably recognized many of his symbols.

Years ago, Governor Jimmy Carter entered the Democratic presidential primaries in the United States as a virtual unknown. Carter had such a huge smile that cartoonists regularly drew his caricature with an exaggerated smile and a mouthful of teeth. Soon he was challenging the frontrunners. A political cartoon at that time depicted a scene in which a large train locomotive was roaring down the tracks about to overrun the two previous Democratic Party frontrunners. The cow catcher (the grill at the bottom front of the locomotive) was in the shape of Carter's smile and teeth. Now place this image into a vision—"I saw a black, monstrous, smoke-spewing machine with the teeth of a man, about to devour two fleeing men"—and imagine trying to interpret that vision thousands of years later. This is close to the apocalyptic imagery of Daniel and the challenge we face.

> "The four great beasts are four kingdoms that will rise from the earth."

We are helped in Daniel with occasional explanations of the visions. Thus, Daniel's vision of the four beasts in Daniel 7, for example, is explained to him: "The four great beasts are four kingdoms that will rise from the earth" (Dan. 7:17). So while we may be uncertain

---

1. Tremper Longman III, *Daniel,* NIV Application Commentary (Grand Rapids: Zondervan, 1999), 177.

of some of the specific details (which kingdoms are these?) we can be confident in the major interpretation (these beasts represent world kingdoms).

Evangelical interpretation of Daniel 7 – 12 reflects a wide spectrum of views. Perhaps here more than in any other prophetic book the differences between dispensational premillennialism and amillennialism are most acute. For most evangelicals, Daniel 7 – 12 has much to say about the future and is interconnected with our understanding of New Testament texts on the end times like the book of Revelation. We should be cautious, however, about being too dogmatic in regard to many of the texts in Daniel 7 – 12. It might be wise to recall Daniel's comments on one of his own visions: "I was appalled by the vision; it was beyond understanding" (8:27).

> "I was appalled by the vision; it was beyond understanding."

DANIEL 7 — THE FOUR BEASTS

Daniel 7 introduces the apocalyptic section of Daniel and the major themes that will run like threads throughout the rest of the book. Longman identifies these themes as: (1) the horror of human evil, particularly as it is concentrated in the state; (2) the announcement of a specific time of deliverance; (3) repentance that leads to deliverance; (4) the revelation that a cosmic war stands behind human conflict; (5) judgment as certain for those who resist God and oppose his people; and (6) the equally certain truth that God's people, downtrodden in the present, will experience new life in the fullest sense in the future.[2]

In this chapter Daniel sees a vision of four beasts: a lion, a bear with three ribs in his mouth, a leopard with four wings and four heads, and a terrifying fourth beast unlike any other, with iron teeth and ten horns. Daniel is given an explanation of the vision in 7:17 – 18. These animals represent kingdoms. Thus the vision of Daniel 7 is similar in many respects to Nebuchadnezzar's vision in Daniel 2, also a vision representing four kingdoms.

Which kingdoms are these? There are two major views regarding the sequence of empires in the ancient world and how they relate to Daniel 2 and 7. Traditionally, evangelical scholars have maintained that the book of Daniel dates to the sixth century BC and was actually written

The Persian King Darius the Great, Persepolis (5th century BC).

© Livius.org

---

2. Ibid., 178 – 79.

A Comparison of the Two Major Traditional Views of Daniel 2 and 7			
Man in Daniel 2	Beasts in Daniel 7	Traditional evangelical view	Alternate view
Gold head	Lion	Babylon	Babylon/Assyria
Silver chest, arms	Bear	Medo-Persia	Media
Bronze belly, thighs	Leopard w/4 heads	Greece	Persia
Clay and iron feet	Fourth beast	Rome/revived Roman Empire	Greece

A coin with a portrayal of Antiochus Epiphanes.

by Daniel. Since the book is inspired by God, it contains much predictive prophecy, which includes the last two kingdoms. Thus they identify the four world kingdoms as Babylon, Medo-Persia, Greece (i.e., the Hellenistic empire established by Alexander the Great), and Rome (or a future kingdom descended in some way from Rome, i.e., a revived Roman Empire). On the other hand, almost all nonevangelical scholars note that many events mentioned in Daniel 7–12 took place during the Greek period (third and second centuries BC), long after the death of Daniel. They conclude that the book was pseudonymous and written after the events of the third and second centuries BC that the book describes. Thus they identify the four kingdoms as Babylonia, Media, Persia, and Greece. In recent years, a few evangelical scholars—while maintaining their belief in predictive prophecy and authorship by Daniel—have nonetheless argued from historical and exegetical evidence to suggest a similar view of the kingdoms, that is, that the fourth beast stands for Greece/Alexander the Great.[3]

Recently, Longman has suggested a third option—that it might be best to view all four kingdoms as symbolic (note that the numbers four and ten are highly symbolic numbers), "representing the fact that evil kingdoms (of an unspecified number) will succeed one another from the time of the Exile to the time of the climax of history, when God will intervene and once and for all judge all evil and bring into existence his kingdom."[4]

Daniel's vision is not just of the pagan world empires, however. He also sees God himself in this vision. Daniel describes God as "the Ancient of Days," sitting on a throne of fire with blazing wheels (7:9) (compare Ezekiel's vision in Ezekiel 1). Remember that Daniel's central theme is that God is sovereign and rules over all, in spite of how things look. Daniel also sees "one like the son of man, coming with the clouds of heaven" (7:13). Jesus will apply this title to himself and

> Daniel describes God as "the Ancient of Days," sitting on a throne of fire with blazing wheels.

---

3. See, for example, John H. Walton, "The Four Kingdoms of Daniel," *Journal of the Evangelical Theological Society* 29 (1986): 25–36.

4. Longman, *Daniel*, 190.

Part 2:
The Major Prophets

Daniel 7 and the European Union?

One of the most interesting and controversial images in the book of Daniel is that of the "ten-horned beast." Daniel refers to this beast repeatedly (7:7 – 8, 20, 24). Drawing from Daniel's imagery, John likewise mentions this "ten-horned beast" several times in the book of Revelation (12:3; 13:1; 17:3 – 16). This beast has been the subject of much speculation, especially from some popular prophecy writers who are convinced that most of the imagery used in biblical prophecy refers specifically to entities in our current day.

In searching the contemporary world for an entity that corresponds with the "ten-horned beast," several writers over the past forty years have concluded that the "ten-horned beast" of prophecy refers to the present-day European Union. Most of them arrived at this conclusion by making the following assumptions: (a) the "ten-horned beast" refers to a revived Roman Empire; (b) since the Roman Empire was largely in Europe, then Europe today must be the new embodiment of that empire; (c) the ten horns on the beast refer to nations; and (d) these must be European nations. The European Union, or EU (often referred to as the European Common Market in earlier literature) seems to fit the profile, and several popular writers are convinced that the EU is the "ten-horned beast," indicating the end times are very near. Is such an identification valid?

The European Union is a peaceful alliance of European nations, joined together primarily for trade and other economic reasons. In 1973 the EU was made up of nine countries (Belgium, Germany, France, Italy, Luxembourg, the Netherlands, Denmark, Ireland, and the United Kingdom). Thus they seemed very close to becoming a ten-nation coalition. When Greece joined the EU in 1981, the number of nations grew to ten! Now there was a ten-nation coalition of European nations, just like the ten-horned beast in Daniel and Revelation. End times writers of the 1970s and 1980s such as Hal Lindsey proclaimed rather confidently that the ten-member European Union was indeed the ten-horned beast, and that the revived Roman Empire of prophecy would soon emerge out of the EU. These startling facts, according to pop prophecy writers, proved quite clearly that the events of the end times were unfolding before our very eyes. Indeed, the end was very near!

In 1981 this argument could at least find some support in the current geopolitical situation. For many this argument was therefore quite convincing, and many people actually believed that the end-time events of Daniel and Revelation were beginning and would soon escalate. However, nothing happened and time passed. The end did not come. Two more countries (Spain and Portugal) joined the EU in 1986, bringing the number to twelve members. Over the years since then an additional fifteen countries have joined the EU (Austria, Finland, Sweden, Cyprus, the Czech Republic, Estonia, Hungary, Latvia, Lithuania, Malta, Poland, Slovakia, Slovenia, Bulgaria, and Romania), bringing the membership of the EU up to 27, where it stands at the time of this writing. In what sense can this 27-member alliance be the fulfillment of the biblical

continued on next page…

ten-horned beast? The confident identification of the ten-horned beast with the EU has proved to be over-speculative and misleading. Perhaps some of the sensationalist writers of the 1970s and 1980s owe their readers an apology.

Not only does the number of members not match the prophetic imagery, but a close historical and geographical study of the Roman Empire also reveals numerous points of incongruity with the modern European Union. For example, quite a few of the countries currently in the EU were not part of the Roman Empire in the first century, and many of them were never part of the Roman Empire. Large portions of Germany and the Netherlands fall into this category, as do Denmark, Ireland, Finland, Sweden, the Czech Republic, Estonia, Latvia, Lithuania, Poland, and the Slovak Republic. In addition, several large, critical regions of the first century AD Roman Empire are not even in Europe. These regions included countries such as Egypt and Libya, which were extremely important to the Roman Empire since they provided a large percentage of the empire's food supply. Numerous other non-European countries were important regions in the Roman Empire as well (Morocco, Algeria, Tunisia, Israel, Jordan, Lebanon, Syria, and Turkey, although Turkey has applied for membership in the EU). Even if the ten-horned beast referred to a revived Roman Empire, in what sense should it be restricted to Europe?

In more recent years, other pop prophecy writers have abandoned the EU theory and argued that the United Nations is the fulfillment of the ten-horned beast prophecy. Again, the evidence is flimsy and the argument is based largely on sensationalism and an unfounded conviction that the end time events *must* be taking place in *our* lifetime.

Guards from the palace of Darius I, King of Persia.

© Livius.org

make a direct connection to this text, stating, "They will see the Son of Man coming on the clouds of the sky, with power and great glory" (Matt. 24:30; see also Matt. 26:64; Mark 13:26; 14:62; Luke 21:27).

Quite a lot of controversy has occurred among evangelicals in recent years over the identity of the strange fourth beast. From the ten horns of the terrible fourth beast, one horn rises to power and wages war against the saints. Many interpreters connect this to the beast/Antichrist of Revelation 13. This person tries to subdue God's people and "change the set times and the laws," but God (the Ancient of Days) defeats him and establishes his everlasting kingdom.

DANIEL 8—THE RAM AND GOAT

In chapter 8 Daniel sees a vision of a two-horned ram and a one-horned goat. Unlike the beasts of Daniel 7, these two animals are specifically identified for Daniel by the angel Gabriel, who states, "The two-horned ram that you saw represents the kings of Media and Persia. The shaggy goat is the king of Greece, and the large horn between his eyes is the first king. The four horns that replaced the one that was broken off represent the four kingdoms that will emerge from his nation but will not have the same power" (8:20–21). Thus most scholars agree that the shaggy goat is Alexander the Great and the four horns represent his four generals, who split up his empire upon his death: Ptolemy ruling over Egypt, Seleucus ruling over Syria and Babylonia, Lysimachus ruling over Thrace and Asia Minor, and Cassander ruling over Macedonia. The specifics regarding the action of the "little horn" that comes out of one of these four (8:9–14) describes the historical actions of Antiochus Epiphanes, who ruled over the Seleucid kingdom (including Palestine) from 175–163 BC. Antiochus committed terrible atrocities against the Jews who were back in the land of Palestine. He also sacrificed a pig on the altar in Jerusalem, destroyed all copies of the Torah he could find, and executed anyone who kept copies.[5]

> The shaggy goat is Alexander the Great, and the four horns represent his four generals who split up his empire upon his death.

---

5. Robert B. Chisholm Jr., *Handbook on the Prophets* (Grand Rapids: Baker, 2002), 311–12.

The four horns of Daniel 8:20–21 and perhaps the four heads of the leopard in Daniel 7:6 represent the four generals who split up the empire of Alexander the Great.

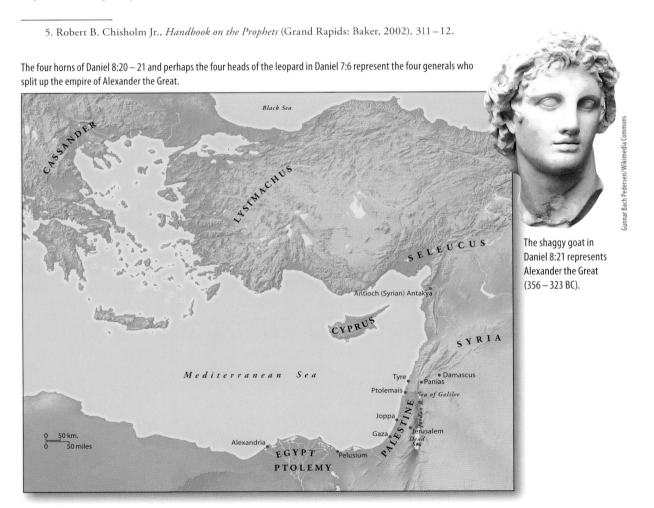

Gunnar Bach Pedersen/Wikimedia Commons

The shaggy goat in Daniel 8:21 represents Alexander the Great (356–323 BC).

DANIEL 9 — A PROPHET'S PRAYER AND THE "SEVENTY SEVENS"

Daniel 9 opens with a reference to Jeremiah's prophecy that the desolation of Jerusalem would last seventy years (see the discussion on "Jeremiah's Seventy Years of Exile" in chapter 11). In light of the promise to Jeremiah, Daniel prays to Yahweh (note the use of Yahweh here instead of Elohim, used throughout the rest of Daniel), confessing the sins of Israel and petitioning for the restoration of Jerusalem. Daniel's entire prayer (9:4–19) is similar in content and style to the rest of the prophets and is based on Deuteronomy, as are most of the other prophets.

> The term "seven" or "week" probably refers to a seven-year period.

While Daniel is still praying, the angel Gabriel appears and answers Daniel's prayer by giving a complicated apocalyptic expanded explanation of Jeremiah's seventy years. The term "seven" or "week" used in this passage probably refers to a seven-year period. Thus "seventy sevens" (9:24) is probably either a literal reference to 490 years or a symbolic reference to a long but complete period of time. Interpreters also differ on how to understand 9:26–27. Does 9:26–27 refer to Antiochus Epiphanes and the terrible events of his reign or to the future Antichrist described in the New Testament? Perhaps we should see this text with a near view/far view understanding and see Antiochus Epiphanes as the near view fulfillment, foreshadowing the future Antichrist (the far view). Likewise, most evangelicals view the ultimate fulfillment of 9:24 as connected to the life, death, and return of Jesus Christ.

DANIEL 10–12 — THE FINAL VISION

In this final section of Daniel, we are given a brief glimpse of the heavenly realities that lie behind human conflict.[6] Daniel has a vision of a coming war, a vision that leaves him mourning for three weeks. Then an angelic figure appears to him and tells him that he wanted to come to him earlier but that "the prince of the Persian kingdom resisted me twenty-one days. Then Michael, one of the chief princes, came to help me" (10:13). This intriguing text implies that there may be territorial spiritual powers that are hostile to God and his angels (see also Deut. 32:8; Psalm 82; Eph. 6:12; Rev. 12:7). Having been assisted by the angel Michael, the angelic speaker has now been able to overcome the hostile "prince of the Persian kingdom" and come to Daniel to explain the upcoming war.

> In this final section of Daniel, we are given a brief glimpse of the heavenly realities that lie behind human conflict.

In Daniel 11, the angel tells Daniel in a rather detailed manner about numerous conflicts and struggles that will occur in Palestine during the third and second centuries BC. Inheriting the dismantled empire of Alexander during this time, the Seleucid dynasty ruled over Syria and Babylonia, while the Ptolemy dynasty ruled over Egypt. The angel in Daniel 11 refers to the Seleucids as "the king of the north" and the Ptolemies as "the king of the south." These two powers fought over control of Palestine throughout this period, and Daniel 11 recounts

---

6. Longman, *Daniel,* 245.

The New Testament writers often draw material from Daniel, especially when discussing prophetic events. Daniel's description of God on his throne and the "Son of Man, coming with clouds of heaven" (7:9 – 14) is no doubt the background imagery for New Testament texts that proclaim Jesus' second coming in the clouds (Mark 13:26 – 27; Luke 21:27 – 28; Matt. 24:30 – 31; Rev. 1:7, 12 – 18). Likewise, New Testament passages such as Mark 13 and Revelation 6 – 18 that deal with the great tribulation and/or the fall of Jerusalem connect to Daniel 9:24 – 27 and 11:40 – 12:13. Strong echoes of these texts in Daniel can also be seen in 2 Thessalonians 2 and in Revelation 19 – 22.

that struggle in some detail.[7] While this chapter covers quite a span of history (down to the Maccabean revolt), Antiochus Epiphanes plays the role of prototypical antagonist. Once again, some interpreters see these references as completely tied to the events of the third and second centuries BC, while others see some of these prophecies as dealing with the future, especially regarding the Antichrist. Texts like Daniel 11:31 appear to refer both to actions of Antiochus and to those of a future antagonist (Matt. 24:15). Once again we are helped by a near view/far view approach, whereby Antiochus Epiphanes fulfills the prophecy in the near view but still functions as a typological foreshadowing of a future temple desecration, as explained by Jesus (Matt. 24:15).

Ultimately, as Daniel 12 explains, the angel Michael will bring about victory, culminating in the resurrection from the dead (12:2 – 3). This is one of the few verses in the Old Testament that speaks of the resurrection of the dead. Throughout the prophetic books the hope of the future was usually based on a promise of the physical restoration of Israel and the nations to Jerusalem and the Promised Land. Daniel gives the added encouragement that even those who have died will rise again, some to everlasting life and some to shame and everlasting contempt.

> Ultimately, as Daniel 12 explains, the angel Michael will bring about victory, culminating in the resurrection from the dead.

---

7. For a good discussion on the historical events mentioned in this chapter, see Chisholm, *Handbook on the Prophets,* 318 – 27; and John E. Goldingay, *Daniel,* Word Biblical Commentary (Dallas: Word Books, 1989), 293 – 306.

» FURTHER READING «

Regarding the genre of apocalyptic, see the following:

Collins, John J. *The Apocalyptic Imagination: An Introduction to Jewish Apocalyptic Literature*. Grand Rapids: Eerdmans, 1998.

Grabbe, Lester L. and R. D. Haak, eds. *Knowing the End from the Beginning: The Prophetic, the Apocalyptic and Their Relationships*. JSPSup 46. London: T & T Clark, 2003.

Sandy, D. Brent. *Plowshares and Pruning Hooks: Rethinking the Language of Biblical Prophecy and Apocalyptic*. Downers Grove, IL: InterVarsity Press, 2002, 103–28.

For general exegetical help on Daniel 7–12, see the following:

Baldwin, Joyce G. *Daniel*. Tyndale Old Testament Commentaries. Downers Grove, IL: InterVarsity Press, 1978.

Chisholm Jr., Robert B., *Handbook on the Prophets*. Grand Rapids: Baker, 2002.

Goldingay, John E. *Daniel*. Word Biblical Commentary. Dallas: Word Books, 1989.

Longman III, Tremper. *Daniel*. NIV Application Commentary. Grand Rapids: Zondervan, 1999.

» DISCUSSION QUESTIONS «

1. Is the European Union a plausible fulfillment of the ten-horned beast of Daniel 7? Why not? Does the United Nations appear to be a plausible fulfillment of Daniel 7? Why do some popular prophecy writers make such claims? Should they admit their errors?

2. Identify the "Ancient of Days" and "one like a son of man" in Daniel 7. What role does each of them play in that chapter?

3. How has the description of the "Ancient of Days" in Daniel 7:9 influenced the way people envision God? What is the symbolism behind the terms and description of God in Daniel 7:9?

1. Using the resources listed above, or other resources available to you that are approved by your professor, discuss the career of Antiochus Epiphanes and how events in his life correspond to texts in Daniel 11.

2. Read Daniel 10:13 – 14, Deuteronomy 32:8, Psalm 82, Ephesians 6:12, and Revelation 12:7 and discuss the possibility of territorial spirits. Are these spirits demons? Fallen angels? Pagan gods?

3. Discuss how Daniel 10 – 12 would have given encouragement to the exiles. Also, how does this passage give encouragement to believers today?

PART 3

The Book of the Twelve

Introduction to the
Book of the Twelve

For most of the twentieth century, Old Testament scholars usually approached the twelve Minor Prophets as individual books, analyzing them individually in a similar fashion to Isaiah, Jeremiah, and Ezekiel. Usually they were rearranged and placed among the Major Prophets in chronological order and then discussed in their historical context (i.e., the prophets of the Assyrian period—Jonah, Amos, Hosea, Micah, Isaiah; the prophets of the Babylonian period—Zephaniah, Habakkuk, Jeremiah, Nahum, etc.). More recently, numerous Old Testament scholars have suggested that while historical setting is very important, nonetheless, canonical order is also significant to the theological meaning of the books. This is true especially regarding the Minor Prophets, and a current trend in Old Testament scholarship is to study the Minor Prophets as a single book, called the "Book of the Twelve."[1]

> A current trend in Old Testament scholarship is to study the Minor Prophets as a single book, called the "Book of the Twelve."

ANCIENT EVIDENCE

This fragment from the Dead Sea Scrolls preserves the end of Zephaniah and the beginning of Haggai, indicating that the twelve minor prophets were all probably on one scroll (150 – 125 BC).

In the apocryphal book of Sirach (also called Ecclesiasticus), written around 200 BC, the writer mentions Isaiah (Sir. 48:23), Jeremiah (Sir. 49:6), Ezekiel (Sir. 49:8) and then the Twelve Prophets (Sir. 49:10), indicating that by the year 200 BC the twelve Minor Prophets were viewed as a unit. Likewise, in the earliest manuscripts of this literature, both in Hebrew and in the translated Greek, the Minor Prophets are collected onto one scroll. Furthermore, early counts of the books of the Old Testament by writers such as Josephus indicate that they counted the twelve Minor Prophets as one book.[2] It is also not mere coincidence that the number 12 has special symbolic significance.

SUPERSCRIPTIONS AND CHRONOLOGICAL ORDER

Six of the twelve books (Hosea, Amos, Micah, Zephaniah, Haggai, and Zechariah) open with a specific historical superscription. For example, Hosea 1:1 begins, "The word of Yahweh that came to Hosea son of Beeri during the reigns of Uzziah, Jotham, Ahaz and Hezekiah …" Likewise, these six books are in chronological order, Hosea being the earliest and Zechariah the latest. The other six (Joel, Obadiah, Jonah, Nahum, Habakkuk, and Malachi), however, contain no specific opening historical superscription, making it difficult to date some of them with assurance, and indicating, perhaps, that historical

---

1. See, for example, James D. Nogalski and Marvin A. Sweeney, *Reading and Hearing the Book of the Twelve,* SBL Symposium Series 15 (Atlanta: Society of Biblical Literature, 2000), and Christopher R. Seitz, *Prophecy and Hermeneutics: Toward a New Introduction to the Prophets,* Studies in Theological Interpretation (Grand Rapids: Baker, 2007).

2. David L. Peterson, "A Book of the Twelve?" 4, and Paul L. Redditt, "The Production and Reading of the Book of the Twelve," 14, in Nogalski and Sweeney, *Reading and Hearing the Book of the Twelve;* J. Gordon McConville, *Exploring the Old Testament: A Guide to the Prophets* (Downers Grove, IL: InterVarsity Press, 2002), 133. Note, however, that while the concept of the Book of the Twelve as a unit was firm very early, the exact order varied, and the Septuagint order differs slightly from the order of the Masoretic Text, which our English Bibles follow.

Canonical Order and Historical Superscription in the Book of the Twelve		
Book	**Historical Superscription?**	**Date from the Superscription**
Hosea	Yes	786 – 746 BC
Joel	No	
Amos	Yes	786 – 746 BC
Obadiah	No	
Jonah	No	
Micah	Yes	750 – 687 BC
Nahum	No	
Habakkuk	No	
Zephaniah	Yes	640 – 609 BC
Haggai	Yes	520 BC
Zechariah	Yes	520 BC
Malachi	No	

dating for these books was not overly important to the early writers or editors. These six undated books are fairly evenly distributed among the six dated books.

CONNECTIONS WITHIN THE BOOK OF THE TWELVE

Why are these twelve books in this particular canonical order? What is the connection between them? Numerous observations have been made in recent years noting a host of thematic and "catchword" interconnections within the twelve books. Seitz argues that Hosea serves as an introduction to the Book of the Twelve and that the final verses of Hosea serve as a motto for the Twelve, as Psalm 1 does for the Psalter. Hosea 14:9 reads: "Who is wise? He will realize these things. Who is discerning? He will understand them. The ways of Yahweh are right; the righteous walk in them, but the rebellious stumble in them."[3]

Other scholars have suggested that the Book of the Twelve is "framed" with a similar theme that opens and closes the larger unit. Thus Hosea opens

> Numerous observations have been made in recent years noting a host of thematic and "catchword" interconnections within the Book of the Twelve.

---

3. Seitz, *Prophecy and Hermeneutic,* 215.

the unit, stressing the theme of the love of Yahweh (esp. Hosea 1–3), and Malachi closes the unit with the same thematic emphasis (Mal. 1:2).[4]

Numerous connections between adjacent books have been noted. For example, Joel 3:16 ("Yahweh will roar from Zion") ties Joel to the following book of Amos, which opens with "Yahweh roars from Zion" (1:2). Likewise, Amos ends with a judgment on Edom (9:12), and the following book of Obadiah focuses on the end of Edom.[5] At the end of Habakkuk, the prophet states, "Let all the earth be silent before him [Yahweh]" (Hab. 2:20); and early in Zephaniah, the prophet declares, "Be silent before Yahweh the Lord" (Zeph. 1:7). The last two units of Zechariah are called "oracles," and the following book of Malachi is introduced as an "oracle."

> Amos ends with a judgment on Edom, and the following book of Obadiah focuses almost entirely on the end of Edom.

Recently, several scholars have suggested that the Book of the Twelve is loosely connected around the central theme of "the day of Yahweh" (see the discussion of the "day of Yahweh" in chapter 20). Primary texts in the Book of the Twelve that deal with the day of Yahweh directly include Hosea 9:5; Joel 3:14–2l; Amos 5:18–20; Obadiah 15; Micah 2:4; Habakkuk 3:16; Zephaniah 1:7–16; Haggai 2:23; Zechariah 14:1; and Malachi 4:1.[6]

Paul House points to the character of God as the focal point of the Book of the Twelve. As each book adds to the characterization of God, House suggests, there is a threefold movement or development of the emphases. In Hosea through Micah, warnings dominate the depiction of Yahweh. Next, in Nahum through Zephaniah, judgment texts dominate.

> Recently, several scholars have suggested that the Book of the Twelve is loosely connected around the central theme of "the day of Yahweh."

Finally, in Haggai through Malachi, "renewal metaphors take precedence," pointing toward the restoration.[7] Note the similarity between House's analysis of theological movement in the Twelve and the synopsis of the prophetic message that we have been following for the preexilic prophets: (1) You (Israel/Judah) have broken the covenant; you had better repent! (2) No repentance? Then judgment! (3) Yet there is hope beyond the judgment for a glorious future restoration.

The same lack of consensus about the theological or literary cohesion of the Twelve holds true for the study of the book of Jeremiah, which is not one of the Twelve. The thematic relationships or literary connections between the various portions is not always clear, a fact that has caused a great amount of scholarly debate. In addition, even though several portions

---

4. John D. W. Watts, "A Frame for the Book of the Twelve: Hosea 1–3 and Malachi," in *Reading and Hearing the Book of the Twelve,* ed. Nogalski and Sweeney, 209–17.

5. Redditt, "The Production and Reading of the Book of the Twelve," 14–15; McConville, *Guide to the Prophets,* 133–34.

6. Peterson, "A Book of the Twelve?" 4, 9; Rolf Rendtorff, "Alas for the Day! The 'Day of the Lord' in the Book of the Twelve," in *God in the Fray: A Tribute to Walter Brueggemann,* ed. Tod Linafelt and Timothy K. Beal (Minneapolis: Fortress Press, 1998), 186–97.

7. Paul House, 'The Character of God in the Book of the Twelve," in *Reading and Hearing the Book of the Twelve,* ed. Nogalski and Sweeney, 125–45.

of Jeremiah are in tight chronological order, the book as a whole is not. Nonetheless, while the historical context of each unit in Jeremiah is significant, no attempt to cut the book apart and reassemble the pieces in chronological order would be fruitful. Rather, the book functions in its canonical form as a unified anthology connected by the various literary and thematic features spelled out in this chapter, and it should be read and studied as it now stands. The same should probably hold true for the Book of the Twelve; it should be read as a literary unit without denying the complex and varying devices that make this anthology hold together.

» FURTHER READING «

House, Paul R. *The Unity of the Twelve*. Bible and Literature Series 27; JSOT Supplement 97. Sheffield: Almond Press, 1990.

Nogalski, James D., and Marvin A. Sweeney, eds. *Reading and Hearing the Book of the Twelve*. SBL Symposium Series Number 15. Atlanta: Society of Biblical Literature, 2000.

Seitz, Christopher. *Prophecy and Hermeneutics: Toward a New Introduction to the Prophets*. Grand Rapids: Baker, 2007.

CHAPTER 19

Hosea

"For I desire steadfast love and not sacrifice, the knowledge of God rather than burnt offerings."

(Hos. 6:6 NRSV)

OVERVIEW OF HOSEA

Setting

Hosea 1:1 ties the prophet's ministry first of all to a series of Judahite kings: Uzziah (783–742 BC); Jotham (742–735 BC, although he became co-regent in 750 BC); Ahaz (735–715 BC); and Hezekiah (715–687/686 BC). Thus Hosea's ministry spans much of the eighth century BC. During his early years, Hosea would have overlapped with Amos and Jonah, and during his later years, he would have been contemporary with Isaiah and Micah. Hosea 1:1 also connects Hosea's ministry to the reign of the Israelite king Jeroboam II (796–746 BC). Hosea does not mention the six weak kings who ruled briefly in Israel between the death of Jeroboam and the fall of Israel to the Assyrians (722 BC), probably signaling that he is treating them as insignificant.

In the later years of Hosea, the Assyrians grow strong as Israel grows weak, and eventually the Assyrians overrun the entire area.

The later part of the eighth century was a tumultuous time for Israel and Judah (see chapter 2, "The Prophets in History"). The early years of Hosea's ministry were times when Israel was strong and prosperous, while the Assyrians were weak. In the later years of Hosea, however, the Assyrians grow strong as Israel grows weak, and eventually the Assyrians overrun the entire area. In 734 BC the Assyrians defeat the Israelite/Syrian alliance in the Syro-Ephraimite war. In 722 BC the Assyrians conquer Israel and destroy Samaria, the capital. In 701 BC the Assyrians unsuccessfully besiege Jerusalem. Hosea's message is delivered in this tumultuous context.

At the beginning of Hosea's ministry Israel's borders extended as far north as Lebo (Hamath).

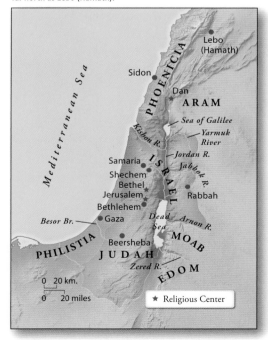

By the end of Hosea's ministry the Assyrians controlled most of the area.

Message

Hosea's message is typical of the preexilic prophets and follows the standard three-point pattern: (1) You (Israel/Judah) have broken the covenant; you had better repent! (2) No repentance? Then judgment! (3) Yet there is hope beyond the judgment for a glorious future restoration. Hosea's charges against Israel and Judah are likewise the common prophetic indictments: idolatry, social injustice, and religious ritualism. Hosea has very little to say about the nations, so in this regard his message is slightly different than that of Isaiah, Jeremiah, and Ezekiel.

Jeroboam constructs calf idols and declares, "Here are your gods, O Israel, who brought you up out of Egypt." Depicted is an Egyptian ruler bowing before an Apis bull (c. 600 BC).

The book of Hosea does not follow any tight organizational structure. Like many of the prophetic books, it is more like an anthology, a collection of speeches, events, and oracles. Hosea 1–3 centers on his marriage to Gomer and the symbolism of her unfaithfulness. Its lyrical nature stresses the emotional aspects of Israel's disobedience. Hosea 4–14 is a loose collection of oracles and speeches that cover the entire range of the three-part prophetic message. As part of a covenant lawsuit (note 4:1), it stresses the legal component of violating the covenant.

> Hosea's message is typical of the preexilic prophets and follows the standard three-point pattern.

HOSEA 1–3 — HOSEA'S MARRIAGE AND YAHWEH'S MARRIAGE

As we have seen, Isaiah, Jeremiah, and Ezekiel all use the image of an unfaithful wife to illustrate Israel's and Judah's idolatry. Chasing after

---

The Dangers of Syncretism

Religious syncretism is the mixing together of customs and rituals involved in worshipping different gods. In general, as Israel and Judah slide into apostasy, they don't drop the worship of Yahweh completely (although Israel does at times), but they simply incorporate the worship of other gods into their religion. They want Yahweh to be part of a pantheon-like system. They want to continue to sacrifice and burn incense to Yahweh along with worshipping Baal and other gods. They are also quick to apply Yahweh's name and acts of salvation to pagan idols. Thus in 1 Kings 12:28, for example, King Jeroboam constructs calf idols for Israel and blasphemously declares, "Here are your gods, O Israel, who brought you up out of Egypt." Yahweh, however, absolutely and without any ambiguity rejects this concept, comparing it to adultery. Like a husband, he is jealous of his wife and does not approve of her playing the harlot and sleeping around. This tendency of Israel and Judah to fall into syncretism is one of the reasons that Yahweh uses the husband/wife imagery so frequently. Yahweh's people cannot mix worship of Yahweh with worship of idols or other unclean things. He demands total obedience and faithfulness. What does this characteristic of God imply for us today?

foreign gods is compared to a woman's chasing after other lovers, indeed, to the rejection of the husband by an adulterous wife. This imagery is especially powerful and very personal in Hosea because the unfortunate prophet is directed to live it out in his own life and heartbreaking marriage.

In Hosea 1:2 Yahweh instructs the prophet to "take to yourself an adulterous wife" (lit. "a woman of prostitutions" or "a prostituting woman"). The text is not overly clear as to when exactly her promiscuous, immoral behavior started. Three possibilities are put forward by Old Testament scholars: (1) Gomer was a prostitute when Hosea found her and married her; (2) Gomer had promiscuous tendencies and became a prostitute after Hosea married her; and (3) Gomer merely represents a typical Israelite woman, who was a "prostitute" in the sense that she worshipped other gods along with the rest of Israel (i.e., the national idolatry is equated to prostitution).[1] The first option (she was a prostitute when Hosea married her) is probably the best option, fitting the text and the context better than the others.

Hosea obediently marries a woman named Gomer, who bears three children. Regarding the first child, Hosea 1:3 mentions that Gomer "bore *him* a son," perhaps implying

> Yahweh instructs the prophet to "take to yourself an adulterous wife."

---

1. The third view is favored by Douglas Stuart, *Hosea-Jonah,* Word Biblical Commentary (Waco, TX: Word Books, 1987), 26–27.

The Valley of Jezreel, where Jehu slaughtered the entire royal family of the previous dynasty.

that Hosea was indeed the father. Neither of the other two births is described in this way, perhaps casting some doubt on who the father of the second two children was.

Yahweh names the first child "Jezreel" and then explains his choice of names (1:4–5). Jezreel means "God sows," but it also refers to the valley where Jehu (former king of Israel and founder of the current ruling dynasty) ended the previous dynasty by slaughtering the entire royal family (see 2 Kings 10–11). The name "Jezreel" thus reminds the current dynasty of how they came to power. Ironically, Yahweh uses it to inform them of their demise: they will end up like the dynasty before them.

> The second child is named "Lo-Ruhamah," which means "not loved."

The second child is named "Lo-Ruhamah," which means "not loved." Yahweh explains that this child symbolizes the fact that Yahweh will no longer love or forgive the house of Israel. Thus he is predicting the coming destruction of Israel in 722 BC. On the other hand, Yahweh adds, "I will continue to love Judah, and I will save them." Thus Jerusalem is delivered from the Assyrian siege in 701 BC.

The name of the third child is perhaps the most ominous, for the child is named "Lo-Ammi," which means "not my people." Recall from our study of Isaiah, Jeremiah, and Ezekiel that the oft-repeated foundational formula statement of the covenant relationship was: "I will be your God; you will be my people; I will dwell in your midst." When Yahweh names this third child "not my people," it is an indication that the covenant between Yahweh and Israel is shattered. However, in Hosea 1:10–11 Yahweh looks to the future and declares that the Israelites will be like the sand on the seashore (a fulfillment of the Abrahamic covenant, Gen. 22:17).

> When Yahweh names this third child "not my people," it is an indication that the covenant between Yahweh and Israel is shattered.

Hosea 2 appears to be a poetic reflection on the symbolism of Hosea 1. Apparently Gomer abandons Hosea, because in Hosea 2 Yahweh speaks of how his unfaithful wife turns to other lovers, refusing to even acknowledge the good things he has given to her (2:5–8). Yet in spite of all this, Yahweh declares that he will take her back and be her husband again (2:14–20). In so doing, he reverses the judgmental names of Gomer's children, declaring, "I will say to those called 'Not my people,' 'You are my people'" (2:23). Then, to further illustrate the point, Yahweh instructs Hosea to take his wife Gomer back and to love her again. The analogy is clear, underscoring how deep and spectacular the love of Yahweh is. To restore and love Israel and Judah again after they had abandoned Yahweh for other gods is like a jilted husband taking his wife back and loving her again after she has been continuously involved in adulterous affairs, even prostitution.

Hosea's Relationship Images

The Old Testament prophets use three major images to illustrate the relationship between Yahweh and his people: (1) a king and his subjects; (2) a father and his child; and (3) a husband and his wife. Hosea employs all three images.

HOSEA 4–13—THE COVENANT LAWSUIT AND THE COMING JUDGMENT

Legal terminology is used in Hosea 4:1, "Yahweh has a charge to bring against you who live in the land." The word translated as "charge" implies a covenant lawsuit. The main indictments are then listed. There is no faithfulness, no love, and no "knowing of God." There is only "cursing, lying and murder, stealing and adultery," sins taken straight out of the Ten Commandments. Compounding the problem, as Isaiah, Jeremiah, and Ezekiel also point out, the priests are the ones leading the apostasy (4:4–9).

> The charge of participating in prostitution had both a literal and a figurative element.

Hosea continues to use the analogy of prostitution. Forms of the Hebrew word for prostitution are used 22 times in Hosea, with 12 of those occurrences appearing in Hosea 4–5. It is a fitting, ironic analogy because cultic prostitution was a common element in Baal worship, in which the Israelites were involved. So the charge of participating in prostitution had both a literal and a figurative element. The Israelites were participating in literal, physical prostitution in their Baal worship, and they were also participating in figurative, symbolic prostitution as they abandoned Yahweh and turned to worshipping foreign gods.

> The people believed that they could sin as much as they wanted to and worship other gods if they wanted to as long as they kept the basic religious rituals of Yahweh worship.

Throughout Hosea 4–13 Yahweh often refers to the northern kingdom of Israel as Ephraim. Ephraim was the largest and most influential of the ten northern tribes of Israel and is thus used to represent all of them. Remember that when the northern kingdom, Israel, was formed, their first king set up golden calves at Dan and at Bethel for the people to worship. Apparently, by the time of Hosea, the two main idolatrous worship centers for Israel were in Bethel and Gilgal. The word "Bethel" means "house of God." In an obvious parody and wordplay, Hosea refers to this cultic worship center instead as "Beth Aven," which means "house of iniquity" (4:15, 5:8; 10:5).

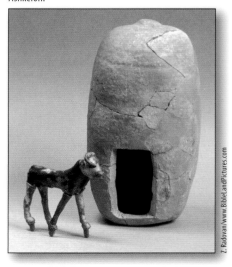

Calf idols were common throughout Palestine and Egypt. This calf image and shrine were excavated at Ashkelon.

As has been pointed out several times, one of the indictments against Israel made by the prophets is that of religious ritualism. That is, the people believed that if they performed the religious rituals, then everything would be all right. They could sin as much as they wanted to and worship other gods if they wanted to as long as they kept the basic religious rituals of Yahweh worship. Yahweh, of course, consistently rejects this. In Hosea 6:6 he declares, "I desire faithful love [loyal love toward others, i.e., mercy, as in some translations], not sacrifice; the knowledge of God rather than burnt offerings" (NRSV). Jesus quotes this verse twice (Matt. 9:13; 12:7) to rebuke the hypocritical piety of the Pharisees.

In Hosea 8:1 Yahweh states clearly that Israel has broken his covenant. Even though they cry out hypocritically, "O our God, we acknowledge you," their actions show otherwise, for they have set up their own royal dynasties that Yahweh did not approve and have built calf idols to worship (8:4–6). Thus, Yahweh declares poetically, "They sow the wind" (i.e., sin) "and reap the whirlwind" (i.e., judgment) (8:7).

> Hosea is quite explicit regarding the destruction of Israel and their expulsion from the Land.

Hosea is quite explicit regarding the destruction of Israel and their expulsion from the Land. In 9:3 he states, "They will not remain in Yahweh's land." Likewise in 10:7 he declares, "Samaria and its king will float away like a twig on the surface of the waters."

Hosea 11 uses the father/child imagery. Yahweh reflects on the past like a father reflecting back to the time when his child was a toddler. "Out of Egypt I called my son," Yahweh reminisces, referring to the exodus story. He continues with the father analogy, saying, "It was I who taught Ephraim to walk, taking them by the arms." Here Yahweh is using the image of a parent holding the hands of his toddler and helping the child to take his first tentative steps. It is therefore with anguish that Yahweh cries out, "How can I give you up, Ephraim?" (11:8). He then states that he will not destroy them completely (like Admah and Zeboiim, cities destroyed with Sodom and Gomorrah). And afterward,

Hesed (Faithful, Loyal Love)

An important Hebrew word in Hosea is *hesed*. This word means "love," but it also contains a strong nuance of faithful, loyal love (like the enduring love of a strong, mature marriage). This is an important theological word, occurring over 246 times in the Old Testament. Half of these occurrences are in Psalms, where some translations often render *hesed* as "mercy" (KJV), while others render it as "lovingkindness" (NASB) or "unfailing love" (NIV). "Unfailing love" or "loyal love" probably captures the nuance of the word the best. It reflects the kind of love Yahweh has for his people, but Yahweh also uses this word to describe how he expects his people to love him and to love others.

Hosea uses *hesed* six times (2:19; 4:1; 6:4, 6; 10:12; 12:6). While Isaiah and Jeremiah stress justice and righteousness as foundational virtues, Hosea adds *hesed* ("loyal love") to that combination, implying that faithfulness in love is as critically important as justice and righteousness. In Hosea 2:19, Yahweh states, "I will betroth you to me forever; I will betroth you in righteousness and justice, in *hesed* and compassion." On the other hand, *hesed* was one of the things Israel lacked, as evidenced by their unfaithful behavior. Yahweh accuses them of this in the central charges leveled against them early in Hosea 4, "There is no faithfulness, no *hesed*, no acknowledgment of God in the land." Likewise, catch the irony of 6:4, as Yahweh tells Ephraim and Judah that "your *hesed* is like the morning mist, like the early dew that disappears." This is also the word used in the oft-quoted Hosea 6:6, "For I desire *hesed*, not sacrifice." In 10:12 Yahweh uses the term figuratively, telling them to "sow for yourselves righteousness, reap the fruit of *hesed*" (cf. 8:7). Then in 12:6 the call to repentance includes maintaining justice and *hesed*.

From the palace of Sennacherib, a scene showing the inhabitants of Lachish being led into exile, while their leaders are being tortured.

Yahweh continues, his lion's roar will not be the roar of judgment, but the roar that calls his people back from their scattering (11:10–11).

Hosea 12–13 returns to the sin of Israel and the impending judgment. For much of Hosea's life, Israel was prosperous economically, but in Hosea 12:7–8 Yahweh accuses them of economic dishonesty. Twice in this section (12:9; 13:4) Yahweh declares, "I am Yahweh your God, who brought you up out of Egypt," stressing that his character is expressed through the exodus, the central salvation event of the Old Testament. Recall also that, when Israel first established the calf idols, the king declared that the calf idols were the gods that brought them up out of Egypt (1 Kings 12:28). Remember too that it was the construction of a golden calf that nearly destroyed Israel early in their relationship with Yahweh (Exodus 32).

Hosea 14 is a final plea for repentance, stressing how Yahweh will heal and restore them if they will only repent. The book ends with a proverb-like word of wisdom and warning: "Who is wise? He will realize these things. Who is discerning? He will understand them. The ways of Yahweh are right; the righteous will walk in them, but the rebellious stumble in them."

> Hosea 14 is a final plea for repentance.

NT Connection: "Out of Egypt I Called My Son"

In Hosea 11:1, in regard to the deliverance of Israel through the exodus, Yahweh states, "Out of Egypt I called my son." In Matthew 2:14–15, Joseph is directed to take the baby Jesus to Egypt, to protect him from Herod. When Jesus returns from Egypt, Matthew cites it as a fulfillment of Hosea 11:1. This kind of fulfillment is called "typology," reflecting the sense in which historical actions and entities in the Old Testament (the near view) are prophetic of future messianic fulfillment (the far view). In this type of prophecy/fulfillment, Jesus comes as the perfect Israel, completing and fulfilling all that literal Israel failed to do and to be.

» FURTHER READING «

Garrett, Duane. *Hosea, Joel*. New American Commentary. Nashville, TN: Broadman & Holman, 1997.

Smith, Gary V. *Hosea, Amos, Micah*. NIV Application Commentary. Grand Rapids: Zondervan, 2001.

Stuart, Douglas. *Hosea-Jonah*. Word Biblical Commentary. Waco, TX: Word Books, 1987.

» DISCUSSION QUESTIONS «

1. What does the unfaithful wife imagery in the prophets say to us today about our relationship with God? To what extent does God desire an intimate and emotional relationship from us? Does this relationship make him vulnerable?

2. Why does God command Hosea to marry a woman with a bad reputation?

3. Discuss the difficulty in taking back a spouse who has been unfaithful. How does this difficulty relate to God's relationship to us?

» WRITING ASSIGNMENTS «

1. Discuss the three relational images in Hosea (king/subjects; father/child; husband/wife) in regard to intimacy and emotional response. Which one is the most intimate and emotional? Why does Yahweh use this image?

2. In today's world how does the offense of a speeding ticket differ in its consequences and its emotional effects from the offense of an adulterous affair in a marriage? Which image (speeding ticket or adulterous affair) best illustrates sin and its effect? Which image reflects the more popular thinking of people in America regarding sin? Why?

3. Summarize the main points of Hosea 14.

CHAPTER 20

Joel

"Return to Yahweh your God, for he is gracious and compassionate, slow to anger and abounding in love." (Joel 2:13)

OVERVIEW OF JOEL

Setting

The prophet Joel is not mentioned anywhere else in the Old Testament outside the book of Joel, and thus little is known about him. Likewise, the book of Joel gives no indication of the time in which it was written. Unlike many of the other prophetic books, no Israelite or Judahite kings are mentioned that would allow scholars to date the book with precision. Based only on the content of the book, many scholars have concluded that it was written just before either the Assyrian invasion of Israel (late eighth century BC) or just before the Babylonian invasion of Judah (late seventh to early sixth century BC). The latter view seems to have the strongest support. On the other hand, some older scholars argued for an even earlier date (ninth century), while the recent trend among many scholars is to favor an early postexilic date (late sixth to early fifth century BC).

> Joel skips the first point of the standard prophetic message.

Message

Many of the specific descriptions of judgment that the prophets proclaim on Israel and Judah come directly from Deuteronomy 28. Much of Joel's message is closely connected to his extensive description of a locust plague. Thus Joel appears to draw directly from the warning judgment of Deuteronomy 28:38, 42, "You will sow much seed in the field but you will harvest little, because locusts will devour it.... Swarms of locusts will take over all your trees and the crops of your land." Unlike most of the other prophets, Joel skips the first point of the standard prophetic message ("You have broken the covenant" — idolatry, social injustice, religious formalism), apparently assuming the broken covenant. He does frequently call for repentance as he focuses on point two, "Judg-

Middle Eastern locusts, related to the grasshopper.

ment," and then moves to point three, "Future hope and restoration." That is, Joel skips over listing the many covenant violations and simply focuses on the resultant curse from Deuteronomy, apparently assuming that his audience is well aware of their guilt. He does, however, include a call to repent as well as a picture of future restoration and a section of judgment on the nations.

Structurally, the book of Joel breaks down into two halves, with 2:18 functioning as the hinge. Each of the two halves also contains two units. Thus the structure is as follows:

I. The Judgment
    1:2–20 The coming locust invasion (perhaps a near view), and a call to repentance
    2:1–17 The coming locust invasion (perhaps a far view), and a call to repentance
II. Yahweh's response
    2:18–32 Future restoration (the giving of Yahweh's Spirit)
    3:1–21 Judgment on the nations

House suggests that Joel continues the central focus on "warning" that unites the first six books (Hosea to Micah) within the Book of the Twelve.[1] Yet Joel also reminds the readers that Yahweh is slow to anger and that he will always relent if his people will only repent. In this sense Joel reflects the theology of Hosea 1–2 and tempers the focus on judgment coming in Amos.

---

1. Paul House, "The Character of God in the Book of the Twelve," in James D. Nogalski and Marvin A. Sweeney, *Reading and Hearing the Book of the Twelve,* SBL Symposium Series 15 (Atlanta: Society of Biblical Literature, 2000), 131–32.

Locust Plagues in the Ancient Near East

Plagues of locusts moving across the land were a recurring and terrifying phenomenon in the Ancient Near East (like hurricanes for those today on the Gulf Coast and tornadoes for those in the "tornado alley" of the midwestern and southern United States). In the Ancient Near East the locusts normally bred in the region south of Egypt (modern Sudan) and then migrated north in February-March, following the prevailing wind. Locust swarms can cover up to 400 square miles, each square mile containing over 100 million insects, each of which normally consumes its own weight each day![1]

The seriousness of locusts in the Ancient Near East is perhaps indicated by the large number of words that the ancient languages had for various kinds of locusts. The Old Testament uses nine different words for locusts (four different words are used in Joel) and in Akkadian (the language of the Babylonians and Assyrians) there are eighteen different words. The analogy between a locust plague and an invading human army was all too obvious, and Joel is not the only one to make use of it. Such metaphoric usage of locust plagues occurs in Sumerian, Egyptian, Ugaritic, and Neo-Assyrian texts.[2]

---

1. John H. Walton, Victor H. Matthews, and Mark W. Chavalas, *The IVP Bible Background Commentary: Old Testament* (Downers Grove, IL: InterVarsity Press, 2000), 760.
2. Ibid., 760–61.

JOEL 1:1 – 2:17 — THE LOCUST PLAGUES

The first two units of Joel (1:2 – 20 and 2:1 – 17) both describe locust plagues. Numerous interpretive questions arise out of these chapters. Is this locust plague literal or is it symbolic of an invading army (i.e., Assyrians or Babylonians)? Is the plague in Joel 1 different from that in Joel 2? Why are they described differently? Scholars differ in their answers; however, the most probable interpretation is to take Joel 1 as a reference to a literal, historical locust plague that has already happened. This locust invasion is but a wake-up call from Yahweh. Thus in 2:1 – 17 Yahweh uses the locust plague imagery to describe, figuratively and poetically, the coming human army invasion (either the Assyrians or the Babylonians).

> The first two chapters of Joel both describe locust plagues.

Joel 1:2 – 3 indicates that this particular locust plague was one of the worst in their memory. Joel 1:4 uses four different words for the locusts. Scholars are uncertain whether these words refer to different stages of development in the life cycle of locusts or whether they refer to different species. Probably the point is that wave after wave of locust swarms have passed through the land, each wave stripping the land of vegetation even further.

Note the sarcastic irony of 1:5 as Joel calls on the sleeping drunkards to wake up and weep because there will not be any more wine. Joel 1:11 – 12 underscores the agricultural disaster in the wake of the locust invasion. Joel lists eight different crops or fruits that will be destroyed, underscoring the extent of the devastation (listing "seven" would have represented completion or totality; "eight" poetically implies an extent beyond totality).[2]

In light of the locust disaster, in Joel 1:13 – 14 the prophet calls for repentance. Dressing in sackcloth and fasting were the outward signs of repentance. In the book of Jonah sackcloth and fasting are the repentant actions of the Assyrians in Nineveh that cause Yahweh to avert the judgment coming on them. Here Joel calls on Israel's priests (1:13) and elders (1:14) to repent with fasting and sackcloth to avert the coming judgment, which Joel refers to as "the day of Yahweh" (1:15).

Joel 2 continues to speak of a locust invasion, but now Joel is probably using the locust figuratively to describe a coming Assyrian or Babylonian invasion. Keep in mind that most of Joel is poetry, and the figurative, colorful description of the locusts marching in straight lines and scaling the walls of cities should be interpreted as a poetic description of the coming invasion. As the other prophets do, Joel

A scene of threshing the harvest in the hills of Judea. Joel 2:24 includes abundant harvest on the threshing floors as part of the restoration blessing.

Library of Congress/LC-matpc-00041/www.LifeintheHolyLand.com

2. Robert B. Chisholm Jr., *Handbook on the Prophets* (Grand Rapids: Baker, 2002), 369.

reminds his audience that this invasion is not by chance or at the whim of foreign nations. Rather, it is Yahweh himself who brings this invasion to Israel. Joel paints the picture of Yahweh leading the invading army: "Yahweh thunders at the head of his army; his forces are beyond number, and mighty are those who obey his command. The day of Yahweh is great; it is dreadful. Who can endure it?" (2:11).

In Joel 2:12–17 the prophet makes another impassioned plea for repentance. "Return [*shūv*] to me with all your heart.... Rend your heart and not your garments" (2:12–13). These verses point to the need for inward repentance and not hypocritical outward-only repentance. Joel uses the Hebrew word *shūv* (turn, repent) much like Jeremiah does. If the people will *shūv* (turn) to Yahweh, then he will *shūv* (turn) away from judging them. Joel 2:14 is very similar to Jonah 3:9, posing the question, "Who knows but that he [Yahweh] may turn [*shūv*] and have pity." The reason they can even pose that question (when they truly deserve judgment) is the character of Yahweh described in Joel 2:13 — Yahweh is "gracious and compassionate, slow to anger and abounding in love [*hesed*], and he relents from sending calamity." The word translated as "relent" (occurring both here and in Jonah 3:9) implies changing one's mind about something. The prophets

> Joel reminds his audience that this invasion is not by chance or at the whim of foreign nations.

The Day of Yahweh (the LORD)

The English phrase "day of the LORD" is a translation of the Hebrew "day of Yahweh." The prophets use this phrase to refer to a time in the future (either near or far) when Yahweh will intervene into human history in a dramatic and decisive way to bring about his plan, including both judgment and blessing/salvation.

Thus the "day of Yahweh" will be a time of future judgment on Israel and Judah because of their covenant disobedience (Isa. 3:18–4:1; Amos 5:18–20), but it also includes a time of judgment on the foreign nations that have oppressed or harmed Israel or Judah (Isa. 13:1–22; Obad. 15). Likewise, the prophets will describe the time of future restoration and blessing, both for Israel/Judah and for the nations, as part of the "day of Yahweh" (Isa. 11:10–12; Joel 3:14–18). While "day of Yahweh" is the major terminology for this concept, the prophets also use several synonyms such as "that day," or "the day" in reference to the "day of Yahweh."

The "day of Yahweh" is an important theme running throughout most of the prophetic material. Used frequently in Isaiah, it is also quite prominent in the Book of the Twelve, playing a central thematic role in several key passages (Joel 2:28–3:21; Zeph. 1–3). As mentioned earlier, several scholars have even suggested that the "day of Yahweh" is a central unifying theme for the Book of the Twelve.

The New Testament appropriates this term as well, likewise using a range of terms such as "that day," "those days," or "the great day" synonymously with "the day of the Lord." Joel's prophecy in 2:28–31 described the outpouring of Yahweh's Spirit on the "day of Yahweh." Luke identifies the outpouring of the Spirit on the day of Pentecost as the fulfillment of Joel's prophecy (Acts 2:17–21), thus indicating that certain aspects of the "day of Yahweh" began to be fulfilled at the time of Christ's first coming. Usually, however, the New Testament writers use the term "day of the Lord" and its synonyms to refer to the time of Christ's return (Mark 13:24; 1 Cor. 5:5; 1 Thess. 5:2; 2 Thess. 2:2; 2 Peter 3:10, 12).

often run up against the theological mystery of how Yahweh's total and complete sovereignty fits with his gracious character and his inclination to respond positively to prayer and repentance in order to change things. The prophets (and Jonah makes this extremely clear) often declare judgment as imminent, a done deal, something Yahweh has announced as certain. At the same time, they plead with the people to repent, because if they repent, Yahweh will "change his mind" or "change the plan" and not send the judgment. Joel 2:13 stresses that this gracious response of Yahweh is part of his character.

> If the people will *shūv* (turn) to Yahweh, then he will *shūv* (turn) away from judging them.

In Joel 2:1 the prophet states, "Blow the trumpet in Zion." This trumpet call would be warning the people of the invasion, calling them to flee to the fortified fortress of Jerusalem (similar to Jer. 4:5). Joel 2:15 repeats this command, "Blow the trumpet in Zion," but in contrast, this trumpet now summons the people together to fast and mourn (signs of repentance).

FUTURE RESTORATION

Because Joel 2:13 is true, Yahweh does not totally destroy his people, and instead he promises a future for them. Joel 2:18 is a transition, stating that Yahweh will indeed take pity on them. In the verses that follow (through verse 32), Yahweh drives away the northern army and restores his people to the Land, which will become fertile again. The result? Sounding very similar to Ezekiel, Joel states, "Then you will know that I am in Israel, that I am Yahweh your God" (2:27).

An Assyrian portrayal of the siege of Lachish, a city in Judah. "They charge like warriors; they scale walls like soldiers. They all march in line" (Joel 2:7).

Caryn Reeder

The Spirit of Yahweh

The Spirit of Yahweh plays a major theological and prophetic role in Isaiah, Ezekiel, Joel, Micah, and Zechariah. In these prophetic books, as well as in other texts in the Old Testament, the Spirit of Yahweh is integrally associated with three central interrelated characteristics of Yahweh: his presence, his power, and his revelation. Unlike New Testament believers, followers of Yahweh in the Old Testament do not regularly or routinely receive the Spirit. Yahweh sends his Spirit upon special people at special times for specific purposes. The Spirit of Yahweh is closely related to Yahweh's presence, and thus when the Spirit comes upon an individual, it brings special divine power and enablement. Often that power and enablement is in regard to revelation and wisdom or understanding, thus leading to oracles and prophecy.

One of the characteristics that Isaiah attributes to the great coming Davidic king (the Messiah) is that he will be empowered by the Spirit of Yahweh. For example, in Isaiah 11, the prophet proclaims, "The Spirit of Yahweh will rest on him — the Spirit of wisdom and of understanding, the Spirit of counsel and of power, the Spirit of knowledge and of the fear of Yahweh" (Isa. 11:2). In Isaiah 42:1 the Spirit empowers the Servant to carry out justice, a connection also repeated and expanded in Isaiah 61:1 – 3.

In Joel and Ezekiel, however, Yahweh proclaims a radically new concept regarding his Spirit and the coming messianic era (Joel 2:28 – 29; Ezek. 36:27; perhaps faintly foreshadowed in Isa. 32:15). In these verses Yahweh reveals that in the coming messianic era he will pour out his Spirit on every one of his people. As part of the new covenant, Yahweh promised that he would write his law in the hearts and minds of his people and enable them all to know him (Jer. 31:33 – 34). In Jeremiah, Yahweh does not reveal how this will happen. In Joel 2 and Ezekiel 36, however, the prophecy becomes clear. Yahweh promises to put his Spirit within people, empowering them to know him, to be obedient to him, and to speak prophetically of him.

At the very beginning of his public ministry, Jesus identifies himself as the coming one empowered by the Spirit that Isaiah spoke of. In Luke 4:18 Jesus quotes directly from Isaiah 61:1, "The Spirit of the Lord is on me." Throughout the Gospels the Spirit is active in Jesus' life, evidence that he is indeed the Spirit-empowered Davidic king/deliverer that Isaiah had promised (Isa. 11:1 – 4).

Yet, as in the Old Testament prophets, the New Testament also underscores the important event in which God pours out his Spirit to dwell within each of his followers. Jesus explains and expounds on much of this in John 13 – 17.[1] Then, as mentioned above, at Pentecost the Spirit actually comes and fills each follower of Christ (Acts 2). Peter makes the obvious connection, citing Joel 2:28 – 32 to explain what has happened. The role of the Spirit in the book of Acts, both as the indwelling presence of God and as the empowering force for the early expanding church, is evidence that the prophecies of Isaiah, Ezekiel, and Joel are being fulfilled and that the messianic age has indeed dawned.

---

1. M. Turner, "Holy Spirit," in *New Dictionary of Biblical Theology*, ed. T. Desmond et al. (Downers Grove, IL, and Leicester, England: InterVarsity Press, 2000), 555 – 56.

As he did in Ezekiel, in Joel 2:28 – 32 Yahweh promises to pour out his Spirit on his people. Joel 2:28 – 29 stresses the point that all kinds of people (sons, daughters, old, young, men and women) will receive the Spirit of Yahweh. This is in sharp contrast to all earlier occurrences when Yahweh gave his Spirit. Normally he gave his Spirit only to a few select people at a few special times in history, people like Moses or King David or the prophets. Now Yahweh is promising to give his Spirit to all of his people, indicating a remarkable shift or change to something new. Remember that the Spirit of Yahweh is closely connected throughout the Old Testament to three themes: presence, power, and revelation from Yahweh. Thus the promise of the Spirit implies that people will know and experience the presence of Yahweh in a new way, that they will have knowledge of him in a new way, and that this new presence and knowledge will bring enabling power to these people.

This pouring out of the Spirit is connected to the day of Yahweh (2:31), a time when Yahweh will roar in judgment. Astronomical signs will occur. The sun will grow dark (as in the plague of Exodus 10:21 – 29) and the moon will turn blood red. "Everyone who calls on the name of Yahweh," however, "will be saved" from this judgment (Joel 2:32), a text quoted by Paul in Romans 10:13.

JOEL 3:1 – 21 — JUDGMENT ON THE NATIONS

Joel 3 continues to look to the future but shifts the theme from future restoration of Israel to future judgment on the nations. As with many other prophecies, this one seems to include near view and far view features in close proximity. Specific nations are mentioned and cited for their atrocities against Israel (3:1 – 8), but the strong poetic language of 3:12 – 18 seems to move beyond the near view, in keeping with our understanding of the "day of Yahweh." As in Joel 2:30 – 31, astronomical signs accompany the coming of Yahweh in judgment (3:15 – 16). Joel also mentions a fountain flowing out of Yahweh's house (the temple) as Ezekiel describes in Ezekiel 47:1 – 12. Also as in the case of Ezekiel, Joel concludes his prophecy with a stress on the presence of Yahweh, dwelling on Zion in Jerusalem (3:17, 21).

A *shofar* (trumpet) made from a ram's horn. Frequently the prophets refer to blowing the trumpet to announce the coming judgment (Assyrians or Babylonians). Joel mentions the *shofar* twice (2:1, 15). The other prophets use this term a total of twenty times.

Joel 2:28 – 29 stresses the point that all kinds of people (sons, daughters, old, young, men and women) will receive the Spirit of Yahweh.

» FURTHER READING «

Allen, Leslie C. *The Books of Joel, Obadiah, Jonah and Micah*. The New International Commentary on the Old Testament. Grand Rapids: Eerdmans, 1976.

Baker, David W. *Joel, Obadiah, Malachi*. NIV Application Commentary. Grand Rapids: Zondervan, 2006.

Garrett, Duane. *Hosea, Joel*. New American Commentary. Nashville: Broadman & Holman, 1997.

Stuart, Douglas. *Hosea-Jonah*. Word Biblical Commentary. Waco, TX: Word Books, 1987.

» DISCUSSION QUESTIONS «

1. Discuss whether the locust plague in Joel 2 is literal or figurative.

2. What is included in the term "day of Yahweh"?

3. What is the Old Testament theological significance of Yahweh promising to pour out his Spirit on all people (Joel 2:28 – 32)?

» WRITING ASSIGNMENTS «

1. Compare the description of the "day of Yahweh" in the Old Testament with the "day of the Lord" in the New Testament.

2. Explain Peter's use of Joel 2:28 – 32 in Acts 2.

CHAPTER 21

Amos

"Let justice roll on like a river. . . ."

(Amos 5:24)

OVERVIEW OF AMOS

Setting

Amos provides a very specific historical setting for his prophetic words. Amos 1:1 dates his prophecy to the reigns of Uzziah, king of Judah (783–742 BC), and Jeroboam II of Israel (786–746 BC). Furthermore, Amos dates his prophecy to "two years before the earthquake," apparently referring to a severe earthquake that everyone in his time remembered.

Also, note that this reference to "two years before the earthquake" implies that Amos's message did not stretch out over a long period of time, as did Jeremiah's and Hosea's, but covered a very short period, perhaps only a few months.

> Although Amos is from Judah, his message is directed against Israel.

Although Amos is from Judah, his message is directed against the northern kingdom, Israel. As mentioned earlier, during Jeroboam's reign Israel experienced a time of prosperity, enjoyed especially by the upper classes.

Remember also that the northern kingdom of Israel fell into idol worship immediately after splitting away from Judah and Jerusalem (1 Kings 12). They created new worship centers with calf idols at Bethel, Dan, and (apparently) at Gilgal.

Message

Amos delivers the same basic message as do the rest of the standard preexilic prophets:

1. You (Israel/Judah) have broken the covenant; you had better repent!
2. No repentance? Then judgment! Judgment will also come on the nations.
3. Yet there is hope beyond the judgment for a glorious future restoration, both for Israel/Judah and for the nations.

The ruins of Samaria, the capital of the northern kingdom Israel.

Golf Bravo/Wikimedia Commons

Amos, however, stresses points one and two, especially the themes of broken covenant (sin) and impending judgment. He directs his prophecy of impending judgment specifically at Israel. Unlike many of the other prophets, Amos does not have oracles of hope and future restoration scattered throughout his book. No hope or future restoration is mentioned until right at the end of the book in Amos 9. Like the other prophets, Amos's indictment on Israel centers on three main sins: idolatry, social injustice, and religious ritualism. Social injustice is a particularly pervasive theme in Amos, especially Yahweh's concern for and anger over the neglect and oppression of the poor. Amos levels scathing critiques at the selfish, self-centered, decadent wealthy class (both men and women) who exploit the poor to increase their wealth. This message is especially relevant to us today at a time when Christians in North America have unprecedented wealth, while much of the world (both here and abroad) lives in poverty and struggles to survive.

> Amos stresses points one and two, especially the themes of broken covenant (sin) and impending judgment.

Canonically, Amos lies in the middle of the opening unit of the Book of the Twelve, which focuses on Yahweh's warning of judgment. Also, as mentioned earlier, Joel 3:16 ("Yahweh will roar from Zion") anticipates and connects to the extensive lion imagery in Amos. Likewise, Amos ends with a judgment on Edom (9:12), and the destruction of Edom is the focus of the next book in the canon (Obadiah). In addition, the locust plague imagery, so important in Joel, resurfaces in Amos twice (4:9; 7:1). Finally, as throughout the Book of the Twelve, Amos describes the terrible, dreadful "day of Yahweh" (5:18–20).

The Man Amos

In contrast to Joel, we are given quite a bit of information about Amos. He is called a "shepherd" (1:1; 7:14), a term that might better be understood as "a breeder of sheep." Amos is probably the owner of a substantial flock and not just the simple shepherd who watches over them. He also refers to himself as one who takes care of sycamore-fig trees. Thus, in contrast to many of the other prophets who come from priestly families (Jeremiah, Ezekiel), Amos is a shepherd/farmer by occupation. Remember also that Amos is from Judah (the southern kingdom) but he preaches against Israel (the northern kingdom). Thus Yahweh chooses a farmer from Judah to travel to Israel and deliver a scathing polemical message against the wealthy ruling families there. Not surprisingly, the critical message from this rustic prophet from the south was not well received by the sophisticated upper classes that controlled Israel, the northern kingdom.

> Yahweh chooses a farmer from Judah to travel north to Israel and deliver a scathing polemical message against the wealthy ruling families there.

AMOS 1–2—"FOR THREE SINS, EVEN FOR FOUR, I WILL SEND FIRE"

After identifying Amos and the time of his prophecy in Amos 1:1, Amos 1:2 introduces the message of the book by declaring, "Yahweh roars from Zion." The word translated as "roars" is specifically used in regard to lions, so Amos is comparing Yahweh metaphorically to a dangerous lion. Keep in mind that Amos prophesies in a time before electric lights, cars, and rifles, things that minimize the fear of lions, even in Africa. In his day, if you were traveling on the open road on foot or were in the open field plowing and you heard the roar of a lion, it would strike terror in your heart. Yahweh is compared metaphorically to a lion because he is dangerous and, like a hungry lion, he is circling around his prey for the kill. Amos also declares that Yahweh "thunders," a reference to the loud, frightening thunder of a storm. Ironically, however, the thundering of Yahweh brings a terrible drought instead of a rainstorm. Droughts were part of the warning curses that would come upon Israel if they broke the covenant with Yahweh (Lev. 26:19; Deut. 28:22–24).

The ruins of Ashkelon, a Philistine city. Amos pronounces judgment against the Philistines in 1:6–8.

In the first major unit (Amos 1:3–2:16) Yahweh declares judgment on six surrounding foreign nations: Damascus (i.e., Aram or Syria), Gaza and Ashdod (i.e., Philistia), Tyre, Edom, Ammon, and Moab. Next he proclaims judgment on Judah and then Israel. The specific offenses cited for the surrounding nations are sins of cruelty and violence, often relating to selling groups of people into slavery. The sins of Judah are rejecting Yahweh's law and following other gods. In each case, Yahweh introduces the judgment oracle with the phrase, "For three sins of X, even for four, I will not turn back my wrath." The formula-like phrase "for three sins, even for four" is simply a poetic way to say "These people have committed numerous sins." In each of the first seven oracles (against the six foreign nations and Judah), Yahweh pronounces the same judgment, "I will send fire" (1:4, 7, 10, 12, 14; 2:2, 5).

> The list of wrongs that Yahweh cites against Israel includes a mix of social, sexual, and religious sins.

The focus of this unit, however, is on Israel. In fact, the sequence of judgments on the other nations serves a rhetorical function for an Israelite audience. As they hear each judgment pronounced on their neighbors, no doubt they would have responded with a hearty "Amen!"—agreeing with the appropriateness of the judgment on their enemies. Even Judah was an enemy, and they would have been in favor of judgment on their kinfolk to the south. However, after proclaiming judgment on the neighbors all around Israel, Yahweh then zeroes in on the primary culprit—Israel herself. At this point the chorus of "Amen!" would no doubt cease as Yahweh directs his primary oracle of judgment at Israel. In essence, by including them in the list of foreign nations to be judged, Yahweh is treating Israel as a foreign nation.

> Yahweh is extremely serious about the issue of social justice, especially regarding the needs and rights of the weak and the poor.

The list of wrongs that Yahweh cites against Israel includes a mix of social, sexual, and religious sins. Israel is charged with selling the "righteous" and needy for silver or even for a pair of shoes (2:6). They trample the heads of the poor into the dust and deny justice to these oppressed ones (2:7). Fathers and sons are sharing the same girl, probably a concubine or a cult prostitute (2:7).

Part of their exploitation was taking the very garments that the poor needed to keep warm at night. These garments were given in pledge, probably as collateral for a loan to pay an extorted debt. The wealthy people of Israel then used these garments to lounge on as they drank their wine (paid for by money taken from the poor) before their altars of worship. Their hypocrisy and complete indifference to the plight of the poor infuriates Yahweh. Although Yahweh promises to send fire on the other seven nations in this unit, in regard to Israel he changes images, promising instead to "crush" them as a heavily loaded cart crushes small things that it runs over. One of the theological truths emerging clearly out of this passage is that Yahweh is extremely serious about the issue of social justice, especially regarding the needs and rights of the weak and the poor.

AMOS 3–4—THE LION HAS ROARED

Amos 3:1–2 reminds the Israelites of their origins as a special people brought up by Yahweh out of slavery in Egypt. The implication is that they are all the more culpable for forsaking

Lions were the most feared of the wild animals.

Yahweh and committing so many serious sins. In Amos 3:3–8 the prophet asks seven questions, all of which have obvious answers. In English this would be like asking, "Do bees buzz?" The first five questions are proverb-like questions, most of them alluding to lions capturing prey or birds captured in traps. Question six moves a little closer to the main point by asking, "When a trumpet sounds in a city [i.e., announcing the approach of an invading army], do not the people tremble?" Question seven is the climactic question in this rhetorical sequence: "When disaster comes to a city, has not Yahweh caused it?" (3:6). The answer is again obvious. The coming judgment on Samaria (capital of the northern kingdom Israel) will not be a random, coincidental event, but a specific course of action brought about by Yahweh. Amos 3:7–8 declares that the lion (Yahweh) has roared (judgment) and that he has revealed this coming judgment to his prophets who are compelled to proclaim it.

Next Amos describes the judgment with colorful, sarcastic, poetic—yet very grim—language, "As the shepherd snatches two legs or a piece of an ear from the lion's mouth, so the Israelites who live in Samaria will be rescued with only the corner of a bed or the cushion of a couch" (3:12, HCSB; most of the newer translations such as ESV, NLT and NRSV also reflect this understanding of the verse, while NIV appears to miss the sense of the second half of the verse somewhat). Amos 3:14 highlights the judgment upon the golden calves that Israel worshipped at Bethel. In 3:15 Amos declares that all of the great luxurious mansions that the wealthy Israelites have been living in will be destroyed.

> Amos calls these wealthy women "cows," a reference that probably did not sit well with them.

The scathing sarcasm of Amos continues in chapter 4. He castigates the wealthy women of Samaria for oppressing the poor and crushing the needy while only being concerned about their "drinks." Amos calls these wealthy women "cows," a reference that probably did not sit well with them. He tells them that they will be dragged out and taken away with fishhooks. "Go on to Bethel and sin!" Yahweh tells the Israelites sarcastically, since that is what they like to do anyway (4:4–5).

Yahweh then declares that he has already tried to get the Israelites to repent by warning them repeatedly through numerous lesser judgments, but each time the result was the same: "Yet you have not returned to me" (4:6, 8, 9, 10, 11). The serious result of this repeated failure to repent comes in 4:12: "Prepare to meet your God, O Israel."

AMOS 5 — YAHWEH DEMANDS JUSTICE, NOT RITUAL

Amos 5 is a powerful chapter stressing the importance of social justice and underscoring that the religious rituals of Israel cannot replace the requirement to live justly, especially in regard to the poor. The chapter starts out with a lament (a funeral eulogy) over the imminent fall of Israel. Amos 5:3 presents the terrible casualty rate—only 10 percent will survive. Starting in 5:7, the theme of justice dominates the chapter. The Israelites are accused of trampling on the poor and exploiting them. Those who have no socioeconomic power are regularly denied justice in the courts, where the bribery system favors those in power with money (5:11–13). Yahweh demands of his people that they "maintain justice in the courts" (lit. "gates," where court was held; 5:15). The consequence for this lack of justice is described in 5:18–20—the terrible day of Yahweh is coming. Likewise, in light of their total lack of concern for justice, their hypocritical worship not only fails to please Yahweh but is actually annoying to him: "I hate your religious feasts.... I will have no regard for your offerings.... I will not listen to the music of your harps" (5:21–23). What is the sound that Yahweh wants to hear? "Let justice roll on like a river, righteousness like a never-failing stream!" (5:24).

> Amos reveals the terrible casualty rate— only 10 percent of the people will survive.

AMOS 6—JUDGMENT ON THE WEALTHY AND COMPLACENT

Amos 6:1 includes the wealthy and complacent people of Zion (i.e., Jerusalem, capital of Judah) along with those in Samaria as recipients of this prophecy of judgment. Amos, the rustic farmer, describes these wealthy, self-centered people: "You lie on beds inlaid with ivory.... You dine on choice lambs and fatted calves.... You strum away on your harps like David.... You drink wine by the bowlful" (6:4–6). However, Amos declares, they are not concerned in the least over the spiritual situation in the country. "Therefore," Amos proclaims, "you will be among the first to go into exile; your feasting and lounging will stop" (6:7).

AMOS 7:1–8:3—FOUR VISIONS

In this unit Yahweh gives Amos four visions that portend the coming judgment. The first vision is one of a terrible locust plague (similar to that in the book of Joel). Amos pleads with

Beitin (biblical Bethel), where Israel had established a sanctuary for idol worship.

Courtesy of www.HolyLandPhotos.org

Yahweh, declaring that "Jacob [Israel] is so small" (7:2). The size and scope of the locust invasion made Israel look small and defenseless. In response to Amos's plea, Yahweh relents.

In the second vision it is fire, rather than locusts, that ravages the land. Recall how the book of Amos began. In the opening unit Yahweh said he would send fire on each of the six foreign nations contained in the list (1:4, 7, 10, 12, 14; 2:2) as well as on Judah (2:5). Now in 7:3–4 Yahweh sends fire on Israel. Amos again cries out that Jacob (Israel) is so small that she won't survive, so Yahweh once again relents.

In the third vision Yahweh talks to Amos about a wall (7:7–9). This passage contains some Hebrew text that is difficult to translate. Most English translations have followed the traditional understanding of this passage, translating the central term in question as a "plumb line." A plumb line is a weight on a string used to be sure that something—in this case, a stone wall—is exactly vertical. If it was not, then it could easily fall over. Thus Yahweh holds a plumb line to a wall that represents Israel, implying that, like a crooked "out of plumb" wall, it will easily fall. However, the majority of recent Old Testament scholars favor translating this term as "tin," which is used in contrast to strong materials such as iron or bronze. Thus Yahweh is mocking the defenses of Israel, saying that their walls are weak, only made of tin. This understanding connects with Amos's cry in the first two visions (Jacob is too small).

> Yahweh is mocking the defenses of Israel, saying that their walls are weak, only made of tin.

Amos 7:10–17 is an interruption between visions three and four. This passage is biographical in nature and describes Amos's encounter with Amaziah, a high priest of sorts, who was in charge of the sanctuary at Bethel (where the calf idol was worshiped). Amaziah reports to King Jeroboam concerning Amos's words of judgment against the king. Then Amaziah confronts Amos, calling him a "seer" (another name for prophet) and telling him to return back home to his native country of Judah and not to prophesy against Bethel anymore. In a self-indicting statement, Amaziah declares, "This is the king's sanctuary and the temple of the kingdom" (7:13), thus inadvertently acknowledging that the sanctuary at Bethel was not Yahweh's sanctuary.

> The time is ripe for judgment on Israel.

Amos responds by saying that he is neither a prophet nor the son of a prophet, probably indicating that he was not part of the "schools" or guilds of professional prophets that apparently existed. On the other hand, Amos declares, he was only a shepherd and keeper of sycamore-figs and Yahweh was the one who told him to proclaim judgment on Israel. In essence, the reaction of Amaziah points out that there was no repentance in response to Amos's message. The official reaction is that given by Amaziah, who tells Amos to quit prophesying against them and to return home. Amos then confronts the priest Amaziah and informs him of the coming judgment on him and his family as well as the exile of the nation of Israel (7:17). Amos's fourth vision is described in 8:1–3. The vision is a basket of ripe fruit. Yahweh explains the significance: the time is ripe for judgment on Israel.

AMOS 8:4–9:10—JUDGMENT ON ISRAEL

Yahweh chastises Israel for economic dishonesty in the marketplace as well as buying and selling the poor (8:4–6). He once again describes the coming judgment (8:7–9:10). How-

Ruins of the foundation of the altar for idol worship in Dan.

ever, toward the end of this section Yahweh indicates that a remnant will survive: "Yet I will not totally destroy the house of Jacob" (9:8).

AMOS 9:11 – 15 — FINALLY, HOPE AND RESTORATION

After eight and a half chapters of pointing out sin and promising judgment, Amos concludes with a few verses of future restoration. Yahweh declares that he will restore David's fallen tent (in fulfillment of the Davidic covenant) (9:11). This text promises a Davidic king that will also rule over the nations (9:12). Keep in mind that the northern kingdom, Israel, had thrown off the rule of the Davidic kings in the south more than 80 years earlier. Amos's prophecy points to a time of future reunification under a Davidic king. Furthermore, Amos continues by pointing to a time when Israel would return back to the land and be prosperous once again (9:13 – 15).

> Amos concludes with a very few brief verses describing the future restoration.

» FURTHER READING «

Carroll R., M. Daniel. *Amos*. New International Commentary on the Old Testament. Grand Rapids: Eerdmans, forthcoming.

Mays, James Luther. *Amos*. The Old Testament Library. Philadelphia: Westminster, 1969.

Motyer, J. A. *The Message of Amos: The Day of the Lion*. The Bible Speaks Today. Leicester, England and Downers Grove, IL: InterVarsity Press, 1974.

Smith, Gary V. *Hosea, Amos, Micah*. NIV Application Commentary. Grand Rapids: Zondervan, 2001.

Stuart, Douglas. *Hosea-Jonah*. Word Biblical Commentary. Waco, TX: Word Books, 1987.

On the Christian responsibility toward poverty:

Blomberg, Craig. *Neither Poverty nor Riches*. NSBT. Downers Grove, IL: InterVarsity Press, 2001.

Sider, Ronald J. *Rich Christians in an Age of Hunger,* rev. ed. Nashville: W Publishing Group, 1997.

» DISCUSSION QUESTIONS «

1. Discuss Yahweh's concern with justice and the proper treatment of the underclass (the poor and weak). Discuss this situation for the church today. Who are the poor or the socioeconomic underclass today? Do they receive the same justice in our courts that a wealthy person gets? Does this vary from country to country today? What should your attitude be if you encounter injustice taking place?

2. Discuss how your relationship with God should affect your relationship with people. Explain how your attitude and actions toward people relate to your worship of God.

» WRITING ASSIGNMENTS «

1. Trace the theme of social justice throughout Amos.

2. Discuss the different images used in Amos for judgment.

CHAPTER 22

Obadiah and Jonah

"Should I not be concerned about that great city?"

(Jonah 4:11)

OVERVIEW — THE NON-STANDARD PROPHETS

Obadiah prophesies against Edom shortly after the fall of Jerusalem to the Babylonians in 586 BC.

Other than Daniel, all of the prophets that we have studied so far can be categorized as "standard" prophets in that, with only slight variations, they all follow the standard three-part prophetic message. Daniel, Obadiah, Jonah, and Nahum, however, do not follow that pattern. We can label them "non-standard" prophets. None of them directs their spoken message to Israel or Judah. Obadiah preaches against Edom; Jonah and Nahum (discussed in chapter 24) preach against Nineveh (Assyria). Daniel's message is about world empires (discussed in chapters 17 and 18). However, each plays an important role in the progression of the central message developed in the Book of the Twelve (warning, judgment, restoration).

OBADIAH — THE END OF EDOM

Obadiah prophesies against Edom shortly after the fall of Jerusalem to the Babylonians in 586 BC. Edom, which had often schemed with Judah as an ally, turns against Judah when Babylonian victory becomes obvious and joins in the plundering of Judah when the nation falls. Obadiah prophesies that judgment will fall on Edom for what they did to Judah. Recall that Jeremiah also prophesies against Edom during this same period (Jer. 49:7–22). Indeed, there are numerous similarities between Jeremiah 49:7–22 and the short book of Obadiah. In several prophetic books Edom appears to represent symbolically all the nations of the world that will come under Yahweh's judgment (Joel 3:19; Amos 1:11–12; 9:12). Some scholars have suggested that Obadiah is located canonically right after Amos because Amos declares judgment on Edom right at the end of his book (9:12).[1]

Edom is located to the southeast of Judah (see map). Edom had strong fortresses securely located within a rugged mountain range. Jeremiah alludes to their mountain cities in 49:16: "You who live in the clefts of the rocks, who occupy the heights of the hill." Obadiah appears to allude to their mountain dwellings in verse 4 ("Though you soar like the eagle and make your nest among the stars") as well as in verses 8–9.

Obadiah prophesies the future restoration of Judah (17–21). In contrast to the complete end of Edom, the people of Israel, who are now exiles, will flourish and actually rule over the mountains of Edom.

The land of Edom.

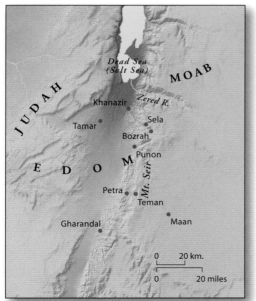

1. J. Gordon McConville, *Exploring the Old Testament: A Guide to the Prophets* (Downers Grove, IL: InterVarsity Press, 2002), 133; Christopher R. Seitz, *Prophecy and Hermeneutics: Toward a New Introduction to the Prophets* (Grand Rapids: Baker, 2007), 138–39, 237.

OVERVIEW OF JONAH

Setting

Unlike Hosea and Amos, the book of Jonah does not contain an opening statement that connects the book to the reign of particular Israelite or Judahite kings. Neither does the book present itself as the words of the prophet from Yahweh or as an oracle from Yahweh through the prophet. In fact, in literary style the book of Jonah resembles historical narrative more than the style of the traditional prophets. The book of Jonah is a story about the prophet Jonah rather than a collection of oracles and prophecies like the other prophetic books. Jonah's proclaimed prophetic word from Yahweh is just one short sentence (3:4). It is the story of Jonah, as well as the words of Yahweh to him, that presents the prophetic message in this book.

> The literary style of the book of Jonah resembles historical narrative more than that of the traditional prophets.

The book of Jonah, however, identifies the main character with some specificity, calling him "Jonah, son of Amittai" (1:1) and thus clearly connecting him to the prophet in 2 Kings 14:25 called "Jonah, son of Amittai." In 2 Kings 14:25, the prophet Jonah is placed during the reign of Jeroboam II (786–746 BC), and he is thus a contemporary of Hosea and Amos. As described in 2 Kings 14:23–25, Jonah's prophetic role during the reign of Jeroboam is somewhat surprising. In spite of the negative assessment of Jeroboam ("he did evil in the eyes of Yahweh"), Jonah delivers the word of Yahweh, proclaiming that Jeroboam would be successful in expanding Israel's borders north to Lebo Hamath, thus incorporating much of Syria (Aram), including Damascus. This area was probably wrested from Assyrian control, and Jeroboam's ability to expand into this area reflects the internal weakness of Assyria at that particular time in contrast to the growing power and prosperity of Israel. At Lebo Hamath, Israel's new northern border touches on the southern borders of a region controlled by an Assyrian provincial ruler.

Many scholars doubt the historicity of the book of Jonah, arguing that the details in the book do not fit the historical situation in Assyria, indicating to them that the book is an allegorical story written much later by one who was not as familiar with Assyria (these scholars usually doubt the reality of the great fish episode as well). In their arguments, however, these scholars often fail to place the book of Jonah into the very specific time of Assyrian history that the book itself indicates (a time of Assyrian weakness); thus, they often look to the later time period of Neo-Assyrian

The city of Petra in the mountains of Edom was built by the Nabateans, who replaced the Edomites in this region.

© Holger Mette/www.istockphoto.com

Jonah's world.

power and dominance (which comes after Jonah) to determine what is "normal" in Assyria. For example, they question the title "king of Nineveh" (Jonah 3:6) because the numerous Assyrian historical records regularly use "king of Assyria." Likewise, they argue that the important role of the nobles (3:7) is not in keeping with normal Assyrian practice. Furthermore, many of them note that in the thousands of historical Assyrian records there is no mention of the decree or repentance mentioned in Jonah.

> There are virtually no historical royal Assyrian written records from the time period in which Jonah lived.

However, a careful and close study of Assyrian history during the specific time of Jeroboam's reign (786–746 BC) reveals a political situation in Assyria that was quite different from that of later years. First of all, there are virtually no historical royal Assyrian written records from this time period, so the lack of direct corroboration is an argument from silence. Second, the records that are available come from provincial rulers, indicating perhaps the unique power and independence that they enjoyed during this time period and that Tiglath-pileser III will end when he comes to power in 745 BC. Thus most of the arguments against the historicity of Jonah based on Assyrian history can be answered just by focusing the analysis of the Assyrian political situation to the specific time frame for Jonah identified in 2 Kings 14:25.

Message

The book of Jonah is one of the "non-standard" prophetic books, and thus the message of the book cannot be summarized by the three-part prophetic message so common in many of the other prophetic books. Furthermore, the book of Jonah is a story rather than collected oracles and spoken messages, and thus the meaning lies in the actions and words of the story's two central characters (Jonah and Yahweh). Because of the book's narrative form, determining the central message of Jonah (the book) is neither a straightforward nor an easy task, and scholars remain divided over this issue.

Perhaps it is best to ask what role the book of Jonah plays within the prophetic books. As these books move the biblical story along from Israel's and Judah's covenant abandonment through the consequential judgment toward Yahweh's gracious messianic restoration, including that of the Gentiles, how does Jonah fit in?

First of all, the story in the book of Jonah provides commentary and reflection on the rest of the prophetic books, probably serving as a foil for underscoring the disobedience and failure to repent of Israel and Judah. The prophets preach for generations to Israel and Judah, pleading continuously for the king, his nobles, and the people to repent and turn to Yahweh, and warning them continuously over and over of the coming judgment. Unbelievably, nothing happens. No one, from the king down to the lowest servant, repents and turns to Yahweh (with only a few notable exceptions). In the book of Jonah, the contrast is staggering. Without pleading, begging, or arguing, the reluctant prophet delivers one brief warning statement: "Forty more days and Nineveh will be destroyed" (3:4). At this point everyone in the city, from the king down to the very lowest in the city (the animals are included too!), repents and puts on sackcloth and ashes. Incredibly, what happens in Nineveh is what should have happened in Israel and in Judah, but didn't.

> Incredibly, what happens in Nineveh is what should have happened in Israel and in Judah, but didn't.

It is also important to ask how Jonah's message fits with the specific books that surround it in the Book of the Twelve, particularly in regard to the nations. Remember that a regular feature in the prophetic message of the Major Prophets Isaiah, Jeremiah, and Ezekiel is that the nations will not only be judged but will also participate in the future glorious restoration as they turn to Yahweh and worship him. Hosea, the first prophet in the Book of the Twelve and serving as the introduction to the Twelve, does not address the nations at all. Joel proclaims judgment on the nations but says nothing about turning to Yahweh in the future. Obadiah proclaims the end of Edom, with the country of Edom probably representing all of the hostile foreign nations that oppressed Judah or Israel. Next in the canon is Jonah, qualifying the message of the first four Minor Prophets and reminding everyone that even the terrible Assyrians could be delivered if they repented, thus connecting to prophecies like Isaiah 19:23–25, where Assyria is included into the people of God.

> Even the terrible Assyrians could be delivered if they repented.

The underlying cause of this deliverance is the character of Yahweh. Frequently in the Book of the Twelve, Yahweh's love, compassion, and mercy are stressed.[2] The book of Jonah proclaims that Yahweh feels love, compassion, and mercy, not just for Israel and Judah, but also for foreign cities like Nineveh.

---

2. Seitz, *Prophecy and Hermeneutics,* 235.

Structurally, the book of Jonah breaks into two main units (Jonah 1–2 and Jonah 3–4). Jonah 1–2 contains numerous elements that are paralleled in Jonah 3–4.[3] For example, there is an ironic comparison between the captain, sailors, and ship that are about to perish in Jonah 1 and the king, people, and city that are about to perish in Jonah 3.

Jonah runs away toward Tarshish, at the other end of the world.

JONAH 1 — THE DISOBEDIENT PROPHET

In the opening verses of Jonah, the word of Yahweh comes to Jonah, commanding him to go and preach against Nineveh (the major city of Assyria). Jonah, however, disobeys. In fact, he flees from Yahweh (lit. "from the presence [face] of Yahweh"). Jonah runs away toward Tarshish, probably a port city on the coast of Spain; that is, at the extreme other end of the Mediterranean Sea and as far away from Nineveh as possible. As Jonah runs away from Yahweh and the task Yahweh assigned to him, the Hebrew text poetically captures his movement geographically (and theologically?) through the repeated use of the word *yārad* ("to go down"). Thus Jonah "goes down" to Joppa (1:3), pays his fare, and then "goes down" into the ship (1:3). He is unaware of the storm because he had "gone down" below deck and fallen asleep (1:5).

Likewise, another colorful Hebrew wordplay runs through Jonah 1. In 1:4 Yahweh hurls (*tūl*) a great wind on the sea, against the ship. In 1:5 the sailors fear and each call out to their own god. Then they hurl (*tūl*) the cargo of the ship into the sea in order to lighten it, but to no avail. In 1:15 they hurl (*tūl*) Jonah into the sea, and the sea immediately grows calm. At that point, in contrast to 1:5, the sailors now fear Yahweh, and they offer sacrifices and vows to him.

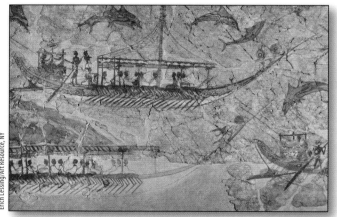

Erich Lessing/Art Resource, NY

Numerous peoples sailed the Mediterranean during the second and first millennia BC. Depicted are Minoan vessels from 1700 BC.

Yahweh "appoints" a great fish (Hebrew doesn't distinguish between fish and mammals like whales; the word here refers to any fish-like animal that swims in the water) to swallow Jonah, who remains inside the fish for three days and three nights. In the literary mythology of the Ancient Near East there was a common theme or figure of speech that it took three days for someone who died to actually reach Sheol, the abode of the dead. Some scholars suggest that the three days and three nights in the fish allude (poetically) to this theme, indicating that the fish is bringing Jonah back from the place of the dead. Indeed, in Jonah 2:1 the prophet cries out from the depths of Sheol (translated as "the grave"). Other scholars think the time reference here merely points to the time it took the fish to reach land and deposit Jonah on dry ground. Most

---

3. See the discussion in Robert B. Chisholm Jr., *Handbook on the Prophets* (Grand Rapids: Baker, 2002), 408–9.

Nineveh became even greater after the time of Jonah. Sennacherib and Ashurbanipal built great palaces. In this scene from Ashurbanipal's palace, a lion wounded by the king is dying.

likely, however, the three days Jonah spent in the fish parallel the three days he is supposed to spend in Nineveh (3:3), underscoring once again the parallel between Jonah 1–2 and Jonah 3–4.

JONAH 2—PRAYER AND PRAISE FROM INSIDE THE FISH

From inside the fish, Jonah prays to Yahweh. The form of this prayer follows that of several psalms classified as "Individual Declarative Praises," in which the psalmist presents a testimony of praise for how Yahweh has delivered him. Jonah's prayer is very similar. Based on Jonah 2:2, some scholars suggest that Jonah actually died, only to be resurrected by Yahweh. However, others note that the language is poetic, and sinking down into the sea could be described poetically quite appropriately as descending down into the grave (Sheol). Note the occurrence once again of the Hebrew word *yārad* ("to go down") in 2:6. Once more Jonah "goes down," this time to "the roots of the mountains" (the depths of the sea). However, in contrast, this time Yahweh "brings him up" (the opposite word from *yārad*) from the pit to deliver him.

JONAH 3—THE REPENTANCE OF NINEVEH

After Jonah is discharged from the fish onto the dry ground, Yahweh tells him once again to go to Nineveh. This time Jonah obeys and goes to Nineveh. In 3:3 the text presents some background information about Nineveh. Translators and commentaries alike have different views on how best to translate and understand this verse. A literal reading of the Hebrew renders the following: "Now Nineveh was a great city to God, a going of three

The Great Fish and Miracles in the Bible

In regard to the historicity or believability of the great fish story, older conservative commentaries frequently cited a story of a nineteenth-century sailor who was washed overboard and swallowed by a whale, only to survive and emerge from the whale later. These writers seemed to be concerned with demonstrating that this story could have really happened — that it is believable. First of all, however, there is no evidence that this nineteenth-century story ever really happened. Second, and more importantly, these writers are missing the point; that is, this story is about Yahweh's miraculous intervention into human history. By definition, miracles are supernaturally caused events that contradict the norms of nature. We also miss the point if we seek to legitimatize the miracle by supposedly showing that it does not contradict the laws of nature and that it really could have happened. Likewise, we miss the point and deny the power of Yahweh if we dismiss biblical miracles as things that could not have happened.

The plagues Yahweh sends on Egypt and the parting of the Yam Suph (Red Sea) should not be explained away as things that really could have happened naturally (e.g., as associated with a volcano eruption). The Bible presents these events as Yahweh's special miraculous works. Biblical miracles (starting with Genesis 1:1 and ending in Revelation 22), both in the Old Testament and in the New, are not to be explained away with scientific explanations, but rather find plausibility or believability in the sovereign power of God. Once we accept Genesis 1:1, that God created the heavens and the earth, then the other biblical miracles should not be too hard to accept. Certainly, the God who created the heavens and earth can part the Red Sea or have Jonah swallowed by a great fish.

days." In the past, many scholars took this phrase to indicate the size of Nineveh, that is, it took three days to walk across it. Some English translations still read this way. However, there were no cities in the Ancient Near East so large that it took three days to walk across, and excavations of ancient Nineveh indicate that it (and other large cities of the day) could be crossed quite easily on foot in less than a few hours. Other scholars have suggested that three days refers to the length of Jonah's trip to get there, and others have suggested that it refers to the size of the surrounding area under Nineveh's jurisdiction. The best understanding, however, is probably that put forward by Douglas Stuart. He argues (convincingly) that the phrase "great city to God" is a statement about the importance of Nineveh to God. The three days mentioned refers to the protocol required for a state visit to such an important city. That is, Nineveh was of such importance internationally (and, ironically, even to Yahweh), that if another ruler sent an emissary there, the emissary could not just deliver his message and quickly depart, which would be impolite and insulting, but rather was required to stay three days.[4] He would probably normally deliver his message on the third day.

> "Three days" refers to the protocol required for a state visit to such an important city.

Jonah, however, delivers his brief message of judgment after only one day. "Forty more days," he declares, "and Nineveh will be destroyed" (3:4). Incredibly, the Ninevites believe

---

4. Douglas Stuart, *Hosea-Jonah,* Word Biblical Commentary (Waco, TX: Word Books, 1987), 486–88.

the message. The text states (ironically) that they believe *God,* thus indicating that they accepted Jonah's message as coming from God. The Ninevites, from the greatest (the king and his nobles) to the least (the poor — indeed, even the cows!), then declare a fast and put on sackcloth. Fasting and wearing sackcloth is a sign of repentance. Again, the shocking thing about this repentance by the Ninevites is that it is in strong contrast to the lack of repentance in Judah or Israel, as proclaimed by the rest of the prophets!

In Jonah 3:7–9 the king of Nineveh and his nobles issue a decree calling on all people and even the animals to fast and plead with God. In 3:10 God responds to their repentance by removing the coming judgment. Several important Hebrew words connect this section together in ironic wordplay. The first word is *shūv,* a term discussed at length in chapter 10 (Jeremiah 1–10) and a central word in Jeremiah. *Shūv* literally means "to turn from" or "to turn to." Another important term is *rā'āh.* This word is often translated as "evil," especially when it is used to describe the actions of people. This is the word used in Jonah 1:2, translated in the NIV as "wickedness." "Preach against Nineveh," Yahweh tells Jonah in 1:2, "because its wickedness [*rā'āh*] has come up before me." Yet this word is also used frequently of Yahweh's actions and intentions, usually in terms of judgment against people for their sin. In those cases, many translations such as the NIV translate *rā'āh* as "disaster" or "calamity." Yet using different translations for this word does not allow the readers of the English text to catch the wordplay. I suggest translating this word as "bad stuff." Thus people do "bad stuff" (*rā'āh*), that is, sin, wickedness, and so forth. Yahweh, in his justice, brings "bad stuff" (*rā'āh*) upon sinful people: judgment. The other critical term used here, and in the similar passage in Joel 2:13, is *niham,* which means "to grieve, relent, be sorry about, or change one's mind."

So, how do these words play together? In Jonah 3:8 the king of Nineveh makes a declaration. The Hebrew literally reads: "Let man and beast be covered with sackcloth and may they cry out strongly to God. May each person turn (*shūv*) from their 'bad stuff' (*rā'āh*) way and from the violence which is in their hands. Who knows? God may 'change his mind' (*niham*) and turn

> The shocking thing about this repentance by the Ninevites is that it is in strong contrast to the lack of repentance in Judah or Israel.

Sennacherib, king of Assyria, leading a campaign from his chariot, in this detail from a relief from Nineveh (690 BC).

> "You are a gracious and compassionate God, slow to anger and abounding in love [*hesed*], a God who relents [*niham*] from sending calamity [*rā'āh*]."

(*shūv*) from his anger and thus we will not be destroyed." Jonah 3:10 describes God's response: "God saw what they did; that they turned (*shūv*) from their 'bad stuff' (*rā'āh*) way (or road, path). Thus God 'changed his mind' (*niham*) concerning the 'bad stuff' (*rā'āh*) which he had said he would do to them and he did not do it."

JONAH 4 — YAHWEH'S COMPASSION AND JONAH'S ANGER

The wordplay continues on into 4:1–2. Literally, the Hebrew of 4:1 reads: "It [the actions of God in 3:10] was 'bad stuff' (a form related to *rā'āh*) to Jonah, great big 'bad stuff' (*rā'āh*)." The Hebrew word for "great" is used several times in Jonah: Yahweh hurls a *great* wind on the sea (1:4); the sailors fear a *great* fear (1:10, 16); Yahweh sends a *great* fish (1:17); and Nineveh is a *great* city to Yahweh (3:3). Ironically, now Jonah sees Yahweh's compassionate removal of judgment as a *great* "evil" or "bad stuff." Jonah then states, in essence, "I knew this would happen!" Jonah knew this because he knows the basic character of Yahweh, which Jonah expresses in 4:2: "You are a gracious and compassionate God, slow to anger and abounding in love [*hesed* — remember our discussion of this word in chapter 19 concerning Hosea], a God who relents [*niham*, changes his mind] from sending calamity [*rā'āh*]."

This verse is very similar to Joel 2:13, underscoring how important this statement is to the overall theology of Jonah (and the Book of the Twelve). This verse stresses the compassionate, gracious character of Yahweh. The prophets never take a fatalistic view of impending judgment. Yahweh is gracious and will always respond to repentance.

The remainder of Jonah 4 contrasts the attitude of pouting, self-centered Jonah with the compassion of Yahweh. Miraculously, Yahweh causes a huge plant to grow up to provide Jonah with shade. When Yahweh then takes away the shade, Jonah becomes angry. Yahweh rebukes Jonah, asking why he is so concerned with the death of the plant but has no compassion or concern whatsoever with the 120,000 people in Nineveh (4:5–11). Yahweh, in contrast to Jonah, is quite concerned with these people.

The book of Jonah has an interesting and humorous ending. In Hebrew, the last verse literally reads, "And I, should I not take pity upon Nineveh the great city, in which there are 120,000 people who do not know their right hand from their left, and *lots of cows*?" Earlier in Jonah 3:7, the king had proclaimed a fast of repentance that included the animals, probably expressing the extensive extent of the fast and repentance (in contrast to Judah and Israel). Humorously, Yahweh seems to allude to the repentance of the animals, as his closing words in this book express his compassion on them as well, rhetorically (and humorously) implying that even dumb cows who repent can be delivered (again, underscoring the obstinate refusal to repent in Judah and Israel).

» FURTHER READING «

Allen, Leslie C. *The Books of Joel, Obadiah, Jonah and Micah*. The New International Commentary on the Old Testament. Grand Rapids: Eerdmans, 1976.

Bruckner, James. *Jonah, Nahum, Habakkuk, Zephaniah*. NIV Application Commentary. Grand Rapids: Zondervan, 2004.

Chisholm, Robert B. *Handbook on the Prophets*. Grand Rapids: Baker, 2002, 406–416.

Stuart, Douglas. *Hosea-Jonah*. Word Biblical Commentary. Waco, TX: Word, 1987, 423–510.

» DISCUSSION QUESTIONS «

1. How does the message of Jonah relate to the rest of the prophetic message? In what way is Jonah a "foil" for the message of the other prophets?

2. Why was Jonah reluctant to go to Nineveh? What does the book of Jonah teach us about obedience? World missions?

» WRITING ASSIGNMENTS «

1. Compare and contrast Jonah 1–2 with Jonah 3–4. Focus especially on comparing and contrasting the Jonah/captain/sailors/boat/fish episode with the Jonah/king/people/city/plant episode. Be sure to include attitudes, actions, and declarations. Also note when people want to die and when they want to live.

CHAPTER 23

Micah

"And what does Yahweh require of you?
To act justly and to love mercy and to walk humbly
with your God." (Micah 6:8)

OVERVIEW OF MICAH

Setting

Micah is one of the six Minor Prophets in the Book of the Twelve that is tied tightly into a specific historical context by the opening verse. Micah 1:1 states that Micah prophesied during the reigns of Jotham, Ahaz, and Hezekiah (750–687 BC). Note that these are all kings of Judah. Micah prophesied against both Israel and Judah, but he does not mention any of the kings of Israel. Perhaps he did not recognize their legitimacy.

> Micah is a contemporary of Hosea, Isaiah, and Amos.

As mentioned in the Introduction to the Book of the Twelve, the Minor Prophets like Micah that have historical headings are in chronological order. Micah is a contemporary of Hosea, Isaiah, and Amos. This was the time during which Assyria rose to power, destroying Samaria (the capital of Israel) in 722 BC and then besieging Jerusalem in 701 BC.

Message

Micah's message is typical of the preexilic prophets and follows the standard three-point pattern: (1) You (Israel/Judah) have broken the covenant; you had better repent! (2) No re-

---

Jeremiah and Micah

Around the year 609 BC, nearly one hundred years after Micah's prophetic ministry, a verse from Micah (3:12) was quoted in defense of Jeremiah. The prophet Jeremiah had been arrested because, in his temple sermon (Jeremiah 7, 26), he had proclaimed the destruction of Jerusalem. His accusers were demanding that he be executed — indeed, his life seemed to hang by a thread. Some of the elders of the land, however, cited Micah's story in defense of Jeremiah:

> [They] said to the entire assembly of people, "Micah of Moresheth prophesied in the days of Hezekiah king of Judah. He told all the people of Judah, 'This is what Yahweh Almighty says:
> "'Zion will be plowed like a field,
> Jerusalem will become a heap of rubble,
> the temple hill a mound overgrown with thickets.'
> "Did Hezekiah king of Judah or anyone else in Judah put him to death? Did not Hezekiah fear Yahweh and seek his favor? And did not Yahweh relent, so that he did not bring the disaster he pronounced against them? We are about to bring a terrible disaster on ourselves!" (Jeremiah 26:17–19)

The use of Micah 3:12 by these elders of the land proved effective, and Jeremiah's life was spared. The citation of Micah 3:12 in a trial setting provides us with helpful insight as to how the earlier prophets were viewed by people in Judah later in history. It is also interesting to note that Micah was cited instead of Isaiah, indicating perhaps that the "Minor Prophets" were not at all "minor" in regard to importance. Finally, the fact that the people in Jeremiah's time were aware of Micah, Hezekiah, and the deliverance of Hezekiah from the Assyrians further underscores how foolish their rejection of Jeremiah's message was.

pentance? Then judgment! (3) Yet there is hope beyond the judgment for a glorious, future restoration. Similarly, Micah levels the three common prophetic indictments against Israel and Judah: idolatry, social injustice, and religious ritualism.

The book of Micah is very similar to Isaiah, only much shorter. In fact, several passages in Micah resemble passages in Isaiah (e.g., Micah 4:1–3 is nearly identical to Isaiah 2:1–4). Since they were contemporaries and both probably living in Jerusalem, it is likely that they knew each other and were very much aware of each other's prophetic ministry.

While the overall message of Micah is not difficult to determine, the organizing structure is not readily discernible. Like Jeremiah, Micah is an anthology — a collection of oracles and visions that are loosely connected structurally but that combine to present a clear prophetic warning and future promise. Although scholars disagree on the details, most acknowledge that the book appears to break down into three main units (Micah 1–2; Micah 3–5; and Micah 6–7). However, each of the units contains elements of both central themes (judgment and restoration).

Not much is known about the man Micah. His name means "Who is like Yahweh?" Jeremiah 26:18 indicates that Micah was still well known nearly one hundred years after the end of his ministry.

> Micah 3:12, declaring the death sentence on Jerusalem, falls in the exact center of the Book of the Twelve.

Within the canon, then, Micah is connected to Isaiah because they are historical contemporaries and some of their texts are the same. Yet Jeremiah's quotation of Micah connects these two as well, even though Jeremiah comes much later. Some have also noted that Micah falls in the exact middle of the Book of the Twelve. In fact, the verse that falls in the exact center of the Book of the Twelve is Micah 3:12, the verse that the elders of the land cited in Jeremiah … a verse declaring a death sentence on Jerusalem.[1]

MICAH 1–2 — PUNISHMENT AND PROMISE

Micah 1:1 places Micah into a firm historical context, but this opening verse also summarizes the prophet's message: "The word of Yahweh given to Micah … the vision he saw concerning Samaria and Jerusalem." Samaria was the capital of the northern kingdom, Israel, and Jerusalem was the capital of the southern kingdom, Judah. Frequently the prophets will use the two capitals to represent each entire nation. The "vision" Micah refers to in 1:1 is described in 1:2–7 — Yahweh comes roaring down from heaven in judgment on Israel and Judah.

In Micah 1:10–16 the prophet proclaims coming judgment through wordplay

Discovered at the Red Sea port of Aqaba was this signet ring of Jotham (742–735 BC), one of the kings of Judah who reigned during the days of Micah.

Smithsonian Institution

---

1. Christopher R. Seitz, *Prophecy and Hermeneutics: Toward a New Introduction to the Prophets* (Grand Rapids: Baker, 2007), 128.

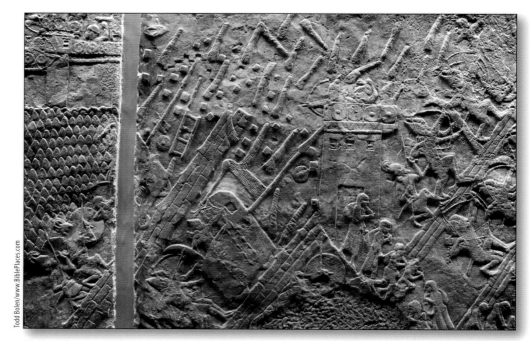

Micah 1:13 has a warning for the city of Lachish. Not long after that, the Assyrians conquer Lachish, as this panel from Sennacherib's palace in Nineveh illustrates.

using the names of cities. For example, in 1:10 Micah declares, "Tell it not in Gath." The city name "Gath" sounds like the Hebrew word for "tell." Throughout this unit Micah will use wordplay based either on similar sounds or similar meanings of words. To illustrate how this works, if these were cities in the United States, the sound-alike wordplays would be like saying, "I will deal with Dallas and cleave Cleveland." The meaning-related wordplay would be like saying "I will grind Little Rock into little pebbles." All of the cities Micah lists lie in the region to the southwest of Jerusalem called the Shephelah. The order of the cities is probably the invasion route that the Assyrians will follow as they move up from the coastal plains toward Jerusalem. Also note that the opening declaration, "Tell it not in Gath," is a quote from David (2 Sam. 1:20). With David in the context, it is interesting to note that Micah follows a route from Gath to Adullam. At one of the low points of David's life, he flees from Saul along the very same route, running from Gath to Adullam (1 Sam. 22:1).

In 2:1 the prophet declares "Woe!" to those who plan iniquity and evil (*ra'ah*) on their beds. This iniquity and "evil" is then described as illegal economic practice—defrauding people of their lands and houses. The Land, remember, was a gift and an inheritance from Yahweh. Extortion and defrauding people out of their land was a serious injustice. Therefore, Yahweh declares in 2:3, "I am planning disaster against this people." The word for disaster (*ra'*) is related to the word *rā'āh* translated as "evil" in 2:1. As we discussed in chapter 22, recall that basically *rā'āh* means "bad stuff." The wordplay here is that these people are planning "bad stuff" (stealing houses and lands), so Yahweh is planning "bad stuff" (judgment) on them.

At the end of Micah 2 the tone changes abruptly, and in 2:12–13 Yahweh suddenly speaks of the future restoration when he will regather the remnant of Israel. Once again Israel will have a king riding before them (as promised in the Davidic covenant), but it will be Yahweh himself who actually leads them (2:13).

MICAH 3–5—LEADERS, JUSTICE, AND THE COMING ONE

Micah 3 focuses on the corrupt leaders of Israel and their lack of concern for justice. Social and economic justice is a huge issue for most of the prophets, and Micah is no exception. Yahweh holds the leaders of the land responsible for justice, and when the leaders themselves are the central culprits for injustice, they incur the wrath of Yahweh. The wrathful judgment of Yahweh is ironically declared to be "justice," meted out to those who have had no concern for "justice" in the land (3:8–9). Because the leaders in Israel were not standing for justice but instead furthering injustice, Yahweh declares that on their account, "Zion will be plowed like a field, Jerusalem will become a heap of rubble." As mentioned above, this text from Micah will be quoted by the elders of the land in Jeremiah 26:18. But note the context of both passages. In Micah this verse comes as a statement of judgment on the leaders for their injustice. In Jeremiah, it is cited at the trial of Jeremiah (a serious incident of injustice). Thus the citation of this verse in Jeremiah 26 implies the judgment of the prophet Micah on the leaders of Jeremiah's day as well.

> Micah 3 focuses on the corrupt leaders of Israel and their lack of concern for justice.

The Temple Mount area today. Micah prophesies that Yahweh's temple will be established and that people from the nations will stream to worship there in peace.

Todd Bolen/www.BiblePlaces.com

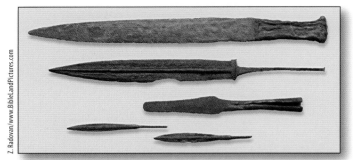

Various metal weapons. Micah's vision of peace is one where implements of war are forged into farming implements.

Micah 3 ends with a picture of Jerusalem being torn down in judgment. In contrast, Micah 4 opens with a picture of future restoration when Jerusalem will be raised up. As mentioned above, Micah 4:1–3 is nearly identical to Isaiah 2:1–4. Yet as Micah describes the glorious time of future restoration, he paints a picture of Yahweh's people worshiping him that includes the Gentile nations (a fulfillment of the promise to Abraham in Genesis 12:3). Micah 4:1–5 presents Jerusalem as restored, but it also describes a time of peace among the nations, a peace brought about by the justice of Yahweh's reign (4:3). The nations themselves will "beat their swords into plowshares and their spears into pruning hooks" (4:3). Likewise, part of this restoration includes regathering the weak, scattered exiles and forming them into a powerful nation with a strong king (4:8 — probably an allusion to the Davidic covenant promise of a righteous king).

> The nations will "beat their swords into plowshares and their spears into pruning hooks."

In Micah 5:2–5 the prophet proclaims that the Coming One will be a shepherd and that he will establish peace. In Micah 4:3 the prophet describes the future restoration as a time of peace — when swords would be hammered into plowshares. Here in 5:4–5 Micah connects the coming peaceful

Peace and the Coming Messiah

In contrast to the tumultuous times in which the prophets preached, they proclaim that the coming Messiah (King, Shepherd, Servant) will bring about a time of peace. They proclaim that it is because of sin and corrupt leadership that Israel/Judah does not enjoy peace now. However, the Coming One will change things and will, indeed, be characterized by peace. Thus Isaiah 9:6 assigns the title "Prince of Peace" to the Messiah. Ezekiel 34 further develops this theme, declaring that the coming shepherd will be a Davidic messianic ruler (Ezek. 34:23–24) who will play a critical role in the covenant of peace that Yahweh will establish (Ezek. 34:25–31). Micah 5:4–5 adds to the theme of peace by declaring that "he [the coming shepherd] will be their peace." The New Testament likewise speaks to the theme of peace frequently. "Peace I leave with you," Jesus tells his disciples in the upper room just prior to the crucifixion (John 14:27). "Peace be with you!" Jesus states several times in his post-resurrection appearances (Luke 24:36; John 20:19, 21, 26). Paul will explain that the death of Christ brought peace between God and believers, bringing reconciliation to the relationship (Rom. 5:8–11; 2 Cor. 5:18–21; Eph. 2:14–17; Col. 1:20–22).

age to the image of the shepherd. Indeed, Micah declares that the shepherd himself will be their peace.

Furthermore, Micah notes, the coming deliverer will come from the town of Bethlehem. The additional designation Ephrathah is added to Bethlehem to distinguish this Bethlehem from two other towns with the same name, thus designating this particular town with precision. This was the town in which David was born, so Micah's prophecy not only identifies the town in which the Messiah will be born but also connects the Messiah to the Davidic covenant.

> The shepherd himself will be their peace.

In contrast to the promised peace for Yahweh's people, Yahweh promises wrath upon those who oppose him (5:5b–15). Probably referring to the Assyrians in a figurative sense to represent all hostile enemies (5:5b–6), Yahweh describes a time when the tables will be turned and the enemies of his people will be destroyed.

MICAH 6–7 — THE PRESENT AND THE FUTURE

In a fashion similar to Isaiah 1, Micah 6 opens with the prophet presenting a "covenant lawsuit" against Israel. When Yahweh made the Mosaic covenant with Israel in Deuteronomy, he figuratively called on "heavens and earth" to be witnesses to the covenant agreement, that is, to the fact that Israel pledged to be faithful and live according to the stipulations in Deuteronomy. Now that Israel has abandoned Yahweh and the law of Deuteronomy, Yahweh summons these original witnesses (heavens and earth) to testify against Israel.

> Micah proclaims that the coming deliverer will come from the town of Bethlehem.

Micah 6:6–8 is one of the most powerful texts in Micah. In 6:6–7 the prophet speaks rhetorically for the people, asking what level of ritual worship would be acceptable to Yahweh. He asks about increasingly difficult levels of ritual, moving from the normal (but very expensive) sacrifice of a calf, to the outrageous (thousands of rams), to the unthinkable (one's firstborn). What is it, he demands to know, that Yahweh wants out of us? The answer comes in 6:8. Yahweh does not want more meaningless ritual. He has shown us what he wants and what is good, Micah declares. Yahweh desires of his people that they do justice, that they love *hesed* (loyal, faithful love), and that they walk humbly with Yahweh (a daily relationship). Here Micah pulls together several major themes of the prophetic literature. Yahweh is much more concerned that his people are actively involved in bringing about justice than he is about the rituals of worship. Likewise, he wants his people to be zealous about faithful, loyal love (*hesed*) both toward him and

In modern Bethlehem, the Church of the Nativity is built over the site traditionally believed to be the birthplace of Jesus.

toward other people. Finally, Yahweh desires humility of his people. In humility — that is, recognizing the glory and the power of Yahweh in contrast to our weakness and sinfulness — we are to walk with Yahweh in constant, daily relationship.

In contrast, Micah 6:9 – 7:6 presents Yahweh's ire at the social injustice that Israel was practicing (dishonest scales, false weights, violence, lying, bribes, etc.). They have abandoned Yahweh's laws to follow the statues of Omri and Ahab (the most corrupt and pagan kings of Israel's history) (6:16).

On the other hand, in the midst of this sin and in the context of coming judgment, Micah declares that he will watch and wait in hope for God his savior (7:7).

Yet at the end of the book, Micah returns to the theme of hope and future restoration (7:14 – 20). Remember that Micah's name means "Who is like Yahweh?" In 7:18 he asks a similar question ("Who is a God like you?"), noting that Yahweh is a God who "pardons sin and forgives the transgression of the remnant." Micah declares that Yahweh is a God who delights in *hesed* (loyal, faithful love; NIV "mercy"). At the end of the book, Micah highlights the connection between the promised restoration and Yahweh's original promise/covenant to Abraham made in Genesis (7:20).

> Yahweh is a God who delights in *hesed*.

» FURTHER READING «

Allen, Leslie. *The Books of Joel, Obadiah, Jonah, and Micah*. New International Commentary on the Old Testament. Grand Rapids: Eerdmans, 1976.

Barker, Kenneth L., and Waylon Bailey. *Micah, Nahum, Habakkuk, Zephaniah*. New American Commentary. Nashville: Broadman & Holman, 1998.

McComiskey, Thomas E., ed. *The Minor Prophets: An Exegetical and Expository Commentary*. Vol. 2: *Obadiah-Habakkuk*. Grand Rapids: Baker, 1993.

Smith, Ralph L. *Micah-Malachi*. Word Biblical Commentary. Waco, TX: Word, 1984.

1. Discuss the meaning and application of Micah 6:6–8 for Christians today.

2. What did the promise of peace entail for the ancient audience in Micah's day? How does the New Testament use the theme of peace? How does the promise of peace relate to us today?

» WRITING ASSIGNMENTS «

1. Trace the theme of leaders throughout the book of Micah, describing the actions of the bad leaders and contrasting that with the action of the coming Messiah.

2. Discuss the theme of justice in Micah.

CHAPTER 24

Nahum and Habakkuk

"... the righteous will live by their faith."

(Hab. 2:4)

NAHUM — THE END OF NINEVEH

Nahum is one of the "non-standard" prophets in that he does not follow the three-part prophetic message that most of the rest of the prophets follow. This is because he preaches against Nineveh, the capital city of Assyria and not against Judah or Israel.

> Nahum counterbalances Jonah, showing that the repentance of the Ninevites/Assyrians was short-lived.

Within the Book of the Twelve, Nahum is one of the six books that does not have a clear historical superscription in the first few verses that identifies the specific historical setting (and date) of the book. However, Nahum refers to the fall of Thebes (3:8) as a past event — Thebes was destroyed by the Assyrians in 663 BC — and he refers to the fall of Nineveh — destroyed by the Babylonians in 612 BC — as a future, prophesied event. So we are probably safe to place Nahum's prophecy between 663 and 612 BC.

Recall that earlier in the Book of the Twelve, Jonah recounted how Nineveh had repented and been delivered from imminent destruction. Nahum counterbalances Jonah, showing that the repentance of the Ninevites/Assyrians was short-lived. After the events in Jonah take place, Assyria rises to power and dominates the Ancient Near East, extending its control all the way into Egypt. Yahweh uses the Assyrians to judge the

The Great Temple of Amun in Thebes, Egypt. "Are you better than Thebes ... yet she was taken captive" (Nah. 3:8 – 10). Cushite power was centered at Thebes, which was overrun by the Assyrians in 665 BC.

northern kingdom of Israel, but throughout the earlier prophets he regularly proclaims judgment on the Assyrians as well. Nahum spells out the destruction of Nineveh, the capital of Assyria, the very city that had earlier responded so favorably to Jonah. In this sense, within the Book of the Twelve, Nahum is similar to the "Oracles Against the Nations" seen repeatedly in Isaiah, Jeremiah, and Ezekiel.

Paul House suggests that Nahum introduces the second unit within the Book of the Twelve, a unit that focuses on the judgment of Yahweh (even though other themes are still present) and the certainty that this judgment is coming soon. Repentance has not come; therefore, the terrible consequences will start to unfold.[1]

The basic message of the book of Nahum is judgment on Nineveh. The opening verses (1:1–11) underscore Yahweh's patience but also his wrath: "Yahweh is slow to anger and great in power; Yahweh will not leave the guilty unpunished" (1:3). The literary structure of the rest of the book is chiastic, and can be outlined as follows:

1. Paul House, "The Character of God in the Book of the Twelve," in James D. Nogalski and Marvin A. Sweeney, *Reading and Hearing the Book of the Twelve,* SBL Symposium Series 15 (Atlanta: Society of Biblical Literature, 2000), 126, 137–38.

A relief panel showing the Assyrian king Ashurbanipal sitting pleasantly with the queen in his garden and eating a feast. Yet look carefully at the tree on the left side of the panel. The head of one of Ashurbanipal's enemies, King Teumman of Elam, hangs from a branch!

Todd Bolen/www.BiblePlaces.com

A¹ Assyrian king taunted/Judah urged to celebrate (1:12–15)
   B¹ Dramatic call to alarm (2:1–10)
      C¹ Taunt (2:11–12)
         D¹ Announcement of judgment (2:13)
            E Woe oracle (3:1–4)
         D² Announcement of judgment (3:5–7)
      C² Taunt (3:8–13)
   B² Dramatic call to alarm (3:14–17)
A² Assyrian king taunted as others celebrate (3:18–19)[2]

The Assyrians were famous throughout the Ancient Near East for their cruelty. Nahum prophesies that when the end comes to Assyria, those who have suffered by their hands will rejoice: "Everyone who hears the news about you claps his hands at your fall, for who has not felt your endless cruelty?" (3:19).

OVERVIEW OF HABAKKUK

Setting

The book of Habakkuk is one of the six books in the Book of the Twelve that contains no historical superscription tying the prophecy to a specific king or specific time in history. Likewise, little information about the prophet himself is provided. However, Yahweh tells Habakkuk in 1:6 that he is raising up the Babylonians (lit. Chaldeans) to judge Judah. Thus the message of the book implies a setting just prior to one of the Babylonian invasions of Judah (597 BC or 586 BC). Some scholars suggest that the book may contain some earlier material that perhaps predates the battle of Carchemish (605 BC), the battle that established Babylon as the most powerful military force in the region. Thus, historically, Habakkuk was a contemporary of Jeremiah.

Message

In general, Habakkuk follows the standard three-part message of the preexilic prophets: (1) You (Judah) have broken the covenant; you had better repent! (2) No repentance? Then judgment! (3) Yet there is hope beyond the judgment for a glorious future restoration. In the book of Habakkuk, Yahweh stresses that he will use the Babylonians as his agent to bring judgment on Judah but that he will also then judge the nations (including the Babylonians). Habakkuk, in the meantime, must continue to trust in Yahweh for his own deliverance, while waiting for the coming judgment on Judah and the nations.

Within the Book of the Twelve, Habakkuk combines with Nahum and Zephaniah to state clearly that the day of Yahweh is coming soon both for the nations (especially Assyria and Babylonia) and for

Yahweh tells Habakkuk that he is raising up the Babylonians to judge Judah.

In the context of coming judgment, Habakkuk provides a model of faith for the remnant to embrace.

---

2. Robert B. Chisholm Jr., *Handbook on the Prophets* (Grand Rapids: Baker, 2002), 428, citing G. H. Johnston, "A Rhetorical Analysis of the Book of Nahum" (Ph.D. diss., Dallas Theological Seminary, 1992), 46–214.

Judah. In this context of imminent judgment, Habakkuk provides a model of faith for the remnant to embrace.[3]

While Habakkuk's basic message is similar to that of the other prophetic books, the style of this book is quite unique. Habakkuk 1 and 2 are not composed of messages preached to the people, but rather they are a dialogue between the prophet Habakkuk and Yahweh. In this sense the style is similar in some respects to Wisdom Literature. The concluding prayer in Habakkuk 3 is a psalm, apparently written to be sung accompanied by stringed instruments. However, while the style of the book is a dialogue between Habakkuk and Yahweh, the message of the book (the point of recording the dialogue) is directed at the people.

Habakkuk can be outlined as follows:

(1:1)	Heading
(1:2–4)	Habakkuk's opening question—"Why doesn't Yahweh do something about the injustice in Judah?"
(1:5–11)	Yahweh's answer—"I am doing something; I'm raising up the Babylonians."
(1:12–2:1)	Habakkuk's response—"How can that be right?"
(2:2–20)	Yahweh's answer—"Wait, for this judgment is most certainly coming."
(3:1–19)	Habakkuk's final conclusion—"I will wait for the judgment and rejoice in Yahweh."

HABAKKUK 1:1–4—"WHY DOESN'T YAHWEH DO SOMETHING ABOUT THE INJUSTICE IN JUDAH?"

The terrible religious and social situation in Jerusalem and throughout Judah that the book of Jeremiah describes provides the background situation for understanding Habakkuk's lament concerning the prevalence of injustice that he sees in the land. The prophet feels like he is crying out in vain: "How long, O Yahweh, must I cry out for help, but you do not listen?" (1:2). Violence and injustice are common, Habakkuk complains, and the wicked prevail over the righteous. Thus the law is paralyzed, he continues, and justice is perverted (lit. twisted, bent).

"How long, O Yahweh, must I cry out for help, but you do not listen?"

HABAKKUK 1:5–11—YAHWEH'S ANSWER: "I AM RAISING UP THE BABYLONIANS TO JUDGE JUDAH."

In Habakkuk 1:5–11 Yahweh responds by informing Habakkuk that he is raising up the Chaldeans (i.e., Babylonians). Habakkuk had asked why Yahweh makes him "look" at injustice (1:3). Here Yahweh begins his response by telling him to "look" at the nations—to see justice unfolding (1:5). Yahweh then describes what he will see: the Babylonian army as it sweeps across the region, easily conquering fortified city after fortified city. Yahweh describes them as "ruthless and impetuous" (1:6) as well as "feared and dreaded" (1:7). Their army contains large units of swift cavalry that can sweep through areas rapidly, adding to the fear and terror of their victims. The Babylonian army laughs at fortified cities, Yahweh declares, describing them as men "whose own strength is their god" (1:11).

---

3. House, "The Character of God in the Book of the Twelve," 139.

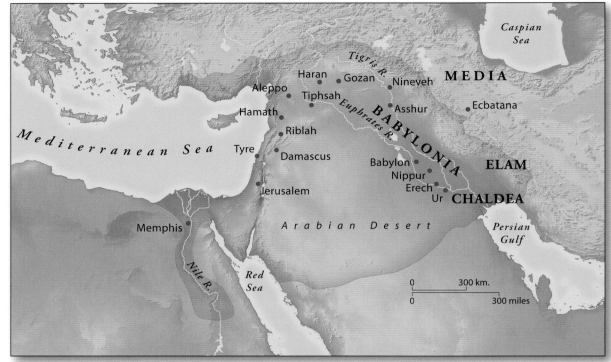

The Chaldeans originated to the south of Babylonia, but during the seventh and sixth centuries BC they ruled Babylonia and the name Chaldean became synonymous with Babylonian.

HABAKKUK 1:12 – 2:1 — HABAKKUK'S RESPONSE: "HOW CAN THAT BE RIGHT?"

The theme of Yahweh raising up a foreign power to judge Israel or Judah occurs fairly frequently in the prophets. Habakkuk, however, seems shocked at Yahweh's solution to the injustice in Judah. Habakkuk apparently wanted Yahweh to intervene in Judah and bring about justice without judging the entire nation. The prophet is disturbed that Yahweh would bring about justice by punishing Judah through the agency of someone even more unjust than they are. Habakkuk addresses Yahweh as being "from everlasting," probably a reference to Yahweh's faithful protection of Israel throughout its history. He also calls Yahweh "my Holy One" (1:12), leading to his statement that Yahweh's eyes are too pure to look on such evil. Likewise, the prophet addresses Yahweh as "O Rock" (1:12), a symbol of power, steadfastness, and protection. Can "the Rock" allow the wretched Babylonians to destroy Judah?

> Habakkuk is shocked at Yahweh's solution to the injustice in Judah.

In Habakkuk 1:14 – 17 the prophet employs an extensive metaphor comparing the rampaging Babylonian army to a fisherman. The victims of the Babylonians are like fish that are caught by hooks and nets. It is interesting to note how Jesus later takes the fisherman metaphor (used also in Jeremiah 16:16 and Amos 4:2 as a metaphor for judgment) and

Originally, Chaldea was a region in southern Babylonia. During the time of Assyrian domination of Babylonia (eighth century BC), the Chaldeans were able to continue a guerilla-type resistance against Assyria. When Assyrian power started to decline, a Chaldean dynasty consolidated power in both Chaldea and Babylonia. This Chaldean dynasty ruled during the time of the Neo-Babylonian Empire (seventh to sixth centuries BC). Thus the Chaldeans are the dynastic leaders of Babylonia. The Old Testament prophets will often use the terms "Chaldeans" and "Babylonians" in parallel or interchangeably. Jeremiah, a contemporary of Habakkuk, uses the term Chaldean often (46 times). Usually the NIV will translate the Hebrew term "Chaldean" into English as "Babylonian" for clarity. Thus in Habakkuk 1:6, Yahweh states that he is raising up the "Chaldeans," and the NIV translates this as "Babylonians."

reverses it into a metaphor for deliverance and salvation ("I will make you fishers of men" Matt. 4:19).

In Habakkuk 1:5, Yahweh told the prophet to "look" at the nations to see what he was doing. At the end of Habakkuk's questioning response in 1:12–2:1, however, the prophet declares that he will stand watch and "look" to see how Yahweh will answer his question, apparently expecting Yahweh to change his mind.

HABAKKUK 2:2–20—YAHWEH'S ANSWER: "WAIT, FOR THIS JUDGMENT IS MOST CERTAINLY COMING."

Yahweh, of course, does not waver from his plan of action. He responds to Habakkuk's questioning by telling the prophet to write this revelation down so that many would be able to read it (2:2). Yahweh also instructs Habakkuk to wait patiently for the judgment (2:3). Regardless of Habakkuk's objections, the Babylonians will most certainly come upon Judah in judgment, but then they will also be judged themselves.

> Yahweh tells Habakkuk to wait patiently for the judgment.

In Habakkuk 2:4–5 Yahweh contrasts two people. One appears to represent the Babylonians—arrogant and greedy, "gathering to himself all the nations" (2:5). The other person, however, is in stark contrast. This one is a righteous person who, in the midst of the death and destruction brought on by the Babylonians, will live because he believes in Yahweh—that is, he remains faithful to Yahweh. Yahweh apparently directs this comment to Habakkuk and to the remnant, those who continue to trust in Yahweh, accepting his judgment on Judah and awaiting the coming judgment on Babylon as well.

Yahweh has not altered his plans to raise up the Babylonians to judge Judah. In his response to Habakkuk, however, Yahweh does clearly point out that judgment will also come on the Babylonians for their evil, violence, and other sinful behavior. Habakkuk 2:6–20 contains five "Woe!" passages, judgments in the form of funeral dirges sung over the Babylonians by their victims, listing the sins of the now-defeated Babylonians. Habakkuk 2:6–8 underscores extortion and stealing; Habakkuk 2:9–11 points to unjust or illegal gain. The next "woe" text is Habakkuk 2:12–14, describing the empire (lit. "city") built on violence. Habakkuk 2:15–17 focuses on drunkenness and related shameful behavior as well as violence associated with drunkenness. The fifth "woe" is because of idolatry (2:18–19).

> Yahweh points out that judgment will also come on the Babylonians for their evil, violence, and other sinful behavior.

The "woe" judgments are interrupted by two contrasting statements about Yahweh. The Babylonians will be humiliated and shamed, but the knowledge of the glory of Yahweh will be spread throughout the earth "as the waters cover the sea" (2:14; also in Isa. 11:9). Likewise, in contrast to the lifeless, impotent idols that the Babylonians have built, Yahweh sits in his holy temple, and all the earth is silent before him (2:20). This verse also probably provides a connection to the following book of Zephaniah, who in 1:7 calls on everyone to be silent before Yahweh, who is inaugurating the day of Yahweh in judgment.

HABAKKUK 3:1–19 — HABAKKUK'S FINAL CONCLUSION: "I WILL WAIT FOR THE JUDGMENT AND REJOICE IN YAHWEH."

The final chapter in Habakkuk differs from the rest of the book because the entire chapter is a psalm, set apart from the rest of the book by both an opening superscription (3:1) and a closing dedication subscription (3:19b). In 3:2 Habakkuk seems to accept Yahweh's plan spelled out in Habakkuk 2, calling on Yahweh to renew his deeds today, as in the past. Yet, in his address to Yahweh, Habakkuk adds, "in wrath remember mercy" (3:2b).

Habakkuk 3:3–7 describes the conquering warrior Yahweh coming up from the south (the places mentioned are south of Judah) in awesome power — the earth shakes, the nations tremble, the mountains collapse (3:6). In 3:8–15 the prophet describes the wrath of

Yahweh, raging against the sea and rivers. Habakkuk uses extensive figurative language in this passage. The arrows of Yahweh, for example, probably represent lightening bolts. The sea, the object of Yahweh's rage, probably represents the hostile nations, although allusions to exodus events such as the parting of the Red Sea are also present. Habakkuk 3:13 proclaims that Yahweh is not just judging the hostile nations, but he has come to deliver his people and his "anointed one," a messianic reference to the coming Davidic king.

Habakkuk describes the terror within him resulting from this horrific vision of Yahweh's wrath. Yet based on his faith in Yahweh's promises (2:4), Habakkuk looks hopefully and expectantly to the future. Even though the Babylonians will come and destroy Judah, Habakkuk will wait, knowing that Yahweh will judge them as well. Even in judgment, Habakkuk proclaims that he will rejoice in Yahweh his Savior (3:18).

> Based on his faith in Yahweh's promises, Habakkuk looks hopefully and expectantly to the future.

Music and musical instruments were important in the Ancient Near East, as this Assyrian relief shows. Habakkuk 3 is written as a song.

Werner Forman Archive/The British Museum

» FURTHER READING «

Achtemeier, Elizabeth. *Nahum-Malachi*. Interpretation. Atlanta: John Knox Press, 1986.

Bruckner, James. *Jonah, Nahum, Habakkuk, Zephaniah*. NIV Application Commentary. Grand Rapids: Zondervan, 2004.

Longman III, Tremper. "Nahum." In *The Minor Prophets: An Exegetical and Expository Commentary*. Edited by Thomas Edward McComiskey. Grand Rapids: Baker, 1993.

Robertson, O. Palmer. *The Books of Nahum, Habakkuk, and Zephaniah*. New International Commentary on the Old Testament. Grand Rapids: Eerdmans, 1990.

Smith, Ralph. *Micah-Malachi*. Word Biblical Commentary. Waco, TX: Word Books, 1984.

On Habakkuk 2:4, see the following:

Seifrid, Mark A. "Romans." In *Commentary on the New Testament Use of the Old Testament*. Edited by G. K. Beale and D. A. Carson. Grand Rapids: Baker, 2007, 608–11.

» DISCUSSION QUESTIONS «

1. How does the book of Nahum relate to the book of Jonah?

2. What is the relationship between the terms "Chaldean" and "Babylonian"?

3. What does Habakkuk mean when he says, "The righteous will live by his faith" (2:4)? How does Paul use this verse in Romans 1:17?

» WRITING ASSIGNMENTS «

1. The book of Habakkuk consists of a dialogue between the prophet Habakkuk and Yahweh. Follow the conversation by answering the questions below.

    a. Habakkuk cries out to Yahweh in 1:2–4 because of the situation in Judah. What was the situation that Habakkuk complains about, and what does he want Yahweh to do?

    b. Yahweh answers in 1:5–11. What is it that Yahweh is planning to do?

    c. Read 1:12–13. Does Habakkuk accept Yahweh's answer? What question does Habakkuk ask Yahweh?

    d. What does Habakkuk resolve to do in 2:1?

    e. What does Yahweh tell Habakkuk to do in 2:3?

f.   Yahweh then lists five "woes," describing five groups of people on whom judgment will come (2:6, 9, 12, 15, 19). List the five groups. Are the people in these groups Israelites or Babylonians?

g.   After this discussion with Yahweh, what does Habakkuk say in conclusion in 3:16 – 19?

h.   Summarize the main message of Habakkuk. How does it apply to us today?

2.   Discuss the similarities and differences between the meaning of Habakkuk 2:4 in the book of Habakkuk and the way that Paul uses the verse in Romans 1:17 and Galatians 3:11. Consult and engage with a good commentary on Romans such as Moo (NICNT), Cranfield (ICC), Morris (Pillar), Mounce (NAC), Schreiner (BECNT), or Dunn (WBC).

CHAPTER 25

Zephaniah

"Be silent before the Sovereign LORD,

for the day of the LORD is near."

(Zeph. 1:7)

OVERVIEW OF ZEPHANIAH

Setting

Zephaniah is one of the six prophetic books in the Book of the Twelve that opens with a historical superscription. His ministry is placed during the reign of Josiah, one of the few good kings of Judah (640–609 BC). Thus Zephaniah overlaps with the beginning of Jeremiah's ministry. Not surprisingly, much of the language of Zephaniah is very similar to Jeremiah's. Also, remember that Josiah was quite an exception to the rule; the kings before him (primarily Manasseh, 687–642 BC) and the kings after him (Jehoiakim and Zedekiah) all turned away from Yahweh. Zephaniah's message of judgment, like Jeremiah's, appears directed at disobedient Jerusalem—there is no mention of Josiah's short-lived reforms in Zephaniah.

> The word of Yahweh comes to Zephaniah toward the end of the Neo-Assyrian era.

The word of Yahweh comes to Zephaniah toward the end of the Neo-Assyrian era. For much of the first half of the seventh century BC, the two main powers in the Ancient Near East were Assyria (the most powerful) and Cush (rulers of Egypt and challengers of Assyrian power). The Cushites ruled Egypt from 710 BC until 663 BC, during which time relations between Egypt and Judah were close, both commercially and militarily. Indeed, throughout the first half of the seventh century BC, the Cushites maintained a strong presence throughout Palestine. The end of Cushite rule in Egypt was marked by the tumultuous destruction of Thebes by the Assyrians in 663 BC, a scant thirty years or so before the prophetic ministry of Zephaniah began. This significant event marked the high point of Assyrian expansion and, ironically, the beginning of the Assyrian decline. Zephaniah prophesies in this context.

Message

Zephaniah's message is typical of the preexilic prophets and follows the standard three-point pattern: (1) You (Judah) have broken the covenant; you had better repent! (2) No repentance? Then judgment! (3) Yet there is hope beyond the judgment for a glorious future restoration. Zephaniah's indictments against Judah are likewise the common prophetic

A wall painting from Thebes depicting Cushite princes bowing to the Egyptian king. In the late eighth century BC, however, the Cushites conquered and ruled over Egypt.

An aerial view of Megiddo. King Josiah was killed in battle by the Egyptians near here as the Egyptian army marched north to fight the Babylonians (609 BC).

Todd Bolen/www.BiblePlaces.com

indictments: idolatry, social injustice, and religious ritualism. The stress in Zephaniah is on judgment and restoration.

Within the Book of the Twelve, Zephaniah closes out the subunit of Nahum-Habakkuk-Zephaniah, which focuses on judgment. Zephaniah emphasizes the day of Yahweh—a central theme in the Book of the Twelve—more than any of the other prophets. Zephaniah clearly ties the day of Yahweh to two quite different aspects. This coming day will be a time of judgment on rebellious Judah as well as on the surrounding haughty nations that defy Yahweh. Yet it will also be a time of blessing on the faithful remnant of Judah along with those Gentiles from among the nations who come to worship Yahweh. Thus the day of Yahweh is linked to judgment and to restoration, both for Judah and for the nations.

At the end of Habakkuk, the prophet declares, "Yahweh is in his holy temple; let all the earth be silent before him" (Hab. 2:20). The book of Zephaniah, which follows in the Book of the Twelve, apparently connects to this phrase by stating near

> Zephaniah emphasizes the day of Yahweh—a central theme in the Book of the Twelve—more than any of the other prophets.

the beginning, "Be silent before Yahweh the Lord" (Zeph. 1:7). In connection to his central theme, however, Zephaniah drives home the ominous reason for this silence: "for the day of Yahweh is near."

There is no consensus among scholars regarding how to outline the prophecies of Zephaniah. As has been noted several times, the prophetic books are more like anthologies than modern essays and thus are often not easy to outline. Likewise, between the various identifiable units in Zephaniah are complex transitional passages that can connect with both the preceding and the following sections, adding to the difficulty of determining when units start and stop. One of the more traditional ways to outline Zephaniah is as follows:

1:1	Superscription
1:2–2:3	The day of Yahweh will bring judgment
2:4–15	Judgment on the nations
3:1–8	Judgment on Jerusalem
3:9–13	Restoration of Jerusalem and the nations
3:14–20	Rejoicing in Yahweh's salvation

ZEPHANIAH 1:1—THE SUPERSCRIPTION

The book of Zephaniah opens with an unusual superscription: "The word of Yahweh that came to Zephaniah son of Cushi, the son of Gedaliah, the son of Amariah, the son of Hezekiah, during the reign of Josiah son of Amon king of Judah." In addition to the fact that Zephaniah's father was named *Cushi* ("Cushite"), the genealogy of Zephaniah is unusual in the prophetic literature because it goes back four generations, a feature unique among the identifying lineages of the prophets. Scholars are divided on the reason.

Those who identify the Hezekiah of Zephaniah's lineage with King Hezekiah see the royal connection as a reason for the extra-long genealogy. It is possible that the reforms of Hezekiah may be implicitly connected to the upcoming reforms of Josiah, thus giving a reason for connecting Zephaniah back to his royal ancestor. Also, note that Hezekiah was the king during the great Assyrian/Cushite collision (715–687 BC), the events of which provide much of the background for the oracle in Zephaniah 2:1–3:13.

On the other hand, several scholars question whether this Hezekiah is to be identified with the famous king. They suggest that the citing of four generations of ancestors was required in order to establish Zephaniah's legitimate Judahite heritage, a legitimating that was required precisely because his father was named "Cushite." The evidence, however, appears to weigh in favor of identifying Zephaniah's ancestor Hezekiah with the earlier king.

> Within the prophetic literature, the genealogy of Zephaniah is very unusual.

ZEPHANIAH 1:2–2:3—THE DAY OF YAHWEH WILL BRING JUDGMENT

Unlike Jeremiah, Zephaniah skips over any call to repentance and opens with an extended description of the terrible wrath of Yahweh that will accompany the coming day of Yahweh. Zephaniah uses the term "that day" in reference to the day of Yahweh throughout

Zephaniah the Son of Cushi, "the Cushite"

For several generations prior to Zephaniah, the geopolitical world of the Ancient Near East was dominated by the struggle between the Assyrians and the Cushites (who ruled Egypt). In light of this historical context, it is perhaps not all that surprising that Zephaniah mentions Cushites three times in his three short chapters.

However, it is perhaps unusual to be informed at the beginning of the book that Zephaniah's father is named "Cushi," or "the Cushite." In light of the important role that genealogies usually play throughout the Ancient Near East and certainly in the Old Testament, it is valid to explore the implications of Zephaniah being the son of a man named Cushi. The Hebrew term *Cushi* (lit. "Cushite") clearly refers to the kingdom of Cush, an African kingdom located on the Nile to the south of Egypt. It is logical to suppose that the owner of the name Cushi would be related to Cush in some manner. This is even more pertinent when a date for the birth of Zephaniah's father is estimated (perhaps around 685 BC). At that time, Cush was one of the two major world powers.

Recall from chapter 2 that in 701 BC Sennacherib, the Assyrian king, drove the Cushites out of Israel and down into Egypt. However, the Assyrians did not completely subdue the Cushites at that time, and the African kingdom subsequently quickly reemerged as a significant power in the region, routing the Assyrians in 674 BC and sending the proud army of Esarhaddon back to Assyria in defeat. Soon after, however, the Assyrians returned and, led by Ashurbanipal, marched into Egypt to finally subdue the Cushites. On this campaign, Ashurbanipal took numerous vassal kings with him, including Manasseh, the king of Judah and the grandfather of Josiah.

It was during this tumultuous time, when the Cushites were extremely involved in the commercial, diplomatic and military affairs of Judah, that Zephaniah's father was born and given the name "Cushite." It is interesting to note that Jeremiah 36:14 refers to an official in Jerusalem with a great-grandfather named "Cushi." This individual would probably have lived at about the same time period as Zephaniah's father. Thus we know of two Israelites living in Jerusalem around the turn of the seventh century that have the name "Cushi." Perhaps it was a popular name.

Scholars have suggested four plausible reasons why someone might be named Cushi: (1) the person was actually an ethnic Cushite; (2) the person had dark skin and looked like a Cushite; he may even have had a Cushite mother, father, or grandparent; (3) he was born in Cush, even if he had Judahite parents; or (4) he was given the name Cush in honor of the Cushites, recognizing the importance of Cush as an ally against the Assyrians. The historical context suggests that Cushite soldiers, diplomats, and traders would have been in Judah frequently during this time; thus, any of the four scenarios described above would have been possible.[1]

---

1. J. Daniel Hays, *From Every People and Nation: A Biblical Theology of Race,* New Studies in Biblical Theology (Downers Grove, IL: InterVarsity Press, 2003), 121–27.

this section (the term occurs 17 times in 1:2–2:3). In the opening verses (1:2–3), Yahweh declares that his judgment will be on the entire creation; indeed, as in the flood judgment during the time of Noah, this day of Yahweh will entail a reversal of the creation story. Yahweh will sweep away men and animals (created on day 6) as well as birds of the air and fish of the sea (created on day 5). Likewise, in the wordplay of the final half of 1:3,

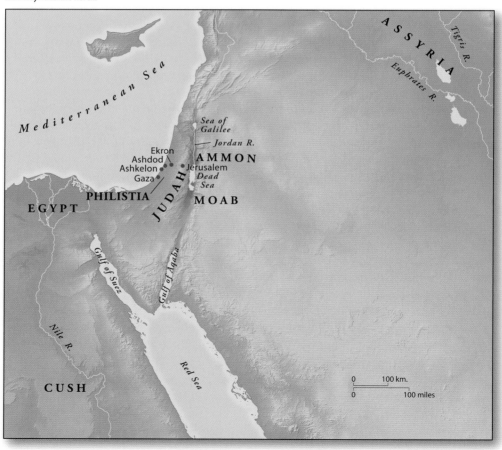

Zephaniah stresses that the day of Yahweh is near.

Yahweh alludes to reversing creation when he states that he will cut off *adam* (mankind) from the face of the *adamah* (earth, dirt, ground, the substance that Adam was created from). The severity of this imagery is similar to Jeremiah 4:23, in which the prophet declares, "I looked at the earth, and it was formless and empty; and at the heavens, and their light was gone." The day of Yahweh is not going to be some minor disciplinary action, but rather an earthshaking event comparable to the Genesis flood.

The focus of this section is judgment on Jerusalem and Judah, especially because of their blatant idolatry (1:4–6). Zephaniah stresses that the day of Yahweh is near (1:7, 14) and that the accompanying judgment will fall on the nobility (1:8), the corrupt priests (1:4,

Zephaniah 2:4–15 moves around the points of the compass: Philistia to the west, Moab and Ammon to the east, Cush to the south, and Assyria to the north.

6, 9), and the wealthy (1:10–13, 18), including those who are merely complacent (1:12). However, the final line of 1:18 indicates (at least poetically) that the entire world will be consumed by Yahweh's jealous wrath.

Zephaniah 2:1–3, however, inserts a warning and an exhortation to "seek Yahweh." In contrast to the destruction of the arrogant and haughty leaders of Judah, Zephaniah calls on humble and obedient people to seek Yahweh. This exhortation closes with a call to seek righteousness and humility in order to find shelter from Yahweh's wrath.

ZEPHANIAH 2:4–15—JUDGMENT ON THE NATIONS

The judgment oracle in Zephaniah 2:4–15 covers the four points on the compass—Philistia to the west (2:4–7), Moab and Ammon to the east (2:8–11), and then the two most powerful nations in the region, Cush to the south (2:12), and Assyria to the north (2:13–15). The connection between Cush and Assyria is important. The final defeat of the Cushites by the Assyrians and the accompanying destruction of the Cushite power center in the Egyptian city of Thebes in 663 BC marked the height of Assyrian expansion. Ironically, as mentioned above, this event also marked the beginning of the downfall of Assyria, for Yahweh proclaims judgment on the Assyrians for such violence.[1]

---

1. Michael Floyd, *Minor Prophets, Part 2*, The Forms of the Old Testament Literature (Grand Rapids: Eerdmans, 2000), 212–13.

The citadel of Rabbah Ammon, capital of the Ammonites, was located on this hill, now in the middle of modern Amman, capital of Jordan. Several of the prophets prophesied judgment on the Ammonites.

Ruins of ancient Ashkelon, one of the five main Philistine cities.

The NIV translates Zephaniah 2:12 as follows: "You too, O Cushites, will be slain by my sword." What is puzzling about this translation is that the expansion in the following verses (2:13–15) pronounces judgment quite clearly on *Assyria,* not Cush. The solution to this puzzle lies in the questionable translation that the NIV follows in this verse. There is no future tense verb (imperfect) in the Hebrew of 2:12, but only a verbless clause with a pronoun (even though there are numerous imperfect verbs in the verses that follow dealing with the judgment on the Assyrians). Literally, then, Zephaniah 2:12 would read: "You also, O Cushites; slain of my sword are they." Grammatically and contextually, it is probably preferable to translate and understand 2:12 as a current statement of fact, describing the Assyrian sack and devastation of Thebes in 663 BC, rather than a prophecy of coming judgment.[2]

Thus, as in Isaiah, the Cushites as an imperial Gentile power that did not acknowledge Yahweh fell under the same judgment of Yahweh that the other powers experienced. Yahweh judged Cush through the Assyrians, whom he had raised up. But then Yahweh likewise used that action by the Assyrians as the basis for pronouncing and predicting judgment on the Assyrian empire as well.

ZEPHANIAH 3:1–8—JUDGMENT ON JERUSALEM

In Zephaniah 3:1–8 Yahweh returns to proclaiming judgment on Jerusalem. The stress of this unit is that Jerusalem will not accept any discipline or correction from anyone, in-

---

2. Hays, *From Every People and Nation,* 127–28; Floyd, *Minor Prophets,* 212–13.

cluding Yahweh, even in spite of Yahweh's judgment on the nations (3:6) and his faithfulness to Israel throughout the years (3:5). Like Jeremiah, Zephaniah lists as the culprits the very leaders of Jerusalem—nobility/officials, false prophets, and priests (3:3–4). At the end of this unit, however, Zephaniah confronts the faithful (probably the same group called humble and obedient in 2:3) with an exhortation to "wait" (in faith) for the day of Yahweh to come. This is similar to Habakkuk's conclusion, "Yet I will wait patiently for the day of calamity" (Hab. 3:16).

> Jerusalem will not accept any discipline or correction from anyone, including Yahweh, even in spite of Yahweh's judgment on the nations.

ZEPHANIAH 3:9–13—RESTORATION OF JERUSALEM AND THE NATIONS

The nation of Cush reappears for the third time in Zephaniah 3:9–10, in a passage describing the future ingathering of Yahweh's people:

> Then will I purify the lips of the peoples,
> that all of them may call on the name of Yahweh
> and serve him shoulder to shoulder.
> From beyond the rivers of Cush
> my worshipers, my scattered people,
> will bring me offerings (Zeph. 3:9–10).

Following a typical pattern in the prophets, Zephaniah shifts from proclaiming destruction to prophesying restoration. Just as he had been announcing destruction on both Jerusalem and on the nations, he now declares restoration for both groups. In 3:9–10 Zephaniah delivers a promise of salvation for all the peoples of the earth. Then in 3:11–13 he briefly describes salvation for the people of Israel. Interestingly, 3:9–10 contains numerous allusions and connections to the Tower of Babel story in Genesis 11.

Just as the languages (lit. "lips") of the peoples are confused in Genesis 11, so the "lips" are purified in Zephaniah 3:9. The implication is that the effects of the Tower of Babel are being reversed. In a similar fashion, Zephaniah refers to "my scattered people" (lit. "daughter of my scattering"), perhaps an allusion to the scattered people in Genesis 11, where the judgment of Yahweh brought about the breakdown and destruction of international order (resulting in the scattered situation of Genesis 10). In contrast, Zephaniah paints a future picture of salvation, depicting a dramatic restructuring of the entire world order (alliances, enemies, etc.) in which the nations and Judah join together to worship Yahweh. To typify those foreign nations that stream to worship Yahweh, Zephaniah refers to the area "beyond the rivers of Cush" (3:10), a clear reference to the African kingdom of Cush and the southern regions beyond. In a role similar to that which Ebedmelech plays in the book of Jeremiah, the Cushites in the book of Zephaniah are depicted as a paradigm representing the inclusion of the nations (Gentiles) into the people of God.

> Zephaniah paints a future picture of salvation, depicting a dramatic restructuring of the entire world order in which the nations and Judah join together to worship Yahweh.

Throughout the Old Testament the nations enter into the covenant or the "people of God" in two different ways. The first way is historical, as individual foreigners (like Ruth, Rahab, Ebedmelech, etc.) become part of Israel/Judah through faith, intermarriage, naming, and so forth. The other avenue of entrance into the people of God is eschatological. As we have seen throughout the prophets, Yahweh points to a glorious time in the future when the nations will join his people in worshipping him. The short book of Zephaniah includes both aspects, focusing on the foreign Cushites as the paradigm. The first aspect is seen through Zephaniah's physical father named Cushi, introduced in the opening verse of the book, and the second aspect is revealed through his typical prophetic picture of the great restoration, when Yahweh gathers together all peoples, even those from beyond the rivers of Cush.[3]

> His people are rejoicing in the streets in celebration, and Yahweh himself, in loving care, so delights in his people that he breaks out in joyous singing as well.

ZEPHANIAH 3:14–20—REJOICING IN YAHWEH'S SALVATION

The final unit in Zephaniah ends on a positive note. One feature of the day of Yahweh is that at that time Yahweh will bless both Jerusalem and the nations. Yahweh will restore his scattered people and reside with them as King of Israel (3:15). Part of the punishment of Israel/Judah was the loss of Yahweh's presence, but in the deliverance of 3:15–17, Yahweh declares that he will be with them to protect them and save them.

Zion (Jerusalem) is thus called upon to rejoice at this future promise (3:14). This salvation is so spectacular that Yahweh himself joins in the happy singing (3:17).

Thus Zephaniah ends with a wonderful picture of restoration. Yahweh is reigning as king, having subdued all enemies. There is no longer any reason to be afraid, and all oppression has been ended. His people are rejoicing in the streets in celebration, and Yahweh himself, in loving care, so delights in his people that he breaks out in joyous singing as well.

---

3. Hays, *From Every People and Nation,* 129–30.

» FURTHER READING «

Bruckner, James. *Jonah, Nahum, Habakkuk, Zephaniah*. NIV Application Commentary. Grand Rapids: Zondervan, 2004.

Floyd, Michael H. *Minor Prophets, Part 2*. The Forms of the Old Testament Literature. Grand Rapids: Eerdmans, 2000.

Hays, J. Daniel. *From Every People and Nation: A Biblical Theology of Race*. New Studies in Biblical Theology. Downers Grove, IL: InterVarsity Press, 2003.

Robertson, O. Palmer. *The Books of Nahum, Habakkuk and Zephaniah*. New International Commentary on the Old Testament. Grand Rapids: Eerdmans, 1990.

Smith, Ralph L. *Micah-Malachi*. Word Biblical Commentary. Waco, TX: Word Books, 1984.

» DISCUSSION QUESTIONS «

1. Zephaniah 3:17 states of Yahweh that "he will rejoice over you with singing." First discuss the context and meaning of 3:17. Then discuss whether the reference to the singing of Yahweh is literal or figurative. That is, does God really sing? Give reasons for your answer.

2. Both Isaiah and Zephaniah portray the Cushites (Black Africans) as part of the Gentile inclusion that becomes the people of God. Likewise, it appears that Zephaniah's father was connected in some way to Cush. How does this affect our theology regarding race?

» WRITING ASSIGNMENTS «

1. In the context of Zephaniah 2:3, discuss the relationship between humility, obedience, and righteousness. Also, how does this verse relate to Habakkuk 2:4–5?

2. Explain the difference in how amillennialists and premillennialists would interpret the fulfillment of Zephaniah 3:14–20.

CHAPTER 26

Zechariah

"I am coming, and I will live among you," declares Yahweh. "Many nations will be joined with Yahweh in that day and will become my people." (Zech. 2:10 – 11)

THE POSTEXILIC PROPHETS

The postexilic prophets are Haggai, Zechariah, and Malachi. They bring the prophetic corpus to a close, reiterating the main prophetic promise and pointing forward to the coming of the Messiah.

As the books of Jeremiah, Ezekiel, and 2 Kings so vividly describe, the southern kingdom, Judah, had remained obstinate in refusing to heed the preexilic prophets. The kings and people of Judah insisted on worshipping foreign idols, violating the Deuteronomic norms of social justice and yet believing that their practice of temple rituals would keep them in Yahweh's good graces, in spite of all the preexilic prophetic warning. Finally, in 587–586 BC, Yahweh's judgment was unleashed, and the Babylonians destroyed Jerusalem and carried off most of the people into exile.

> The return to the Land after the exile hardly signaled a return to the old days of blessing in the Promised Land, as spelled out in the book of Deuteronomy.

In 539 BC King Cyrus conquered Babylonia, bringing the displaced Hebrew exiles and their distant homeland under Persian control. In 538 Cyrus issued a decree that allowed the Hebrews to return to their homeland. Over the next one hundred years or so, several waves of Hebrew exiles returned. As they rebuilt, they struggled to restore their identity and proper worship of Yahweh. After a faltering start, they managed to rebuild a scaled-down temple. Economically and politically they remained weak and under Persian domination. Thus the return to the Land after the exile hardly signaled a return to the old days of blessing in the Promised Land, as spelled out in the book of Deuteronomy. There was no Davidic king on the throne, and Israel remained under foreign domination. Even though they did rebuild the temple, there is no mention of Yahweh coming in spectacular fashion to dwell in the temple, as he did when Solomon finished the first one (1 Kings 8:10–11).

Yet the preexilic prophets had prophesied a future glorious time of restoration when a righteous Davidic king would rule with justice, when Gentile nations would acknowledge

This clay cylinder describes the capture of Babylon by Cyrus, King of Persia, and also presents the king's policy to allow displaced peoples to return to their homeland.

the power of Yahweh and join Israel in worshipping him at his Jerusalem temple dwelling, and when Israel would know a time of peace and prosperity. The contrast between this picture and the reality that the returned exiles faced was quite stark.

The postexilic prophets underscore the obvious conclusion that the return of the rag-tag Hebrew nation to Palestine was not the glorious time of restoration promised by the preexilic prophets, nor was it a return to the Deuteronomic blessings ("the way things were") of the past. They also point to the disobedience of the past generations and the consequential judgment of the exile as a lesson that should teach the postexilic community to obey and to remain faithful to Yahweh. However, the postexilic prophets also affirm that the promised restoration/salvation has at last begun. Haggai, Zechariah, and Malachi proclaim that the new community back in the Land lives between the beginning of the restoration and the ultimate consummation, which still lies in the future. The postexilic community is in an interim period, and they are exhorted to live and worship Yahweh faithfully as they await the coming of the One who will bring all of the glorious prophetic promises to fruition.

> The postexilic prophets underscore the obvious conclusion that the return of the rag-tag Hebrew nation to Palestine was not the glorious time of restoration promised by the preexilic prophets.

OVERVIEW OF ZECHARIAH

Setting

Like Haggai, Zechariah dates his message by references to the Persian King Darius, who ruled the Persian Empire from 522 to 486 BC. In the first eight chapters, the book of Zechariah contains three specific dates, all tied to the reign of Darius, ranging from 520 to 518 BC. This makes Zechariah a contemporary with Haggai, who dates his message at 520 BC. Zechariah is introduced as the "son of Iddo," apparently one of the priests that initially returned to the land with Zerubbabel (Neh. 12:4, 16). Like Ezekiel, Zechariah appears to have been a priest; indeed, portions of the book of Zechariah have features similar to those in the book of Ezekiel.

The "Gate of All Nations" at Persepolis, a capital city of Darius I of Persia.

© mustafa can/www.istockphoto.com

Message

Within the Book of the Twelve, Zechariah is part of the final unit (Haggai, Zechariah, and Malachi), a unit that emphasizes the restoration. Zechariah's name means "Yahweh remembers," and his name relates to the theme of the book. Yahweh has not forgotten his people, and he promises that

The Persian Empire under Darius I. Judah became one of many small provinces in the mighty Persian Empire.

salvation/restoration is on the way. One of the longest books of the Twelve, and with an emphasis on salvation rather than judgment, Zechariah provides a closing contrast with the opening unit of the Twelve (Hosea to Micah). Even more than Haggai and Malachi, Zechariah is often quite oriented to the future, though he does still address the current situation, often exhorting the people to repent and to obey Yahweh. Zechariah also incorporates the central prophetic theme of contemporary social justice into his message (7:8–10).

> Zechariah's name means "Yahweh remembers."

In Part One of this book we noted that the prophets focus much more on their day and time than on the future. Zechariah is different in this regard, and unlike typical prophets such as Jeremiah, he does focus more on the future than on the present. This makes sense, for Zechariah comes after the judgment that the preexilic prophets warned about, and his central task was to reorient the postexilic community toward the expectation of the promised restoration. This shift in emphasis makes Zechariah more eschatological than the standard preexilic prophets. Likewise, in keeping with this shift Zechariah often employs the imagery of "apocalyptic" literature[1] (see the discussion of "Apocalyptic Literature" in chapter 3).

---

1. J. Gordon McConville, *Exploring the Old Testament: A Guide to the Prophets* (Downers Grove, IL: InterVarsity Press, 2002), 254–55.

Like Haggai, which comes before it in the canon, the book of Zechariah is concerned about rebuilding the temple. The temple in Zechariah should probably be viewed as part of the prophetic phenomenon we have labeled as "near view/far view." That is, during Haggai and Zechariah's time, actual construction began on a physical second temple (the "near view"). However, like Ezekiel, Zechariah continually points to something bigger and greater connected to the temple (the "far view"). Related to the temple theme, as usual, is the promise of Yahweh's presence.

> Like Haggai, the book of Zechariah is concerned about rebuilding the temple.

As Zechariah looks to the future, he also connects to the preexilic theme regarding the Gentile inclusion into the people of Yahweh. Like many of the other prophets, Zechariah proclaims judgment on the nations (9:1 – 8), but he then also looks beyond that judgment to describe the nations streaming to Jerusalem to worship Yahweh and to receive the ensuing blessings (2:10 – 11; 8:22).

Zechariah breaks down into two major units. Zechariah 1 – 8 is organized around the historical superscriptions (dates) and is primarily prose. Zechariah 9 – 14 is composed of two "oracles" (the Hebrew translated as "oracle" also means "burden") without historical superscriptions and contains a large amount of poetry. Thematically, however, numerous common themes and catchwords unite the two parts into a unified message.

The structure of Zechariah can be described generally by the following outline:

Part One (Zechariah 1 – 8)
1:1 – 6   Introduction and call to repentance
1:7 – 6:8   Eight night visions
6:9 – 15   Symbolic crowning of the high priest

Ruins of the great terrace from the city of Persepolis, a capital of Persia under Darius I.

© Lumo.org

ZECHARIAH 1:1 – 6 — INTRODUCTION AND CALL TO REPENTANCE

Zechariah 1:1 identifies the book as the word of Yahweh that came to the prophet Zechariah. As mentioned above, the date (520 BC) is tied to the Persian King Darius, a reminder that Jerusalem was still under foreign domination. Sounding much like the preexilic prophets (especially Jeremiah), Zechariah immediately quotes Yahweh as calling on the people to repent (*shūv*). "Turn [*shūv*] to me ... and I will return [*shūv*] to you" (1:3). Don't be like your forefathers, who did not listen or obey, Yahweh warns. Those disobedient forefathers are gone, Yahweh observes ominously, but his word given through the prophets lives forever (1:4 – 6). Unlike in the time of Jeremiah, this time the people repent (*shūv*), acknowledging the just judgment of the exile (1:6).

ZECHARIAH 1:7 – 6:8 — EIGHT NIGHT VISIONS

The historical superscription of Zechariah 1:7 provides the setting for the eight night visions contained in the next six chapters. While this date is three months after the opening date of Zechariah 1:1, when compared with Haggai 1:15 we note that these visions occurred only five months after Zerubbabel began rebuilding the temple. An angel (called the "angel of Yahweh" in 1:12) accompanies each vision to explain it to Zechariah. The visions are probably best understood from within the "near view/far view" perspective. In the near view, the visions described the current situation of rebuilding the temple and reactivating the high priests and other leaders. In the far view, the visions look to the future New Jerusalem and the coming messianic Servant of Yahweh.

> In the far view, the visions look to the future New Jerusalem and the coming messianic Servant of Yahweh.

The first vision is of four horses/horsemen (although the exact number is not specifically stated). The angel who answers Zechariah's questions is one of the horsemen. The horses/horsemen have been surveying the entire world and are now reporting back to Yahweh that the world is at rest. The angel of Yahweh then asks Yahweh how long he will stay angry with Jerusalem and Judah, citing the seventy years length of judgment pronounced in Jeremiah 25 (see the discussion of "seventy" years in chapter 11). Indicating an end to the time of judgment on Judah, Yahweh then speaks kindly and promises to return to Jerusalem (remember the importance of Yahweh's presence) and see to it that the city is rebuilt. Thus this first vision certifies that Yahweh will bring about the promised restoration.

In the next vision (1:18 – 21) Zechariah sees four horns, a representation of the powerful nations who destroyed and scattered Israel and Judah. The number four probably represents the four points of the compass, indicating that Israel's enemies were all around them. But Zechariah also sees four craftsmen (apparently with the power to carve up and destroy horns), who will terrify the horns and throw them down, thus announcing the end of the nations that had brought judgment on Israel and Judah. This is a theme that we have seen repeatedly throughout the prophets.

The third vision (2:1–13) is of a man with a measuring line, surveying Jerusalem in preparation for reconstruction. Recall the numerous verses in Ezekiel 40–48 depicting the measurement of the future temple. In Zechariah, however, the angel who interprets for the prophet sends another angel to tell the "surveyor" that there is no need to lay out the location for the walls because the new city will not need walls. Yahweh himself will dwell in the city, and his fire around it will provide any defense needed. The point of the vision is that the future restored Jerusalem will be safe and at peace. This is in contrast to the situation in the book of Nehemiah, where the walls (and the gates) were critical for the defense and survival of the postexilic community. Note also that just as the image of "no walls" represents peace and safety, so in Revelation 21 John makes the same point by declaring that in the New Jerusalem the gates will never be shut, even at night.

In the next vision (3:1–10), Zechariah sees the current high priest, Joshua, exchanging his dirty clothes for clean ones. This symbolizes a cleansing and restoration of priestly leaders (recall how corrupt they were in the preexilic prophetic books, especially in Jeremiah), although it is possible that this action also represents the cleansing of the entire community. Yahweh then promises that his servant, the Branch (whom Jeremiah 23:5 identifies as a future Davidic king), is coming, a stone with seven eyes who will "remove the sin of this land in a single day" (3:9). While the cleansing and reinstitution of the priesthood meant that the priests could carry out the annual Day of Atonement, Yahweh points their hopes toward the day when his servant will take care of all sin in a single act.

The two central leaders in Jerusalem at this time were Joshua, the high priest, and Zerubbabel, the governor. The fourth vision purified and re-established the high priest, Joshua. The fifth vision (4:1–14) focuses on the governor, Zerubbabel. In this vision Zechariah sees two olive trees supplying a lamp with oil. The angel identifies the two trees as Yahweh's anointed leaders (Joshua and Zerubbabel). The lamp is probably to be associated with the temple. The angel declares that Zerubbabel will overcome the huge obstacles (the "mighty mountain") and complete the temple. Yahweh's word proclaims that Zerubbabel will do this, "not by might nor by power, but by my Spirit" (4:6). Recall that the

> There is no need to lay out the location for the walls because the new city will not need walls.

An olive tree in the Middle East today. Zechariah sees a vision of two olive trees supplying oil to a gold lampstand.

© Angela Sorrentino/www.istockphoto.com

prophets (and the rest of the Scriptures) consistently make a direct connection between the presence of Yahweh and his empowering Spirit.

The sixth vision (5:1–4) is of a huge flying scroll, big enough to be very easy to read. The scroll announces judgment on thieves and those who swear falsely in Yahweh's name. The postexilic prophets call on the rebuilt community in Jerusalem to obey the law of Moses and to live righteously as they wait expectantly for the coming day of Yahweh.

> The prophets consistently make a direct connection between the presence of Yahweh and empowerment through his Spirit.

The seventh vision (5:5–11) symbolizes cleansing and the removal of sin. Zechariah sees a basket with a woman inside, representing iniquity. The Hebrew word "iniquity" is a feminine conjugated word; thus, in the symbolic world of the prophets, "iniquity" is represented by a woman. The angel pushes the woman ("iniquity") down into the basket and places a heavy lid on it. Then two other women—who do not represent iniquity, but who are perhaps angels—use their stork-like wings and fly off with the basket to take it to Babylonia, the fitting place to which iniquity should be banished. Yet the vision may also suggest that those who disobey Yahweh and continue to practice iniquity could face being exiled once again.

The eighth and final vision (6:1–8) describes four horse-drawn chariots (note their similarity with the horses in the first vision of 1:7–17). The chariots proceed from the presence of Yahweh, and with his power they patrol the entire world, apparently establishing justice. Note that in the first vision the "riders" questioned when justice would come (1:11–12). Now it has come, especially in the north. In the "near view," this is perhaps referring to the judgment on Babylon that occurred twenty years earlier, when the Persians conquered the city. Yet it also probably has a "far view" as well, describing a future time when the day of Yahweh would bring justice on the entire world (a theme running throughout the prophets).

Female Angels with Wings

It is interesting to note that in our popular culture we generally portray angels as women with big white wings. This image is especially entrenched in our Christmas pageants. However, this image is fairly rare in the Bible, and it probably was developed from Zechariah 5:9, even though the women in that text are not actually identified as angels. Elsewhere in the Old Testament angels look much like humans, although specific descriptions are vague. Yet in some other texts, strange "angel-like" heavenly beings are described in some detail. Recall the four living creatures of Ezekiel's vision (Ezek. 1:4–24), each with four faces, with four wings, and covered with eyes. Imagine using Ezekiel's "angels" as our model for Christmas pageants instead of Zechariah's! Which image of angels is more valid? What do angels really look like? Do the Christmas angels that appear to the shepherds at the birth of Christ have wings (Luke 2:8–15)?

ZECHARIAH 6:9–15—SYMBOLIC CROWNING OF THE HIGH PRIEST

In this passage Zechariah is told to carry out a symbolic crowning of the high priest, thus unifying the priesthood and royalty in the task of rebuilding the temple.

ZECHARIAH 7:1–14—JUSTICE IS STILL REQUIRED, NOT JUST RITUAL

A delegation comes to the temple to ask of Yahweh if they should continue to fast and mourn for the fall of Jerusalem and the exile (since the exile was over). Yahweh answers in a way that we saw frequently in the preexilic prophets. He is much more concerned with social justice than with the details of ritual. Yahweh declares what he really wants from them: "Administer true justice; show mercy and compassion to one another. Do not oppress the widow or the fatherless, the alien or the poor. In your hearts do not think evil of each other" (7:9–10).

> Yahweh is much more concerned with social justice than with the details of ritual.

ZECHARIAH 8:1–23—FUTURE RESTORATION

This chapter focuses on the future restoration. Yahweh promises to come and dwell among his people again in Jerusalem (8:3). The people will be regathered to the Land and will live in peace and prosperity (8:4–13). Connecting back to the Abrahamic promise of Genesis 12:2, Yahweh once again tells Judah and Israel that they "will be a blessing" (8:13). Yahweh then interjects an exhortation and a warning concerning truthfulness and justice (8:14–19). Finally, Yahweh paints the familiar prophetic picture of the nations of the world streaming to Jerusalem to worship him (8:20–23).

ZECHARIAH 9:1–11:17—ORACLE 1: THE ADVENT AND REJECTION OF THE COMING ONE

The second part of Zechariah (9–14) focuses on the coming time of restoration and the establishment of Yahweh's kingdom. The "near view/far view" approach will continue to be helpful for us in interpreting this section. Note that although Zechariah in general contains

NT Connection: The Gospels and Zechariah 9–14

The Passion Narratives of the Gospels quote from Zechariah 9–14 frequently to demonstrate that Jesus was the Messiah that the Old Testament prophesied. Matthew 21:4–5 and John 12:14–15, for example, cite Zechariah 9:9–10 regarding the Messiah's humble entry into Jerusalem mounted on a donkey. Likewise, Zechariah 11:12–13 (30 pieces of silver thrown to the potter) is connected, along with Jeremiah's prophecy, to Judas's betrayal of Jesus (Matt. 27:9). John 19:37 states that the piercing of Jesus side on the cross is the fulfillment of Zechariah 12:10. Finally, Zechariah 13:7 ("strike the shepherd and the sheep will be scattered") is cited in Matthew 26:31.

a large amount of messianic material, this particular unit (9 – 14) is especially rich with passages that the New Testament will connect to Jesus.

> Zechariah 9 – 14 is especially rich with passages that the New Testament connects to Jesus.

Zechariah 9 – 11 covers many of the same restoration themes that we encountered in the preexilic prophets, although Zechariah adds a few new details and "twists." The unit starts off with judgment on the nations (9:1 – 8), similar to the familiar "oracles against the nations" that we saw in the preexilic prophets. Next, amid shouts of joy, the righteous King arrives, coming in power and bringing peace over all the nations, yet at the same time, ironically, riding humbly and gently on a donkey (9:9 – 10). Yahweh, the great divine warrior, crushes all his enemies but saves and protects his own people on "that day" (the day of Yahweh; 9:11 – 17).

Zechariah 10:1 – 11:3 likewise contains numerous prophetic themes. Yahweh proclaims his anger against the shepherds (leaders of Israel), and in contrast, he points to the coming "cornerstone" from Judah. Yahweh will restore all of Israel, bringing them back from Egypt (symbolizing the south) and Assyria (symbolizing the north). Similar to the rejection of Yahweh's servant in Isaiah 53, however, Zechariah 11:4 – 17 portrays the unthinkable — the people reject Yahweh's shepherd. Thus the unit closes with judgment.

ZECHARIAH 12:1 – 14:21 — ORACLE 2: THE ADVENT AND ACCEPTANCE OF THE COMING ONE

The final unit of Zechariah stresses the day of Yahweh. He delivers Jerusalem from the attack by the nations (12:1 – 9). The people mourn and repent of their rejection of Yahweh (and his shepherd) and Yahweh forgives them, cleanses them, and re-establishes his covenant with them (12:10 – 13:9). The passage is brought to a climax with the traditional covenant formulation: "They are my people/Yahweh is our God" (13:9). Finally, the day of Yahweh brings about the establishment of his great universal kingdom, with Yahweh ruling from Jerusalem and the nations streaming to worship him (14:1 – 21).

» FURTHER READING «

Boda, Mark J. *Haggai, Zechariah*. NIV Application Commentary. Grand Rapids: Zondervan, 2004.

Floyd, Michael H. *Minor Prophets, Part 2*. The Forms of the Old Testament Literature. Grand Rapids: Eerdmans, 2000.

Smith, Ralph L. *Micah-Malachi*. Word Biblical Commentary. Waco: Word Books, 1984.

On the use of Zechariah in the New Testament, see especially:

Bauckham, Richard. *The Climax of Prophecy: Studies in the Book of Revelation*. Edinburgh: T & T Clark, 1993.

Beale, G. K., and D. A. Carson, eds. *Commentary on the New Testament Use of the Old Testament*. Grand Rapids: Baker, 2007.

Duguid, Iain. "Messianic Themes in Zechariah 9 – 14." In *The Lord's Anointed: Interpretation of Old Testament Messianic Texts*. Edited by Philip Satterthwaite. Carlisle: Paternoster, 1995.

» DISCUSSION QUESTIONS «

1. Summarize the setting and the message of the postexilic prophets.

2. Discuss the reconstruction of the temple by the postexilic community and the near view/far view concept regarding the temple.

3. Discuss the context of Zechariah 4:6. How could the principles in this verse be applicable for us today?

» WRITING ASSIGNMENTS «

1. Discuss the differences and similarities between what Zechariah says about the future temple and what Ezekiel says in Ezekiel 40 – 48.

2. Discuss the differences between an amillennial view and a premillennial view of the fulfillment of Zechariah's prophecies regarding the temple in Jerusalem.

3. Trace and discuss the theme of the presence of Yahweh throughout the book of Zechariah. How does this Old Testament theme relate to the New Testament theology of the presence of God? Discuss similarities and differences.